# EARLY INDIAN HISTORICAL TRADITION AND ARCHAEOLOGY

**Reconstructing Indian History & Culture**
**ISSN 0971-3824**

1. Society in Ancient India / Sures Chandra Banerji.
   (ISBN 81-246-0000-7)
2. Political Thought in Ancient India / G.P. Singh.
   (ISBN 81-246-0001-5)

Reconstructing Indian History & Culture, no. 3

# EARLY INDIAN HISTORICAL TRADITION AND ARCHAEOLOGY

## Purāṇic Kingdoms and Dynasties with Genealogies, Relative Chronology and Date of Mahābhārata War

**G.P. SINGH**
Ph. D., F.R.A.S. (London)

D.K. Printworld (P) Ltd.
**NEW DELHI-110015**

**Cataloging in Publication Data — DK**

Singh, G.P. (Girish Prasad), 1942-

Early Indian historical tradition and archaeology.
(Reconstructing Indian history & culture; no. 3).
Includes index.

1. India — History — To 324 BC 2. India — History — 324 BC – 1000 AD 3. India — History — 1000 – 1526. 4. India — Antiquities. 5. Archaeology — India. 6. India Historical geography. I. Title. II. Series : Reconstructing Indian history & culture; no. 3.

**ISBN 81-246-0005-8**

*First Published in India in 1994*
2nd impression in 2004



*Published and printed by*
**D.K. Printworld (P) Ltd.**
*Regd. office* : *'Sri Kunj'*, F-52, Bali Nagar
New Delhi - 110 015
*Phone* : (011) 2545-3975, 2546-6019; *Fax*: (011) 2546-5926
*Email* : dkprintworld@vsnl.net
*Web* : www.dkprintworld.com

# Preface

IN mankind's history, India's is the longest literary tradition that began with the *Ṛgvedic* hymns, which were indisputably composed at a time when many a great old-world civilization lay in the wombs of futurity. And almost equal is the antiquity of *Purāṇa-Saṁhitā*: the single, original *Purāṇa* that, with the rolling centuries, emerged as a ramified system—embodying eighteen distinct works like *Barhma Purāṇa, Viṣṇu Purāṇa, Bhāgavata Purāṇa, Śiva Purāṇa, Matsya Purāṇa, Kūrma Purāṇa, Skanda Purāṇa, Bhaviṣya Purāṇa, Liṅga Purāṇa, Vāyu Purāṇa*, . . .

Its antiquity apart, early Indian historical tradition is formidable in its sheer immenseness (!), with endless possibilities of research and fresh interpretations—though, judged by its contemporary parameters, it is not 'historiography'. Yet some of the time-honoured sources—*Vedic Saṁhitās, Brāhmaṇas, Purāṇas, Srutis* and *Smritis, Dharmaśāstras*, epics (the *Rāmāyaṇa* and the *Mahābhārata*), *tantra* manuals, and myriad Buddhist and Jaina texts, have greatly helped historiographers sharpen their perspectives on India's remote past.

Bulky and often crowded with legendary matters of various kinds, the *Purāṇas*, (which form the essential basis of my study), tell fascinating stories of gods and godlings of Hindu mythology, bringing home to us the prowesses and possibilities of divine principles. They refer to the creation, renovation, and destruction of the universe, among their diverse speculative/philosophical reflections. Also contained in them are narrative accounts of the old-world dynasties that ruled different regions of India : from a primeval king, Manu Vaivasvata to the last great Hindu ruler of Northern India, Prithvirāja Cauhāna, which all I have tried to analyse in my modest effort to prove the historicity of the *Purāṇic* writings.

My account of the ancient kingdoms/dynasties, together with their genealogies and relative chronologies, is the outcome of my historical researches into the *Purāṇic* records, and how these, in turn, are corroborated by other traditional writings, and now increasingly by archaeological evidence. I have also focussed on the much-debated 'date' of the Mahābhārata War.

I am indebted to all the scholars whose works I have relied upon for writing this book.

I am aware of the errors which, despite my best possible care, have crept into the study. While I must, therefore, apologise for my shortcomings, I would gratefully look forward to suggestions/comments on the content or the format of the book.

(G.P. SINGH)

# Contents

# Abbreviations

| | |
|---|---|
| *ABORI* | *Annals of the Bhandarkar Oriental Research Institute*, Poona. |
| *ACAI* | *Astronomical Method and its Application to the Choronology of Ancient India.* |
| *Agn.* | *Agni Purāṇa.* |
| *AI* | *Ancient India-Bulletin of the Archaeological Survey of India*, New Delhi. |
| *AICL* | *Ancient India as Described in Classical Literature.* |
| *AIHA* | *Aspects of Indian History and Archaeology.* |
| *AIHT* | *Ancient Indian Historical Tradition.* |
| *AIMA* | *Ancient India as Described by Megasthenes and Arrian.* |
| *AISH* | *Ancient Indian Social History.* |
| *AIT* | *Ancient India as Described by Ptolemy.* |
| *Ait. Br.* | *Aitareya Brāhmaṇa.* |
| *Antiquity* | *A Quarterly Review of Archaeology*, Cambridge, England. |
| *Ar. Ant.* | *Ariana Antiqua.* |
| *ASB* | *Asiatic Society of Bengal*, Calcutta. |
| *ASIAR* | *Archaeological Survey of India, Annual Reports.* |
| *As. Res.* | *Asiatic Researches (Comprising History and Antiquities, the Arts, Sciences, Ethnology and Literature of Asia).* |
| *AV.* | *Atharvaveda.* |
| *BDCRI* | *Bulletin of the Deccan College Research Institute*, Poona. |

| | |
|---|---|
| *Bhāg.* | *Bhāgavata Purāṇa.* |
| *Bh. Sv.* | *Bhārata Sāvitrī (An in-depth historical study of the Mahābhārata)* by Vasudeva Sharan Agrawala, Vols. 1 and 2, 2nd. edn., Delhi, 1977, Vol. 3, first edn., Delhi, 1968. |
| *Bhv.* | *Bhaviṣya Purāṇa.* |
| *BI* | *Buddhist India.* |
| *BIS* | *Bibliotheca Indica Series (a Collection of Oriental Works)* Asiatic Society, Calcutta. |
| *Bmd.* | *Brahmāṇḍa Purāṇa.* |
| *Bmv.* | *Brahmavaivarta Purāṇa.* |
| *Br.* | *Brahma Purāṇa.* |
| *Br. Saṁ.* | *Bṛhat (Vārāhī) Saṁhitā.* |
| *BRWW* | *Buddhist Records of the Western World.* |
| *CAGI* | Cunningham's *Ancient Geography of India,* Varanasi, 1979. |
| *CAI* | *Coins of Ancient India from the Earliest times down to the Seventh Century* A.D. by A. Cunningham, London, 1891. |
| *CASR* | Cunningham's *Archaeological Survey of India, Annual Reports.* |
| *CCBM* | *Catalogue of Coins in the British Museum, Ancient India,* by John Allan, London, 1936. |
| *CCIM* | *Catalogue of Coins in the Indian Museum* (Calcutta), by V.A. Smith, Oxford, 1906. |
| *CHI* | *Cambridge History of India,* Vol. 1, Ancient India. |
| *Chro. An. Ind.* | *Chronology of Ancient India.* |
| *CII* | *Corpus Inscriptionum Indicarum.* |
| *CMI* | *Coins of Medieval India.* |
| *CSARM* | *Classical Studies in Ancient Races and Myths.* |
| *DDEI* | *Dates and Dynasties in Earliest India.* |
| *Dip.* | *Dipavaṁsa.* |
| *DPPN* | *Dictionary of Pāli Proper Names.* |
| *EAB* | *Ethnology of Ancient Bhārata.* |
| *EB* | *Encyclopaedia Britannica.* |
| *EHD* | *Early History of the Dekkan.* |

| | |
|---|---|
| *EHI* | *Early History of India.* |
| *EHIDS* | *Early Hindu India : A Dynastic Study.* |
| *EIP* | *Early India and Pakistan to Ashoka* by M. Wheeler, London, 1968. |
| *Ep. Ind.* | *Epigraphia Indica*, Delhi. |
| *ESAI* | *Ethnic Settlements in Ancient India.* |
| *GAGI* | *Geographical Essays Relating to Ancient Geography of India.* |
| *GAII* | *Geographical Names in Ancient Indian Inscriptions (Upto 650 A.D.)* |
| *Gar.* | *Garuḍa Purāṇa.* |
| *GDAMI* | *Geographical Dictionary of Ancient and Medieval India.* |
| *GEB* | *Geography of Early Buddhism.* |
| *GESM* | *Geographical and Economic Studies in the Mahābhārata, Upāyana Parva,* by Motichandra, Lucknow, 1945. |
| *Go. Br.* | *Gopatha Brāhmaṇa.* |
| *GP* | *Geography of the Purāṇas.* |
| *HA* | *History of Antiquity.* |
| *HAI* | *History of Ancient India.* |
| *HASL* | *History of Ancient Sanskrit Literature.* |
| *HCIP* | *History and Culture of the Indian People.* |
| *HCSL* | *History of Classical Sanskrit Literature.* |
| *HGAI* | *Historical Geography of Ancient India.* |
| *HHK* | *Hindu History of Kashmir.* |
| *HIL* | *History of Indian Literature.* |
| *HLI* | *Historical and Literary Inscriptions.* |
| *HPL* | *History of Pāli Literature* by B.C. Law, 2 Vols., Delhi, 1983. |
| *HRIAS* | *Historicity of Rāmāyaṇa and the Indo-Aryan Society in India and Ceylon.* |
| *HSL* | *History of Sanskrit Literature.* |
| *Hv.* | *Harivaṁśa.* |
| *IAC* | *Indo-Asian Culture*, New Delhi. |
| *IAR* | *Indian Archaeology*—A Review, New Delhi. |

| | |
|---|---|
| *IC* | *Indian Culture*, Calcutta. |
| *IETBJ* | *India as Described in Early Texts of Buddhism and Jainism.* |
| *IGI* | *Imperial Gazetteer of India.* |
| *IHQ* | *Indian Historical Quarterly*, Calcutta. |
| *IHR* | *Indian Historical Review*, Delhi. |
| *Ind. Alt.* | *Indische Alterthumskunde* by Chr. Lassen, Vols. 1 and 11, 2nd edn., Leipzig, 1867-73. |
| *Ind. Ant.* | *Indian Antiquary* (*A Journal of Oriental Research*), Bombay. |
| *Ind. Co.* | *Indian Coins.* |
| *INM* | *Index to the Names in the Mahābhārata.* |
| *IP* | *India as known to Pāṇini : A Study of the Cultural material in the Aṣṭādhyāyī.* |
| *ITP* | *India in the time of Patañjali.* |
| *JA* | *Journal Asiatique*, Paris. |
| *JAOS* | *Journal of the American Oriental Society.* |
| *JASB* | *Journal of the Asiatic Society of Bengal*, Calcutta. |
| *JBBRAS* | *Journal of the Bombay Branch of the Royal Asiatic Society*, Bombay. |
| *JBHU* | *Journal of the Benares Hindu University*, Benares. |
| *JBORS* | *Journal of the Bihar and Orissa Research Society*, Patna. |
| *JGRI* | *Journal of the Ganganath Jha Research Institute*, Allahabad. |
| *JGRS* | *Journal of the Gujarat Research Society.* |
| *JIH* | *Journal of Indian History*, Trivandrum. |
| *JNSI* | *Journal of the Numismatic Society of India.* |
| *JOIB* | *Journal of the Oriental Institute*, Baroda. |
| *JRAS* | *Journal of the Royal Asiatic Society of Great Britain and Ireland*, London. |
| *JRASB (L)* | *Journal of the Royal Asiatic Society of Bengal Letters*, Calcutta. |
| *JS* | *Jainist Studies* by Otto Stein, ed. by Jina Vijaya Muni, Ahmedabad, 1948. |
| *JUPHS* | *Journal of the U.P. Historical Society*, Lucknow. |

| | |
|---|---|
| *Kat. Sar. Sag.* | *Kathāsaritsāgara.* |
| *Krm.* | *Kūrma Purāṇa.* |
| *LAIJC* | *Life in Ancient India as depicted in Jaina Canon and Commentaries.* |
| *Lg.* | *Liṅga Purāṇa.* |
| *MAINWO* | *Monumental Antiquities and Inscriptions in the North-Western Provinces.* |
| *MASI* | *Memoirs of the Archaeological Survey of India.* |
| *Mats.* | *Matsya Purāṇa.* |
| *Mbh.* | *Mahābhārata,* ed. with Hindu trans. by Pt. Shreepāda Damodar Sātavalekar, Pāradi, Gujarat, 1968-1981-82. |
| *Mbh. Ko.* | *Mahābhārata Kosha* (*A Descriptive Index to the Names and Subjects in the Mahābhārata*) by R.K. Rai, Varanasi, 1982. |
| *Mhv.* | *Mahāvaṁśa.* |
| *Mkd.* | *Mārkaṇḍeya Purāṇa.* |
| *NAGG* | *Notes on the Ancient Geography of Gandhara* by A Foucher, Delhi, 1974. |
| *NRPO* | *Notes on the Races and Peoples of Oudh.* |
| *OIB* | *Original Inhabitants of Bhāratavarṣa.* |
| *Pan. Br.* | *Pañcaviṁśa Brāhmaṇa.* |
| *PDKA* | *Purāṇa text of the Dynasties of the Kali Age.* |
| *Pdm.* | *Padma Purāṇa.* |
| *Periplus.* | *Periplus of the Erythraean Sea,* tr. from the Greek and annotated by W.H. Schoff, London, 1912. |
| *PHAI* | *Political History of Ancient India.* |
| *PIHC* | *Proceedings of the Indian History Congress.* |
| *PK* | *Paurāṇic Kosha* by R.P. Sharma. Varanasi, VS. 2028. |
| *POC* | *Proceedings of the All India Oriental Conference.* |
| *PPIP* | *Prehistory and Protohistory of India and Pakistan.* |
| *PTS* | *Pāli Text Society,* London. |
| *RAENIT* | *Racial Affinities of Early North Indian Tribes.* |
| *Raghu.* | *Raghuvaṁśa.* |
| *RBK* | *Record of the Buddhistic Kingdoms (the Travels of* |

| | |
|---|---|
| | *Fa-hien, 399-414 A.D.)* |
| *RV* | *Ṛgveda.* |
| *Śat. Br.* | *Śatapatha Brāhmaṇa.* |
| *SBA* | *Sacred Books of the Aryan Series,* Delhi. |
| *SBE* | *Sacred Books of the East,* Oxford. |
| *SGAMI* | *Studies in the Geography of Ancient and Medieval India.* |
| *SI* | *Select Inscriptions bearing on Indian History and Civilisation.* |
| *Siv.* | *Śiva Purāṇa.* |
| *Skd.* | *Skanda Purāṇa.* |
| *SPHI* | *Studies in the Proto-History of India.* |
| *SPRH* | *Studies in the Purāṇic Records on Hindu Rites and Customs.* |
| *Tai. Ar.* | *Taittirīya Āraṇyaka.* |
| *Tai. Br.* | *Taittirīya Brāhmaṇa.* |
| *Tai. Sam.* | *Taittirīya Saṁhitā.* |
| *Val. Ram.* | *Vālmīki-Rāmāyaṇa.* |
| *Val. Ram. Ko.* | *Vālmīki-Rāmāyaṇa Kosha* by R.K. Rai, Varanasi, 1965. |
| V.E. | *Vikrama* Era. |
| *VI* | *Vedic Index of Names and Subjects* by A.A. Macdonell and A.B. Keith, 2 Vols. (1st edn. London, 1912), 3rd edn. *Indian Text Series,* 1967. |
| *Vmn.* | *Vāmana Purāṇa.* |
| *Vrh.* | *Varāha Purāṇa.* |
| *Vṣṇ.* | *Viṣṇu Purāṇa.* |
| *Vṣṇ. Dh.* | *Viṣṇu-Dharmottara Purāṇa.* |
| *Vy.* | *Vāyu Purāṇa.* |
| YCTI | Yuan Chwang's *Travels in India (A.D. 629-45).* |
| ZFKDM | *Zeitschrift Für de' Kunde d'es Morgenlaṅ- dische.* |

# 1

# Introduction

THE primary purpose of undertaking this research work is to provide a comprehensive historical account of ancient Indian kingdoms and dynasties with their genealogies and chronology, as recorded in the *Purāṇas.* The *Purāṇic* kingdoms and dynasties comprise those of the Solar and Lunar race of both the pre- and post-Bhārata war period and the Bārhadratha dynasty (*c* 1151-513 B.C.) of Magadha, the Pradyota dynasty (*c* 513-411 B.C.) of Avanti, the Bimbisārian, Śaiśunāga, Nanda, Maurya, Śunga and Kānva dynasties that ruled sucessively over Magadha and other kingdoms from the sixth century to the first century B.C., the Andhra or Sātavāhana dynasty that reigned in western India and the Deccan from the first century B.C. to the third century A.D., kingdoms and dynasties of the post-Sātavāhana period, some contemporary minor dynasties of the kings of both indigenous and foreign origins, who ruled over different parts of India between the third century B.C. and the sixth century A.D., the Nāga dynasties that reigned in Central and Northern India between the second century B.C. and the fourth century A.D, the Vākāṭaka and the Gupta dynasties that ruled contemporaneously over the kingdoms of the Deccan and U.P. and Bihar respectively from the third to the sixth century A.D. and the Pratihāra, Paramāra, Cauhāna and Cālukya (representing the four Rajput families of Agnikula) dynasties that ruled over various kingdoms in Northern India in the post-Harṣa period (*c* 650-1200 A.D.).

The work is broadly based on the *Vedic*, Epic, *Purāṇic*, Jain and Buddhist traditions as well as other literary, historical and archaeological evidences. For making an accurate historical study of the subject, we have placed our reliance on the combined testimony of all. They are, actually, complementary to each other. Ancient Indian historical traditions have been copiously recorded in the Sanskrit, Prākṛt and Pāli literature about the subject under review. H.D. Sankalia, who has reasonably maintained an equitable balance between the traditional and archaeological data in the treatment of the subject relating to the kingdoms and dynasties and towns and cities as described in the epic and *Purāṇic* literature,[1] observes that "traditions, whether epic or *Purāṇic*, Jain or Buddhist or purely local, have an important role to play in helping unravel our past culture and civilization."[2] He has attached great importance to the epic and *Purāṇic* tradition from both historical and archaeological points of view. In fact, tradition and archaeology constitute two wheels of the chariot of ancient Indian history and culture. The *Purāṇas* contain genuine historical tradition, which finds, to some extent, corroboration in archaeology. This can fairly be attested to by the statement of R. Morton Smith (Deptt. of Sanskrit and Indian Studies, University of Toronto, Canada) : ". . . the *Purāṇa* makes a good historical sense, consistent with the idea of archaeology."[3]

The antiquity of the *Purāṇas* goes back to the *Vedic* age, which can amply be substantiated by the evidences recorded in the *Vedic* literature. The composition, compilation and classification of the *Purāṇas* went on concurrently or simultaneously with those of the *Vedas*. The *Purāṇas*, like the *Vedas*, were composed by different sages and seers at different times. They were first compiled and edited by the great sage Vyāsa (who became popularly known as Vedavyāsa, after having collected the *Vedic* hymns and compiled them and classified the single *Vedic* into four *Saṁhitās*). There was originally only one *Purāṇa-Saṁhitā*, whose authorship is very often attributed to Vyāsa. Later it was ramified by him into 18 principal branches. We have some concrete evidences from the original sources (the *Vedic*, *Brāhmaṇic* and *Purāṇic*)[4], to confirm it. The said *Purāṇa Saṁhitā* originally contained the details to the beginning of the *Kali-Yuga*. The recording of events of the later period in the *Purāṇas* further continued. Most of the *Purāṇas* were further recast or rewritten, modified, enlarged and edited in their present form some time between *c* 500 B.C. and *c* 500 A.D. and in the post-Gupta period, which will be discussed in detail little later. After having divided the *Purāṇas* into 18 main parts, Vyāsa composed the *Mahābhārata* dividing it into 18 parts and incorporating therein some information which was both identical with and additional to that of the *Purāṇas*. The tradition of dividing, re-arranging and re-interpreting the *Purāṇas* originally set by Vyāsa was further followed by his disciples.

It is striking to note that ancient Indian historical tradition was originally compiled by the *Sūtas* on the basis of the information collected from the families of priests and others during the *Vedic* period. It was their principal duty to keep the genealogical records and arrange the traditional genealogies (*Vaṁśāvalis*) of the royal families. They were, actually, employed by the kings to chronicle the events of their reigns as well as that of their ancestors. Thus, they were not only the chroniclers of events, but also the custodians or preservers of tradition. It is undeniable that both the *Sūtas* and *Māgadhas* adorned the courts of kings, but the former were not the bards, as held by some scholars; only the latter can be placed under the category of either bards or panegyrists.[5] The identification of *Sūtas* with bards is not valid, as the latter is not a suitable equivalent for the former mentioned in the original *Purāṇic* texts. Though it is not possible to speak on the subject with authority, but at least this much can be said with certain amount of confidence that some sort of distinction was definitely maintained between the two in the remote past.

It was Vyāsa who first taught the *Itihāsa* (which denotes actual traditional history)—Purāṇa (which signifies any old tale or events of the ancient past of whether quasi-historical or mythological nature or that happened and existed in former times) tradition to one of his distinguished disciples, Romaharsana (or Lomaharsana), who belonged to the class of *Sūta* (popularly known as *Sūta* Romaharsana). He in turn taught it to his son Ugrasravas and six disciples, at least five of whom were *Brāhmaṇs.*[6] Thus, tradition was handed down from generation to generation. It is noteworty that the *Itihāsa-Purāṇa* tradition had three "main constituents—myth, genealogy and historical narrative" (*ākhyānas, upākhyānas, gāṭhās,* etc.). Ever since the *Vedic* age, the *Itihāsa-Purāṇa* existed as inter-twined or inter-related. Both had become synonymous and were complementary to each other. In the beginning no clear distinction was made between the two. But, subsequently, they developed as two distinct subjects of special study. In the *Yājñavalkya Smṛti* (1.3) and the *Viṣṇu Purāṇa* (3.6.28) the *Purāṇa* (in the sense of *Itihāsa-Purāṇa*) has been mentioned as one of the fourteen branches of learning.

The antiquity of *Itihāsa-Purāṇa* tradition can also be proved. The earliest reference to the word *'Purāṇa'* occurs in the *Ṛgveda.*[7] In the same text it has been again used in the form of a *gāthā* or narrative.[8] In the *Atharvaveda* the *Purāṇa* has been used first singularly along with the three other *Vedas*[9] and then conjointly with *Itihāsa* in the form of historical narrative.[10] In some of the *Brāhmaṇas* too, the *Itihāsa-Purāṇa* have been used together and it has been categorically stated that they were composed along with the *Vedas*, they very much form as one of its parts and they are equally important.[11] In the *Āraṇyaka*[12] and *Upaniṣadas*[13] also, the *Itihāsa-Purāṇa* have been mentioned along with the *Vedas*.

The *Purāṇas* appeared as writ-large or in the enlarged form of the *Vedas.* That is why, the *Itihāsa-Purāṇa* have been referred to in the *Vedic* and *Purāṇic* literature[14] and some other reliable sources as the fifth *Veda* (*Itihāsa Purāṇaṁ pancama Vedānaṁ Vedaṁ*) along with other four *Vedas.* The information supplied by Kauṭilya is also worth quoting. According to him, the three *Vedas*, the "*Sāman, Ṛc* (*Ṛg.*) and *Yajus* are the threefold (scripture). The *Atharva-Veda* and the *Itihāsa-Veda* are also the *Vedas.*"[15] He also defines the *Itihāsa* as, '*Itihāsa* means the *Purāṇa, Itivṛtta* (history), *Ākhyāyika* (tale), *Udāharaṇa* (illustrative story), the *Dharmaśāstra* and the *Arthaśāstra.*[16]

The *Itihāsa-Purāṇa* and the *Vedas* were closely related and equally important. But from one particular *Purāṇic* text it appears that the *Purāṇas* were considered relatively more important than the *Vedas.*[17] For the correct interpretation, explanation and analysis of the data contained in the *Vedas*, the sound knowledge of the *Itihāsa-Purāṇa* was essential which is evidenced by both the *Mahābhārata*[18] and the *Purāṇas.*[19]

Some of the *Purāṇa* texts call themselves as "*Purātana Itihāsa* (ancient history) in support of their historicity, which can be testified to by the evidences furnished therein.[20]

Apart from the *Purāṇas*, the *Itihāsa-Purāṇa* tradition includes the two epics—the *Rāmāyaṇa* and the *Mahābhārata.* The *Mahābhārata*, in particular bespeaks the truth as it is said in the text that it is not only a reliable history, but the best of all the available histories of the contemporary period. It is further stated that this history is well attested by the *Purāṇas* and the *Vedas.*[21] From the first and the last *parvans* of the *Mahābhārata* it distinctly appears that this history bearing the name "*Jaya*" (*Jayonametihāsa . . .*") was originally composed by *Kṛṣṇa Dvipāyana Vyāsa*. It is said to be a treasure-house of knowledge.[22] That the *Mahābhārata* is part of history, can be supported by the statements of V.S. Agrawala[23] and C.V. Vaidya.[24]

The age of the *Purāṇas* may now fairly be considered on the basis of both the internal and external evidences, the former being therein and the latter in some other relevant sources. The '*Kaliyugarājavṛttānta* of the *Bhaviṣya Purāṇa* appears to be the oldest of all other *Purāṇic* details. It existed before *c* 500 B.C., as it appears from the *Āpastamba Dharmasūtra*. The dynastic account of the rulers of the *Kali* Age was first compiled in it towards the end of the second century A.D. during the reign of the Sātavāhana king Yajña Śri Śātakarni (*circa* A.D. 165-195). The text in the revised form very much existed in the middle of the third century A.D. Its antiquity is further supported by the fact that the *Matsya*, which was finally completed before the end of the third century A.D. (as it covers the accounts only up to the end of the rule of the Andhras or *Sātavāhanas*), borrowed its account from the *Bhaviṣya*. The *Vāyu* and *Brahmāṇḍa* (two other early *Purāṇas*) also borrowed their accounts from the *Bhaviṣya* in the fourth century A.D., as it appears from the *Purāṇic* evidence itself. This particular fact has also been highlighted by Pargiter.[25] Here it may profitably be added that the *Bhaviṣya Purāṇa* contains the accounts up to the times of Prithvirāja Cauhāna, so far as the ancient period is concerned, otherwise, the account has been carried forward to the times of Akbar, which shows only the periodical additions made in the text. Thus, no particular date can be assigned to what we find in the present form.

Since the *Vāyu, Viṣṇu, Brahmāṇḍa* and *Bhāgavata* contain the dynastic accounts upto the rise of the Gupta power before the time of Samudragupta (*c* 335-80 A.D.), they must have existed before *c* 400 A.D. Later some events up to the times of the Vākāṭakas, whose power was shattered some time in the second quarter of the sixth century A.D., were recorded in them. It seems that these were finally completed by the end of the sixth century A.D. Some additions were, of course, made in the *Bhāgavata* between 600 and 800 A.D., as it appears from the text itself. The *Harivaṁśa* existed before *c* 400 A.D. The *Agni* was composed before *c* 400 A.D., but some additions were made in it between *c* 500 and 900 A.D. The *Kūrma, Mārkaṇḍeya, Padma, Brahma* and the *Skanda Purāṇas* were also in existence before *c* 600 A.D. It has been specifically observed by Pargiter that "verses praising gifts of land are quoted in various land-grants that are dated; and some of those are found only in the *Padma, Bhaviṣya* and *Brahma Purāṇas* and thus indicate that those *Purāṇas* were in existence before A.D. 500 and even long before that time. Some of those verses which occur in grants of the years 475-6 and 482-3 are declared in some grants to have been enunciated by Vyāsa in the *Mahābhārata*."[26]

The *Brahmavaivarta, Liṅga, Vāmana* and *Viṣṇudharmottara Purāṇas* were completed before *c*. 700 A.D.

The '*Vaṁśānucarita*' (genealogical) and '*Vaṁsa*' (dynastic) sections of the *Purāṇas* constitute two very important of the five by which they are chiefly characterised (*Purāṇapañcalakṣaṇam*).[27]

The *Purāṇas,* in general, have preserved the traditional accounts of the dynasties ruling in India from a primaeval king Manu Vaivasvata (son of Vivasvāna) down to the times of the last great Hindu ruler of Northern India, Prithvirāja Cauhāna. However, the trustworthiness of the *Purāṇic* accounts of the pre-Bhārata war period is less than that of the post-war period.

The historical credibility of the dynastic and genealogical accounts of the pre-Bhārata war period is less than that of the post-war period.

The historical credibility of the dynastic and genealogical accounts of the post-Bhārata war period, particularly from the sixth century B.C. to the rise of the Guptas, as provided in the *Matsya, Vāyu, Viṣṇu, Brahmāṇḍa, Bhāgavata and Bhaviṣya Purāṇas,* is a well-established fact. The *Bhaviṣya* is especially important for the history of the *Rajputa* period to the twelfth century A.D. These six *Purāṇas* constitute very faithful historical records. They have preserved highly valuable accounts of the subject with the help of which we can throw some new light on the dark or obscure aspects of ancient political history. V.A. Smith has also admitted that "... the most systematic record of the Indian historical tradition is that preserved in the dynastic list of the *Purāṇas* . . . modern European writers have been inclined to disparage unduly the authority of the *Purāṇic* lists, but closer study finds in them much genuine and valuable historic tradition."[28] H.H. Wilson has also expressed more or less the same view. He has clearly stated that the dynastic lists of the kings of the post-war period preserved in the *Purāṇic* historical records offer political and chronological particulars. Their general accuracy has also been accepted by him. It has also been pointed out that some Gupta and Andhra rulers as mentioned in the *Purāṇas,* find confirmation in the inscriptions on columns of stones, on rocks and on coins deciphered by archaeologists.[29] Col. Tod has emphatically asserted that "... In the absence of regular and legitimate historical records,there are, however, other native works, which in the hands of a skilful and patient investigator would afford no despicable material for the history of India. The first of these are the *Purāṇas* and genealogical legends of the princes, which obscured as those are by the mythological details, allegory . . . contain many facts that serve as beacon to direct the research of the historian . . ."

"It is said that Indians have no history and that they do not possess any historical instinct. This erroneous opinion about the Hindus owes its origin to the fact that the first literature to which the west came in contact was either the poetical or sacerdotal literature of India in which one would not naturally expect much of the historical knowledge. The *Purāṇas* . . . never attracted much attention to the historical treasures buried in them. The literature of the *Brāhmaṇa* was always supplemented from the earliest times by the literature of the *Kṣatriya* kings . . . compiled in *Vaṁśābalis* or chronicles."[30]

As they stand, the *Purāṇic* genealogies are partly legendary and partly historical. The names of some kings are historically authenticated, but some names are hypothetical. We find some fabrications, interpolations and distortions in the genealogical lists of the

*Purāṇas.* The genealogies are, no doubt, chronologically arranged; the regnal years of the individual kings as well as the total duration of the dynasties are given, etc. but some figures are inflated and arbitrary. However, they are of some considerable importance for the purpose of chronological computation and interpretations, particularly, in the context of the end of the one dynasty and the beginning of other. The chronological sequence in the dynastic accounts of the *Purāṇas* are also, to some extent, broken. The details have also been jumbled up in such a way that sometimes it becomes difficult to separate one from the other—dynastic and genealogical wise. The veracity of the *Purāṇas* is darkened by the shadow of these defects. However, the evidence as a whole cannot be put aside as wholly unworthy of credence or discarded simply because it contains discrepancies and suffers from the lack of coherence.

Apart from the dynastic chronology there are some chronological data in the *Purāṇas,* which constitute the sheet-anchor of ancient Indian chronology. The data concerned help us fix the date of the great Bhārata battle and the beginning of *Kaliyuga,* on the basis of which the dates of subsequent events are fixed. The data also show the period that had elapsed between the two rulers and the two dynasties. However, the exact chronology cannot be determined. The data based on *Saptarṣi* era or an astronomical era used by astronomers for making calculation not by years or decades, but by centuries on the basis of the movements of the heavenly bodies in conjunction with certain planets, are not much useful for our historical purposes, as it was not an historical era based on any memorable historical event. No exact chronology can be determined on the basis of the data concerned but only some tentative inferences can be drawn from it. However, the historical importance of the *Purāṇic* chronology, as a whole, cannot be dismissed.

F.E. Pargiter, while making distinction between the Brāhmaṇical tradition as recorded in the Vedas, the *Brāhmaṇas* and other *brāhmaṇic* literature and the *Kṣatriya* tradition as recorded in the two epics and the *Purāṇas,* so as to judge their comparative historical value, has observed that the historical tradition in the *Vedic* and other *brāhmaṇic* literature is not reliable and they do not make any historical sense, since they give us notices of ancient times from the *brāhmaṇic* and religious points of view. "*Vedic* literature is not authoritative in historical matters, and conclusions drawn from it are not criteria for estimating the results yielded by historical tradition in the epics and *Purāṇas.*"[31] Further "the lack of the historical sense was a special characteristic of the *brāhmaṇs.* The *Vedic* texts, notoriously, are not books of historical purpose, nor do they deal with history."[32] The *Brāhmaṇs,* according to him, failed to compose genuine history, fabricated incorrect stories and fables and neglected to revise or harmonize historical tradition. They did not maintain the distinction between history and mythology, rather they confused both by mythologizing history and giving mythology an historical garb. Thus, there was a total lack of the historical sense among the *brāhamaṇs.* But the "*Purāṇic brāhmaṇs* preserved a large mass of *Kṣatriya* and popular tradition which was inconsistent with brahmanic stories and tenets".[33] Further, the "lack of the historical sense in ancient Indian literature is a commonplace, but it does not hold entirely good as regards *Kṣatriya* tradition. Before the invention of writing, genealogies, ballads and tales are practically the only literature of an historical kind that can exist. Genealogies are essentially chronological . . . and have also an historical character. Royal genealogies certainly do not lack the historical sense, and those *Kṣatriya* tales and ballads are generally consistent in their historical conditions . . ."[34] While making a statement in a comparative fashion, he writes, "Though historical works about ancient India are wanting, yet tradition has handed down fairly copious genealogies of the ancient dynasties. These state the succession of kings and in that way are historical. They are almost the only historical data found in Sanskrit books as regards ancient political development." . . . The genealogies form the basis by which the investigation of tradition for historical ends may be tested. They supply the best chronological clue, for the *Vedic* literature . . . is not a sure ('trustworthy') guide in historical matters."[35]

I am not in perfect agreement with Pargiter, so far as the historical authenticity of at least the *Ṛgveda* is concerned. We find some contradictions in his statements. On the one hand, being greatly influenced by what Macdonell said, "History is the one weak spot in Indian literature. It is, in fact, non-existent. The total lack of the historical sense is so characteristic that the whole course of Sanskrit literature is darkened by the shadow of this defect, suffering as it does from an entire absence of exact chronology",[36] he has heaped heavy accusations on the non-*Purāṇic Brāhmaṇs* and cast his doubt on their historical sense. But, on the other, he has maintained that they also contributed something to our historical knowledge. Actually, Macdonell's statement is general and not about any particular category of literature. Moreover, this is untenable. But Pargiter, unfortunately, applied his statement only to the *brāhmaṇic* literature. Quite contrary to it he has admitted that the greatest brahmanical book, the *Ṛgveda*, contains historical allusion i.e. contemporary persons and events and there are some "plain statements in the genealogies and tradition, which assign him a definite place in the scheme of Aryan expansion in North India." But "contemporary historical notices in the *Ṛgveda* therefore remain chronologically vague, and by themselves yield little information that can be co-ordinated for historical purposes."[37]

We cannot totally ignore the historical value of the *Vedic* tradition since it is also identical with that of the *Purāṇic* tradition, so far as some rulers of the Solar and Lunar dynasty are concerned. The *Vedic* data also help us ascertain their antiquity. It is, of course, undeniable that their genealogies are not arranged chronologically or otherwise. The historical importance of the *Vedas* has been sufficiently highlighted by F. Max Müller.[38] U.N. Ghoshal, on the basis of his study of the historical traditions preserved in the *Vedic Saṁhitās, Brāhmaṇas*, epics and the *Purāṇas,* has also accepted that "the historical sense had dawned upon the Indians at the beginning of their history."[39] A.K. Warder has also expressed more or less the same view.[40] A.B. Keith has candidly stated that early India was not destitute of historical tradition. He observes, "That, the *Vedic* texts, the *Saṁhitās* and the *Brāhmaṇas* are not books of historical purpose, is notorious."[41] Notwithstanding his statement, Pargiter has repeatedly stated that the *brahmaṇic* literature does not contain the historical material.[42] The allegations levelled by Pargiter against the *Brāhmaṇs* in the context of historical validity of their writings have also been dismissed by Jayachandra Vidyalankar[43] and P.V. Kane.[44] As a matter of fact, the *Vedas* and the *Purāṇas* are the two important sources of tradition as history. It is altogether different thing that the *Purāṇic* accounts of the subject are more elaborated and amplified than the *Vedic* ones. It goes without saying that Pargiter has placed his reliance only on the epic and *Purāṇic* tradition for his writings on the subject concerned.

Pargiter has not drawn information from the Buddhist and Jain literature, the reason being as stated by himself, "it is of no real help : it is religious, does not deal with history any more than *Vedic* literature . . ."[45] But this is not a valid reason, because they are very useful for our purpose. Before we proceed to prove that they bear the historicity and are of great help for our purpose, here it is imperative to prove first the relevance of the data obtained from the epics for dealing with the subject concerned.

The data contained in *Vālmiki-Rāmāyaṇa* relating to the Solar and Lunar dynasties of particularly the pre-Bhārata war period are helpful for filling in the gaps in the *Purāṇic* accounts of the subject. The details provided in the *Mahābhārata* about the genealogies, kingdoms, towns and cities of the rulers of Lunar dynasty, particularly of Puru's line of the pre-Bhārata War period, the expansion of the Pauravas in the Ganga-Yamuna Doab in the later *Vedic* period and the growth of urban centres, etc. are supplementary to the details obtained from the *Purāṇas.* The information supplied in the same text about the Pauravas of the post-war period is also of considerable historical importance.

Some other literary sources like the *Garga Saṁhitā*—the *Yuga Purāṇa* section (composed some time between *c.* 144 B.C. and 400 A.D.), *Svapnavāsavdatta* of Bhāsa (*c* 53-41 B.C.), *Mṛcchakatika* of Śudraka (placed between the fifth and seventh century A.D.), *Harṣacarita* of Bāna (A.D. 606-647) and *Kathāsaritsāgara* of Somadeva (ascribed to the eleventh century A.D.) are also important for corroborating the evidence of the *Purāṇic* literature about the dynasties of the early historical period.

The Jaina historical traditions recorded in the canonical texts, *Uttarādhyayana* (*Sūtra*), *Kalpasūtra* (*Bṛhat*), *Āvaśyaka Cūrni* and *Jambuddīvapaṇṇati* or *Jambudvipa-Prajñāpati—Saṁgraha*—(*c* A.D. 700), and non-canonical texts (of both ancient and medieval periods), *Tiloyapaṇṇati* or *Trailōkyaprajñāpati* of Yativṛṣabha (a *Prākṛt* text ascribed to *c* A.D. 176), the *Harivaṁśa Purāṇa* of Jinasena (*c* A.D. 783), the *Uttarapurāṇa* of Gunabhadra (*c* A.D. 898), which is a latter part of the *Ādi Purāṇa* of Jinasena, *Dhavala* (*c* A.D. 780) of Virasena, *Jayadhavala* (*c* A.D. 837) of Jinasena Svāmin, *Trilokasāra* of Nemicandra (*c* A.D. 973) and other Digambara works, the *Paṭṭāvalis—Titthogāli—Painna*, an old Prākṛt text, *Tirthoddhāra Prakarana* and *Tapāgaccha*—paṭṭāvali (based on the *Śvetāmbra* tradition), *Vicāraśreni* (*c* A.D. 1304) of Merutunga, *Prabhāvakacarita* (*c* A.D. 1277) of Prabhācandra, *Vividha Tirtha-Kalpa* (*c* A.D. 1332) of Jinaprabhā Sūri and other *Śvetāmbara* works, the *Pariśiṣṭaparvan* (*Sthavirāvalīcarita*) of Hemacandra (1088-1172), *Vasudevahindi* (an authentic Jain version of the *Bṛhatkathā*) of Dharmadāsa, etc. supplement the *Purāṇic* accounts of the dynasties of both pre and post-historical times, in general, and of the dynasties from the Pradyotas to the Guptas, in particular. But the dynastic lists of kings are incomplete and the total reign-period as given by the Jaina scholars are not fully reliable. The comparative use of the Jaina chronological tradition and the *Purāṇic* and Buddhist tradition in respect of the dynastic chronology has yielded some satisfactory result.

The Buddhist historical tradition recorded in the Canonical Pāli texts (ascribed to the period extending from the fifth to the first century B.C.) : the *Vinaya Piṭaka*,. the *Dīgha Nikāya, Majjhima Nikāya, Saṁyutta Nikāya* and *Khuddaka Nikāya*—(*Jātakas, Sutta Nipāta* and *Udana*—the three of the sixteen books of this *Nikāya*), the post-Canonical two great Pāli chronicles of Ceylon—the *Dipavaṁśa* (an ancient Buddhist historical record *c.* 410-432 A.D.) and the *Mahāvaṁśa* (ascribed to *Mahānāma, c* 459-477 A.D.) and Commentaries—the *Samanta-pāsādikā* (on the *Vinaya Piṭaka*) and *Sumangalā-Vilāsini* (on the *Dīgha Nikāya*) written by Buddhaghosa, an Indian Buddhist scholar, in Ceylon in the first-half of the fifth century A.D., the Sanskrit-Buddhist texts—the *Bodhisattvāvadāna-Kalpalata* of Kshemendra (*c* 1028-1089 A.D.) of Kashmir, the *Divyāvadāna, Mahāvastu* and *Lalitavistara* (a kind of Buddhist *Purāṇa*), etc. in general, are extremely important for supplementing the *Purāṇic* accounts of kingdoms and dynasties of both pre- and post-Bhārata war period to the second century B.C. The two Ceylonese Chronicles, one commentary—the *Samanta-pāsādikā* and one Sanskrit Buddhist text, *Divyāvadāna*, are of special importance for examining the historical authenticity of the *Purāṇic* evidence with regard to the genealogies and chronology of the dynasties from the sixth century B.C. to the end of the age of the Mauryas. The data contained in the Buddhist sources as a whole help us fill in several vacuums in the *Purāṇic* accounts of the subject under discussion. The *Purāṇic* tradition has, no doubt, variant form.

The archaeological reports of the excavated sites are of a great help for us for not only proving the existence and antiquity of the towns and cities that flourished in different parts of India in the pre-Bhārata war period, in general, and in the Ganga-Yamuna Doab in the first and second half of the first millennium B.C., in particular, during the rule of the Solar and Lunar dynasties, but also for throwing some light on the settlement-patterns of the natives. Some other archaeological evidence like coins and inscriptions help us confirm the *Purāṇic* list of kings of various dynasties. The archaeological data provided by A. Cunningham in some of his important works[46] serve as a trustworthy guide for ascertaining the actual geographical position of the remains of ancient kingdoms, their capital cities, etc. We have sufficient archaeological evidence to confirm the epic and *Purāṇic* tradition, so far as the emergence, growth and decline of the early urban centres are concerned.

Ancient Indian historical tradition also finds reflection in some of the non-Indian sources. In this connexion the Classical (Greek and Roman) tradition is worth noting. The chronological tradition of ancient Hindus, as recorded by Megasthenes (*c* 303-298 B.C.) in his "*Indica*" and further quoted by Pliny (*c* 23-79 A.D.) in his "*Natural History*", Arrian (*c* 130-172 A.D.) in his "*Indica*" and Solinus (third century A.D.), testifies to the fact that from the earliest times to Alexander or Candragupta 153 kings ruled for 6,451 years and three months. This is not only important for supporting the evidence that the genealogies were maintained by the *Purāṇic* chroniclers, but also for computing the

*Purāṇic* and Classical chronological data in a comparative manner for determining the date of Bhārata battle. The data provided in the Geography of Ptolemy (first-half of the second century A.D.) relating to both the Solar and Lunar dynasties, the towns and cities of both Lower and Upper Gangetic region etc. and interpreted by various other scholars have been used as supporting evidence.

Some threads of the *Purāṇic* data have also been picked up from the accounts of two celebrated Chinese travellers, Fa-hien (*c.* 399-414 A.D.) and Hiuen-Tsang (*c.* 629-645 A.D.) and woven into the texture of the history befitting to the context.

The information supplied by Abul-Fazl Allami in his '*Ain-i-Akbari*'[47] is helpful for chronological interpretations in connection with fixation of the date of Bhārata battle and the beginning of the *Kali-Yuga*.

The data brought to light by Sir William Jones,[48] Capt. F. Wilford,[49] John Bentley,[50] Colebrooke[51] and Dr. Bühler[52] on the basis of their researches are very useful for making a thorough investigation into the *Purāṇic* dynastic genealogies and chronology.

Some noted Indian and foreign scholars like F. Max Müller,[53] H.H. Wilson,[54] F.E. Pargiter,[55] J.F. Fleet,[56] J. Kennedy,[57] R. Morton Smith,[58] V.A. Smith,[59] A.S. Altekar,[60] D.R. Mankad,[61] V.R.R. Dikshitar,[62] A. Banerji Shastri,[63] A.D. Pusalker,[64] R.G. Bhandarkar,[65] D.R. Bhandarkar,[66] C.V. Vaidya,[67] Harprasad Shastri,[68] Vasudeva Sharan Agrawala,[69] R.C. Hazra,[70] K.P. Jayaswal,[71] Jayacandra Vidyalankar,[72] M. Krishnamachariar,[73] A.K. Majumdar,[74] E.J. Rapson,[75] S.N. Pradhan,[76] H.C. Raychaudhuri,[77] B.C. Law,[78] R.S. Tripathi,[79] Romila Thapar[80] and Kota Venkatachalam[81] by throwing light on the dynastic, genealogical and chronological aspects, etc., have contributed a lot to the enrichment of our knowledge about the subject concerned.

The history of the *Purāṇic* researches carried out by both oriental and occidental scholars during last more than a century is too long to be covered here as it is neither necessary nor desirable. However, there is an ample scope for throwing new light on the subject with the help of all available sources.

Ancient Indian historical tradition has not yet been meticulously examined with the aid of different historical traditions and other relevant information. The work of this type is still a desideratum. The analyses and interpretations of the data contained in the primary and secondary sources have been made with relative judgment. The methodological technique applied in the treatment of the subject is entirely different from that of others.

The present research work, hopefully, will restore several broken chains in the political and cultural history of Ancient India. It will open up a new avenue for the reconstruction of ancient Indian history from the dynastic, genealogical and chronological points of view. Some of the important aspects of *Purāṇic* tradition of historiography find expression in the treatment of the present subject. The work, as a whole, will be useful for historians, indologists and archaeologists.

## References and Notes

1. (a) "Archaeology and Tradition" and (b) "Prehistoric Colonization in India : Archaeological and Literary Evidences", in *AIHA* (eds. S.P. Gupta and K.S. Ramachandran, Delhi, 1977), pp. 277-81 and pp. 299-311 respectively; see also his *Prehistory of India* (Delhi, 1977), pp. 179f; *PPIP* (Poona, 1974), pp. 400-5, 555-58.
2. *AIHA*, p. 281.
3. *DDEI* (ed. J.L. Shastri, Delhi, 1973), Preface, see also pp. 1-3.
4. *AV*, 11, 4, 7, 24 (Where the word *Purāṇa* has been mentioned along with the three *Vedas, Ṛg., Sāma* and *Yajur*, which shows its antiquity); *Śat. Br.*, 13. 4.3. 12-13; *Go. Br.*, Purvabhāga, 2.10 (for the composition of the *Itihāsa-Purāṇa* along with the *Vedas*); *Krm.*, 1, 50, 10-11, 1, 50, 20-21; *Pdm. Sṛṣṭikhaṇḍa*, 1, 50-52; *Pātālakhaṇḍa*, 70, 62; *Mats.*, 53, 4-7; *Bhāg.*, 5,3; *Devi Bhāgavata*, 5, 3, 17; *Vrh.*, 112, 69; *Śiv.*, *Revākhaṇḍa*, 1, 23-30 (the *Purāṇic* evidence in this regard is more explicit than the *Vedic* and *Brāhmaṇic* ones).
5. For details see F.E. Pargiter, *AIHT* (Delhi, 1972), pp. 15-24; V.S. Pathak, *Ancient Historians of India* (Bombay, 1966), pp. 21 ff.
6. *Vṣṇ.*, 3, 4, 6-10; *Krm.*, 1, 1, 2-8; 1, 50, 13-14; *Vy.*, 43, 137-48; *Pdm.*, V, 1, 2, 11-14, 27; *Bmd.*, iv, 4, 67 f; *HV*, 1, 11, 16. According to the *Mats.* (164, 16) the *Ādi-Purāṇas* and *Vedas* were recited by *Brāhmaṇs*. The *Lg.* (1, 39, 61) clearly states that the *Itihāsa* and *Purāṇa* became separate from each other at much later stage.
   The *Itihāsa-Purāṇa* have been defined in the Sanskrit literature in various ways, i.e. records of the past events, ancient records of the occurrences, etc. See *Mbh. Ādi Parva*, 1, 16; *Bmd.*, 1, 1, 173; *Pdm.*, v, 2, 53; *Yaska's Nirukta*, 2.3.1.42 (as explained by *Durgācārya*),3, 19.4.6 particularly for an equal importance of the *Itihāsa-Purāna* and the *Vedas*. In the *Amarakośa* (1.5.4) of Amara Siṃha, *Itihāsa* has been referred to as "*Itihāsaḥ Purāvṛttaṃa*".
7. *RV*, 3, 5, 54, 9; 3, 5, 58, 6.
8. *Ibid.*, 9, 6, 99, 4.
9. *AV*, 11, 4, 7, 24.
10. *Ibid.*, 15, 1, 6, 11-12.
11. *Śat. Br.*, 11.5.6.8; 11.5.7.9; 13.4.3.12-13; 14.6.10.6; *Go. Br.*, 1.10.2.10.
12. *Tai. Ar.*, 2, 9.
13. *Bṛhadāraṇyaka Upaniṣada*, 2.4.10., See also *Vājasaneyi Brāhmaṇa Upaniṣada*, 2, 4, 10.
14. *Go. Br.*, 1.10; *Chāndogya Upaniṣada*, 7.1.2 :
    "ऋग्वेदं भगवोऽध्येमि यजुर्वेदं सामवेदमाथर्वणं चतुर्थमितिहासपुराणं पञ्चमं वेदानां वेदम्"
    *Shreemada Bhāgavata*, 1.4.20 :
    "इतिहास–पुराणं च पञ्चमो वेद उच्यते"
    *Shreemada Bhāgavata*, 3.12.39 :
    "इतिहास–पुराणानि पञ्चमं वेदभीश्वर . . . . . . . . . . . . ."
    *Mats.*, 53, 3. In Patañjali's *Mahābhāsya* also it is said that :
    " चत्वारो वेदाः . . . . . . . . . . . . . इतिहास पुराणम् . . . . . . . . . . . . . ."
    See also *Nyāyadarśana*, *Vātsyāyanabhāṣya*, 4.1.62.
15. *Arthaśāstra*, Bk. 1, Ch. 3.
16. *Ibid.*, Bk. 1, Ch. 5.
17. *Nāradiya Purāṇa*, 2, 24, 17.
    वेदार्थादधिकं मन्ये पुराणार्थं वरानने।
    वेदाः प्रतिष्ठिताः सर्वे पुराणे नात्र संशयः।।
18. *Ādi Parva*, 1, 204.
    इतिहासपुराणाभ्यां वेदं समुपबृंध्येत्।
    विभेत्यल्पश्रुताद् वेदो मामयं प्रहरिस्यति।।

19. *Vy.*, 1, 201-3; *Nārada Purāna, Uttarabhāga*, 24, 18.
20. *Vy.*, 103, 48, and 51.
    इमं यो ब्राह्मणो विद्वानितिहासं पुरातनम ।
    श्रृणुयाद् श्रावयेद्वापि तथाऽध्यापयतेऽपिच ।।
    x x x x x
    धन्यं यशस्यमायुस्यं पुण्यं वैदैश्च समतम् ।
    कृष्णद्वैपायनेनोक्तं पुराणं ब्रह्मवादिनः ।।
    *Mats.*, 72, 6 (also 17.6). See also *Bmv., Uttarakhaṇḍa*, 133, 5 (for *Itihāsa-Purāṇa* on the basis of the statement of *Sūta*).
21. *Ādi Parva*, 1, 17 f, 24-25, 48-52, 62-63; 11, 31,-33; 56, 15-16.
22. *Ibid.*, 56, 19, 25-27; *Svargārohana Parva*, 5, 39, and 43.
23. *Bh. Sv.*, Vol. 1, pp. 17, 21, 27-30, 48-52, Vol. 3, p. 229.
24. *The Mahābhārata : A Criticism* (Delhi, 1966), pp. 50 ff.
25. *AIHT*, p. 50; *PDKA* (London, 1913), pp. vii-viii, xii-xiv, xxiv-xxv.
26. *JRAS*, 1912, pp. 248-55, quoted in *AIHT*, p 49.
27. *Krm.*, 1.1.12; *Bmv., Uttarakhaṇḍa*, 133, 6; *Devi Bhāgavata*, 1.2.18.
28. *EHI* (Oxford, 1924), p. 11.
29. *Tr. Vṣṇ.* (Calcutta, 1961), Preface, pp. lxviii-lxlx, lxx.
30. Srisa Chandra Vidyarnava, "*Paurāṇik* Chronology in the *Matsya Purāṇam c.f. SBA*, Vol. 1 (ed. J.D. Akhtar, Delhi, 1972), App. VIII, lxx-xciii.
31. *AIHT*, p. 14.
32. *Ibid.*, p. 61.
33. *Ibid.*, pp. 61-63.
34. *Ibid.*, p. 60-61.
35. *Ibid.*, p. 11.
36. *HSL* (first pub., Oxford, 1899, 3rd. edn., Delhi, 1972), pp. 10-11.
37. *AIHT*, pp. 1-2.
38. *HASL* (Varanasi, 1968), pp. 11, 57-59.
39. *The Beginnings of Indian Historiography and other Essays* (Calcutta, 1944), pp. 21-23, 50-52.
40. *An Introduction to Indian Historiography* (Bombay, 1972), pp. 15-25.
41. *HSL* (first Pub. Oxford, 1920, Delhi, 1973), pp. 144-45; *JRAS*, 1914, pp. 739, 1031 note, 1915, p. 143 note.
42. *AIHT*, p. 2.
43. *Bhāratiya Itihāsa Kī Ruparekha* (Prayag, 1933), Pt. 1, pp. 239-47.
44. *History of Dharmaṣāstra* (Poona, 1963), Vol. 5, Pt. 2, pp. 845-49.
45. *AIHT*, p. 14.
46. *CAGI* (Varanasi, 1979), pp. 40-44, 88 f., 303-94, 402 f; *CAI* (London, 1891) and his archaeological reports.
47. Tr. into English by Col. H.S. Jarrett and annotated by Sir Jadu Nath Sarkar (Delhi, 1988), Vol. 2, pp. 15-16 ("*Era of the Hindus*" with notes).
48. "On the Chronology of the Hindus" (which was written in Jan. 1788 on the basis of Pt. Radha Kanta Sharma's '*Purānārthaprakāshā*', based on the *Bhāgavata Purāna* and first pub. in *As. Res.*, 1799) pub. in *As. Res.*, Delhi, 1979, Vol. 2, pp. 107-13; also Lord Teignmouth (ed.) *The Works of Sir William Jones* (in 13 Vols.), Vol. IV, London, 1807, pp. 36-46.
49. "Chronology of the Hindus" in *As. Res.* (Delhi, 1979), Vol. 5, pp. 241-92; "An Essay on the Sacred Isles in the West with other Essays connected with other essays that works" in *As. Res.* (Delhi, 1979), Vol. IX, pp. 84-210 (for kings and their Chronology).

50. "On the Principal Eras and Dates of the Ancient Hindus" (first written in 1796) pub. in *As. Res.* (Delhi, 1979), Vol. V, pp. 315-43; "On the Hindu System of Astronomy and their connection with History in Ancient and modern times" in *As. Res.* (Delhi, 1979), pp. 225 ff. (It was first pub. in *As. Res.*, Vol. VIII, 1809, pp. 195-244).
51. "The *Saptarṣi* Era" in *As. Res.*, Vol. IX (first pub. 1811 and then Delhi, 1979), pp. 323-76.
52. "Hindu Chronology" in *EB* (11th Edn.), Vol. 13, pp. 499-500.
53. *HASL*, pp. 264-69.
54. Tr. *Vṣṇ* (Calcutta, 1961), pp. 277-391; Tr. Vols. 1-X (ed. F. Hall, London, 1864-70).
55. *AIHT*, pp. 90-119, 253-89; *PDKA*, pp. 2-73; "Ancient Indian Genealogies and Chronology" in *JRAS* (London, 1910), pp. 11-56; "Earliest Indian Traditional History" in *JRAS*, 1914, pp. 267 ff; *Mkd.* (tr. *BIS*, *ASB*, Calcutta, 1904).
56. "The *Kali-Yuga* Era" in *JRAS*, 1911.
57. "The *Purāṇic* Histories of the Early Aryas" in *JRAS*, 1915.
58. *DDEI Intr.*, pp. 1-386; "The Early Chronology of India" in *JAOS*, Vol. 77, No. 2, April-June, 1957; No. 4, Dec. 1957.
59. *EHI* (4th edn. Oxford, 1924), pp. 41-48.
60. "Can we Reconstruct Pre-Bhārata War History" ? in *JBHU*, Vol. IV, pp. 183-223; also his presidential address, Section I : "Archaic and Early Cultural HIstory", Indian Hist. Congress, 3rd Session, Calcutta, 15-17 Dec., 1939.
61. "Studies in *Purāṇic* History, genealogies and Chorology in Modern Times" in "*Purāṇa*", Vol. 4, 1962, No. 1, pp. 3-22; ed. *Garga-Yuga Purāṇam* : A Chapter from the *Garga-Saṁhitā* (Vallabhvidyanagar, Gujarat, 1951), also his paper on *Yugas* and *Manvantras* in *IHQ*, Vol. XVIII, pp. 208-30.
62. "The *Purāṇa* : A study in *IHQ*, Vol. VIII, pp. 747-67; The *Matsya Purāṇa* : *A Study*, Madras, 1935.
63. "On Ancient Indian Historical Tradition" in *JBORS*, Vol. XIII, pp. 62-79.
64. "Conception of History in Ancient Indian Literature", in *Our Heritage* (Calcutta, 1964), Vol. 12, Pt. 2, pp. 35-52; *Studies in Epics and Purāṇas of India* (Bombay, 1955), pp. 1-48; "Progress of Indic Studies" 1917-42, Silver Jubilee Vol. Pub. by *BORI*, Poona, 1942, pp. 139-52; "Traditional History from the Earliest Time to the Accession of Parikshit" in *HCIP* (The *Vedic* age, Bombay, 1965), pp. 271-322; "From the Accession of Parikshit to the End of the Bārhadratha Dynasty" in *Ibid.*, pp. 323-33, also *cf. Historians and Historiography on Modern India* (ed. S.P. Sen, Calcutta, 1973), pp. 32-34 (particularly about the Andhra dynasty).
65. *EHD* (Delhi, 1979), Intr. 1-IV, pp. 8-23; A peep into the Early History of India (Varanasi, 1978), pp. 19-36.
66. *Carmichael Lectures on the Ancient History of India*, c. 650-325 B.C. (Calcutta, 1918-19).
67. See *JBBRAS*, 1925, pp. 155 ff.
68. See his papers on the *Mahā-Purāṇas* in *JBORS*, Vol. XV, pp. 323-40.
69. *Matsya Purāṇa, A Study* (Varanasi, 1963).
70. *SPRH* (Dacca, 1940), pp. 208-12.
71. *JBORS*, 1915, 1917, 1919, 1933; *History of India c. 150-350* A.D. (Lahore, 1933); also "Historical Data in the *Gargi Saṁhitā* and the *Brāhmin* Empire" in *JBORS*, Vol. XIV (1928), pp. 397-421.
72. *Op. cit*, Pt. 1, pp. 239 f; Pt. 2, pp. 89 ff.
73. *HCSL* (Delhi, 1974), pp. Int., pp. xxxviii-xliii, XLix-XLviii, XLxxvi f.
74. *EHIDS* (first Pub. Dacca, 1917, reptd. Delhi, 1981), Vol. 1, pp. 6 ff; Vol. 11, pp. 353 ff.
75. "The *Purāṇas*" in *CHI* (Delhi, 1962), Vol. 1, Ancient India, pp. 264-84.
76. *Chro. An. Ind.* (Varanasi, 1979), pp. 61-248.
77. *PHAI* (6th edn., Calcutta, 1953), pp. 12-84, 205-29, 264-530.

78. "Countries and Peoples of India" (Epic and Paurāṇic Sources") in *ABORI*, Vol. XVII (1936),, Pt. 111, pp. 223 ff and in *GAGI* (Varanasi, 1976), pp. 128-67; *IETBJ* (Varanasi, 1980), pp. 34-80, 87-135.
79. *HAI*, (Delhi, 1985), pp. 112-14, 182-91.
80. "*Purāṇic* Lineages and Archaeological Cultures" in *AISH* (Hyderabad, 1984), pp. 240 ff; "The Tradition of Historical Writing in Early India" in *ibid*., pp. 268 ff; "Origin, Myths and the Early Indian Historical Tradition" in *ibid*., pp. 294 ff; "Genealogy as a Source of Social History" in *ibid*., pp. 326-60 and in *IHR*, Vol. II, No. 2 (Jan. 1976), pp. 259-81; *From Lineage to State* (Bombay, 1984), pp. 130-42.
81. *The Plot in Indian Chronology* (Vijayawada, 1953), pp. 23 f, 38 f, 80 ff; *Chronolgy of Ancient Hindu History* (in two parts, Vijayawada, 1957), Pt. 1, pp. 34 f, 90 ff. See also The *Matsya Purāṇam; SBA*, Vol. 1 (ed. J.D. Akhtar, Delhi, 1972), pp. 125-340 & APP. I-X for the views, articles and notes of various scholars including H.H. Wilson, Bentley, Wilford and B.C. Majumdar.

# 2

# From Manu Vaivasvata to the Accession of Parīkshit

## General Background

ACCORDING to ancient Indian historical tradition, as recorded in the *Purāṇas*, all the kings and chiefs ruling over various kingdoms throughout India during the period concerned belonged to different dynasties that sprang from Ikṣvāku of the Solar race, Purūravas of the Lunar race and Sudyumna, constituting three separate stocks descended from Manu Vaivasvata. The *Purāṇic* texts, while tracing back all the royal lineages to Manu, have assigned nine sons to him. They were Ikṣvāku, Nābhāga or Nṛga, Dhṛṣṭa, Śaryāti, Nariśyanta, Prāṁśu, Nābhānediṣṭha, Karūṣa and Pṛṣadhra (traditionally called nine Mānavas)[1]. The reliability of this list can be tested only on the basis of the collated text.

Manu is further said to have divided the Indian territories among his sons. Ikṣvāku, the eldest and chief among them and the progenitor of the Solar dynasty, obtained Madhyadeśa with its capital at Ayodhya.[2] His descendants continued to rule over there for the longest period of history, i.e. till the rise of the Nandas. Nābhāga and his successors (called Nābhāgas), probably, reigned in the midlands of the Gangetic Doāb and from them descended the Rathitaras, who were *Kṣatriyan Brāhmaṇs*.[3] The kingdom founded on the southern bank of the river Yamuna is ascribed to him, but Nābhāgas' line played no conspicuous part in the traditional history, probably because of their conquest by the rulers of Purūravas' line. Ambarisa, son of Nābhāga was the ruler of Sindhudvipa[4] but no confirmatory evidence is adduced in support of this view. Dhṛṣṭa, from whom sprang number of clans collectively known as Dhārṣṭakas[5] and reckoned sometimes as *Kṣatriyas*, sometimes as *Brāhmaṇas* and sometimes as *Vaiśyas*, ruled over Vāhika country, generally identified with Punjab,[6] but not in the Bāhlika region as stated in *Śiva Purāṇa*.[7] Śaryāti founded the dynasty of Ānarta. Actually the kingdom of Ānarta (Ānartadeśa Northern Saurāṣṭra, Gujarat) was named after his son Ānarta. He and his successors ruled over this kingdom with its capital at Kaśasthali, which was later named as Dvāravati or Dvārakāpuri.[8] This can also be partly confirmed by the epigraphic evidence.[9] Nābhānediṣṭha is believed to have founded the Vaiśāla dynasty. The rulers falling directly in his line (Vaiśālakas) reigned in the country of Viśālā, which was in Vidisa (Bhilsa or Besnagar) region or Eastern Malava and Avanti or Western Malava in Central India. This can be easily distinguished from the kingdom of Vaiśāli (Basārh in

North Bihar in eastern India), which was later built by a king, Viśāla, one of the descendants of Manu.[10] There is much confusion about Nariṣyant's offspring. Some *Purāṇas* refer to them as the Śakas.[11] If so, they settled in Central Asia outside India, where their descendants became widely known as the śakas, but it is always open to doubt. Nariṣyanta is correctly mentioned in some *Purāṇas*[12] as a king of the Vaiśāla dynasty. Karūṣa, from whom descended the numerous *Kṣatriya* clans of the Karūṣas and were valiant fighters,[13] occupied the Karūṣa country, which roughly corresponds to the region round the modern Rewa and eastwards to the river Sone.[14] The kingdom, which he established on the bank of the said river, also comprised the Śāhābāda Dist. of Bihar and its southern and western portion in the *Rāmāyaṇa* age. The Karūṣas are also placed in the north, but their country is usually placed upon the paripatra or Vindhya mountains.[15] Pṛṣadhra[16] did not have the fortune of establishing any dynasty because of his exclusion from territorial share as a punishment for killing his *guru*'s (preceptor's) cow. He was degraded to the rank of a *Śudra*. Nothing is known either about Prāmśu or about his descendants.

From the above description it is quite evident that of nine sons of Manu, three,—Ikṣvāku, Śaryāti and Nābhānediṣtha or Nābhāgodiṣṭa,—were very important, as they were the founders of the three noted kingdoms and dynasties at Ayodhya, Ānarta and Vaiśāli respectively. But on the other hand, the dynastic rule over the kingdoms established by Karūṣa, Nābhāga, Dhṛṣṭa and Nariṣyanta soon came to an end, probably because of the persistent attempts of the rulers of the Lunar dynasty to expand the frontiers of their kingdom by subjugating the territories of the former and bringing them under their political hegemony.

Purūravas Aila,[17] the founder of the Lunar dynasty, and his lineage ruled at Pratiṣṭhānapur[18] (Jhūṅsi in Prayāga, situated on the eastern side of the confluence of the Ganga and Yamuna). They formed the second stock. The most prominent dynasties that sprang from the Ailas were known as the Kānyakubjas, Yādavas (divided into several branches, notably, Andhakas, Vṛṣṇis, Bhojas and Haihyas) Ānavas, Druhyus, Turuvasas, Pañcālas, Bārhadrathas, Cedis, etc.

It was Sudyumna (whose parentage is disputable, but his ancestry can be traced back to Manu, because he was his lineal descendant), who first received the town Pratiṣṭhāna, but gave it to Purūravas.[19] After having abdicated his throne at Pratiṣṭhāna, he moved towards Magadha in the east in an attempt to have territorial settlements for his sons. His three sons, Utakala, Gaya and Vinatāśva or Haritāsva, ruling over the Utkala country (Orissa), the town of Gaya in the Magadha region in eastern India and a kingdom in the eastern side bordering the realm of Northern Kurus respectively,[20] formed the third stock. His third son has also been placed in the Western,[21] as well as the Southern region.[22] Utkalas and other clans occupied the hilly tracts from Gaya to Orissa. These three principalities have been designated collectively as the "Saudyumnas". They are said to have "occupied the town Gaya, the country eastward of a line drawn roughly from Gaya to Cuttack and the region north of the Ganges eastward of Videha and the

Vaiśālaka kingdom".[23] Whatever may be the fact, this cannot be denied that their principal dominions were in the eastern region. Their kingdoms were finally annexed by the Ānavas and Kānyakubjas to their respective territories.

The three important dynasties that sprang from Manu were the Solar dynasty with its principal seat at Ayodhya, the Lunar dynasty at Pratiṣṭhānpur and Saudyumna dynasty, which reigned in eastern part of India. It is worthy of note that territorial divisions and their assignments to lineal descendants of the kings of three different stocks, as recorded in the *Purāṇic* tradition, led to the setting up of different kingdoms and sub-kingdoms in early period out of which some lost their independent existence because of their annexations to the neighbouring powerful kingdoms, and some continued to exist till later period because of several factors, which have been analysed subsequently in a proper context.

Here it will be worthwhile to mention the view of H.D. Sankalia. He has pointed out that about 2,250 B.C. the original four Āryan kingdoms founded by four kings : Ikṣvāku, Prāmsu, Sudyumna and Saryāta had developed into so many sub-kingdoms probably by mixing with the original inhabitants.[24] However, no positive evidence has been adduced in confirmation of the hypothesis, particularly relating to their antiquity. The authenticity of the date as suggested by him has been further examined in context of the chronological sequence of the subjects, which figure later.

The historicity of the dynastic lists of royal houses from Manu (Mānavas), Purūravas (Aila) and Sudyumna can, of course, be doubted in absence of the literary data in the form of written tablets, seals or inscriptions on stone or copper, but there are some other literary and archaeological evidences to corroborate the *Purāṇic* accounts. Mr. Sankalia by maintaining a reasonable balance between the *Purāṇic* and archaeological data has proved beyond doubt that the *Purāṇic* tradition is not totally wrong. He also observes that large parts of India such as whole of the Punjab, Uttar Pradesh, Saurashtra and northern Deccan were inhabited by non-Āryan peoples, but it cannot be denied that there was prehistoric colonization of India either by the Āryans or the various *Vedic* or *Purāṇic* tribes. On the basis of the discovery of three or four extensive chalcolithic cultures and Painted Grey Ware culture (PGW) in those parts of India, where the descendants of Manu had different phases of settlements, he has placed his reliance to a reasonable extent on the *Purāṇic* description of the expansion and settlements of Āryans in various phases in eastern, northern, western and central India and of their kingdoms and dynasties founded by different kings.[25]

The popular tradition affirms it that "the royal powers first developed mainly in the Gangetic plain, in the towns, Ayodhya, Mithila, Pratiṣṭhāna and Gaya with an off-lying branch at Kuśasthali on the western sea-coast and apparently two others on the rivers Narbada and Tapti".[26]

Now we will proceed to give a general description of the expansion of descendants of Ikṣvāku of the Solar race in different parts of India and beyond, as well as of their respective kingdoms.

Ikṣvāku's eldest son, Vikukṣi, reigned at Ayodhya.[27] Śakuni, a king of Ikṣvāku line, is said to have got the realm of Uttarāpatha (North-West India) and Vasāti's decendants occupied Dakṣināpatha (the Deccan). Vikukṣi's descendants also colonised the country in the north and south of Meru ("Sumerugiri", i.e. Ilāvṛtavarṣa).[28] Meru and Uttarakuru in north are traditionally placed in Central Asia. Srāvasta, the son of Yuvanāśva and sixth in descent from Kakutstha or Purañjaya, the son of Vikukṣi, founded the city of Śrāvasti (Śrāvastipur)[29] which later became the capital of north Kosala. Śrāvasti (Saheth-Maheth in the Gonda Dist. of U.P.) is situated on the southern bank of Rāpti. It is 58 miles away from Ayodhya in the north. The capital of North Kosala in ancient times was known as Śrāvasti, Candrikāpuri and Dharmapaṭṭana.

One of Ikṣvāku's son known as Daṇḍa, or Daṇḍaka migrated to a region in the south, which was named after him as Daṇḍakāraṇya.[30] This constituted a kind of watershed in their later phase of transmigration from Kosala to Dakṣina Kosala.

The epic account is little different from the *Purāṇic* one. In the *Vālmīki-Rāmāyaṇa* it is said that Ikṣvāku's youngest son Daṇḍa was made ruler of the region between Vindhya and Śaivala mountains. He founded the town, Madhumanta, where he ruled for a long time.[31] The *Mahābhārata*[32] also refers to 100 families of rulers of the Ikṣvāku dynasty. From one of the chief sons of Ikṣvāku, named Nimi, sprang the dynasty that reigned in Videha. He founded the kingdom, known as Jayantapur (later Janakpur), which is identified with Mithila, (the capital of the kingdom of Videha) named after his son Mithi. The Videha line of kings came to be known as Janakas because of this Mithi Janaka.[33] One of the kings of Ikṣvāku line known as Ḍaśāśva is said to have reigned at Māhiṣmati on the river Narbada,[34] but its historicity cannot be affirmed.

No doubt, some of Ikṣvāku's sons became rulers in the east and west of Āryāvarta and in the Madhyadeśa.[35]

Manu Vaivasvata is said to be the originator of the human race, and all the ruling dynasties of the proto-historic India, as mentioned in the *Purāṇas,* sprang from him. But we find that this identity has been made a subject of great dispute.

D.P. Mishra has mistakenly located the homelands of the Mānavas and Purūravas Ailas in the Herat and Bactrian regions respectively. He thinks that "after Manu parted from his brother Yima, the Mānavas first settled in the region of Herat, then in Seistan and finally near Kandahar". On the basis of the *Purāṇic* evidence, that Nariṣyanta, one of the sons of Manu was the progenitor of the Śakas, he has placed the home of Manu and Nariṣyanta in some region of Iran (ancient Ilāpuri). The regions north of Meru (comprising the vast tract extending from the river Oxus to the Arctic Ocean), ruled by some of Vikukṣi's (Manu's grandson) sons, as stated in the *Purāṇas,* has been located in Central Asia. But the settlements of rest of his sons in India are supported by him.[36]

Before we examine the historical validity of the above statements, it will be quite in the fitness of things to cite the further evidence from the epic about the identity of Purūravas, which is of contradictory nature. The story narrated in the *Uttarakāṇḍa*[37] of *Vālmīki-Rāmāyaṇa* (about the birth of Purūravas, the son of Budha and Ilā) creates an impression that Ilā in previous birth known as the king Ilā (son of Kardama) was ruling over Bāhli from where he later migrated to Madhyadeśa (Ganga-Yamuna Doāb) and founded Pratiṣṭhānapur and became its ruler. After his transformation from manhood to womanhood, Ilā gave birth to Purūravas, who obtained the kingdom of Pratiṣṭhānapur. It is said that after the king Śaśabindu occupied Bāhli, Ilā moved to Mid-India. Whatever may be the interpretation of this myth, it is almost certain that here Bāhli has not been used in the context of Bāhlika (=Iranian Balkh=Greek Bactria in the Oxus valley), but Vāhika (Pubjab). This can also be confirmed by the *Purāṇic* evidence. It is clearly stated in the *Matsya Purāṇa*[38] that Purūravas in his previous birth was the ruler of Madradeśa (western Punjab). But, on the other hand, we find that H.C. Raychaudhuri has tried to establish that Bāhli (lying outside the Madhyadeśa) in Central Asia was "the realm of the parents of Purūravas".[39] This may be misinterpretation of the data available in the text concerned. The fact remains that Madhyadeśa was the original home of Purūravas, as well as his parents Ilā and Buddha.

In *Vālmīki-Rāmāyaṇa* itself we find that Purūravas Aila was the the son of the king Buddha of Kāśi. He was the founder of Pratiṣṭhānapur, a kingdom in Madhyadeśa. It was here that he and his descendants ruled for a considerable period of time. Pratiṣṭhāna was also the capital of the king of Kāśi.[40] The *Vedic Samhitā*[41] and the *Mahābhārata*[42] also provide some indication of their original homeland in India. We have already seen that the *Purāṇas* place Manu in Ayodhya and Purūravas in Pratiṣṭhāna near Allahabad.

Thus, we find that neither Manu's nor Purūravas' homeland was in Central Asia. They were rather of Indian origin. The *Vedic*, Epic and *Purāṇic* traditions confirm this truth. Actually, the early Āryans of Bāhlika in the Vaśksu or Cakṣu (Greek Oxus) Valley, Herat and Kandhar, etc., constituting an integral part of Ariana region falling within the geographical boundaries of ancient Bhāratvarṣa, were of different stock and of indigenous origin, and cannot be connected with either of them (Manu or Purūravas). Thus, it will not be reasonable to include them among the early Āryans of Central Asia. D.P. Mishra's view, as quoted above, is merely based on supposition. The *Purāṇic* evidence, which he has furnished in support of his arguments, is of doubtful nature. Nariṣyanta appears only in the few *Purāṇas* as the progenitor of the Śakas and not in all. Thus, it is partial or inferential evidence. Further, the descendants of Vikukṣi (son of Ikṣvāku) had not the original seat in any part of Central Asia. They were, actually, colonists. In fact, some of the descendants of Manu went outside India and colonised some regions, which does not mean that they were the original settlers of that place. There may be some interpolation and confusion in the *Purāṇic* statements, but the fact remains that a number of descendants of Manu expanded over different regions of India as far as the north-west, and became rulers of the respective kingdoms. They founded kingdoms and dynasties in different parts of India itself. There is no doubt, that according to both the *Vedic* and *Purāṇic* tradition, the history of so-called "Indo-Aryans" begins with Manu Vaivasvata, but it will not be fair on our part to fix his location either according to our convenience or to suit any preconceived idea.

P.L. Bhargava does not consider the *Vedic* Manu as a mythical figure. He rather takes him as a historical person. He has attached great importance to the *Purāṇic* genealogies, which trace the origin of all the Āryan ruling families from Manu. But his statement, that a band of Āryans came to India[43] under the leadership of Manu, does not appear to be very much convincing. Because, there is no such *Purāṇic* tradition to support the view. As a matter of fact, the question of coming of Āryans under his leadership from outside to India does not arise. They were the original inhabitants of India. He has attempted to place Manu's descendants (Mānavas) in the vicinity of the river Indus on the supposition that they carried the names of the rivers, Sarayu and Gomati, from this region before they settled in Kosala. But we find that these two rivers were Harirūda or Avestic Haroyu in Herat and Gomal in Afghanistan respectively. He does not support the *Purāṇic* tradition of locating the founders of the dynasties first in Ayodhya and Pratiṣṭhāna. He locates them first in the Indus and Sārasvata region. Pointing to the *Purāṇic* error regarding the placement of different rulers in different regions of India and their respective order, he has observed that "The Aikshvākus ruled in the country of Kosala in later times, and so the *Purāṇic* editors have located their earlier ancestors in Ayodhya, the most ancient city of Kosala. The Pauravas ruled in the country of Vatsa in later times, and so the *Purāṇic* editors have located their earliest ancestors, Sudyumna and Purūravas in Pratishthāna, an ancient city of the Vatsa Country. The Haihaya Yādavas, another dynasty descended from Sudyumna and Purūravas, ruled in Avanti in later times, and the *Purāṇic* editors have, therefore, located their remotest ancestors in Māhiṣmati, the most ancient city of that region. That the location of the early kings of these dynasties in Ayodhya, Pratishthāna and Māhiṣmati is a mistake, is fully proved by older records preserved in the *Purāṇas* and the *Mahābhārata*, which entirely agree with *Vedic* evidence . . ."[44]

We are not in perfect agreement with Mr. Bhargava, so far as the order of settlements of the descendants of Manu in India is concerned. Some of his views appear to be conjectural. In fact, there were several centres of their settlements. In the early *Vedic* age they had settled in different parts of India including the Sapta-Sindhu region. The migration from one place to another within India itself was going on from the time immemorial. The Āryan culture flourished contemporaneously in different parts of India in the *Ṛgvedic* age. It was the later *Vedic* age, which witnessed the further expansion of Manu's descendants in the Gangetic valley and the Sārasvata region. The old theory regarding the origin of the Āryans, as propounded by western scholars and blindly supported by some Indian scholars, does not hold good. All the conventional explanation put forward to establish that Āryans also represented by Manu and his descendants migrated from their original home in Central Asia first to Afghanistan and then to Punjab and Upper Gangetic Doāb can be, unhesitatingly, dismissed in the light of the evidences furnished in the *Ṛgveda*, epics and *Purāṇic* literature. However, this will be dealt with properly at a different place.

F.E. Pargiter, while giving a brief description of the origins of Solar dynasty of Mānava race (whose capital was at Ayodhya), the Lunar dynasty founded by Purūravas Aila at Pratiṣṭhānapur or Prayag (Allahabad) and Sudyumna dynasty that reigned in Eastern India, has made some observations, which are worthy of our notice. According to him, the founder of the Lunar dynasty belonged to the Aila or Āryan race. Placing his reliance on the Indian tradition exclusively, he has made it very clear that the Madhyadeśa or Ganga-Yamuna Doāb was the original homeland of the Ailas or Āryans. "The Aila stock, which began in a small principality at Allahabad, had dominated the whole of North India and down to Vidarbha . . . The Ailas or Āryans . . . conquered and spread out north-west, west and south, and had by Yayāti's time occupied precisely the region famed Madhyadeśa. They possessed that Mid-land definitely and made it thoroughly "their true pure home". . . They expanded afterwards into the Punjab and East Afghanistan, into West India and the north-west Deccan, into East and South Bihar and into Bengal",[45] linguistically called by G. Grierson Outer Band regions.[46] Tradition has preserved copious accounts of the earliest Ailas (Āryans) and their beginnings in India. They elucidate the domination of India by the five tribes *(Pañcjan)* i.e. Anu, Druhyu, Puru, Yadu and Turvasu, descended from Yayāti (one of the descendants of Purūravas Aila), which goes well in accord with the Āryan occupation of India, geographically and linguistically. It was Madhyadeśa around Allahabad from where the Ailas expanded over different parts of India including north-west. The *Purāṇic* accounts of dynasties and genealogies constitute an eloquent testimony to the fact. One of the noteworthy facts, which can be further highlighted, is that neither the north-west nor the Punjab was regarded as their earliest home.

Indian tradition knows nothing of any Aila or Āryan invasion of India from Afghanistan or from any quarter of the N.W. Frontier and their gradual advance from there eastwards. Pargiter observes that ". . . there was an Aila outflow of the Druhyus through the north-west into the countries beyond, where they founded various kingdoms . . . If the Aryans entered India from the north-west, and had advanced eastward through the Punjab only as far as the Sarasvati or Jumna when the *Ṛgvedic* hymns were composed, it is very surprising that the hymn (X. 75) arranges the rivers not according to their progress, but reversely from the Ganges which they had hardly reached . . . It was however a route for any one travelling from the Ganges to the north-west".[47] The advance of the Ailas from Afghanistan into the Pubjab may simply be reversed by his arguments. The passages from *Vālmīki Rāmāyaṇa* (as quoted earlier), which make Ilā king of "Bālhi or Bālhika", have been interpreted correctly by him. He denotes the Vāhlika country in the Punjab.[48] He also does not support the theory that "Ailas or Aryans invaded India through the north-west after separating from the Iranians and entered in two streams. The connection of Persia with India does not prove that the Aryans entered India from that direction.[49] The theory propounded by Grierson, that "the inhabitants of the Midland represent the latest stage of Indo-Aryan immigration . . . and that the latest invaders entered into the heart of the country already occupied by the first immigrants forcing the latter outwards in three directions, to the east, to the south and to the west",[50] has been rejected by him.[51] This theory is also incompatible with the historical tradition of the *Vedic* and *Purāṇic* periods.

We find some contradiction in Pargiter's statements, so far as the origin of the progenitor, Purūravas Aila, is concerned. On the basis of the *Purāṇic* legends and fables he has connected him with the middle Himalayan region and placed outside India. The fables about the birth of Purūravas as well as his parent, Ilā, in the northern country, Ilāvṛta, named after him, has led Pargiter to believe that his origin was in that north region, which includes the countries in and beyond the middle of the Himalayas, which has always been the sacred land of the Indians. It is said that "Purūrava's name Aila occurs in the *Ṛgveda* and appears to be more ancient than the fable of Manu's daughter Ilā. The suggested connexion between Ilā and Ilāvṛta may be ancient and may merit credence". The formation of Ilāvṛta with Brahmavarta and Āryāvarta has also been pointed out. The myth connects even the Sudyumna stock with that same north region and with the Northern Kurus.[52] That, the country Ilāvṛta in the north was the region from which they came, is not a reasonable supposition. Pargiter has himself accepted that this view is based on mythical tradition. He has not given much credence to the tradition (more legendary than historical), which suggests that the region north of the mid-Himalayas was the original sacred outside land of the Āryans. Considering the fact that Pratiṣṭhānapur was their original home and they did not enter India from the north-west, all ideas drawn from the hypothesis may be put aside.

The theory postulated by Pargiter, that Madhyadeśa around Pratiṣṭhāna, later known as Prayaga or Allahabad, was the original home of the Āryans and from here the sons of Manu Vaivasvata spread out in different directions, has been strongly corroborated by H.D. Sankalia[53] on the basis of the combined testimony of the literary and archaeological data and their rational interpretation. He has further observed that "Accepting the *Purāṇic* view that the Āryans originated somewhere in Mid-Western U.P. around Pratiṣṭhān or Allahabad and spread in all directions, we find that this view fits in surprisingly well with the present known origin and distribution and nature of the PGW and the associated Early Iron age culture. Though we do not know the names of the various rulers at this time except through the *Purāṇas* and late *Vedic* texts . . . We might say that the *Purāṇas* had probably in view the rise and spread of the P.G.W. culture and its authors."[54] Further, "Pargiter's view would very well suit the likely origin and spread of the painted Grey Ware Culture and the various other pottery cultures such as the black-slipped and black-and-red wares found at various sites in U.P., Bihar and West Bengal, might be regarded as antecedent cultures belonging to various indigenous people, particularly the Sudyumnas or the Easterners"[55] . . . who proceeded northwestwards from the Midlands ("the region around Allahabad)".[56]

Pargiter's view relating to the origin of the Lunar dynasty at Pratiṣṭhāna is, of course, very logical, but his statements that the Mānavas (of the Solar race) and the Sudyumnas were of non-Āryan stocks, are not correct at all. The evidence, which he has produced in support of his view, renders the theory hardly tenable. His statements, that the

Mānavas, who held all the rest of India including the three kingdoms of Ayodhya, Videha and Vaiśāli, belonged to Dravidian stock, and the Ayodhya realm was non-Aila (non-Āryan), and it was not subdued by the Ailas rather influenced by them,[57] run contrary to the truth. The *Purāṇic* genealogies of the Solar race in no way land support to his view, and, hence, it can be disposed of as a fanciful notion. The Mānavas were, no doubt, of Āryan stock. It is absurd to locate the Dravidians at Ayodhya in mid-Āryāvarta or middle Gangetic plain. It goes without saying that the Dravidians' original home has been in the far South since time immemorial. Pargiter's inference that the names of the early kings of the Mānava stock were sanskritized in course of time; in Oudh there was a mixture of language and here the Midland language had not established itself so firmly as it had in the west and south,[58] has not been drawn from any relevant source.

Likewise, he has wrongly identified the Sudyumna stock with the Mundas of the Mon Khmer race on the ground that they were ruling over territories located in South-Bihar and Orissa in the east.[59] He has not given any satisfactory explanation in support of this identification. Influenced by Grierson's linguistic explanation of the Munda language and the "Pronominalized Himalayan languages",[60] he has unreasonably placed them under this group. His attempt to establish some connexion between Sudyumna (so-called Kimpuruṣa) and the Uttar Kurus[61] has also not yielded any positive result. In every respect the evidence of language is not in harmony with the *Purāṇic* accounts of the origin of this dynasty. In fact, the Saudyumnas were also one of the branches of the Solar race.

## THE SOLAR DYNASTY

While turning to four pre-eminent kingdoms of the Solar dynasty : Ayodhya of Ikṣvākus, Videha of Janakas, Vaiśāla (also Vaiśāli) of Vaiśālakas and Kuśasthali of Sāryātas (with their principal dominion in Oudh, North Bihar, Malwa in Central India and Gujarat in Western India), mention may first be made of Ayodhya, which is considered to be the most ancient city.

### Ayodhya Dynasty

Ayodhya (in the district of modern Faizabad in U.P.), situated on the banks of the river Sarayu, was the capital of Kosala Janapada, which roughly corresponds to the Oudh (or Avadha) region.[62] It has been in existence since the *Vedic* age, which can fairly be substantiated by the evidences furnished in the *Vedic* literature. The earliest allusion to this city with eight cakra (palaces) and nine gateways occurs in the *Atharva Veda Samhitā* (10.1.2., 31). This shows that the kingdom of Kosala with its capital at Ayodhya was colonised during the later *Vedic* period. The reference to the city of Ayodhya in the *Taittirīya Āranyaka* (27.2.3) of the Krishna *Yajurveda* is exactly similar to that of *Atharva Veda*. Manu, the famous ruler of Solar dynasty is said to be the builder of this ancient city,[63] which covered an area having a length of twelve Yojanas and breadth of three

Yojanas.[64] From Vālmīki's description of the capital of the kingdom of Kosala it is clear that Ayodhya was not in any way inferior to our modern cities. No doubt, in ancient India, city civilization had reached a high level of development or the pinnacle of glory. Ayodhya is believed to be one of the seven famous cities of ancient times.[65]

Manu's son, Ikṣvāku, became the first ruler of Ayodhya.[66] In the *Rāmāyaṇa* of Vālmīki as well as in the *Purāṇas* the royal family of Ayodhya is well represented as being descended from a king named Ikṣvāku. The names of many kings of the Ikṣvāku dynasty are found in the *Vedic* literature. The earliest reference to a prince named Ikṣvāku occurs in a passage of the *Ṛgveda*.[67] Pāṇini (*sūtra*, VI. 1.171; VI 4.174) and Patañjali (IV. 2.104; 11.298) also refer to Ikṣvāku of Kosala kingdom.

In the pre-Rāma period of the line of Ikṣvāku there were sixty four kings as it appears from the *Purāṇic* records.[68] But, on the other hand, we find that the *Rāmāyaṇa*[69] contains a list of only thirty five kings down to Rāma. The *Rāmāyaṇa* genealogy after getting examined in detail, is found erroneous. That is why it is generally contradicted and the *Purāṇic* genealogy of the Ayodhya dynasty accepted. This is not very astounding because the *Rāmāyaṇa* is brāhmaṇical poem, and the *Brāhmaṇs* lacked the perfect historical sense. However, some of the important characters and their deeds and achievements, as depicted in the *Purāṇas* and other relevant sources, may be mentioned here.

The kingdom of Ayodhya rose to very great eminence under Māndhātā (or Māndhātṛ), son of Yuvanāśva-II of the Ikṣvāku family. He married Bindumati, daughter of a Yādava king, Śaśabindu. He was not only a famous king, but also a great conqueror. He has been called a *Cakravartin* and a *Samrāt*, because he conquered surrounding kingdoms and brought them under his imperial authority and established paramount position over more or less extensive regions.[70] He extended his sway over the neighbouring Kānyakubja kingdom and the realm of Pauravas. He entered into a long contest with the Druhyu king, Arudha or Angāra, on the confines of the Punjab and ultimately conquered him. Consequently, the next Druhyu king, Gāndhāra, moved to the north-west and gave his name to the Gāndhāra country. Māndhātā is also believed to have exercised his supremacy over the Ānavas in the north and other rulers.[71] As a result of the disturbances caused by his conquests, the three great movements occurred contemporaneously among the Haihayas, Ānavas and Druhyus.

Māndhātā and his three sons, Purukutsa, Ambarisa and Mucukunda,[72] probably carried their arms south to the river Narmada as the tradition indicates. Their periods saw the extension of the Āryan culture towards the river Narmada and the land of the Nāgas, who were aborigines or indigenous primitive Non-Āryan peoples.

Māndhātā's third son, Mucukunda, who was a famous king, built and fortified a town on the bank of the river Narmada between the Vindhya or Paripatra and Ṛkṣa (Satpura) ranges, which was later conquered by the Haihaya king, Mahiṣmant, who named it Māhiṣmati, the modern Māndhātā on an island in the river.[73] From the story as narrated in the *Harivamśa* it appears that the town, Māhiṣmati, existed long before the time of

Mādhava and Sattvata, who are said to be the contemporaries of Mucumunda. It was also the capital of Arjuna Kārtavirya, a famous Haihaya king. The details of identification of this capital city based on an archaeological evidence befitting to the context have been provided later separately in a section, which deals with the kingdom of the Haihayas. Actually, there is no uniformity in the *Purāṇic* accounts about the foundation or the original ownership of this city, as it appears from the available contradictory evidences, which have been cited subsequently in the relevant place. Mucukunda built another town named Purikā on the south bank near the Ṛkṣa range. Both the above mentioned towns were probably his capitals. However, his kingdom did not survive long. The supremacy of Ayodhya soon waned because of the two primary factors. Firstly, some of the kingdoms of the Lunar dynasty rose into local prominence, and secondly, Māndhātā's conquests resulted in the disturbances, which led to the outbreak of three great movements spearheaded by the Haihayas, Ānavas and Druhyus.

The kingdom of Ayodhya for some time passed through a crisis. Satyavrata (*Roman*=Triśanku) after being installed on its throne married Kaikeya princess.[74] If this statement is accepted, the Kaikeya dynasty and all the other Punjab kingdoms comprising the Śivis, Madras and Sauviras had come into existence before his time. Satyavrata was suceeded by his son Hariścandra, whose son Rohita is said to have built a fortress-town, Rohitapura,[75] which has been identified with Rohtas in the districts of Shāhābād in Bihar.[76]

Hariścandra's eighth successor, Bāhu, a king of Ayodhya, was driven from his throne by the Haihayas, Tālajaṅghas and their allies, the Śakas, Kāmbojas, Yavanas, Pāradas and Pahlavas, five foreign tribes from the north-west. The foreign tribes after having conquered Ayodhya settled down therein. They were called *Kṣatriyas* and observed *Brāhmaṇical* rites. They kept the kingdom in their possession for more than twenty years. Afterwards, Bāhu's son, Sagara—one of the greatest sovereigns of the Solar dynasty, defeated the Haihaya-Tālajaṅghas and regained Ayodhya. He extended his campaign and subdued all the other enemies in North India. He crushed the Haihayas in their own territories and annihilated their dominion. He was determined to exterminate those tribes who had meanwhile settled down in his territories, but because of intercession of his family priest Vasiṣṭha he spared their lives, but reduced them to a great social and religious degradation.[77] Like other *Kṣatriya* tribes they were degraded to the rank of the *mlecchas*. However, there seems to be some reason to distrust the tradition. The people like the Śakas and Yavanas do not figure in Indian history before the second century B.C. In all probability, only the Haihayas and the Tālajaṅghas might have invaded the kingdom and other tribes might have been included in the list some time after the second century B.C. Therefore, the historical authenticity of the *Purāṇic* evidence about the subjugation of the foreign tribes concerned may be doubted. There is every reason to believe that the Haihayas after having captured the cities of Kāśis and the Vatsas might have put the kingdom of Kosala under the siege. The Haihayas tribe also known as Haihaibans, Haiya, Hyobans, Ho, Hurihobans and Hiya, all synonymous with the Haihaias people, are said to be "a portion of the original population inhabiting the hilly and jungly districts between the rivers *Kali* and forest Tista, the tract which includes Avadh".[78] After defeating the Haihayas on the Narmada Sagara subdued the Yādava ruler of Vidarbha, but made peace by marrying his daughter and was received with honour by the Śurasena Yadavas. His name and fame soon spread far and wide as a famous monarch. Many petty Āryan or Purāṇic kingdoms continued to flourish in the region subdued by him until the *Mahābhārata* war and even later. According to some *Purāṇas*,[79] Sagara also defeated the Kelisparaśas, the Māhiṣakas, Dārvas, Cholas and Khaśas.

When Sagara established his empire over North India, some of the important kingdoms that survived were the Videha, Vaiśāli and Ānva kingdoms in the east, Kāśi in Madhyadeśa, Turvasu's line in the hilly country of Rewa and the new kingdom of Vidarbha of the Yādava branch on the river Chambal. The period following his death saw the rise of several new kingdoms. Some of the overthrown dynasties appear to have generally recovered themselves. The Yādavas of Vidharbha seem to have extended their authority northward over the Haihaya territory. 'Cidi', the son of Kaiśika, founded the dynasty of Caidya kings in Cedi, the country lying along the south of the Yamuna. Lompada founded a separate kingdom the position of which is not yet well ascertained. The Ānva kingdom in the east, the nucleus of which was Aṅga, also flourished.

Ayodhya rose into prominence again under Amśumāna's second successor, Bhagiratha, and latter's third successor, Ambariṣa, son of Nābhāga. It appears from the genealogies that Ayodhya line remained divided with two rival groups of kings for about six or seven generations after Kalmāṣapāda's time, which synchronises with the expansion of the Paurvas and Bhāratas. It was Dilipa II Khatvāṅga, who united these two lines and re-established the single monarchy. His immediate descendants were Raghu, Aja and Daśaratha,[80] and by this time the kingdom acquired the name Kosala. Its capital Ayodhya reached to a pinnacle of glory during the time of Daśaratha. This imperial city was a metropolis of substantive empire situated on the river Sarayu. It was a well-planned city. It was intersected by broad streets. It was during his time twelve *yojanas* or about ninety six miles long and three *yojanas* or about twenty four miles broad. It had magnificent buildings, high mansions adorned with waving flags all around, ornamental gates, beautiful gardens, etc. The city was also well fortified with strong walls, deep trenches, garrison of arches and well equipped with sophisticated weapons. It was full of artisans, traders and merchants from various countries. It had all the paraphernalia of sovereignty and pride and pomp of royalty.[81] The ancient city of Ayodhya or Sāketa, according to A. Cunningham, "is said to have been twelve *yojanas* or nearly hundred miles in circumference, for which we should probably read twelve *kos* or twenty four miles—an extent which the old city, with all its gardens, might once possibly have covered. The distance from the Guptā Ghāt on the west to the Ram Ghāt on the east is just six miles in direct line, and if we suppose that the city with its suburbs and gardens formerly occupied the whole intervening space to a depth of two miles, its circuit would have agreed exactly with the smaller measurement of twelve *Kos* . . . The twelve *yojanas* of the *Rāmāyaṇa* which is equal to forty eight *kos*, being considered too small for the great city of Rama, the *Brāhmaṇs* simply added hundred *kos* to make the size tally with their own extravagant notions. The present city of Ayodhya, which is confined to the north-east corner of the old site is just two miles in length by about three quarters of a mile in breadth . . . There are no high mounds of ruins, covered with broken statues and sculptured pillars, such as mark the sites of other ancient cities, but only a low irregular mass of rubbish heaps from which all the bricks have been excavated for the houses of the neighbouring city of Faizabad . . . This city . . . is built chiefly of materials extracted from the ruins of Ayodhya. The two cities together occupy an area of nearly six square miles or just about one-half of the probable size of the ancient capital of Rama . . ."[82]

Another important city of the kingdom popularly known as Sāketa is generally identified with Ayodhya. Their identity can, of course, be established with the help of some relevant sources. However, opinion differs among scholars. In several passages of the *Rāmāyaṇa* and in the *Raghuvaṁśa*[83] of Kālidāsa, Ayodhya and Saketanagara have been used synonymously as the capital of *Rājā* Daśaratha and his sons. In one of the *Purāṇas*[84] also Ayodhya has been identified with Sāketa. F.E. Pargiter,[85] Cunningham[86] and Csoma de Koros[87] have described them as identical. Hemachandra refers to Sāketa, Ayodhya and Kosala as the names of one particular city.[88] Sāketa has been identified with Sujankot on the river Sai in the Unnao district.[89] Ayodhya (A-yū-t-ye) of Yuan-chung or Hiuen-Tsang "is apparently the Shaki or Sāket . . . this was ten *yojanas* south-east from the Holi village, which was three *yojanas* south from Kanauj . . ."[90] Buddhist[91] and Jain literature[92] generally refers to Sāketa as another capital of the Kosala kingdom. However, some Buddhist works like *Aṅguttara Nikāya* (III.169), Ghata *Jātaka* (II.82) and *Samyutta Nikāya* (III.140) also refer to Ayodhya as its capital. Sāketa, a city of hoary antiquity, was regarded as one of the six chief cities of India during the Buddhist period. In a Jain text it is described as one of the ten capital cities of India. In the *Abhidhāna-Paddipika* of Moggalana Thera[93] Sāketa is included in the list of twenty ancient cities of India. Actually, Ayodhya and Sāketa (like other ancient holy cities, Kāśi-Varanasi or Pratiṣṭhān-apur-Prayag) were the twin capital cities of the whole Kosala Janapada. That is why T.W. Rhys Davids, while describing both as the same observes that "They were possibly adjoining like London and Westminster".[94] Both Sāketa and Ayodhya were considered to be one city down to the fifth century A.D.

The Kosala kingdom during Daśaratha's time had friendly relations with the eastern kingdoms of Videha, Aṅga and Magadha, the Punjab kingdoms of Kekaya, Sindhu and Sauvira, the western kingdom of Saurastṛa, the Dākṣinātya kings and Kāśi in the middle region of North India. The kingdom of Kosala was, no doubt, colonised during the later *Vedic* period. Daśaratha's contemporaries were, on the one hand, the Yādavas, who under the noted *king* Madhu had a powerful kingdom extending from Yamuna to Gujarat and, on the other, the Pauravas, who had at least four states in the Ganga-Yamuna Doāb with North Pañcāla branch specially prominent. Rāma, one of the four sons of Daśaratha, succeeded to the throne of Ayodhya. He was in the real sense of the term its last famous sovereign. The names of Daśaratha and Rāma also figure in the *Ṛgveda*.[95] Keeping in view the geneological order of the descendants of Ikṣvāku, we find Rāma as the sixty fifth king in the Solar dynasty.

Rāma's brothers obtained kingdoms elsewhere. Bharata obtained the Kekaya kingdom, which was the province of his mother, and also Sindhu, i.e. Upper Sind. The Kekayas were settled in the Western Punjab between Gāndhāra and the Beas. From the *Rāmāyaṇa* it appears that the Kekaya territory was beyond the Vipāśa or Beas and extended upto the borders of ancient Gāndhāra *Janapada*. The journey from Ayodhya to the Kekaya capital *Rājagṛha* or *Girivraja* covering a distance of about 650 miles took seven days.[96] The capital of the Kekayas has been identified with Girjak or Jalalpur on the river Jhelam.[97] The Greek writer Arrian places the 'Kekians' on the river Saranges, which is obviously a tributory of the Hydraotes or the Rāvi.[98] The Kekaya kingdom during the time of Bharata was constantly under the attack of the Gandharvas. His two sons Takṣa and Puṣkara conquered Gāndhāra (the Peshawar-Rawalpindi region) from the Gandharvas and reigned there in Takṣaśilā and Puṣkaravati or Puśkalāvati (its two ancient capitals—eastern and western) respectively. This particular evidence as recorded in the *Purāṇas*[99] and the *Rāmāyaṇa*[100] can also be corroborated by the statements of Cunningham,[101] J. Burgess[102] and W.H. Schoff (translator and annotator of a 'Greek text of the first century A.D.).[103] V.S. Agrawala has also pointed out that the Pushkalas of *Mārkaṇḍeya Purāṇa* were the people of the Gāndhāra region.[104] Puṣkalāvati has been archaeologically identified with modern Prang and Chārsadda villages (seventeen miles north-east of Peshawar) situated near the junction of the Suvastu (Swāt) with Kubha (Kabul).[105] The remains of the great city Takṣaśilā have been found in the vicinity of Shah-dheri, one mile north-east of Kāla-ka-Sarai station on North-Western Railway, twenty miles north-west of Rawalpindi.[106]

The *Viṣṇu Dharmottara Purāṇa* (Venkatesvara press, Bombay, 1912, pt. 1, chs. 200-217) provides a picturesque description of the situation, which led Bharat to conquer Gāndhāra and found Takṣaśilā and Puśkarāvati (or Puśkalāvati). Actually, the Gandharvas (of Gāndhāra) to whom the *king* Shailusa had extended his patronage, by their cruelty, violent and outrageous activities had struck terror in the hearts of all the rulers of North-Western India. Yudhājita, the ruler of Kekayadeśa (which stood in close proximity to Gāndhāra) and the maternal uncle of Bharata, because of being disgusted with the highhandedness of Sailusa of Gāndhāra decided to inflict heavy punishment on the Gandharvas, and, thus, in order to carry out his plan successfully he with the mutual consent of all the rulers concerned sent his emissary to Rāma at Ayodhya. Thereafter, Bharata, complying with the order of his elder brother marched towards Gāndhāra along with his army. It took several days for him to reach there. While traversing through Matsya, Shurasena, Kurukṣetra, Shālva and Śivi-deśa, he reached Kunindadeśa after crossing the rivers Gauri, Satlej, Irāvati, etc. After reaching Gāndhāra he along with king Yudhājit entered into a fierce battle with Gandharvas led by their king Shailusa and eventually, defeated them. Sailusa was beheaded. His descendants attacked Bharata, but were ultimately defeated. Thus, after having exterminated and extirpated the Gandharvas, Bharata founded the two new cities—Takṣaśilā and

Puṣkarāvati on two different banks of the Indus river after the names of his two sons (Takṣa and Puṣkara) in order to commemorate his victory, and installed them as the rulers of the cities concerned respectively, and he himself returned to Ayodhya (see *ibid.* 1, ch. 212 ff.).

Lakṣmana had two sons, Angada and Candraketu, to whom were assigned two countries in Kārapatha-deśa near the Himalayas with their respective capitals at Aṅgadiya and Candrabaktra.[107] Here it is worthwhile to mention that the territory of Mallas (with two capitals, Kuśāvati or Kuśinagar and Pava in district of Gorakhpur, U.P.) originally formed the part of Kosala kingdom. Angada was the ruler of Malla-deśa, which was also known as Angada-rājya, and his brother Candraketu or Candrasena founded the kingdom of Candravati. From the *Rāmāyaṇa*[108] it is quite evident that Candraketu was anointed by Bharata in the territory of the Mallas in a city named Candrakānta, which has not yet been identified.

Śatrughna attacked the Śātvata-Yādavas on the west of the Yamuna and after having defeated him killed Mādhava Lavana (Lavanasur), son of Madhu (the founder of the Yādava kingdom at Madhura-Mathura and having a sway over an extensive region extending southward from the Yamuna up to Gujarat and beyond the Vindhya and the Satpura mountains), and established his capital at Mathura in the region thenceforth called Śuraśena and his two sons, Subāhu and Śurasena reigned there. The city of Madhupuri founded by him on the spot, where he killed Lavana,[109] was located in the south-west of Mathura. The epic-*Purāṇic* evidence as furnished above can also be supported by the statements of Thomas Watters,[110] J. Burgess[111] and B.C. Law.[112] Later, Bhima-Satvata, a Yādava ruler, regained Mathura from Śatrughna's son Subāhu.

*Vāyu Purāṇa* (88, 185) and *Raghuvaṁśa* (15, 28) of Kālidāsa also mention Śatrughna as the founder of Madhura (Mathura) in *Madhuvan.* According to *Vālmīki Rāmāyaṇa* (*Uttarkāṇḍa,* 70, 6-9), he took twelve years to make Mathura a beautiful and prosperous city.

Mathura, the capital of the Śurasena Janapada, is generally identified with Maholi—five miles to the south-west of the present town of Mathura.[113] In fact, the ancient Śurasena people occupied Mathura and some of the territory still further south. The Śurasena belonged to the *Yādava* tribe. The *Yādavas* ruled at Mathura for considerable period of time. Śurasena with its famous city Mathura became famous in the epic and *Purāṇic* literature because of its connection with Krishna and *Yādava* tribe, who held Mathura after the death of Kaṁsa. The early Greek writers have also thrown some light on the subject. Arrian (Indica, VIII)[114] on the authority of Megasthenes has also confirmed it that the 'Śourasenoi' or Suraseni possessed two great cities—Methoras' (Mathura) and 'Klisoboras' (Vrindavana or Krishnapur= Gokula). Pliny (*Nat. Hist.* VI, 19) also refers to their towns, 'Methora' and 'Clisobora'. In the Jain texts Śurasena with the capital city Mathura is included in the list of twenty five and half Āryan countries.[115] Archaeologically, Mathura represents the site associated with Painted Grey Ware culture or the Gangetic culture.[116]

Rāma had two sons, Kuśa and Lava. Their periods witnessed the division of the kingdom of Kosala into two parts, viz. Southern (Dakṣina Kosala) and northern (Uttara Kosala) divided by the river Sarayu, and the foundation of two new kingdoms, i.e. Kuśāvati and Śrāvasti.

According to the *Purāṇas*, Kuśa succeeded his father and later became ruler of South Kosala with its capital at Kuśasthali (Kuśāvati) situated at the foot of the Vindhyas.[117] He seems to have extended the Āryan culture in the Vindhya region. But in the *Rāmāyaṇa*, Kuśa has been referred to as a ruler of Kosala with its capital at Kuśāvati,[118] which is modern Kuśinagara or Kuśinara,[119] associated with *Nirvana* of Buddha. The Kuśa *Jātaka* also refers to Okkāku- (of Pāli canon=Ikṣvāku) as a king of Kuśāvati in the Malla country and to his two sons, named Kuśa and Jayampati.[120] Kālidāsa has also mentioned about Kuśa of Ayodhya.[121] On the combined testimony of the *Rāmāyaṇa*, the *Purāṇas* and the Buddhist sources the identity of Kuśāvati and Kuśinagara can, undoubtedly, be established. But, on the other hand, we find that Cunningham identifies it with Kuśapura (Kia-She-pu-lo of Hiuen-Tsang) that is old town of Sultanpur on the Gomati river at a distance of 28 or 30 miles from the present city of Ayodhya (or the ancient Sāketa) in the north. He says that the ancient "Kusapura or Kasapura of Hiuen-Tsang or Kusu-bhavana-pura (identified with Sultanpur) is . . . named after Rama's son, Kusa . . . the site of Kusapura was, no doubt, selected by its founder as a good military position on account of its being surrounded on three sides by the river Gomati or Gumti. . . The ruined fort of Sultanpur now forms a large mound, 750 square with brick towers at the four corners. On all sides it is surrounded by the huts of the ruined town, the whole together covering a space of about half a mile square or about two miles in circuit. This estimate of the size of Sultanpur agrees very closely with that of Kusapura given by Hiuen-Tsang, who describes the place as being ten *li* or 1⅔ miles, in circuit".[122] V.A. Smith has placed the location of Kuśapur in Unāo District.[123]

Lava, son of Rāma, obtained the northern portion of Kosala (the kingdom of Uttarakosala) with Śrāvasti (originally founded by Śrāvasta, son of Yuvanāsva-I, one of the descendants of Ikṣvāku) as its capital city. This city was occupied after deserting the city of Ayodhya.[124] According to Kālidāsa, Ayodhya was the capital of North Kosala.[125] Cunningham, while supporting the *Purāṇic* evidence, ascribes the foundation of the celebrated capital city, Śrāvasti (to the northward of Sāket or Ayodhya), anterior to Rāma. He also admits that during the early period "it formed the part of the kingdom of Ayodhya, as the *Vāyu Purāṇa* assigns it to Lava . . ." He has identified Śrāvasti with the "ruined city of Sāhet-Māhet on the south bank of the Rapti situated between Akaona and Balrampur at five miles from the former and twelve miles from the latter and at nearly equal distance from Bahraich and Gonda". The exact distance of this ruined city from Ayodhya has been fixed fifty eight miles by him,[126] V.A. Smith has placed the ruins of Śrāvasti on the Upper course of the Rāpti in Nepalese territory near the point where the river emerges from the hills.[127]

The kingdom of Kosala approximately coinciding with the Sarayu-Rāpti *doāb* contained three principal cities-Ayodhya, Sāketa and Śrāvasti. According to the epic, *Purāṇic* and Buddhist traditions, Ayodhya seems to have been the earliest capital, but during Buddha's time Ayodhya sank to the level of an unimportant city, while Sāketa and Śrāvasti were two of the six important cities of India.[128] Śrāvasti is one of the P.G.W. sites (in period 1).[129]

The collateral kingdoms established by the sons of four brothers, as noted above, remained in focus for quite some time. Some of them were subsequently taken over by other rival contemporary rulers. Śatrughna's sons were expelled from Mathura by the *Yādava* king, Bhima Satvate, and he and his descendants converted it into a *Yādava* principality. The two states in Gāndhāra were probably absorbed in the kingdom of neighbouring Druhyus. No further account is given either of the principalities of Lakśmana's sons or of Lava's kingdom.

In the post-Rāma period (which marked the end of the *Treta Yuga* and the beginning of *Dvāpara*), in the line of Kuśa there were sixteen kings after him, and Hiranyanābha, whose name figures in the *Purāṇic* genealogical list as a king of Kosala, is unanimously accepted to be the last king and hereafter ends the line of Kuśa.[130] He flourished during the *Mahābhārata* period before the *Kali* age. However, in the line of Lava there were forty kings after him down to the time of Sumitra, out of which fifteen were in the pre-Bhārata war period and rest of the twenty five up to Sumitra were in the post-Bhārata war period, which has been discussed in the next chapter. The last Solar king of Ayodhya of pre-Bhārata war period was Bṛhadbala[131] (son of Visrutavana) of Śrāvasti, who fought on behalf of the Kaurava forces against the Pāṇḍavas and was ultimately killed by Abhimanyu (the son of Arjuna) in the great battle of Kurukśetra. His name as ruler of Kosala also appears in the *Mahābhārata*[132] in the *Sabhā Parva* (27, 1-5) it is said that Bṛhadbala of Kosala was conquered by Bhima. On the basis of the genealogies of Ikṣvāku family that ruled at Ayodhya ninty eight generations can be computed from the time of Manu down to Bṛhadbala of Bhārata war period. Ayodhya, hereafter, played no prominent part in the traditional history. The conquest of Kosala was evidently attributed to the period before the great war. The two chief actors appearing on the political stage were the Pauravas and the Yādavas.

H.D. Sankalia had anticipated as far back as 1975 that "Ayodhya when excavated should give up thick deposits and the earliest should go back to at least 2,500 B.C.".[133] But this has not yet come true. Actually, in absence of any archaeological data no definite date about its antiquity can be postulated.

### The Videha Dynasty

The Videha dynasty sprang from Ikṣvāku's son, Nimi, who is also called Videha. He was the founder of the royal family of Mithila.[134] His name also figures in the *Nimi Jātaka* (*Jātaka* VI, pp. 95-129) as a king of Mithila. The name of his capital city has been called Vaijayantapur in the *Rāmāyaṇa*[135] and Jayantapur in the *Purāṇa*[136] and placed near the hermitage of Gautama *Rishi*. From his son Mithi, whom the *Purāṇas* identify with Janaka

I (Mithi-Janaka), Mithila, the capital of Videha kingdom known both as Mithilapuri and Videhapuri (identified with the small town of Janakapura just within the Nepal border), was named and hence the kings were called Maithilas.[137] But according to the testimony of the *Rāmāyaṇa*, Janaka was the son of Mithi.[138] The name of the great king Janaka also appears in the *Śatapatha Brāhmaṇa* (XI, 6.2.1) and *Jātaka* (6, 30-68). The kings were thus collectively known as 'Janakas'. Janaka, the philosopher king of the Videha, was a great patron of the *Vedic* culture. In the *Bṛhadāraṇyaka Upaniśada* he figures as one of the leading patrons of the *Brāhmaṇical* culture. From the genealogies of the royal family of Mithila, as given in the *Purāṇas*[139] and the *Rāmāyaṇa*,[140] it appears that Janaka I was succeeded by several kings down to the time of Siradhvaja, the father of Sita and identical with Janaka II. He was one of the most celebrated of the Janaka. He killed Sudhavan, the king of Sāṅkāsya (situated on the bank of the river Ikṣumati), in a fierce battle, which followed his refusal to give his daughter Sita in marriage to him, and thereafter placed his own brother Kuśadhvaja on the throne of Sāṅkāsya.[141] Siradhvaja Janaka is supposed to have lived before the *Kali* age.

The geographical position of Sāṅkāsya is not clearly indicated either in the *Rāmāyaṇa* or in the *Purāṇas*. This old city in the Gangetic *doāb*, also mentioned by Pāṇini (IV, 2, 80) and called Seng-Kia-Shi by Fa-hein and Kapitha or Seng-Ka-she by Hiuen-Tsang, has been identified with the modern village, Sankissa or Samkassa or Sakaspura (Pāli Sankassa), situated on the north bank of the river, Ikṣumati, in the Farrukhabad district (2,000 *li* or 333 miles in circuit) north-west or south-east of Kānyakubja or Kanauj at the distance of about 50 miles.[142]

In the line of Nimi there were fifty-two kings after him, who ruled Mithila till it was merged with Vaiśāli some time between the seventh and fifth century B.C. Siradhvaja Janaka was the twenty second king in their dynasty, whose daughter Sita was married to Rāma of Ayodhya. Rāma's three brothers, viz. Lakṣmana, Bharat and Śatrughna, were married to three cousin sisters of Sita, i.e. Urmila, Mandvi and Srutikirti, who were daughters of Kuśadhvaja Janaka, the younger brother of king Siradhvaja Janaka.

Siradhvaja was succeeded by a number of kings. From the genealogical order of the kings of Janaka dynasty it is quite evident that Kshemari Janaka, the thirteenth king after Siradhvaja was the contemporary of king Bṛhadbala of the Ikṣvāku dynasty that reigned at Ayodhya. During the *Mahābhārata* period king Kshemari Janaka as a ruler of Mithila supported the Kauravas in the great Bhārata war, as recorded in many *Purāṇas*. The participation of the Videhas in the Great War and their conquests by Pāndu, Bhima and Karṇa in course of their conquests are referred to in the *Mahābhārata*. In the *Ādi Parva*[143] it is clearly stated that Pāndu defeated the Videhas in Mithila. From the *Sabhā Parva*[144] it transpires that the Pāṇḍava hero Bhima conquered not only the Gandaki and Videhas, but also king Janaka of Videha.

It was Bahulasva's son Kṛti with whom terminated the family of Janaka (Janaka-Vaṁśa). The dynasty of Videha, thus came to its close with Kṛti, the last king, as it appears from the *Purāṇas*.[145]

The three important kingdoms of the *Vedic* period, popularly known as Kāśi, Kosala and Videha, were closely allied to each other. The kingdom of Videha with its capital city Mithila corresponding roughly to ancient Tirabhukti or modern Tirhut in North Bihar was separated from Kosala by the river Sadānira, usually identified with the modern Gandak, which rising in Nepal flows into the Ganges. According to the *Śatapatha Brāhmaṇa*, the origin of Videhan kingdom is traced back to Videha Māthava—the so-called ancestor of the Kosalas and the Videhas. We are told that he accompanied by his priest Gotama Rāhugana carried the sacrificial fire from the banks of the river Sarasvati as far as Kosala and further crossed the river Sadānirā and founded the kingdom of Videha.[146] The *Brahmanisation* of the region is attributed to him by the text. Mithila is some times used to denote the whole country.[147] According to Pargiter, "Videha comprised the country from Gorakhpur on the Rāpti to Darbhanga with Kosala on the west and Aṅga on the east. On the north it approached hills, and to the south it was bounded by the small kingdom of Vaiśāli".[148] We learn from the *Gāndhāra* and *Suruchi Jātakas* (Nos. 406 and 489 respectively) that the whole kingdom of Videha was three hundred leagues in extent consisting of sixteen hundred villages and the capital city was seven leagues in circuit. According to the Jātaka (No. 546), there were four market towns at the four gates of the city. The Mahājanaka Jātaka (No. 539) also provides a brief description of the city with special references to its palaces, walls gates and battlements traversed by streets on every side, etc.[149]

Videha kingdom with the capital Mithila has been also referred to in the Sanskrit Buddhist text. "Vaideha Janapada Mithilāyām Rājadhāyām" occurs in the *Mahāvastu*[150] and "Videhaṣu Janapadeṣu gatvā prabrajitaḥ" in the *Divyāvadāna*.[151] In the *Lalitavistara* the Videha kingdom is described as wealthy and prosperous.[152] In the Jain text the kingdom of Videha is mentioned as one of the twenty five and-a-half Āryan countries and its capital Mithila as one of the important capital cities of ancient India.[153]

### The Vaiśāla (or Vaiśāli) Dynasty

The origin of this dynasty is still shrouded in obscurity. From the epic and *Purāṇic* accounts it appears that the kings of this dynasty, as a whole, were ruling over two different kingdoms, one in Malava region (Vidiśā and Avanti) in central India and other at Vaiśāli (North Bihar) in eastern India at two different periods of history. It is very curious to note that the founders of both the dynasties or kingdoms were commonly known as Viśāla.

The Vaiśālas (or Vaiśālakas) of the Vaiśāla dynasty, that reigned in Malava region, seem to have descended from Manu's son Nābhānediṣṭha. This dynasty was, actually, named after the king Viṣāla, whose name distinctly figures in the *Mārkaṇḍeya Purāṇa*[154] as a ruler of the Vaidiśa (or Vaidiśapur=Vidiśā) kingdom. But, unfortunately, neither his pedigree nor progeny finds mention in the text. However, the existence of Vaiśāla or Viśālā kingdom in the Avanti region can be confirmed by the statements of H.H. Wilson.[155] He has also identified it with Ujjayini (Ujjain), an illustrious city of a great importance in ancient Indian historical tradition. M.R. Kale on the basis of the data provided by Kālidāsa and Hemachandra has also conclusively proved it that there was a region called "Viśālā Avantikā".[156] The names of rulers of this very particular dynasty from Nābhānediṣṭha's son and immediate successor Bhalandana (a very powerful Kśatriya ruler) upto Buddha (including the successors of Rajyavardhana and Bandhumāt) are given in a number of *Purāṇas.*[157] But, details of incidents, which occurred during their times are narrated only in a few of them. Karandhama, one of the noted kings of this dynasty (in the first quarter of the *Treta* age), and his son, Avikṣit, entered into a great conflict with the king Viśāla of Vidiśā. Actually, the attempts on the part of Avikṣit to force Vaiśālinī, the daughter of the said king, to get married to him furnished the pretext for the hostility with the said king. He was captured by the king and his allies and brought to Vaidiśapur, but was ultimately rescued by his father. Both father and son were first besieged by a confederacy of kings, who solidly stood behind the king of Vidiśā. But, finally, Karandhama with the help of his allies including feudal lords and neighbouring kings inflicted a crushing defeat on the king after a pitched battle of three days and finally compelled him to surrender at his feet. Marutta, son of Avikṣit from the daughter of the king was one of great monarchs of antiquity.[158] Marutta had confrontation with the Nāgas. He wanted to exterminate and extirpate them, but saved their lives. The enemies of the rulers of this dynasty were probably no other than the Haihayas, for Vidiśā was for sometime under the control of their chieftain. They all were given a serious blow. Tradition suggests that Haihayas repeated attempts to conquer Vaiśāli were frustrated by the Vaiśāla kings.[159] Marutta's son Nariṣyanta is specifically mentioned in some *Purāṇas*[160] as a king of the Vaiśāla dynasty. He was succeeded by a number of kings.

A few generations after the king Dama of the above dynasty, the *king* Viśāla, son of Tṛnabindu (from Alambuṣā, who is said to have ruled during the third quarter of the *Treta* age, founded Viśālā (called Viśālapuri) or Vaiśāli as the capital of the kingdom.[161] The *Rāmāyaṇa* also begins the dynasty with Viśāla, the founder of the capital Viśālā, wrongly calling him the son of Ikṣvāku from Alambuṣā.[162] There are apparently some errors in the text about the parentage of the founder of this dynasty. The name of Tṛnabindu has, of course, been mentioned in the different context, but without showing Viṣāla as his son.[163] The text is, on the other hand, replete with some valuable information about the history and antiquity of the dynasty and location of the capital city. It is said that Rāma and Lakṣmana accompanied by Viśvāmitra after crossing the Ganges reached the capital city Viśālā. Rāma asked Viśvāmitra to explain the dynastic history of this kingdom and thereafter the latter narrated its whole ancient history. All the three on their way to Mithila are also said to have halted here for one night and were cordially entertained by the *king* Sumati during the time of Daśaratha.[164] This helps us to determine the exact location as well as the antiquity of the kingdom. Cunningham,[165] Thomas Watters,[166] James Legge,[167] Samuel Beal,[168] E.J. Rapson[169] and B.C. Law,[170] on the basis of an archaeological evidence and the information supplied by Fa-hien and Hiuen-Tsang, have reasonably identified the kingdom of Vaiśāli with an old ruined city of the Viśāla (Rājā Viśāla-kā garh) in the modern village called Basārh, about 27 miles north-east of Patna or twenty miles north of Hajipur in North Bihar.

From the genealogical list of the king of the dynasty, as given in the *Purāṇas* and the *Rāmāyaṇa,* which perfectly agrees with each other except one name, it seems that the first king Viśāla was succeeded by nine kings including some prominent ones like Hemachandra, Sucandra, Sahadeva and Somadatta. The genealogy continues down to Pramati or Sumati,[171] who was the contemporary of Daśaratha. It is said that by the favour of Tṛṇabindu all the monarchs of Vaiśāli were long lived, magnanimous and valiant.[172]

After analysing all the available data relating to the subject concerned we come to a definite conclusion that there were two separate branches of the same dynasty ruling over two kingdoms in two different regions of India. Both had, evidently, more or less identical nomenclature. Genealogically and chronologically, we find that the Vaiśāli kingdom of North Bihar was preceded by the kingdom of the Malava region founded by the king bearing the same name—Viśāla or Vaiśāli and Vaiśālakas, were used in anticipation or restrospectively for the whole dynasty,[173] may fairly be disputed. The statements have made confusion worse confounded. Moreover, the accounts of the dynasty, as provided by them, are neither clear not systematic, rather confusing and conflicting.

### The Śāryātas and the Kingdom of Ānarta

Śaryāti, the fourth son of Manu, was succeeded by his son, Ānarta, who founded the kingdom (covering the northern half of the Kathiawaḍ Peninsula, Gujarat) with its capital at Kuśasthali (Kuśasthalipuri), the earliest name of Dvārakā. The capital of the kingdom of Ānarta, which was named after him, was also known as Ānartapuri. The descendants of Ānarta (called the Śāryātas), notably Rocamāna, Reva and Raivata Kukudmin, ruled over the kingdom with its capital at Kuśasthali for a considerable period of time, probably till the rise of the Yādavas. Sometimes after the reign of Raivata Kukudmin the city was captured and destroyed by Puṇyajana Rākṣasas. Soon after it their dynastic rule came to an end. The capital city, Kuśasthalipuri (or Ānartapuri), after its destruction by the Puṇyajanas, remained deserted till the time of Kṛṣṇis, Bhojas and other Yādava tribes,[174] whose full details appear in the Yādavas section on the basis of the epic, *Purāṇic* and archaeological evidences.

The remnants of the Śāryātas after the fall of their kingdom got scattered in different groups. Some of them developed into bands of noble *Kṣatriyas.* Some of them are believed to have formed one of the five branches of the Haihaya-Tālajaṅghas. After the destruction of Haihayas power at the hand of Sagara, they became merged with hill tribes. Whatever may be the facts, it cannot be denied that a considerable section of the Ānarttas continued to exist within their territorial unit till they were fully merged into the Yādava tribe. This is what the *Purāṇic* tradition also indicates.

## THE LUNAR DYNASTY

Purūravas Aila, the progenitor of the Lunar dynasty and the contemporary of Ikṣvāku of the Solar dynasty, ruled at Pratiṣṭhāna (Prayag), the capital city of Madhyadeśa[175] for about sixty four years.[176] Since the expansion of his kingdom northward was limited by the kingdom of Ayodhya and southward by the warlike Kārūṣas, the Ailas began to extend their sway north-westward and eastward along the Ganges. Purūravas was succeeded by his son Āyu at Pratiṣṭhāna, while his another son Amāvasu founded a kingdom with its capital at Kānyakubja (Kanauj). Āyu's eldest son, Nahuṣa, continued the main line at Pratiṣṭhāna, and his another son, Kṣatravṛdha, founded the dynasty that ruled at Kāśi. According to the *Brahma Purāṇa* (chs. 10-12) and in *Linga Purāṇa* (1.63), Nahuṣa, Yayāti and his successors, Puru, Dusyanta and Bharat—all ruled at Pratiṣṭhāpur.

Before we proceed to discuss the rise and fall of kingdom founded by the descendants of Yayāti (son of Nahuṣa), here it will be quite in the fitness of things to throw some light on the dynasties that reigned at Kānyakubja and Kāśi during the period concerned.

### The Kānyakubja Dynasty

Purūravas' son Amāvasu founded a kingdom with its capital at Kānyakubja (Kanauj).[177] The *Purāṇic* genealogy of the kings of this dynasty is full of discrepancies. However, there is a general agreement on the name of the founder of this kingdom. He was succeeded by a number of kings, but the details of their achievements are wanting. This kingdom rose into prominence under its most prominent king, Jahnu, soon after the supremacy of Ayodhya waned. The kingdom by this time became famous as the first Āryan kingdom in the east. During the time of king Kuśa the town Kānyakubja was also known as Kuśasthala after his name. His younger son Amūrtarayas is said to have carved out for himself a kingdom from another portion of the Saudyumna stock in the country known afterwards as Magadha. He was followed by another king named Gadhi. The glory of this kingdom soon dwindled down because of continuous raids of Haihayas and ultimately the dynasty ended with Aṣṭaka's son Lauhi.

Kānyakubja, a famous city in the Gangetic *doāb* of the *Purāṇic* antiquity, was situated to the south-east of Sankāssa or Sankāsya.[178]

### Kāśi Dynasty

Kāśi, celebrated as one of the oldest kingdoms in the Madhyadeśa, finds mention in the *Vedic Saṁhitās, Brāhamaṇas,* the *Rāmāyaṇa,* the *Mahābhārata,* the *Purāṇas,* the Sanskrit Buddhist texts, etc.

The earliest mention of the Kāśi as one of the most ancient peoples of Northern India has been made in the *Atharva Veda.*[179] The city of Kāśi seems to have been situated on the bank of the river Varaṇāvati (later connected with Varanasi), as mentioned in the same *Vedic* text[180] as well as in the *Mahāvastu.*[181] The *Brāhmaṇas* also make incidental notices of the territory of Kāśi.[182] The kingdom of Kāśi has been distinctly mentioned in the *Rāmāyaṇa* showing the association of the people with the Kosalas and Videhas.[183] Purūravas is specifically mentioned therein as a king of Kāśi.[184]

The epic and *Purāṇic* accounts of Kāśi dynasty appear to be a bit inconsistent, so far as the genealogy of kings down to Pratardana is concerned. However, some striking similarity can be noticed between the two and, in fact, they are to some extent supplementary to each other. Having found no scope to harmonise both the dynastic accounts they are preferably given here separately.

According to the *Mahābhārata*, Haryaśva, grandfather of Divōdāsa, was a famous king of Kāśi. He was a renowned conqueror. The Vitahavyas (Haihayas) invaded his kingdom and killed him in a battle, that took place somewhere in the Ganga-Yamuna *doāb*. The Haihayas after killing him entered the capital city of Vatsas (i.e. Kauśāmbi), which was in close proximity to Kāśi. He was succeeded by his son, Sudeva. He was also defeated by the Haihayas, who were in the habit of invading the kingdom constantly. After his death his son, Divodāsa, became the king of Kāśi. After the decline of Haihayas' power, he founded the city of Varanasi on the northern bank of the Ganga, on the southern side of the Gomati (or on the confluence of Gomati and Ganga). This capital city looking like Amarāvati of Indra is said to have been populated by the *Brāhmaṇas, Kṣatriyas, Vaiśyas* and the *Śūdras*. This magnificent city flourished as an emporium of trade. After a brief interregnum, the Haihayas again invaded the kingdom, when Divodāsa was ruling over it. A fierce battle ensued between the two, which continued interruptedly for nearly a couple of years resulting in the death of thousands of supporters of the king. Having found it impossible to continue to rule over his kingdom with depleted treasury and without army, king Divodāsa abdicated the throne and took refuge in the hermitage of Bhāradvāja. His son Pratardana was anointed as Yuvarāja. He was sent by Divodāsa to exterminate the Haihayas. Pratardana, after having crossed the Ganges reached the city of the Vitahavyas and inflicted a crushing defeat on them.[185] It appears that the ancestors of Divodāsa were ruling over the city of the Vatsas and it was Divodāsa, who first founded the city of Varanasi.

A close analysis of the data contained in the *Purāṇas* shows that it was Kṣatravṛddha, son of Āyu in Purūravas line, who first established himself at Kāśi. He was succeeded by Sunahotra or Śutahotra, whose one of the descendants known as Kāśa or Kāśya or Kāśeya founded the kingdom of Kāśi. He was succeeded by Dirghataps, Dhanvantari, Ketuman, Bhimaratha and Divodāsa (called Kāśi-*rājās*), who ruled at Kāśipur. One of the successors of the Haihayas, named Bhadraśrenya (son of Mahiṣmān) and a king of Yadu dynasty, carried his arms eastward, conquered the kingdom of Kāśi and took possession thereof and reigned there for quite some time. Divodāsa (son of Bhimaratha), the famous king of Kāśi, recovered his territory with its capital at Varanasi from Bhadraśrenya's sons after having defeated them. He spared one of his sons, named Durdama, who was very young. Thereafter a *rākṣasa* named Kṣemaka took possession of Varanasi and ultimately desolated the city, as a result of which Divōdāsa abandoned it (afterwards the city was called Avimukta) and built a new capital on the river Gomati on the eastern border of his land. Durdama, a son of Bhardraśrenya, reconquered the kingdom. The Haihayas held the Kāśi territory for some time. The Kāśi kings launched a struggle against the Haihayas and at long last Pratardana, son of Divōdāsa, defeated the Vitihotras (the chief among Tālajaṅgha-Haihayas) and recovered his territory, but Varanasi was still under the occupation of *rākṣasas.* He or his son, Vatsa (also known as Ṛtadhvaja and Kuvalayāśva), carried the victory further and annexed the country around Kauśāmbi, which was then named the Vatsa country. Vatsa's son, Alarka (or grandson or Pratardana), being inspired by Pratardana's success drove the *rākṣasas* out of Varanasi and after killing the *rākṣasa* Kṣemaka re-established the city of Varanasi as the new capital of Kāśi during his long and prosperous reign.[186]

The earliest references to two of the famous kings, Divōdāsa and Pratardana of this dynasty, can be found in the *Ṛgveda Samhitā.* We find in the *Ṛgveda* the name of Divōdāsa,[187] his dynasty[188] and his stone-built 100 cities provided by Indra.[189] This fairly attests to the credibility of the *Purāṇic* statement regarding the founding of the city during the reign of Divōdāsa. Pratardana along with his son Kṣattraśri also figures in the text.[190]

The contemporaneity of Pratardana and Rāma (son of Daśaratha) can very well be proved by the evidence furnished in the *Rāmāyaṇa,* which shows that the former as a king of Kāśi came to Ayodhya to attend the coronation ceremony of Rāma and thereafter returned to his own capital Varanasi.[191]

It has been rightly stated that ". . . the Ikṣvāku king Daśaratha, the father of Rāma, the northern Pāñcāla king Atithigva Divōdāsa, the brother of Ahalyā, Senajit, the southern Pāñcāla king Sārvabhauma and Ṛkṣa II, the sons of Viduratha of the Hastināpur line, Kṛta, the father of Uparicara whose descendant Bṛhadratha I founded Rōmapāda-Daśaratha dynasty of Aṅga, Siradhvaja Janaka, the father of Sita, king Satvant of the Yadu dynasty, and the father of Vitahavya the Haihaya—all these ten kings belonged to the same age, namely the age of Divōdāsa".[192]

It has been accepted by Cunningham[193] and D.L. Eck[194] that "Kāsha" (Kāśi-*rājā*) was one of the early progenitors of the Lunar race. He was succeeded by twenty descendants—all *rājās* of Kāśi amongst whom was the celebrated Divōdāsa.

There are some further evidences to show the rule of Puru dynasty over the kingdom of Kāśi. From the *Rāmāyaṇa* we learn that Puru (son of Yayāti) having his capital at Pratiṣṭhāna ruled over this kingdom.[195] According to the *Mahābhārata,* Bharata, son of Dusyanta and Śakuntalā, was married to Sunanda, daughter of Sārvasena, a king of Kāśi (called-Kāśi-*rājā*).[196] Three daughters of Kāśirājā, named Amba, Ambālikā and Ambikā were brought by Bhiṣma for his brother Vicitravirya.[197] From the *Digvijaya* section of the *Sabhā Parva* of the *Mahābhārata* it is quite evident that Suvandhi, a king of *Kāśi,* was defeated by Bhima.[198] The administration of the kingdom of Kāśi is said to have fallen to the share of Dhataraṭṭha (Pāli=Dhritarāṣtra), represented as a king of the line of Bharata.[199] Before the *Mahābhārata* war, Varanasi was under the possession of

Jarasandha, the king of Magadha. In the *Mahābhārata* war the king of Kāśi (Kāśi-*rājā*) fought on behalf of the Pāṇḍavas and was probably killed in the battlefield at Kurukṣetra. The Bharata line of the Kāśi kings appears to have been supplanted by a new line of Brahmadattas, who were probably of the Videhan origin. The rule of the kings of Brahmadatta dynasty over the kingdom of Kāśi in the post-Bhārata war period extending up to the time of the Buddha, as evidenced by the epics, the *Purāṇas* and the Buddhist literature, has been discussed along with the archaeological details of the capital city in the next chapter, as it does not fall within the purview of the treatment of the subject here.

Here it will be worthwhile to add that the ancient kingdom of Kāśi was situated to the west of the Magadhas, south of the Kosalas and east of Prayaga. The land between the rivers Gomati and the Ganga bounded by the realm of the Vatsas on the east extending up to the confluence of the Ganga and Yamuna formed part of the kingdom. The kingdom with its capital Varanasi also finds mention in the Lalitavistara (pp. 405-6). The *Bodhisatt-Vāvadāna Kalpalatā* (6th Pallava, p. 31) also refers to Varanasi, situated on the bank of the Ganges. The kingdom founded by the Kāśis and named Kāśi after them is said to have been 300 leagues in extent with its capital at Varanasi, which was known by different other names in the past ages.[200] The extent of the city is mentioned as twelve *yojanas*, whereas Mithila and Indapatta (Indraprastha) each are said to be only seven leagues in extent.[201] The city is described in the several *Purāṇas*. Kāśi, Varanasi and Avimuktakṣetra have been used synonymously for the city.[202] Later, it had some other names like Surundhana, Sudassana, Brahmavaddhana, Pusvavati, etc.[203] Pāṇini also mentions Kāśi (iv. 2.116) and its capital Varanasi in a 'Ganga' (iv. 2.97). Ptolemy's 'kassidas'[204] is identical with the kingdom of Kāśi. Kāśi with its capital of Varanasi is included in the list of twenty-five and a half Aryan countries.[205]

**Kingdoms of the Descendants of Yayāti**

Nahuṣa's son and successor named Yayāti (whose capital was at Khāṇḍavaprastha on the bank of the Yamuna) was not only a famous king, but also a renowned conqueror. He is believed to have extended his kingdom widely by conquering not only whole Madhyadeśa, west of Ayodhya and Kānyakubja kingdoms, and the Sārasvata region, but also the north-west and the country west, south and south-east of his territory of Pratiṣṭhāna. He divided his territories among his five sons, Yadu, Turvasu (or Turvasa), Druhyu, Anu and Puru. He installed his youngest son, Puru, as his successor to rule over Madhyadeśa, the southern half of the Ganga-Yamuna *doāb*, with its capital at Pratiṣṭhāna and gave the elde sons the outlying territories. Yadu got the south-west, Turvasu the south-east, Druhyu and north-west and Anu the north and the east. This can be testified to not only with the help of the *Purāṇas*,[206] but also the *Ṛgveda*,[207] the *Rāmāyaṇa*[208] and the *Mahābhārata*.[209] For a better result of our enquiry, we can place our reliance on the combined testimony of all these sources. It seems that Yayāti had extended the boundaries of his empire from the banks of the Sarasvati to the regions far beyond the river Indus i.e. the mountain ranges of Hindukush and the deserts of Siestan. His empire, thus, included whole of the present day Pakistan and Afghanistan. Pargiter, after getting the *Purāṇic* texts collated, has drawn the conclusion that "Puru obtained ancestral kingdom; Yadu's realm lay in the country watered by the river Chambal (Carmaṇvati) Betwa (Vetravati) and Ken (Suktimati); Druhyu's kingdom in the country west of the Yamuna and north of the Chambal; Anu's realm comprised the northern portion of the Ganga-Yamuna plain; Turvasu's kingdom in the territory around Rewa . . ."[210] It has been rightly stated in the *Purāṇa* and the *Mahābhārata* that out of five sons of Yayāti, two (Puru and Yadu) came within the pale of Aryandom and rest of the three were reduced to the rank of the *mlecchas*.[211]

It appears that the Ailas had established the hegemony over the whole of mid-northern India with the exception of the Ayodhya kingdom and had developed into seven kingdoms comprising those of Yayāti's five sons and the two earlier ones Kānyakubja and Kāśi.

According to the *Vāyu Purāṇa*,[212] altogether twenty five dynasties sprang from the descendants of five sons of Yayāti. They carved out several small kingdoms and ruled over them during the period concerned.

## YADU DYNASTY

The rulers of Yadu and Puru dynasties earned great name and fame and found their respective place in the pages of ancient Indian history. One of the notable developments, which occurred among the Yadus, was that the number of their descendants increased, who were divided into two main branches, the Haihayas, who occupied the southern part, and the Yādavas, who held the northern portion of Yadu's territory.

Among the five sons of Yadu, Sahaśrajit was the eldest and the other four were known as Kroṣṭu, Nala (or Nila), Ajita and Raghu. Sahaśrajit's son Śatajita was blessed with three famous sons : Haihaya, Haya and Venuhaya.[213] Here it is significant to note that Yadu's son Sahaśrajit's descendants were named after his grandson, Haihaya (son of Śatajita), and were well known as the Haihayas, whereas the descendants of his another son Kroṣṭu were known, particularly, as Yādvas. The details of the descendants of his other three sons are not available.

### The Haihayas

Haihaya, a king of Yadu's line, was the founder of a dynasty, which was named after him. He was succeeded by Dharma, Dharmanetra, Kunti, Sahajita or Sāhanjawa and many other rulers. The genealogy of the Haihaya branch of the Yādavas is given by a number of *Purāṇas*.[214] Among all the rulers of this dynasty, some were very important, the details of which, as available in the *Purāṇas*, the epics and other relevant sources, are given below.

The Haihayas, actually, prospered in their region of South Malava, and one of their noted kings, Mahiṣmāna, son of Sahajita, is said to have founded the town Māhiṣmati on the bank of the river Narmada.[215] He probably captured the place from Mucukunda's (of the Solar dynasty) successors and gave to it his own name. However, it is a fact to be reckoned with that the first dynasty of Māhiṣmati was of the Haihaya family. One of the Haihaya kings named Bhadraśreṇya (or Rudrasreṇya), son of Mahiṣmāna, marched eastwards and conquered the kingdom of Kāśi, took possession thereof and reigned there for quite some time,[216] till it was taken over by the Kṣhemaka *Rākṣhasas*. His son, Durdama, further recovered the kingdom of Kāśi from them. The Haihayas held the territory of Kāśi till their expulsion from there by the famous Kāśi king, Divōdāsa I.

The Haihaya king Durdama's son Dhanaka was further succeeded by his four sons, Kṛtavirya, Kṛtāgni, Kṛtavarma and Kṛtauja. Kṛtavirya's son, Arjuna, was the sovereign of the seven *dvipas*. He was the most famous and powerful ruler. He has been called the *Cakravartin Samrāta*. His reign was marked not only by the expansion of the kingdom, but also by the economic prosperity.[217] As a great monarch and conqueror he raised the Haihaya power to a great height because of his long reign. He extended his conquest from the mouth of the Narmada as far as the Himalayas. The *Brāhmaṇs* in the lower regions of the Narmada after getting ill-treated by the successors of the Haihaya *king*, Kṛtavirya, fled into Madhyadeśa.

Kṛtavirya's son Arjuna of this Haihaya branch is also credited with having conquered Māhiṣmati, situated on the bank of Narmada, by defeating Karkotak, a Nāga chief ruling over one thousand Nāgas, who had previously settled over there and subsequently made it his fortress capital (Māhiṣmatipuri). The Haihayas established themselves in that part of India by overthrowing the Nāgas of the Narmada region. This is what we learn from the several *Purāṇas*.[218] The facts stated above can also be, more or less, corroborated by the evidences furnished in the epics. In both the *Rāmāyaṇa*[219] and the *Mahābhārata*[220] he is said to be a king of Māhiṣmati. This is further supported by H.D. Sankalia,[221] Morton Smith[222] and others.[223] It was the Karkotaka (Nāga) dynasty from which Durlabhavardhana (seventh century A.D.) of Kashmir claimed his descent. The dwellers of Māhiṣmati were generally called as Māhiṣakas or Māhiṣmakas. There is no doubt that the *Purāṇic* accounts about the original ownership of the city Māhiṣmati is very confusing and contradictory, however the existence of this city during the reign of the Haihaya emperor concerned cannot be doubted. Mr. Sankalia on the basis of both archaeology and tradition has thrown a good deal of light on the antiquity, location and identification of the city. According to him, Māhiṣmati, the famous *Purāṇic* capital city of the rulers of a dynasty known as Haihaya, can be identified either with Maheśvara (Maheśvarapura), situated on the northern bank of the Narmada, about 80 or 96.5 Km. south of Indore (Madhya Pradesh), or with modern Māndhātā in the Nimaḍ (Nimar) District on the basis of the archaeological remains of a prosperous agricultural village at the site with some of the beautiful painted pottery, he has pushed its antiquity back to *c.* 2,000 B.C..[224] The archaeological excavations carried out at the site in 1953-54 show that earlier settlements had taken place on the northern bank of the Narmada, which later developed into a city known as Māhiṣmati or Maheśvara. The initial foundation and the growth of the settlements are said to have occurred about 1,600 B.C. or earlier.[225] Relying more on the archaeological data, chronology, culture-data, etc., as given by recent excavations, than on the *Purāṇic* data, H.D. Sankalia had dated the "Maheswar-Navadatoli Culture" back to 3,000 B.C. and ascribed it to the Haihaya ruler, Sahasrārjuna (Kṛtavirya Arjuna). On the basis of the evidence of the central Indian Chalcolithic culture found at Maheshwar, he has correlated the rise of the Haihayas with this culture in the west and added that with the help of the Bhārgavas the Haihayas initially succeeded in establishing a kingdom on the Narmada at "Mahiṣmati".[226] On the basis of the results obtained from excavations and explorations at "Maheshwar", the antiquity of this ancient city has been traced back to the Prehistoric period (Early Stone Age). The Chalcolithic phase on the Narmada dated by several C-14 dates both by laboratories in America and India prove that "Maheshwar" had been colonized by the people in about 2,000 B.C." It is said that though they lived in wooden, mud-plastered houses . . . still they practised agriculture, as evidenced by several types of grains, oilseeds etc. However, H.D. Sankalia is of the view that these people cannot be identified with any degree of certainty with the *Purāṇic* tribes.[227] Whatever may be the fact, it cannot be denied that the city Māhiṣmati on the Narmada must have come under the occupation of the Haihayas before the Great Bhārata War. Later it might have been colonized by some other people, as it appears from different available dates.

There are also some epigraphic and numismatic evidence to confirm the identification of Māhiṣmati with Maheśvara or Māndhātā. Māhiṣmati in Junagarh Rock Inscription of Rudradāman I (Śaka year 72=150 A.D.) has been clearly identified by D.C. Sircar with modern Maheśvararo Māndhata in the Nimar District.[228] Fleet has also identified Māhiṣmati with the village of Māndhātā in the Nimar District of the Central Provinces. He has further observed that "the territory belonging to Māhiṣmati lay on both banks of the Narmada and consisted of present Nimar Zillah of Indore with parts of the Nimar District of the Central Provinces.[229] A coin bearing the word "Mahisati" of the third century B.C. has also been discovered from Maheśvara itself.[230] Besides, Māhiṣmati figures in a number of inscriptions dated second century B.C., the fifth and thirteenth century A.D.

There are many other scholars, who have proposed more or less the same identification of Māhiṣmati, which we have discussed earlier. We find that all of them have identified it either with Maheśvarapura of Māndhātā, Māndalā, Māhiṣmatipur,[231] the original capital of the country on the upper Narmada. Hiuen-Tsangs Mo-hi-shi-fo-lo-pud-lo, identified with Maheśvarapura, also corresponds to the old town of Māndalā. The kingdom was 3,000 *li* or 500 miles in circuit.[232]

From the *Mahābhārata* it is quite apparent that Sahadeva in course of his *digvijaya* proceeded to conquer Māhiṣmati kingdom on the Narmada then ruled by king Nila after subduing Śurasenas, Navarāṣṭra, Kuntibhoja, Avanti and other countries situated on the banks of Carmaṇvati and Narmada.[233]

According to an old tradition, which is generally accepted, Avanti including

Māhiṣmati belonged to the Haihayas. The early Buddhist literature, which in its present form seems to be earlier than some *Purāṇic* stories, also confirms the truth. According to Mahāgovinda Suttanta (*Digha Nikāya*), Māhiṣsati or Māhiṣmati was the capital of Avanti kingdom.[234] In the *Sutta-Nipāta* commentary (Vol. II, p. 583) also Māhiṣmati is mentioned as an important city. It appears that Avanti was divided into two parts—the northern part having its capital at Ujjayini and the southern part at Māhiṣmati. According to the *Brahma Purāṇa*, the city of Avanti, situated on the banks of the Sipra in the Mālavādeśa with its capital at Ujjayini (or Ujjain, Avantipur) was well-decorated with magnificent buildings, festoons, strong boundary walls, entrance gates, market-complex, trade centres, etc. It was inhabited by the *Brāhmaṇs, Kṣatriyas, Vaiśyas, Śūdras* and other groups including artists, musicians and learned men.[235] Avantika is said to be one of the seven great cities.[236] Patañjali in his *Mahābhāshya* or commentry on *Pāṇini*'s Ashtādhyāyī also refers to Māhiṣmati (III. I. 26) as a city of Western India. Kālidāsa in his *Raghuvaṁśa*, Dandin in his *Daśakumāracarita* and Rājaśekhara in his *Kāvyamīmāṁsā* also refer to Māhiṣmati city.

Kṛtavirya's son Arjuna as well as his compatriots were slewn by Paraśurāma in revenge for ill-treating and killing his father Jamadagni.[237]

Kṛtavirya Arjuna had many sons among whom the five, namely Jayadhvaja, Śura, Śurasena, Bṛṣasena and Madhu were very important.[238] The chief among them was Jayadhvaja, who is stated in one of the *Purāṇas* as the ruler of Avantipur.[239] But from another *Purāṇa* it distinctly appears that not only he, but Arjuna's other sons too, notably, Śura and Śurasena ruled at Avanti.[240] Jayadhvaja's son was Tālajaṅgha, who had many sons, chief of whom was Vitihotra whose son Ānarta (ruler of Gujarata) became very powerful. The Haihayas grew in power and comprised five leading groups, the Vitihotras, Sāryātas, Bhojas, Avantis and Tundikeras, all of whom were called Haihaya-Tālajaṅghas.[241] Their dominion stretched from the Gulf of Cambay to the Ganga-Yamuna *doāb*. They continued their raids and devastated some neighbouring countries, but founded no new kingdom in the countries they overran.

The descendants of Bharata (one of the sons of Tālajaṅgha) were Madhu and Vṛṣaṇa or Vṛṣṇi (also known as Mādhavas and Vārṣneyas), who became popularly known as the Haihaya-Yādavas because of belonging to the Yadu dynasty.[242]

The contradiction in the *Purāṇic* literature about the territories, which they ruled over, is quite apparent. "The Haihayas, Aśmakas and Vitihotras, like the Śurasenas belonged to the great family of the descendants of Yadu, who occupied the countries of the river Chambal in the north and the river Narbada in the south, but it is difficult to identify with precision the kingdoms indicated by these different names. Haihaya is often used almost as a synonym of Yādava to denote the whole group of peoples and the Vítihotras are a branch of the Haihayas. Both the Vitihotras and the Aśmakas are closely associated in literature with the Avantis of west Malwa whose capital was Ujjain (Ujjayin) on the Siprā, a tributory of the Chambal (Carmaṇvati).[243]

The Haihayas were very powerful and ambitious. They left no stone unturned to bring the neighbouring kingdoms under their domination, so as to consolidate their position and to establish themselves firmly. This can be fairly substantiated by their expansion in different directions. They dominated whole Madhyadeśa and Vidisa for quite some time. They had also ravaged the kingdoms of Kānyakubja, Kāśi, Kosala and Vatsa. It is believed that the Kāśis, the Kosalas and the Vatsas were defeated by them.

The Haihayas were, no doubt, checked at several stages in their carreer of conquests. After Paraśurām's time they "recovered their power and extended their conquests into North India, making continual raids, overthrowing kingdoms, founding none, and devastating the countries, which were then overrun by tribes from the north-west also. The *Kṣatriyas* must have perished by thousands. The Haihayas overwhelmed Kānyakubja and Ayodhya, but were arrested by the Vaiśāli kings and afterwards Sagara destroyed all those enemies, rescued India from those evils and re-established peace. The carnage and ruin must have continued nearly a century, and the deplorable condition to which North India was reduced may be imagined by that caused by the Marāṭhas and the Persian and Afghan invasions in the eighteenth century, for the Haihayas occupied the same region as the Marāṭhas, and the two periods are strictly comparable and remarkable alike"[244] The Haihayas also find mention in the classical literature. Ptolemy's "Adeisathroi" is supposed to be the Greek rendering of Hayakshetra or the country of Hayas or Haihayas"[245]

**The Yādavas**

The *Purāṇic* accounts of the expansion of the Yādavas in different parts of India, as well as of the kingdoms, which they ruled over, are neither very systematic nor very clear. We therefore have placed our reliance not only on the *Purāṇas*, but also the *Mahābhārata* and other useful sources dealing with the subject concerned.

The genealogy of the other branch descended from Yadu's son Kroṣṭu and known as the Yādavas proper may conveniently be discussed in two parts, the first from Kroṣṭu to Sātvata and the second from the latter's descendants to the destruction and resettlement of their various offsprings. The first part is covered by a number of *Purāṇas.*[246] But we do not find uniformity in the presentation, so far as the genealogical order of the kings of this part down to Sātvata is concerned. However, they all agree generally, though with considerable variations in some of the names, down to Parāvṛt's sons.

The Yādava branch first developed a great kingdom under its king Śaśabindu (sixth in descent from Kroṣṭu), who was famous as a *Cakravartin,*[247] which implies that he extended his sway over neighbouring countries, which were the Paurava realm on his east and the Druhyu territory on his north. His territories were divided among his sons into many small principalities of which no account is available.

One of the Yādava kings of Kroṣṭu branch was known as Parāvṛta (contemporary of

Karandhama of the Vaiśāli realm of Vidiśā region), whose son Jyāmagha sought his fortune southward in the hilly upper region of the Narmada at Mekals (hills north-west of Chhattisgarh), Mṛttikāvati (capital of Daśārṇa or eastern Mālavā within Cedi kingdom in Madhyapradesh) and in the Ṛkṣa hills (Satpura range), which were all wild and inhabited by Nāgas and other rude tribes. He established himself on the river Suktimati (the Ken) in the hills near its source. He is said to have conquered Madhya-Deśa, i.e. the country along the Narmada, Mekala and the Suktimati mountains. His adventures seem to have resulted in the first settlement of the *Yādava* tribes along the Narmada more to the south and west than before.[248] Suktimati has also been mentioned as a town situated on the bank of Narmada.[249] Pargiter places it in the neighbourhood of Banda.[250] From the *Mahābhārata* it distinctly appears that Sukti, popularly known as Suktipuri, later became famous as the capital city of the Cedis.[251] The Yādavas further moved south and carved out a kingdom on the Tapti, which became popularly known as Vidarbha. This was perhaps one of earliest Āryan kingdoms south of the Vindhyas or in the Deccan. They had, no doubt, established themselves in the north-west portion of the Deccan. According to the *Purāṇic* account of the Yādavas, the kingdom of Vidarbha was founded by Jyāmagha or his son, Vidarbha, whose successors were called Vidarbhas. The name of the earlier capital of Vidarbha country was Kuṇḍinapura or Kauṇḍinyapura, situated about twenty five miles east of Amaraoti on the western bank of the Vardha in Maharastra. And the name of its later capital was known as Bhojakata or Bhojakatapura founded by Rukmin (son of *king* Bhiṣmaka) in Kṛṣṇa's time, which is represented by modern Bhat-Kuli in the Amaraoti district of Berar.[252] The *Padma Purāṇa* refers to a third city of Vidarbha, called Padmapura.[253] The ancient Vidharba kingdom, in fact comprised the valley of Payoṣṇi (modern Pūrṇā) and the middle portion of Tapti and extended on both the banks of the river Varadā corresponding to the western part of Berar.

The Yādava king, Vidarbha, contemporaneous with king Sagara of Ayodhya "sought peace with the Ayodhyā king, advancing south-westward by offering his daughter Keśini in marriage to the latter . . . He then retired towards the Deccan into the country named after him, leaving the whole of northern India to acknowledge the suzerainty of Sagara. After Sagara's death, the Yādavas of Vidarbha extended their authority northward over the Haiṇya country".[254] The three sons of Vidarbha, named Kratha or Bhima, Kaiśika and Lomapada (from Bhojya) founded three sub-lines. Kratha-Bhima, the eldest, continued the main Yādava line of Vidarbha. In the time of *Aitareya Brāhmana* (VII. 34) Bhima was the king of Vidarbha. He was succeeded by his son Kunti in the line of which there were many other rulers. The second son Kaiśika, the king of Cedi, was the progenitor of the Cedis. It was Kaiśika's son Cedi who founded the Cedi line. His descendants known as Caidya kings established themselves in Cedi. The Cedi-Deśa comprising the land between the Chambal and the Ken on the south bank of the Yamuna corresponding to modern Bundelkhand (Jejākabhukti), the Malava region and the adjoining tracts[255] became widely known as the Yādava (including Haihaya branch) kingdom. In the Cedi line, later there were two famous rulers, Damaghosa and his son Śiśupāla, who ruled over Cedi kingdom from different capitals, known as Maheśvara

(Indore), Māndalā, etc. at different times. The location of the territories, over which the youngest son of Vidarbha, Lomapada, and his successors ruled, is not known. One of the important kings of Vidarbha was Bhimaratha, father of the celebrated Damayanti, who was married to the legendary king, Nala of Niṣadha.

The Yādavas seem to have been divided into small kingdoms, but by the time of Daśaratha, one of its noted kings, Madhu (son of Devakṣatra of Kroṣṭu line), who appeared on the scene about ten generations after Bhimaratha, consolidated them to a certain extent. He founded a kingdom on the right bank of Yamuna in Brajabhumi, which was named after him as Madhura or Madhupur (later Mathura), the metropolis of the Yādavas, and extended his territory from the bank of Yamuna to Gujarat. In the *Raghuvaṁśa* (15, 28) of Kālidāsa, the *Anguttra Nikāya* (eds. R. Morris and E. Hardy. PTS London, 1885-1900, 1.167) and the *Ghata-Jātaka* (ed. V. Faushboll, London, 1887, Vol. 4, 81, No. 454) also Mathura finds mention as "Madhura", which was situated in the north and can be distinguished from the Pandya's Madura in the South. The Yādava kingdom of Mathura suddenly fell under the occupation of Subahu, son of Śatrughna, after Madhu's son Lavana was killed by the latter. But soon he was ousted by Bhima Sātvata (son of Satva or Satvat, who was Madhu's fifth successor), the most distinguished king of the Yādavas. Thus, it appears that the Yādava kingdoms in the initial phase were established in the Narmada valley, Vidarbha, Avanti, Daśārṇa (identified with the Vidisa region or Malava) and Mathura.

The second part of the history of Yādavas really begins with Sātvata and his descendants. It also comprises the various families that developed from them. The second phase is relatively more important than the first one, for it witnessed the foundation of several new kingdoms and the further expansion of the Yādavas in other regions and gave a new turn to the history and culture of ancient India.

The extensive Yādava kingdom seems to have been divided among Sātvata's sons, Bhajamāna, Devāvṛdha, Andhaka, Vṛṣṇi and Mahābhoja. The geographical location of Bhajamāna's kingdom is not specified perhaps because of the reason that his descendants might not have attained any distinction. But his sons, Nimi, Kṛkaṇa, etc. are mentioned in the texts. Out of the four dynasties that sprang basically from rest four of them, the three most important were that of Andhakas, Vṛṣṇis and Bhojas. Further, several branches seem to have developed from their descendants. The Andhaka-Vṛṣnis were no doubt, the two very very important sections of the Yādavas. Andhaka had four sons, Kukura, Bhajamāna, Śucikamvala and Bahirsa, but only former two were very important. The descendants of Kukura styled as Kukuras formed the main line of the dynasty, that continued down to the time of Kaṁsa. Bhajamāna's descendants specially known as Andhakas formed another princely line and they all reigned at Mathura, the chief Yādava capital, and its periphery. An important king in the line known as Kṛtavarma, the son of Hṛdika, was contemporary of the Pāṇḍavas. There were four lines of descent of the Vṛṣṇis from Vṛṣṇi's four sons, Sumitra, Anamitra, Yudhājit and Devamidhuṣa. Vṛṣṇi's offspring begins with that of the eldest son (by Gāndhari),

Sumitra, and continues down to Satrājit. Yudhājit's descendants were divided into two families, those of Śvaphalka and Citraka. Vṛṣṇi's youngest son, Anamitra (by Mādri), had a son, Sini, whose descendants were called Sainyas. Akrura, a very important prince of Vṛṣṇi dynasty, belonged to the line of Anamitra. He was further succeeded by his two sons, Devavāna and Upadeva. Devamidhuṣa in the line of Satrājit married an Ikṣvāku princess named Aśmaki and a son named Śūra, popularly known as Śurasena, was born to him. Śurasenas (Greek Sourasenoi) reigned in and around Mathura in the age of the *Mahābhārata*. The country ruled over by the rulers of this dynasty was itself named after them as Śurasena with its capital at Mathura. Śurasena was married to a Bhoja princess named Mārisa. He was the father of ten sons including Vasudeva (the eldest) and five daughters including Pṛtha, Śrutadevā and Śrutaśrava. Pṛtha because of being adopted by the old king, Kuntibhoja, came to be known as Kunti. She was later married to Paurava prince Pāṇḍu and got the fortune of being called the mother of three elder Pāṇḍavas. Śrutadevā was married to a Karūṣa king named Vṛddhaṣarma. Śrutaśrava was given to the Cedi king Damaghosa, the father of Śiśupāla (whose kingdom also called Candeli extended from Mālavā to Mahānadi with several capitals like Nagariva on Narmada, Manipur or Sirapur on Mahānadi, etc.). Vasudeva married Devaki, the daughter of king Devaka, who was one of the sons (including Ugrasena) of Ahuka, the descendants of Kukuras. Balarāma and Kṛṣṇa were the sons of Vasudeva. Kṛṣṇa and Akrura were the two principal chiefs of Vṛṣṇi-Sangha (sometimes Akrura is connected with Andhaka dynasty). The matrimonial alliance of the Andhaka-Vṛṣṇis with the Pāṇḍavas gave a new turn to the contemporary political history of ancient India. Kaṁsa usurped the throne of Mathura after putting his father Ugrasena in prison. Kṛṣṇa ultimately killed Kamsa and reinstated his father as a ruler of the Mathura kingdom.[256] The Yādavas including Andhakas, Vṛṣnis, Kukuras, Bhojas and Sātvatas consolidated their position and in the first phase reigned at Mathura and in its neighbourhood for a considerable period of time.

The historicity of *Purāṇic* details about the Andhaka-Vṛṣṇis can also be proved, to some extent, by the epic, Jaina, Buddhist and other literary accounts of the subject and numismatic, epigraphic and other evidences as well.

The *Ādi Parva*,[257] *Sabhā Parva*[258] and *Śānti Parva*[259] of the *Mahābhārata* frequently refer to the Andhaka-Vṛṣṇis (confederable clans), the "Kukkuras", the Bhojas and the other Yādavas with their people and rulers. Comparatively speaking, the *Śānti Parva* provides very reliable information about their republican system of government. Having reposed their full confidence in the leadership of Kṛṣna they, probably, formed a federal republic. It appears that, particularly, the Andhaka-Vṛṣnis had played jointly a very significant role in the successful functioning of the *Gana-Rājya* or *Sangha-rājya* of the *Mahābhārata* period. Kṛṣṇa on behalf of the Vṛṣṇis and Ugrasena on behalf of the Andhakas were elected as chiefs of the Sangha. Ahuka on the side of the Vṛṣnis and Akrura on the side of the Andhakas led the team of their respective members and took part in the discussion held in the *Sangha Sabha* or Federal assembly. This shows the mutual understanding of these two republican tribes. According to K.P. Jayaswal, "these two . . . had contracted a political marriage between their families.[260] He has referred to their *Sangha* as a "Federal Parliament".

The Jaina texts (*Vasudevahindi*, Bhāvanagar, 1930-31, pp. 77 ff, 110 f, 357 f, *Uttarādhyayana Tikā*, 22. l ff; 2, pp. 37, 39, 45 and *Kalpasūtra Tikā*, 6, pp. 172-78) also refer to the rulers of "Andhagavahni" (Andhaka-Vṛṣṇis) dynasties, that ruled at Mathura. Śurasena, Vasudeva Kunti, "Akura" (Akrura), Kaṁsa and "Uggasena" (Ugrasena) of Mathura, the marriage of Jarāsandha's (of "Rāyaghiha=Rājagṛha) daughter 'Jivājaśa' to Kaṁsa and his death at the hand of Kṛṣṇa, etc. also find mention in them.[261]

The Pāli—"Andhakavenhu", as mentioned in the *Ghata-Jātaka* (iv, pp. 79-89), is the wrong Prākṛt form of Sanskrit Andhaka-Vṛṣṇis. The capital of the Śurasenas has been described as "Uttara-Madhura", which haṣ already been identified with Maholi, five miles to the south west of the present town of Mathura. Vasudeva, "Kānhā" (Kṛṣṇa), "Devagabbha" (Devaki), "Kaṁsabhoga" or Kaṁsabhoja (Kaṁsa of Bhoja dynasty), Vasudeva's descendants, "Ankura" (Akrura) of Vṛṣṇi's dynasty and others, who ruled over the kingdoms of Mathura and Dvāravati or Dvārakā, find mention in the *Jātaka* concerned. The *Jātaka* presents a distorted picture of the subject, to a considerable context, by adding that the Yādavas divided their empire into ten dominions. Vidhurpandita *Jātaka* specifically mentions about the Surasenas. The text refers to their visit to Kuru court in the city of Indapatta (Indraprastha) along with the Macchas (Matsyas), Madras and Pañcālas. The only historical inference which can be drawn from these combinations is that they were all neighbours.[262]

Pāṇini mentions the Andhaka-Vṛṣṇis (vi. 2. 34) as a Sangha in his *Gaṇa-pātha*. One of the chief features of their constitution seems to be a full-fledged party system. Patañjali (II. 295) also refers to the party of Akrura and that of Vasudeva showing that the "followers of each leader were designated in accordance with their respective party leaders".[263] Patañjali in his *Ṃahābhāṣya* (iv. 1.114) also mentions "Ugrasenonāmāndhakaḥ).

The Saṅgha of Kukuras, as mentioned by Kauṭilya in his *Arthaśāstra*,[264] appears to have formed a part of confederation of Andhaka-Vṛṣṇis. The information supplied by him is almost identical with what we find in the *Mahābhārata* and Pāṇini's *Aṣṭādhyāyi*, so far as the age old tradition of Andhaka-Vṛṣṇis of carrying on the administration of their kingdom jointly along the principle of republicanism is concerned.

A silver coin found by A. Cunningham (now in the British Museum) bears the name of tribe called Vṛṣṇi. But on the basis of this discovery it will not be correct to hold that they flourished as early as the fifth century B.C.[265] The high antiquity is beyond dispute. Further, an old coin bearing "Vṛṣṇi rājanyagaṇaṣyatrātāraṣya" confirms the existence of Vṛṣṇi-Ganarājya in the epic period. Their administrative system in the form of a *Gana* or *Sangha* continued probably down to the beginning of *Vikrama* Era (58 B.C.).[266]

The Kukuras also find mention in the Rock Inscriptions of western India ascribed to the first-second century A.D. They clearly figure in Junagarh Rock Inscription of

Rudradāman 1 (150 A.D.).[267] They probably might have lost their existence in the post-Rudradāman period.

Motichandra connects the Kukuras, traditionally a member of the Andhaka-Vṛṣṇis confederation, with Khokharain in Dasuyu *Tahsil* in Hoshiarpur District of Punjab, which is said to be the original homeland of the ancient Kukuras. On the basis of the discovery of a coin from Northern Punjab beyond Lahore he has located the Vṛṣṇis in the same diștrict of Pubjab. The eastern portion of the Punjab between the upper courses of the Rāvi and Bias has been regarded as a place of settlement of the Vṛṣṇis. A class of Vaiśya known as "Barah-senis" living chiefly in the districts of U.P., who claim Agroha (between Rohtaka and Sirsa) in the Hissar District of Pubjab as their original home and are accustomed to write "Vārshneya" (a derivative of Vṛṣṇi) after their names, are believed to be the descendants of the ancient Vṛṣṇis.[268] But no literary evidence can be adduced in support of the connection of the Kukuras or any section of the Vṛṣṇis with Punjab. A single coin of the tribe of unknown provenance is also of no help for determining their exact location or place of settlement in Punjab.

The Bhojas were widely diffused Yādava race. This can be fairly attested to by a categorical statement made in the *Sabhā Parva*[269] of the *Mahābhārata*. Their origin is, of course, shrouded in obscurity. There are divergent accounts of their origin, antiquity, settlements and expansion. There were different branches of this dynasty. However, the reliability of the information, as supplied by some of the Purāṇas, that Mahābhoja, a son of Sātvata, was their progenitor,[270] cannot be doubted.

It is said that Mahābhoja was a pious prince and his descendants—the Bhojas, the princes of Mṛttikāvarapur were called Mārttikāvaras or Mārttikāvatkas.[271] Mārttikāvata also called Saubhanagara, once ruled over by the Bhojas, formed part of the Śālva territory (Śālvadeśa or Śālvapur), which corresponds to modern Virāta (Bairāt in Jaipur, the earstwhile capital of the Matsyas in Rajasthan) and it extended from Alwar to north Bikaner.[272] This justifies the use of "Śālva-Matsyeṣu" conjointly in the *Gopatha Brāhmaṇa* (1.2.9). N.L. Dey has identified Mārttikāvata with Marta in Marwar as the capital of Mṛttikāvati.[273] Pargiter has placed Mārttikāvata in the Śālva country around Mt. Abu.[274] B.C. Law thinks that Śālva country was situated along the western side of the Aravalli hills.[275] According to the *Mahābhārata*, Śālva, a king of Mārttikāvata or Saubhanagara, attacked Dvārakā or Dvāravati (to retaliate the death of his friend Śiśupāla, a Cedi king, at the hand of Kṛṣṇa), entered into a battle with Andhaka-Vṛṣṇis and was ultimately killed by Kṛṣṇa.[276] V.S. Agrawala has placed the capital city of Śālva, as mentioned above, in Ānarta (northern Gujarat),[277] which is not confirmed by any other source. The weight of evidence is in favour of identification of Mārttikāvata city of the Bhojas with Śālva country in Rajasthan, as noted earlier. B.C. Law observers : "The story of Kṛṣṇa's conquest of the Śālva country points to the fact that they were located somewhere contiguously with the Yādavas (of the Aravalli hills).[278]

The Bhojas were widespread in Vidarbha (modern Berar with its capital at Bhojakata or Bhojapur and Avanti region.[279] The Bharhut Inscription also refers to Bhojakata.

Mṛttikāvati (called Mattiyāvai in Jaina canonical text, *Bṛhatkalpa Sūtra Bhāṣya*), the capital of Daśārṇa kingdom (Vidisa or Bhilsa region in Gwalior) or eastern Mālavā, has also been identified with the country of the Bhojas by the side of Parṇāsa (Banas) river.[280] Modern Bhojpur, six miles south-east of Bhilsa might have been one of the earliest kingdoms of the Bhojas in the Mālavā region of Madhya-deśa. Some of the *Purāṇic* texts create an impression that the lineage of Devāvṛdha, one of the sons of Sātvata, were the Bhojas of Mārttikāvata.[281] Pargiter, while connecting Devāvṛdha with the "R. Parṇāsa" ("the modern Banas in west Mālavā)", observes that "he, his son Babhru and his descendants reigned at Mārttikāvata, which was apparently in the Śālva country around Mount Abu".[282] We find some contradiction in his statement, because Devāvṛdha and his descendants and their settlements in the Mṛttikāvati of eastern Mālavā region, which existed before (in pre-Sātvata period) and not in the Marttikāvata of the Śālva region. One may be distinguished from the other.

Ujjain, also called Avantipur, because of being capital of the Avanti kingdom in ancient times, was another capital of the Bhojas in western Mālavā. It is believed that a king named Bhoja later ascended the throne of Ujjain about 757 in *Vikrama* Era and made Dhāravati his capital. Kuntideśa (also called Kamantalapuri, Kāntipuri, Kāntipur and Kuntalapuri in ancient times), identified with the region of modern Kontwar, about 25 miles away from Gwalior in the north, whose remains from archaeological point of view still exist, was one of the very important centres of the Bhojas. A Yādava prince named Kunti-Bhoja was a famous king of this place. He is believed to have founded the capital city of the Bhoja kingdom. He had very friendly relation with the Śurasena king of Mathura. Because of not having any issue, he became the adopted father of his daughter, Pṛtha (sister of Vasudeva and Pāṇḍava's mother), who later became popularly known as Kunti after whom the Bhoja country was named Kuntalapuri.

It has already been stated that the Bhojas were one of the five branches of the Haihayas. The descendants of the Haihayas, the Bhojas, the Avantis and others of Sātvata race, were obviously living like neighbours.

The Bhojas, including Kunti-Bhoja, along with the Śurasenas, Avantis and the king Bhiṣmaka of Bhojamata were, by and large, conquered by Sahadeva in the epic age and were compelled to acknowledge their allegiance and become tributory to Yudhiṣṭhira.[283]

Pargiter deriving his authority from the *Purāṇas* and the *Mahābhārata* has remarked that "The Bhojas were a family among the Haihayas, and yet the name Bhoja is used widely of many Yādavas. Andhaka was the 'great Bhoja' and Devāvṛdha's descendants were Bhojas. Urgasena and his son Kaṁsa (of Mathura) were Bhojas, and so was Kṛtavarman, so also Bhiṣmaka and his son Rukmin of Vidarbha. In fact the Bhojas were widespread, and it would almost seem as if the name belonged to the Yādavas generally, except perhaps the Vṛṣṇis in Gujarat".[284]

The Bhojas were also among the dwellers of the Vindhya region. They probably inhabited the western slopes of the Vindhyas. That is why, the *Purāṇas* place them in

Vindhyavāsin division.[285]

We learn from the Hāthigumphā Cave Inscription (found near Udayagiri Hills, in Prākrit language resembling Pāli, and in Brāhmi script) of Khārvela (ascribed to the second-first century B.C.) that he in the fourth year of the reign led an expedition against the Bhojakas and Rāṣṭrikas.[286] The Bhojakas and Rāṣṭrikas (or Rathikas) of this inscription are said to be ruling chiefs of Vidyādhara settlements ("Vijādharādhivāsa"). The Jaina canonical text, *Jambuddivapaṇṇati* (1.12 : com. Santicandra, Bombay, 1920), connects the Vidyādhara with the Vaitādhya or Vindhya range and speaks of their eighteen settlements. They are regarded as ruling chiefs of sixteen or eighteen Vidyādhara tracts along the Vindhyas.[287] The Bhojakas of the inscription of Khārvela also belonged to the Berar region.

The inscriptions of Aśoka also testify to the fact that the Bhojas were living in his dominion. The Bhojakas along with the Rāṣṭrikas and others find mention in Aśoka's Rock Edicts V and XIII.[288] According to B.C. Law, the Bhojakas, Rathikas and Pitinikas of Aśoka's Rock Edicts concerned "belonged to the Sātvata race" and were "semi-independent ruling people of Aparānta" (south-western region).[289] They also held the present Thana and Kolaba districts of the Bombay presidency. Bhojapura, as mentioned in an inscription dated 882 A.D., has been identified with a village situated on the right bank of the Ganga in the Farrukhabad district.[290] However, they do not fall within the scope of treatment of the subject here.

The earliest reference to the settlements of the Bhojas "as one of the sects of the Sātvats in the southern region" occurs in the *Aitareya Brāhmaṇa* (VIII. 14). In the *Padma Purāṇa*[291] the Bhojas are associated with the Pandyas. The *Mahābhārata*[292] also refers to the Bhojas of southern region. A Bhoja king belonging to the Yadu family of Kerala finds mention in the "Arulal-Perumal and Ranganath inscription.[293] The Yādavas of Devnagiri (Dakṣināpatha), who gradually extended their influence and in course of time established an extensive empire, were also the descendants of Yadu. The Yādava dynasty established during the period concerned rose into prominence at a very later stage. The *Vāyu Purāṇa* makes a mention of a king, Sātadhanva of the Bhoja dynasty, who occupied Dvārakāpuri.[294]

The *Mahābhārata* very categorically refers to the eighteen branches of the Bhojas.[295] The references of the Bhoja country have also been made in the Jaina sources and Pāli Buddhist literature. The Jaina text, *Jambuddivapaṇṇati* (1.12), also speaks of their eighteen settlements.[296] The Bhojas are also mentioned in the *Uttarādhyayana Sūtra*.[297] The *Jātakas* speak of sixteen Bhojaputtas.[298] In the *Sammyutta Nikāya*[299] also we find mention of Bhojaputta. But the texts concerned do not provide details of the countries where the different branches of the Bhojas resided or founded their kingdoms. However, on the basis of the information supplied in the Buddhist and Jain texts, B.C. Law[300] has placed their several branches mainly in the Vindhya and Vidarbha regions.

They, undoubtedly, were spread over different parts of northern, western, central and southern India. It is clearly stated in the *Matsya Purāṇa* that "there were hundred sects or branches of the Yādavas; they were three crores in number and their leader was Kṛṣṇa"[301]

The history of migration of different sections of the Yādvas belonging principally to three dynasties, viz. Andhaka, Vṛṣṇi and Bhoja from their respective original place of abode in general and Mathura in particular, to Dvārakā in Gujarat for seeking a fresh settlement over there, and the subsequent events, which took place during the period concerned are really very interesting and worthy of our attention. In order to maintain the continuity and coherence in the above accounts of the Yādavas, the chronological sequence is broken here. Jarāsandha, a powerful king of Magadha (with its capital at Girivraja), wanted to expand the frontiers of his empire by annexing to it the territories extending from Magadha to Śurasena. Thus, in order to achieve his goal he formed an alliance with Śiśupāl of Cedi, Dantavakra of Kuntideśa, Bhagadatta of Prāgjyotisha, Vasudeva of Pundra, Bhiṣmaka of Vidarbha and other rulers. Kṛṣṇa, taking this alliance as detrimental to him, wanted to break it. However, Jarāsandha gradually rose to the height of power and glory and extended his supremacy around and as far as Mathura, where Kaṁsa, the Yādava king, who had married two of his daughters (Āsti and Prasti), acknowledged him as overlord. His growing strength, power and influence struck terror in the hearts of many rulers including the Yādavas, who ultimately got dispersed in groups in different directions. It is said that eighteen branches of the Bhojas fled from the north to the west because of being scared of him. They concluded a treaty of friendship with the Pāṇḍavas for the survival of their race. Besides, Śurasenas, the Yādava rulers of Kuntideśa along with other neighbouring rulers took shelter in the west. Kaṁsa relying on favour of Jarāsandha tyrannized over his own subjects, but Kṛṣṇa killed him. This aroused Jarāsandha's wrath against Kṛṣṇa and his followers, the Andhaka-Vṛṣṇis and the Bhojas of Mathura. Jarāsandha was bent upon destroying the existence of the Yādavas. He is said to have attacked Mathura altogether seventeen times to take revenge of his son-in-law's death. In the seventeenth encounter with the Yādavas of Mathura he lost two of his commanders, named Haṁsa and Dimbhaka, the former being killed by Balarama and the latter getting drowned in the Yamuna. Thereupon he returned to his capital city, but was instigated by his two daughters (being wives of Kaṁsa) to kill both Balarama and Kṛṣṇa. When he made eighteenth attmept to invade Mathura, Kālayavana, a Yavana chief, simultaneously attacked the city and thereatened Kṛṣṇa. Thus, Mathura was constantly under the attacks of both, one from the east and other from the west. The Yādavas resisted them as far as they could, but felt their position very much insecure. Kṛṣna had an apprehension that their constant invasions of Mathura may prove disastrous to an extent that it could ultimately lead to an extinction of the Yādava race as such. He opposed the idea of combating their combined forces knowing fully well its far-reaching consequences, which bears testimony to his ingenuity, political sagacity and wisdom. The question of future safety of the Yādavas was of greater importance than to enter into battles with them. Thus, he ultimately decided to quit Mathura (thereafter called Ranachora) and to shift his capital to a safer place. He along with the Yādavas moved to the west and founded a new city of Dvārakā exactly at the old site of Kuśasthali, the earliest capital of Ānartadesa (Gujarat), originally built by Śaryati's son, Ānarta or his descendant Raivat near Raivataka hill not far off the sea-coast. The city was also called Ānarttapuri, Dvāravati (i.e. the city of many gates) and Vṛṣṇayandhakapuri. The new city, which was built in the pre-Bhārata war period after getting the earlier one renovated, covered an area of twelve *yojanas* (i.e. 12x4=48 *krosa* or ninty six miles). This magnificent city, called Mahānagari, was one of the seven important cities of ancient India. It was a well planned and fortified city. The domes and minarets of the palatial buildings and temples, fortwalls, gates, gardens, spacious roads, streets, market-complex, the assembly hall of the Yādavas, etc. adorned the city. The architectural design of the city was very attractive. The shifting of the Yādava capital from Mathura in the north to Dvārakā in the west at the behest of Kṛṣṇa constituted a watershed in the politico-cultural history of the Yādavas. The Yādavas inhabiting the new city comprise Andhakas, Vṛṣṇis, Bhojas, Sātvatas, Madhus, Arbudas, Māthurakas, Śurasenas, Visarjanas, Kukuras, Kuntis, Akrura, Dasārha, etc. In fact, a Yādava confederacy was established, but they could not remain united for a long time. Kṛṣṇa returned to Dvārakā after the Great Bhārata battle came to close and Yudhiṣṭhira occupied the throne of Hastināpur. Exactly after thirty-six years of Yudhiṣṭhira's installation on the throne of Hastināpur or towards the close of Kṛṣṇa's life a fratricidal strife started among the Yādavas, including Kṛṣṇa's son Samba, in Prabhāsatirtha near Somnath in which practically the entire Yādava males were ruined. Being perturbed over the destruction of his kinsmen at the hands of one another and their further evacuation, and foreseeing the possibility of submerging of Dvārākā into the sea, Kṛṣṇa sent a messenger to Hastināpur for calling Arjuna to Dvārakā to take back the surviving women and children to different places for their resettlement. Arjuna came to Dvārakā and took with him the remnants of the Yādavas to different places. While retreating from Prabhāsatirtha northwards he reached Pañcanada (Punjab) and going further he was attacked by the rude Abhiras of Rajputana, who forcibly took from him the Yādava women of Andhaka-Vṛṣṇi clan. Arjuna, after having established the Bhojas, particularly Hārdikya's son at Mārttikāvata, Yuvadhāna's grandson on the river Sarasvati and others in Kurukṣetra, brought the bulk of the people including the Andhaka-Vṛṣṇis to Indraprastha (Delhi, about which the details follow little later) and placed Vajra, the only surviving Vṛṣṇi prince (son of Aniruddha or grandson of Kṛṣṇa), as king over them. It is further said that after Arjuna's departure from Gujarat and death of Balaram and Kṛṣṇa in Prabhās-tirtha, the whole Dvārakā city except Kṛṣṇa's palace was submerged by the sea. After the accession of Parīkṣit (Arjuna's grandson or Abhimanyu's son) to the throne of Hastināpur, the Pāṇḍavas in course of their wanderings beheld the sunken city of Dvārakā in the sea. The facts mentioned above are based on the combined testimony of the *Mahābhārata*[302] and the *Purāṇas.*[303] The details of the subject concerned as provided in them are more or less identical except length and breadth of the Dvārakā city, which vary from text to text. Here it will be profitable to add that the *Brahma* (196, 12-15), *Viṣṇu* (V. 23, 9-13), *Harivaṁśa* (*Viṣṇu Parva*, 58, 36) and the *Bhāgavata Purāṇas* (X. 50. 48-54) mention that the total area covered by

Dvārakā city was twelve *yojanas*. Whereas, on the other hand the *Brahmavaivarta* (Ch. 103) and *Bhaviṣya* (*Kṛṣnajanmakhaṇḍ, Uttara.* ch. 103) *Purāṇas* refer to hundred *yojanas*, which is apparently an exaggeration. In the *Varāha Purāṇa* (149, 7-8) the length of the city is said to be *ten yojanas* and breadth five *yojanas*. In the *Padma Purāṇa*, in one place it is two *yojanas* (VI, 200, 66) and in the other (VI, 246. 41) it is thirty *yojanas*. But according to the *Sabhā Parva* of the *Mahābhārata* (13, 49-54) its length was merely two *yojanas* and breadth one *yojana*. However, on the basis of the archaeological excavations and explorations carried out at different parts of the old Dvārakā city in Gujarat in the recent past, whose details follow, a broad consensus has emerged in favour of twelve *yojanas* as its length and breadth. V.S. Agrawala,[304] while comparing the fortified Dvārakā city with the well-fortified Acropolis city of Greece, has observed that the former was wider and stronger than the city-states of Greece.

The epic and *Purāṇic* traditions are also supported to some extent by the Jaina and Buddhist traditions, so far as the foundation of Dvārakā city, its location and settlements of the Yādavas over there are concerned. The Jain text, *Kalpasūtra Tikā* (6, pp. 176 ff),[305] has also highlighted Jarāsandha's attack on Mathura, the migration of the Yādavas to the west, the foundation of Dvārakā city, etc. Another Jaina text, *Uttarādhyayana Sūtra*,[306] clearly states that Dvārakā was situated near the so-called Raivataka hill (Girnar). The *Ghata Jātaka*,[307] while narrating the story relating to Vasudeva (Kṛṣṇa) and his brothers, has made it crystal clear that they after having ruled over a number of states ultimately settled at Dvārakā, on one side of which was hill (Raivataka) and on the other the sea. Any way, on the strength of the epic, *Purāṇic*, Jaina and Buddhist traditions it can be said with greater confidence that Kṛṣṇa's Dvārakā was situated on the sea.

The historical accuracy of the epic and *Purāṇic* details about Dvārakā as a second capital city of the Yādavas can fairly be tested on the basis of the archaeological evidences, which have come to light in the recent past.

It goes without saying that Kṛṣṇa's Dvārakā city of hoary antiquity remained submerged under the sea for several centuries. Attempts have, of course, been made by the historians and archaeologists during last more than a century to determine its antiquity, trace its remains and fix its exact location, and, no doubt remarkable success has been achieved in this direction, but still there are certain problems relating to the subject, which await solution.

On the basis of the information contained in the *Mahābhārata* and the *Purāṇas* it is held that the city of Dvārakā built by the Yādavas under the leadership of Kṛṣṇa was originally situated near the Raivatagiri or Junagarh (ancient Girinagara or Girnar), about 96.5 kms. away from the sea. The possibility of the earliest settlement of the Yādavas in the west (Gujarat) at Kuṣasthali (an island) after getting it renovated and naming it as Dvāravati cannot be precluded or they might have founded second Dvāravati on the sea afterwards. The identification of the city with the area extending from the Raivataka hill to the sea-coast seems to be valid. The fact, as already stated, that on the one side of the city was the hill and on the other the sea, should not be lost sight of. Nalini Kanta

Bhattasali's statement, that the first Dvāravati was situated near the Girnar hill and the second was build on the sea,[308] seems to be quite logical.

Mula-Dvārakā, an island on the south-west coast of Saurashtra, about 22 miles from Prabhāspatan (in the Una Taluka of Junagarh district) or east of Porabandar (also called Sudāmāpuri), is traditionally believed to be the ancient Dvārakā of Kṛṣṇa's time. The people of this village in the Kathiawaḍ still believe that Kṛṣṇa first came to this place from Mathura, stayed here for some time and from here he shifted to modern Dvārakā in ancient Okhamandal (Kathiawaḍ) or the present district of Jamnagar, but the city was destroyed by a tidal wave in the ocean after his death.

There is an archaeological evidence to prove that the sites of ancient cities of Mula-Dvārakā, Mādhavapur (where Kṛṣṇa married Rukmini), Sudāmāpuri (the residence of Kṛṣṇa's friend Sudāmā), etc. are located in the south-eastern corner of Kathiawaḍ.[309] The popular tradition also affirms it. There are some other evidences to show that Mula-Dvārakā was situated on the sea-coast, about three miles away from Kodinar (at very short distance from Prabhāsa), which is represented by a small mound flanked by ruins of temples.[310] Mr. Burgess was perhaps the first man to mention in his Report of 1876 about Mula-Dvārakā extending from the south-west coast of Saurashtra to Porabandar.[311]

Prabhāsa-tirtha or Somanath, a place of hallowed memory of Balarām's and Kṛṣṇa's death following the fratricidal war among the Yādavas there itself resulting into their destruction, etc., was evidently a part of Dvārakā. Taking into account the fact that Prabhāsa (*Adya Prabhāsa* of the *Skanda Purāṇa*), Raivataka-hill and Dvārakā were adjacent to each other, it can be deduced that the remains of the Yādava's Dvārakā must have been somewhere near Prabhāsa and engulfed by the sea not far off.

Pargiter also dealt with the problems relating to identification of the city and its location as early as 1904, but could not reach at any positive conclusion.[312]

The identification of ancient Dvārakā with modern Dvārakā in Okhamandala was rejected by A.S. Altekar in 1925 on the ground of the absence of references to it in literature or inscription, though he accepted the tradition concerning the sunken city into the sea ascribing it to the third century B.C.[313] The date suggested by him about its antiquity does not appear to be very much convincing and hence it can be dismissed as wholly unworthy of our consideration. A.D. Pusalker's arguments put forward in 1945 in support of the location of the old capital of Srikṛṣṇa at the site of modern Dvārakā[314] still hold good.

Modern Dvārakā (containing the famous Dvārakādhisha temple), the political capital of Kṛṣṇa's time, situated on the bank of Gomati stream, where it flows into the Arabian Sea, and the island of Bet-Dvārakā (famous as the pleasure resort of Sri Kṛṣṇa), situated in the Gulf of Kutch, about 30 km. north of present Dvārakā connected with the mainland between Okha and Aramada, have, relatively, received the greater attention of archaeologists than the other sites.

H.D. Sankalia, on the basis of the results obtained from the deep vertical excavation carried out in 1962-63 near the Dvārakadhisha temple jointly with the Department of Archaeology, Gujarat, has drawn the conclusion that there were six habitations or six Dvārakās, and the foundation of the first city of Dvārakā on the sea or on the site of modern Dvārakā goes around the beginning of the Christian era, and not much earlier. The different phases of settlements at Dvārakā according to him continued up to the seventh-eighth century A.D. While dealing with the subject at length on the basis of both literary and archaeological data, he has attempted to establish that the "various places in and around Dvārakā . . . is the Dvārakā mentioned in the *Musala Parva* of the *Mahābhārata*, the *Dvārakāmahātmya* of the *Sakndapurāṇa*, other *Purāṇas* and the *Ghata Jātaka* . . . the Dvārakā described in a great detail as a sacred *tirtha* by the Harivaṁśa probably came into existence after the second submergence in the sea of two earlier Dvārakās, because it gives very minute description of so many temples . . . Dvārakā . . . was twice submerged into the sea and, therefore, the earlier Dvārakā belonged to Shri Krishna . . . the earliest Dvārakā was found at least in the second-first century B.C.-A.D. . . ."[315] He has also very categorically stated that "Even a small and limited excavation at Dvārakā . . . has shown that the stories in the *Purāṇas* about the city being once submerged in the sea are true. However, this event took place not some 5,000 years ago, as popularly believed, but only about the beginning of the Christian era".[316] The dates put forward by him about the antiquity of the city can fairly be disputed.

Modern Dvārakā was, no doubt, built on the ruins of ancient one. Dr. S.R. Rao, a well known archaeologist, and his team taking clues from the *Mahābhārata* that Dvārakā was a port city situated at the point where the river Gomati meets the western sea, further conducted excavation in 1979 in the forecourt or precinct of famous Dvārakādhisa temple, situated near the delta of the Gomati. The remains discovered from here, on the whole, belonged to the period ranging from so-called 1,500 B.C. to the ninth century A.D. and remains of some ancient temples with their walls and sculptures intact, dedicated to Śiva and Viṣṇu, some red polished ware and *Karshapanas*, the copper coins etc. were found. Altogether there were eight phases of settlements at this site. Modern Dvārakā represents the eighth settlements. Several temples were constructed here between 1,500 B.C. and the ninth century. What is most significant is that a pottery found at the site has been dated by the T-L (thermoluminiscence) dating method of about 1,500 B.C. and it is claimed that it belonged to Kṛṣṇa's era—1,500 B.C. which is considered by them as the date of the *Mahābhārata* war. Inspired by the initial success they decided to continue the search for the lost capital city of Kṛṣṇa just off the two main temples in the township. Keeping in view the fact that twelve *yojanas* of land was required for building the Dvārakā City, as stated in the epic, they decided to make search for the city under the sea-water, which began since 1982.

A significant breakthrough was achieved in the field of the discovery or re-discovery of Dvārakā city when a marine archaeological exploration work was undertaken by a team of marine archaeologists from National Institute of Oceanography, Goa led by S.R. Rao in 1982 at the sea-coast of Dvārakā and Bet-Dvārakā. During 1982-1988 six attempts were made by them in this direction and ultimately, in the sixth attmept (November 1987-Feburary 1988) S.R. Rao with the help of two of his associates, M.P. Mishra and S. Bandodkar, succeeded in discovering Kṛṣṇa's ancient city of Dvārakā by diving deep under the water in the vast Arabian sea just off the cost of Dvārakā. It is said that the city was submerged by the Arabian sea "3,500 years ago". They have traced at about nine metres below mean sea level the remains of an inner and outer fortifications of an ancient city, two main gates (inner and outer) attached to the fort-walls flanked by a circular bastion of massive blocks of sandstone, etc. From the inner gateway a flight of steps led to the Gomati river. They found that the bastion wall of the under sea fortification at Dvārakā stands on a foundation of deposited rubble. The remains of a stone temple within the inner fortifications are indicated by a pillar and moonstone. The occurrence of smaller three-holed stone anchors of triangular shape weighing 100 to 140 kg. and other 50 stone anchors has led Mr. Rao to believe that Dvārakā was one of the largest ports of the second millennium B.C. on the Indian coast. The fame of Dvārakā as a proto-hostoric port city is well highlighted. Mr. Rao says that "the *Mahābhārata* age followed the tail-end of the Indus civilization, which finally petered out at around 1,700 B.C. The life of Dwarka city in this post-Harappan age was not extensive and ended with the flooding of the city by the sea, a fact faithfully recorded in the Epic itself. And with this ended what historians refer to as the "first urbanisation" of Dwarka".[317]

The archaeological finds from Bet-Dvārakā, 30 kms. north of Dvārakā, are extremely important. Here the inner and outer fortifications of a city extending landward and seaward up to four kilometres along the eastern coast are believed to be the same, which we find in the Epic as "*Varidurg*" (outer-fortress) and "*Udhadhi-Madhyasthān* (place in the sea), which were submerged because of the rise in the general sea-level in the last 3,500 years. In Bet-Dvārakā too sea-damaged half kilometre long wall of rubble bearing traces of the post-Harappan pottery has been traced just off the shore of the island. A most impressive stone wall 550 metres in perimeter, nine courses of stone masonry of the massive fort wall, four three-holed stone anchors, various shells with lotus (padma) engraved on them etc. were also discovered.

The two archaeological finds from Bet-Dvārakā of great historical importance are worth mentioning here. A post-Harappan votive jar (*kalaśa*) bearing an inscription of seven letters has been found in the sea off Bet-Dvārakā, which has been deciphered by Mr. Rao as : "*Mahi Kutcha Shah Pa*" (Sea Lord protect)—a term said to be used in the *Mahābhārata*. T.L. (Thermo-Luminiscence) dating on this jar shows that it was produced in 1,500 B.C. The inscription may also literally mean "a protector (king) of Mahākaccha". Mr. Rao has placed it between the Indus and the Brāhmi script. In fact, it bears striking similarity with the Brāhmi script. It also stands in marked contrast to the seals of the Harappan period found from Lothal, Rangpur and other places. Mr. Rao has ascribed the inscribed *kalaśa* to the seventeenth-sixteenth century B.C.

A seal made from a shell bearing the image of a three-headed creature with the heads of bull, unicorn and goat has also been discovered from the Bet-Dvārakā sea. Despite being uninscribed, it bears close resemblance to the Indus-type smaller rectangular seals with perforated button at the back.

The finding of the seal concerned reminds us of what is described in the epic and the *Purāṇas*. The *Āraṇyaka Parva* of the *Mahābhārata* makes an incidental allusion to the seals, which have been found in Dvārakā region. According to this text, Kṛṣṇa as a ruler of Dvārakā at one stage had ordered that all citizens, while entering or leaving the city, should carry their seals (*"mudra"*) for showing to the guards, incharge of its security, as a mark of identification.[318] Thus, seals were also used as a security measure in Kṛṣṇa's kingdom. In the same text it is also mentioned that seals (made out of shell) were looking like *padma* (lotus).[319] This exactly finds reflection in the archaeological findings of shells with lotus engraved on them. This also indirectly finds support in the statement made by K.P. Jayaswal in his presidential address to the Seventh All-India Oriental Conference, Baroda, December, 1933, that a passage in the *Mahābhārata* refers to the seals found in the region near Dvārakā.

The economic value of the seals made from shells (called *"śāṅkha"*) has been highlighted in the *Harivaṁśa* (*Viṣṇu Parva*, 58, 57-66). The available evidence gives us an impression that such seals served the purpose of a standard currency. They were the chief means of transaction on which the financial stability of the city greatly depended. The *Padma Purāṇa* (*Svargakhaṇḍa*, 24, 14-16) also contains a passage about the seals concerned. Thus, no doubt, literature and archaeology are supplementary to each other, so far as the seals of Dvārakā are concerned.

The occurrence of late Harappan artifacts such as Chert blades and perforated vessels point to the settlement at Bet-Dvārakā of pre-Kṛṣṇa period to which reference is made in the epic.

S.R. Rao on the basis of his findings connects present Dvārakā and Bet-Dvārakā with the *Mahābhārata* and Kṛṣṇa. He is of the opinion that a few years later than the Bhārata battle (1,500-1,400 B.C.) Dvārakā sank into the sea. But the identification of both the parts of Dvārakā with Kṛṣṇa or the *Mahābhārata* on the basis of the finds of the seventeenth and sixteenth century B.C. cannot be totally accepted. There are several old sites in Somnath and Śaurastra Peninsula whose remains still lie submerged under the sea water. Mr. Rao thinks that in Bet-Dvārakā there were three settlements of the so-called pre-*Mahābhārata* (before 1,500 B.C.), the *Mahābhārata* (1,500-1,400 B.C.) and the post-*Mahābhārata* (third century B.C. onwards) period. The former two are believed to have been engulfed by the sea.

We may differ from Mr. Rao, so far as the date of the *Mahābhārata* war or the antiquity of the *Mahābhārata* and Kṛṣṇa is concerned (which have been subsequently discussed in detail separately), but we do acknowledge his contribution to the archaeological discovery of lost towns and cities (including Dvārakā) of primaeval antiquity in India.

The remains of the temple of so-called Ranachoraji or Kṛṣṇa, the palaces of Kṛṣṇa and his favourite queens, Radha and Rukmini and Jāmbavati (a *candāla* woman, according to *Mahāummagga Jātaka* or *Jataka* VI, p. 421, whose descendants reigned in Dvāravati), many other temples in a village in the northern side of Bet-Dvārakā (having a circuit of twelve km.) and that of a temple of Śaṅkhanārayana in Śaṅkhodvāra *tirtha,* about 1½ miles away from Kṛṣṇa's palace (where Senkhāsur was killed by Kṛṣṇa), etc. constitute monumental evidence to the major settlements of the people at this place. Bet-Dvārakā and Gomati-Dvārakā (or Dvārakā), between which the distance is thirty kms., were politically and culturally connected with each other.

The antiquities found in different parts of Dvārakā of bygone days are in some form or the other associated with the past life of Kṛṣṇa and his family members and kith and kin and the events of their period.

The archaeological discovery of a sunken city, submerged by the Arabian sea in the west, roughly about 3,500 years ago, for which the credit directly goes to the marine archaeologists proves the historicity of details, as provided in the *Mahābhārata* and the *Purāṇas,* about Dvārakā as a city and Kṛṣṇa as a Yādava leader and a versatile genius of his age. Depending on all the available literary and archaeological evidence, here we can plausibly conclude that Dvārakā, a big city (called Mahānagari) covering an area of twelve *yojanas* (i.e. ninty six miles), was divided into four sectors, viz. Mula-Dvārakā, Prabhāsa Tirtha, modern Dvārākā and Bet-Dvārakā. The two sectors—modern Dvārakā, a political capital or the headquarters, and Bet-Dvārakā, a port city and famous as a pleasure resort of Kṛṣṇa, saw the major settlements of the Yādavas before the beginning of the *Kaliyuga.* The city must have come into existence anterior to *c* 1,500 B.C.

The Yādavas and their sub-branches, who spread out over the Aravalli region, Gujarat, Mālavā and the Narmada valley, Vidarbha (Berar), the northern Deccan and the eastern Ganges valley, and the Haihaya-Tālajaṅghas, who were mainly concentrated in the Narmada valley, Mālavā, Central India and the middle Ganges valley, have been archaeologically associated with the Chalcolithic Black and Red Ware (BRW=painted black-on red) culture,[320] which dates back to *c.* 2,000 B.C. The plain BRW in the Ganga-Yamuna *doāb* dates back to *c.* 1,200 B.C. These are the Carbon-14 dates, as suggested by the archaeologists.[321]

**Turvasus**

The line of Turvasu is said to have merged with the Puru family. However, one of his successors was known as Janāpida (son of Śarutha or Varutha), whose descendants founded the kingdoms of Paṇḍya, Cola, Kerala and Kulya (identical with Kollagira or Coorg) and ruled over them respectively.[322] It is quite probable that Turvasu princess may have carved out such kingdoms. They were probably the progenitors of the Dravidas of the south.

**Druhyus**

The Druhyus (after having been pushed out from Rajasthan) are said to have occupied the western part of Punjab. Their main settlement was in Gāndhāra Janapada in north-west, which was named after one of their famous kings, Gāndhāra, son of Aṅgārasetu. Āratta region of this Janapada is said to have been very famous in those days for finest breed of horses. The Druhyus maintained their position permanently within the geographical limits of their kingdom. Five generations afterwards they founded many principalities in the *mleccha* countries in the northern region beyond India.[323]

The *Purāṇic* evidence showing Gāndhāra (one of the kings of this dynasty) as a founder of Gāndhāra kingdom can also be supported by the statements of some other authorities.[324] The *Purāṇic* tradition in this regard also accords with the Buddhist tradition. The *Sumaṅgala-Vilāsini* (the Pāli commentary on the *Digha Nikāya*, p. 389) records that "The kingdom of Gāndhāra was built by the sage Gāndhāra . . ."[325] Actually, his ancestors had already settled in Gāndhāra. Their antiquity as north-western people goes as far back as the *Ṛgvedic* age.[326] According to the *Purāṇic* description, Gāndhāra (modern Kandhar) extended from Takṣaśilā, its eastern capital, to the river Kunar, its western boundary, and from the river Kabul in the south to Swat in the north. Takṣaśilā and Puṣkalāvati, the two cities of this kingdom, were named after Takṣa and Puṣkara, the two sons of Bhārata, which we have already pointed out. The archaeological evidence[327] supports the tradition that the cities were founded at one time.

Āraṭṭa-pradeśa (as mentioned in the *Purāṇas*), according to the *Mahābhārata*, corresponds to a region watered by the Śatadru (Satlaj), Vipāśā (Beas), Irāvati (Rāvi), Candrabhāgā (Chenab) and Vitastā (Jhelum) and the Sindhu comprising Bāhlika, Vasāti, Sindhu-Sauvira, etc. This is said to be a discarded region for the Āryans.[328] Āraṭṭadeśa is generally identified with Pañcanada, i.e. Punjab. A classical (Greek) treatise of the first century A.D. also reveals the truth that "Araṭṭa prākrit form of the Sanskrit "Arāshtra" and identified with "Arāṭṭa" were no other than the people of Punjab.[329] The trans-Indus regions between the Indus and Hindukush were brought by Druhyus under their occupation.

## The Ānavas

The Anus or Ānavas (descendants of Anu) rose to power under two able kings, Mahāśāla and Mahāmanā. The latter has been called a *Cakravartin Samrāta* and lord of the seven *dvipas*. Under his two sons, Uśinara and Titikṣu, the Ānavas divided themselves in two separate branches. One branch headed by Uśinara established separate kingdoms on the eastern border of the Punjab, which was divided among his five sons. His famous son called Śivi Auśinara established himself in Śivapura (capital of Śivistāna or Śivisthāna, a part of Sindh province) and then extending his conquest westwards founded through his four sons the kingdoms of the Vṛṣadarbhas (in the home province of Multan), the Sauviras (in northern part of Sind) the Kekayas (in the modern district of Shahpur between the Jhelum and the Chenab or the western part of the Punjab) and the Madrakas (in the Central Punjab with its capital at Śākala or Sāgala—modern Sialkot in the Lahore division of the Punjab and the surrounding region between the Rāvi and the Chenab or between the Jhelum and the Rāvi). And, thus, they occupied the whole of the Punjab except the north-west corner. They became popularly known as Śivigana (Śivas). Their most prosperous Janapadas were known as Śividesa, Kekaya and Madra. The kingdoms of Uśinara's other sons were those of the Yaudheyas, Ambasthas, Navarāṣṭra and Kṛmis (with city Kṛmila). The Yaudheyas are said to have sprung from Nṛga. And they ruled over some parts of Bikaner and the present Montgomery district. The Yaudheyas Janapada belonged to Nṛga and Ambastha to Subrata; the capital of Kṛsa was Vṛṣalapuri and Nava was the lord of Navarāṣṭra.[330] The city of Śākala, according to the Viṣṇu *Dharmottara Purāṇa*, was thickly populated and prosperous.[331] The Madrakas, the Kekayas and the Uśinaras, no doubt, belonged to the family of Anu. The Ānavas, according the *Vedic* tradition, had settled on the banks of Paruṣṇi. The *Purāṇic* tradition concerned can also be supported, to some extent, in the light of the Jain and Buddhist traditions.[332] The Kekayas of Uttarapatha or the western Punjab settled down in the territory between the Vipāśā or Beas and Gāndhāra. According to the Jain sources, one-half of the Kekayas kingdom was Āryan and the Kekaya city was known as "Seyaviya".[333]

The historical validity of the *Purāṇic* accounts of particularly the Uśinara-Śivi can further be examined with the help of both Indian and foreign sources. In the *Vedic* literature[334] they are described as northerners. In the *Mahābhārata* also Uśinara and his son Śivi and his descendants, Śivis, inhabiting the north west, have been mentioned.[335] H.H. Wilson, while strongly supporting the epic and *Purāṇic* traditions, has stated that the Śivis of the Hindus, as mentioned in the *Mahābhārata* and the *Purāṇas,* and the Sibae, with whom Alexander fought after reaching the confluence of the Akesines (Chenab) and the Hydaspes (Jhelum), are usually associated with the people of the north-west, or the Punjab, and they are the descendants of king Śivi, the son of Uśinara, and also called the Śaivas. "Several of the other tribes of the Punjab are also called the progeny of this prince; and the existence of a people of this name in the proximity of the Indus is fully confirmed by Sanskrit writers.[336] Prof. Lassen has also placed them in the Indus region.[337] Pāṇini (*cf. Kāśika* on IV, 2. 117-18; *Aṣṭādhyāyī*, IV. 2. 52-54)[338] and Patañjali (II. 4.19-comm: on *Kāśika*; and *Mahābhāsya*-IV. 2. 52)[339] mention Uśinaras' country as a part of Vāhikadeśa (Punjab) and the Śibi country as Śaivah (or Śaiba). According to V.S. Agrawala, "Pāṇini names three divisions of the Vāhika country, viz. Kekaya, Uśinara and Madra to which is to be added the fourth division Śavasa. Of these Kekaya and Śavasa may be located between the Jhelum and the Chenab, the first in the south and the second in the north respectively, and Madra and Uśinara between the Chenab and the Rāvi in the north and south respectively. . ."[340] Varāhamihira has also mentioned Śivideśa along with the Yaudheyas, Kekayas, etc. forming the part of Northern India.[341] In the early Buddhist literature, particularly the *Jātakas* they are mentioned as ancient people of India, who settled down in Uttarapatha. From the *Śivi Jātaka* (*Jāt.* IV, 401; V. 210; VI, 419) we learn that Ariṭṭhapura (Pāli form of Aristhapura) was the capital of the

Śivi kingdom. The *Nimi Jātaka* (VI, p. 95 f) mentions a king named Uśinara and his son Śivi without giving much hint about their connection with the Śivi people or kingdom.[342] The other *Jātakas* (*Ummadanti* No. 527; *Vessantara Jātaka* No. 547) also refer to the Śivi kingdom. Their other city was Jetuttara near Chittor. We find that altogether seven *Jātakas* refer to three different locations of the Śivi kingdom.[343] A text-*Bodhisattvāvadāna-Kalpalata* refers to the city of Śivavati, which is said to be identical with the capital of the Śivi country once ruled by the king Śivi. The Śivi country is mentioned in the *Lalitavistara* as well as in the *Mahāvastu* as one of the sixteen *Janapadas*.[344] Their chief city, Śivapura, is mentioned in the Buddhist text-*Mahāmayuri*.[345] The early Greek writers like Megasthenes, Arrian, Ptolemy, Diodorus, Strabo and Curtius have located the country of the Śivis (Siboi, Sibae, etc.) in the Punjab. According to them, they occupied the territory lying on the confluence of Hydespes (Jhelum) and Akesins (Chenab).[364] According to N.L. Dey, one of the early settlements of the Śibis was in the Swat valley,[347] which is not far from the truth.

The archaeological evidence also helps us to identify them. An inscription bearing a date eighty three found at Shorkot in the Jhang district lying between the Rāvi and Chenab, palaeographically assigned to the fifth century A.D., mentions a place, Sibipura, which J.P. Vogel identifies with Śivapura, the capital city of the Śivis.[348] The local tradition also connects Shorkot with the Śivis, who lived in Punjab somewhere between Multan and Lahore. Śibipura mentioned in a Shorkot inscription is also identical with Śivapura, which Patañjali also refers to in his commentary on Pāṇini's *Sūtra* (IV, 2.2) as a locality in north-western India. The epigraphic evidence, as well as the tradition have been supported by A. Cunningham,[349] B.C. Law[350] and V.S. Agrawala.[351]

The Śivis' territory of the *Ṛgveda*, the *Mahābhārata*, the *Purāṇas*, the *Jātakas*, Pāṇini and Patañjali or the Siboi country of the Greek geographers is, no doubt, identical with the Shorkot region of the Punjab, i.e. the ancient Śivapura or Śibipura.

The settlements of the Śivis in Rajasthan can be confirmed by the numismatic evidence. Several coins have been found at Nagari (their capital city), situated about seven miles to the north of Chittor and its surrounding regions. In 1834 Col. Stacy and in 1872 Carllyle and further many others found coins of Śivis at or near Chittor. There are quite a good number of sources,[352] which contain description of such coins. The coins are ascribed to the second century B.C. As a matter of fact, the Śivis, Madras and others migrated from Punjab during Alexander's time (fourth century B.C.) and settled down in Rajasthan. Their diffusion in Punjab, Sind and Madhyamika (Rajputana) was a very important event in the history of ancient India. The coins indirectly lend support to the *Purāṇic* evidence, so far as the settlements of the Śivis in Punjab since time immemorial and the migration of their descendants therefrom to Rajasthan are concerned. It is not altogether improbable that the Uśinara country was at one time the home of the Śivis.

The other branch of the Ānavas under Titikṣu founded a kingdom in the east, which afterwards developed into five kingdoms, named after king Bali's sons, Aṅga (which comprised the modern districts of Bhagalpur and Monghyr and portion of Purnea in

Bihar), Vaṅga (comprising a large part of Central, Southern and Eastern Bengal), Kalinga (Orissa), Pundra (Northern and Western Bengal) and Suhma (comprising the modern districts of Hooghly, Bankura and Burdwan and the eastern portion of Midnapur).[353] The earliest capital of Aṅga kingdom was Mālini, but the name was afterwards changed to Campā or Campāvati, Campāpur after king Campā, the son of Pṛthulākṣa or Pṛthulāsva of Aṅga dynasty.[354] According to Fa-hien, the great kingdom of "Champa" or "Champanagar" was situated three miles west of Bhagalpur or eighteen *yojanas* east from Pātaliputra (Bihar) on the southern bank of the Ganges.[355] Hiuen-Tsang also places 'Chan-po' ("Champa") country on the south side of the Ganges. Thomas Watters adds that the country was ruled for a time by the Aṅga dynasty and it was a large and flourishing city.[356] According to Cunningham, "Champa is an old name of the district of Bhagalpur. The capital was situated on the Ganges at from 140 to 150 *li* or twenty three to twenty five miles, to the east of a rocky hill that was completely surrounded by the river . . . As Patharghata is exactly twenty four miles to the east of Bhagalpur . . . the capital of Champa must have stood either on the same site or in its immediate vicinity. Close by, on the west side, there still exists a large village named Champanagar, and a smaller one named Champapur, which most probably represent the actual site of the ancient capital of Champa".[357] The remains of the city still exist.

**The Pauravas**

With the rise of Paurava kingdom the traditional history of ancient India took a new turn. Puru, the youngest son of Yayāti, had inherited the middle Gangetic region between the Vindhyachal and the Sarasvati on the one hand, and between Oudh and Rajputana, on the other. The Pauravas (descendants of Puru) gradually established a number of kingdoms in Madhya-deśa. The Pauravas, who had their original seat at Pratiṣṭhāna, gradually expanded over the whole of the Ganges and Yamuna plain from the Sivalik hills to Magadha (except Śurasena and Kāśi) and ruled over the kingdoms of Hastināpur, Pañcāla, Cedi, Vatsa, Karuṣa and Magadha (in all of which the ruling families were mainly the Bhāratas) and possibly Matsya.

The Pauravas' settlements in the first phase in the Sarasvati and Upper *doāb* are archaeologically associated with ochre-coloured pottery (OCP) of the late Harappan period, which falls in between "c. 2,200-1,700 B.C." (Carbon-14 dates).[358] The OCP people were probably connected with those of the Copper Hoard and they were not nomads, but lived in simple mud walled as well as sophisticated brick houses.[359] The OCP was first found in the lowest layers at Hastināpur and then at Ahicchatra and other places. Hastināpur also finds a place on the map showing distribution of ochre-coloured ware in the upper Ganga Valley.[360] The archaeological examination of some samples from several sites in the upper Ganges reveals that OCP sites were abandoned because of long exposure to a dry climate or a deluge in the Ganga-Yamuna valley after the seventeenth century B.C.,[361] but this theory has not been widely accepted by others. In the post-Harappan period-second and early first millenium B.C. OCP was succeeded in its second phase by painted grey ware (PGW) whose Carbon-14 dates are not found uniform, but its early phase is generally placed between *c* 1,200-800 B.C.

On the basis of the comparative study of the *Purāṇas* and the *Mahābhārata* the genealogy of Puru's descendants, the first from Puru to Ajamīḍha, the second from Ajamīḍha to Kuru and the third from Kuru Pāṇḍavas, may conveniently be considered; synchronisms of kings can be established and the gaps in the genealogy can be filled in. So far as the first part is concerned, all the *Purāṇas*[362] agree more or less down to Matinara, but from Tamsu to Duṣyanta there is great uncertainty, as the pedigree supplied by the texts is not intelligible. However, from Duṣyanta to Hastin the lists fairly agree. The genealogies, as given in the *Mahābhārata*,[363] are little different and mutually inconsistent. It is significant to add that the comparative study of the *Purāṇas* and the *Rāmāyaṇa* helps us to show the contemporaneity of the Pauravas and Ikṣvākus of Ayodhya.

In fact, the Paurava dynasty was re-established by Duṣyanta after the death of Sagara, the king of Ayodhya. His son by Śakuntala was Bhārata, who has been called *Cakravartin Samrāta*. His successors were called the Bhāratas and the country was named after them as *Bhāratavarṣa*.[364] In the *Mahābhārata* it is clearly stated that :

भरताद्भारती कीर्तिर्येनेदं भारतंकुलम।
ऊपरे ये च पूर्वे च भारता इति विश्रुता।।[365]

It is highly probable that the Bhāratas continued to live united as one great nation. The Purāṇas and the *Mahābhārata*, though not following a scientific system in the genealogical arrangement of the various tribes, still present Bharata as the son of king Duṣyanta and Śakuntala and acknowledge the descent of the Pañcālas and Kurus from Bharata.

The territory of Duṣyanta and Bharata, however, appears to have been shifted to the northern portion of the Ganga-Yamuna *doāb*, for Pratiṣṭhāna is no longer mentioned in the texts concerned and its district was included in the Vatsa realm. Hastināpur is believed to have been their capital and the territory of Bhārata, a great monarch, is said to have stretched from the river Sarasvati to the Ganges.[366] In the early *Vedic* times the Ganga-Yamuna *doāb* and Kurukṣetra-the region between the rivers Sarasvati and Dṛṣadvati, were occupied by the Bhāratas. The *Ṛgveda* (3.23.4) refers to Bhāratas of Sarasvati and Dṛṣadavati region. The *Śatapatha Brāhmaṇa* (5.4.2.1) also places them in the Ganges-Yamuna *doāb*. The same territory was later occupied by the Kurus. However, there is no archaeological evidence to substantiate the expansion of the territory of Bhārata, ascribed to "*c.* 2,500 B.C."[367]

In the Paurava line it was, actually, Bhārata's fifth successor Hastin, son of Suhotra (from Ikṣvāku princess Suvarna), who founded Hastināpura on the bank of the Ganga and made it his own capital.[368] This can be confirmed by both the epic and *Purāṇic* evidences. It had an extent of ten *yojanas*.[369] There is every probability that he might have enlarged it and given it his name. In support of the *Purāṇic* statements regarding the naming of the kingdoms and their capitals after their founders, Pargiter observes : "... countries are said sometimes to have been named after kings, such as Gāndhāra, Ānarta and Sauvīra; and similarly towns, such as Śrāvastī, Hastināpur and Vaiśālī from the kings, who founded them. To assert that such kings are merely eponymous is to disregard the evidence supplied by many countries and all times. One might equally assert that Alexander, Seleucus and Constantine were merely eponymous heroes of Alexandria, Seleucia and Constantinople; or that Columbus, Tasman and Rhodes were mythical persons invented to account for Columbia, Tasmania and Rhodesia. It has been a universal practice to name countries, towns, mountains and rivers, especially in newly discovered regions, after discoverers, conquerors, founders and celebrated men and the same method must have been adopted by the Aryans, who conquered North India and founded new kingdoms and towns there".[370]

The Paurava dynasty further expanded under the descendants of Hastin and resulted in the formation of fresh kingdoms. Paurava was always applied to the main branch at Hastināpur. The three notable dynasties were that of Pauravas, Bhāratas and Ājamīḍhas. Rantideva Sāñkṛti, a cousin of Hastin and a famous Paurava king, had a kingdom with capital Daspura, that encroached into the Yādava territory and lay on the river Chambal. Hastin had three sons : Ajamīḍha, Dvimīḍha and Purūmīḍha, as it appears from the *Purāṇas*.[371] But, in the *Mahābhārata* they figure as Ajamīḍha, Sumiḍha and Purūmīḍha.[372] There can hardly be any doubt that Ajamīdha continued the main Paurava line at Hastināpur. Dvīmīḍha founded a separate dynasty of the Dvīmīḍhas in a new realm, probably, adjacent to the Paurava territory of Hastināpur. Ajamīḍha's realm was divided on his death among his three sons, the main kingdom with its capital at Hastināpur and the two others in the Krivi country, named Pañcāla afterwards.

Before we proceed to present the details of the different kingdoms set up by the rulers of Ajamīdha dynasty, which is the most important out of the three aforesaid dynasties from the historical point of view, it will be profitable here to give a brief outline thereof.

The descendants of Ajamīḍha down to Kuru covering roughly fifteen generations figure both in the *Purāṇas*[373] and the *Mahābhārata*,[374] but they do not go in harmony with each other. From the *Purāṇas* it appears that Ajamīḍha had three wives, Nilinī, Keśinī and Dhumini from whom originated separate dynasties. Ajamīḍha's son, Kaṇva (from Keśinī) was succeeded by Medhatithi, who is said to be the progenitor of the *Kānvāyaṇa Brāhmaṇas*.[375] Ajamīḍha's another son was Bṛhadiṣu from Dhumini, who was further succeeded by Bṛhatkarma, Visvajita, Senajita, etc. One of the four sons of Senajita was Vatsa, king of Avantideśa. Senajita's another son, Rucirāsva was succeeded by many other kings. In the same line there was a king named Nipa whose descendants were called Nipas. The rulers of this dynasty line Samar and his other descentants are wrongly inserted in South Pañcāla line. Ugrayudha is also wrongly called the destroyer of Nipas.[376] Further, Udakasena's son, Bhallāta (Bhallā-tangara-a town was situated near Sulaiman mountain range, which was under the rule of Śasidhvaja) was succeeded by Janamejaya.[377] Ajamīḍha's son, Nila (from Nilini), was the famous ruler of Pañcāla and he was succeeded by Suśanti; Pṛsata and others.[378] Ajamīḍha's another son was Ṛkṣa, whose one of the descendants was Kuru[379] from whom sprang a separate dynasty of great historical importance. According to the *Mahābhārata,* the six sons of Ajamīḍha from his three wives were Ṛkṣa (from Dhumini), Duṣyanta and Parameṣṭhin (from Nili) and Janhu, Jana and Rupin (from Keśini), and from Duṣyanta and Parameṣṭhin sprang all the Pañcālas.[380] This list does not agree with that of the *Purāṇas.*

After having carefully examined the two lists of kings, as inserted in the *Purāṇas* and the *Mahābhārata,* we find that Ṛkṣa, Nila and Bṛhadisu or Bṛhadvasu were prominent among the early successors of Ajamīḍha. The eldest line from his son, Ṛkṣa continued the main Paurava line at Hastināpur and his two other sons, Nila and Bṛhadvasu, founded the dynasties of north and south Pañcāla respectively. The rulers of three dynasties, those of main Paurava line of Ajamīḍha at Hastināpur and of North and South Pañcāla, being the descendants of Bhārata were called the Bhāratas.

We come across some discrepancies in the epic with Purāṇic list of kings falling in the second part till we come to Kuru. However, the third part from Kuru to the Pāṇḍavas as given by the *Purāṇas*[381] and the *Mahābhārata*[382] is comparatively more intelligible.

The *Purāṇic* accounts of the Dvimīdha dynasty is bit confusing. However, there is no doubt that Dvimīdha was succeeded by his son, Yavinar, whose descendants were Kṛta, Ugrayudha, who killed the great Pañcāla ruler Nila, the grandfather of Pṛṣta, and Kṣema, Sumitha or Suvira, Nṛpañjaya and Viratha. They were all known as the Pauravas. The dynastic account as given in the four *Purāṇas*[383] are absolutely correct, but it is wrongly attributed to Ajamīdha by the other two.[384] Whatever may be the fact, we have undeniably very little information about them. We do not find any account of the Purumidha dynasty. From the *Ṛgveda*[385] we learn that his descendants were *Brāhmaṇas.* Thus, it is only the Ajamīdha line, which, relatively, deserves far more serious attention than the other two.

**Pañcālas or the Pañcāla Kingdom**

It is significant to note that the five sons of Bhadrāṣva (also called Bhṛmyaśva and Haryaśva—sixth in descent from Ajamīdha in the line of Nilini or one of the descendants of Nila, the ruler of Pañcāla)—Mudgala, Sṛñjaya, Bṛhadisu, Yaviyāna or Yavinara and Kāmpilya ruled over five different Janapadas or principalities (*Pañca+alam*), which combined together was named Pañcāla after them in the same way as the Punjab obtained name from five rivers (*Pañcanada*). Eversince then it became popularly known as Pañcāla.[386] It comprised Ruhelkhanda, north of the Ganges and east of the upper *doāb,* and south of the Ganges as far as the junction of Chambal and Yamuna, which roughly correspond to Badāyun, Farrukhabad and the neighbouring districts. The country was further divided into two kingdoms : North Pañcāla with its capital at Ahicchatra, identified with modern Rāmnagar in the Bareilly district, and South Pañcāla with its capital at Kāmpilya, which is identical with modern Kāmpil in the Farrukhabad district.[387]

On the basis of the epic-*Purāṇic* evidence it is generally admitted that Ajamīdha's two sons, Nila and Bṛhadvasu, founded the north Pañcāla kingdom north of the Ganges with capital at Ahicchatra and South Pañcāla kingdom south of the Ganges extending from Mākandi on the Ganga to the river Carmaṇvati or Chambal in the South with capital city Kāmpilya respectively.[388]

The northern part of Pañcāla kingdom first rose into prominence under Vadhryaśva, the grandson of Mudgala (the eldest among the said five sons of Haryaśva), who extended the frontiers of his kingdom. The most prominent among the rulers of North Pañcāla were his son Divodāsa, Sṛñjaya, Cyavana, Sudāsa, Somadatta, Sahadeva, Somaka, Pṛṣata and his son Drupada. The names of the rulers of North Pañcāla dynasty, who ruled over the kingdom north of the Ganges are given by some *Purāṇas*.[389] All are in substantial agreement down to Divodāsa's son Mitrayu. Then divergencies occur as regards Mitrayu's son Sṛñjaya and Cyavana. Thereafter, the list assumes the identical character. However, the historical credibility of the *Purāṇic* genealogy can also be proved by other evidence. The *Ṛgveda* also mentions the names of Divodāsa (6, 61, 1), Sṛñjaya and Cyavana (4, 15, 4; 10, 69, 56), Cyavana's son Sudāṣa (7, 18, 22) and one of his descendants Somaka (7, 18, 155). One of the noteworthy features of this dynasty is this that many of its kings played an important part in the early *Vedic* age. All these kings of north Pañcāla were *Kṣatriyan Brāhmaṇs*.

The glory of North Pañcāla dynasty was virtually raised to a great height during the reign of Sudāsa. He embarked upon the policy of conquests and eventually made his kingdom extensive. There is a positive evidence to show that after having defeated the Paurava king Samvaraṇa (son of Ṛkṣa of Ajamidha dynasty) on the Yamuna, he drove him out of Hastināpur and finally conquered his kingdom. Consequently, Samvaraṇa fled away to seek shelter on the banks of the Sindhu, where he remained along with his ministers and other relatives till he recovered his kingdom.[390] Hastināpur passed into the hands of the Pañcālas and remained in their possession for quite some time. That is why it has been recorded in the Buddhist tradition that at one time Hastināpur, the well known chief city of the Kurus, was the capital of Uttara-pañcāla.[391]

About Sudāsa's conquests it has been observed that "his conquests stirred up a confederacy of the neighbouring kings to resist him—Pūru, (Samvaraṇa), the Yādava, (the Yādava king of Mathura), the Śivas (Śivis who were Ānavas), Druhyus (of Gāndhāra), Matsyas (West of Śurasena), Turvaśa (the Turvasu prince apparently in Rewa) and other smaller states. Sudāsa defeated them in a great battle near the river Paruṣṇi (Rāvi) and Pūru Samvaraṇa, took refuge in a fortress near the river Sindhu (Indus) many years."[392] For want of reliable historical information, we are not in a position to judge as to how far this is worthy of credence.

The fortunes of the Pañcālas started fluctuating after the time of Sudāsa, who was further succeeded by his son Sahadeva and grandson Somaka. By this time the kingdom had virtually declined as a result of which, Samvaraṇa, the Paurava king, recovered his ancestral kingdom of Hastināpur, probably, from Somaka and conquered North Pañcāla.

The kingdom of North Pañcāla after some time had sunk into insignificance and later, king Ugrāyudha of the Dvimīdhas after having killed Pṛṣata's grandfather Nila, a North Pañcāla king,[393] annexed his realm. Pṛṣata, the next heir to North Pañcāla, who had taken refuge in Kāmpilya (the capital of South Pañcāla) recovered his kingdom. Actually, Ugrāyudha attacked the Pauravas after Śantanu's death, but was defeated and killed by Bhiṣma, who restored Pṛṣata to his ancestral kingdom of Ahicchatra.

Before further incidents are narrated, here it is worthwhile to make it clear that the South Pañcāla dynasty, which reigned south of the Ganges and was also descended from Ajamiḍha as mentioned above is also given by the *Purāṇas*,[394] but it is intertwined with North Pañcāla. Any way, South Pañcāla under the Nipas in their capital Kāmpilya entered upon a new phase of orientation. Ugrāyudha (of Dvimīdha dynasty) not only conquered North Pañcāla, but also overthrew the dynasty in South Pañcāla. He completely destroyed the Nipas dynasty. This dynasty rose into prominence under one of its kings Brahmadatta of Kāmpilya, as it appears from both the *Rāmāyana*[395] and the *Purāṇa*.[396] He also finds mention in the *Jātaka* (VI, p. 394) and the Jaina *Uttarādhyayana Sūtra* (xiii, 1). His great-grandson Janamejaya Durbuddhi, the last king, was also killed by Ugrāyudha of the Dvimīdhas and the dynasty came to an end. South Pañcāla with its dynasty destroyed ultimately passed under the sway of the Kauravas.

Pṛṣata was succeeded by his son Drupada in North Pañcāla. His reign really proved to be a turning point in the political history of ancient India. The events, which took place during his time are, undoubtedly, of great historical importance.

Just before the outbreak of the Great Bhārata War, Droṇa, whom Drupada had treated with disdain, defeated the latter in a battle and after getting crowned with victory wrested his kingdom with the aid of the Pāṇḍavas and Kauravas, who were his disciples. Drona took possession of both North and South Pañcāla, but he retained only North Pañcāla, north of the Ganges with a capital city Ahicchatra for himself and restored the Southern half of the kingdom to Drupada. As a matter of fact, Droṇa wanted to befriend Drupada for the purpose quite obvious to us. It appears that Drupada received the portion of Pañcāla south of the Ganges as far as the river Çarmaṇvati (Chambal), which had two capital cities, Mākandi and Kāmpilya.[397] The southern portion was merged in the kingdom of Hastināpur after the death of Drupada. The name of Drupada as a ruler of South Pañcāla distinctly figures in some Parvas of the *Mahābhārata*.[398] Drupada was succeeded by his son Dhṛṣṭadyumna, whose son Dhṛṣṭaketu was the king of Cedi and an ally of Yudhiṣṭhira.[399] After the marriage of the Pāṇḍavas to Draupadi, the Pañcāla princess and the daughter of Drupada, the Pañcālas also became the allies of the former.[400] They played very important part in the age of the Bhārata war. After the conclusion of the great war, they shared the fruits of the victory by getting back their lost dominion.

The epic age was evidently marked by the drawing of a clearcut demarcation line between the northern and southern Pañcāla kingdom. The *Mahābhārata* unequivocally speaks of the two divisions, which were effected in partial fulfilment of a treaty between the king of Pañcāla and that of Kuru, after the northern portion had been taken over by the latter. Both the capital cities, Ahicchatra of North Pañcāla[401] and Kāmpilya of South Pañcāla,[402] have been referred to therein. The dominion of the North Pañcālas bounded on the west by the river Ganga is indicated by the *Rāmāyaṇa.*[403] The capital of South Pañcāla has been referred to in the same text as "Kāmpilipuri"[404] We find a very graphic description of Ahicchatra as a city inhabited by *Brāhmaṇas* and other people in the *Padma Purāṇa.*[405] The *Harivaṁśa* makes a mention of Kāmpilya city.[406] The name of the city is also incidentally alluded to in a passage of the *Yajurveda Saṁhitā.*[407]

The early Buddhist and Jain texts also throw some light on the subject dealt with here. It is said the Pañcālas' kingdom contiguous to that of the Kurus was divided into two : Uttarapañcāla and Dakkhinapañcāla, the Bhagirath forming the dividing line between the two.[408] The *Jātaka* stories refer to Kāmpilla (Sanskrit Kāmpilya) as a city of Uttarapañcāla.[409]

The *Kumbhakara Jātaka* (iii, p. 379, No. 408) wrongly describes Kāmpillanagara, situated on the right bank of the Ganges, as the capital of Uttara Pañcāla. According to this *Jātaka,* when king Dummukha, a contemporary of king Naggaji of Gāndhāra, reigned in Uttara Pañcāla, its capital was Kāmpilla. The *Somanassa Jātaka* (iv, op. 444 No. 505) clearly states that once upon a time Uttarapañcāla was included in the Kuru realm.[410] The *Chetiya Jātaka* (No. 422), surprisingly refers to Uttara Pañcāla as a city. The *Brahmadatta Jātaka* (No. 323), refers to Uttara Pañcāla as a city of Kāmpilya *Janapada.* It appears that there was constant political conflict between the Kurus and the Pañcālas for the possession of Uttara Pañcāla. This is why the *Jātaka* stories refer to it both as a part of Kuru kingdom or Kururaṭṭha and of Kāmillaraṭṭha.[411] The information supplied by *Divyāvadāna* (p. 435), that at one particular point of time Hastināpur, the well-known chief city of the Kurus, was the capital of Uttara Pañcāla, is not authenticated by the testimony of the *Mahābhārata,* which we have already produced. "The fact, however, seems to be that the two peoples (Kuru-Pañcālas) were on a state of war with each other from time to time, at one time the Pañcālas annexing a portion of the Kuru country to their realm, and at another, the Kurus establishing their supremacy over the northern division of Pañcāla."[412]

In the Jain texts Pañcāla with its capital at Kāmpilla (Kāmpillapur) is mentioned as one of the twenty five and half Āryan countries. Kāmpilla was one of the ten capital cities of ancient India. Ahiccatta (Ahicchatra) is mentioned as the capital of Jāṅgata.[413] Kāmpilya is also mentioned in the *Uttarādhyayana Sūtra.*[414]

The *Purāṇic* kingdoms and the towns and cities of lower and upper Gangetic regions were also known to classical (Greek and Roman) geographers and historians. Megasthenes (*c.* 302-298 B.C.) refers to the "Passalae", who are identified as the inhabitants of Pañcāla, the lower *doāb.*[415] Ptolemy (middle of the second century A.D.) not only refers to the Pauravas (Porouaroi or Porvaroi), who reigned over the realms between the upper Ganges and Yamuna, and to the Pañcālas (Passala or Passalae) of lower Gangetic region, whose sway is said to have extended from the Himalayas to the

Chambal river, but also to the capital city of Northern kingdom of great antiquity as 'Adisadra', which is identified with Ahicchatra (of the *Purāṇic* list) of Rohilkhanda.[416] The Pabhosa cave inscription (in Brāhmi script) of the time of Udāka ascribed to the end of the first century B.C. also contains the name Adhicchatra.[417] Coins of a king named Achyuta mentioned in Allahabad Stone Pillar Inscription of Samudragupta (*c.* 335-76 A.D.) have been found at ancient Ahicchatra, which is identified with modern Ramnagar in the Bareilly District (U.P.).[418]

The ruins of Ahicchatra are situated about seven miles to the north of Aonla, a town in Bareilly district, and half a mile to the north-east of the village of Ramnagar, which can be testified to by archaeological report based on the excavations carried out by the Archaeological Survey Department in the years 1940-44 at different places within the precinct of brick fortification. Two successive earthen ramparts enclosing a stout-wall of baked brick came to the notice of excavators. Painted Grey Ware (PGW) is also said to have been found there on the basis of which it is conjectured that the rampart should not be earlier than *c.* 500 B.C. The excavators found nine main strata in the total life-span of the city. Coins (square and round) came into use during the Northern Black Polished Ware (NBPW) period. The dates tentatively proposed for the different strata begin with Stratum ix (before B.C. 300), and it is presumed that it became the capital city of Pañcāla ruler not before *c.* 200 B.C.[419] This site is, no doubt, associated with both PGW and NBPW cultures. Most of the sites in the Gangetic valley contain both the PGW and the NBPW.[420] However, the archaeological findings do not permit us to connect the city with Ahicchatra of the epic and *Purāṇic* periods, whose antiquity can be pushed back much earlier to the dates suggested by archaeologists. The excavations have, so far, not revealed anything for establishing the identity of city of the period concerned conclusively. Its existence can, of course, be proved by the present deserted city, which looms majestically over the plain with towering ramparts 3½ miles in circuit. "Kampilya is situated about 28 miles north-east of Fatehgarh in Farrukhabad district (U.P.) on the bank of the Ganga".[421] At this site also both PGW and NBPW were found. Cunningham has located the site of Raja Drupada's palace on the banks of the "Bur Ganga" on the basis of the remains (isolated mounds), which he personally noticed thereat.[422]

Here it will be worthwhile to add that the Bhāratas, represented as the genuine representatives of the noblest of Āryans, appear to have been divided at an early period into two branches. They, however, did not immediately separate, but kept themselves united for a long time under the leadership of one chief, until the reigning family became extinct in its direct line. These two branches were represented eventually by the Kuru-Pañcālas, the latter being afterwards replaced by Pāṇḍavas. The *Ṛgveda* neither mentions the Pañcālas separately nor the Kuru-Pañcālas together. It is, therefore, probable that at that time the Bhāratas continued to live united as one great nation. The Pañcālas represent originally the older and stronger section of the Bhāratas. The Bhāratas became subdivided into two great halves; the Kurus being the leaders of the one, the Pāṇḍavas those of the other set. Samvaraṇa, most likely the last of the Bhāratas in the direct line of succession, after being expelled by the Pañcālas, took refuge in the

Indus region and the Bhārata kingdom suffered a setback. Then followed a long time of anarchy during which the Pañcālas retained their power. The Pañcālas were ultimately ousted by the Kurus. But, at a subsequent period both tribes dwelt as neighbours in Madhyadeśa, the Kurus living north-east of the Pañcālas. Both are often mentioned together leaving behind an impression as if they were combined into one. This is what we find in the *Vedic* literature, the *Purāṇas* and the *Mahābhārata.*

According to the *Aitareya Brāhmaṇa*, the kings of the Kuru-Pañcālas were consecrated to the kingship together with the Vaśas and Uśinaras and got the title of king.[423] They are mentioned together in some other *Brāhmaṇas*[424] and *Upaniṣads* too.[425] Louis Renou, a French authority on the *Vedic* literature, has also pointed out that the *Brāhmaṇas* mention "Kampila", Asandivant, capital of the Kuru, etc. He further states that "Together with the Panchala (formerly the Krivi), the Kuru, who had established themselves in the Doāb, formed the centre of the *Vedic* culture in the period after the hymns."[426]

The *Mahābhārata* also mentions the Pañcālas separately[427] and the Kuru-Pañcālas conjointly like the *Purāṇas.*[428] It has been rightly observed by Gustav Oppert that "The Kurus and the Pañcālas were the two principal tribes of the Bhāratas, who alternately lived in close friendship with or fought against each other in fierce battles. Such a sanguinary and pernicious war forms the legendary subject of the *Mahābhārata,* which has as its special theme the fortunes of the great Bhārata family, but which includes within its voluminous pages and encyclopaedia of ancient Hindu history, geography, divinity and cosmology."[429]

**Kurus**

Saṁvaraṇa's son Kuru, as mentioned in the *Purāṇas*[430] and the *Mahābhārata,*[431] and Kuruśravaṇa of the *Ṛgvedic* age,[432] are considered to be identical.[433] Kuru, because of being very righteous was made king by the people. He raised the Paurava realm to great eminence and extended his sway beyond Prayaga, which implies that he subdued the intervening South Pañcāla territory.

Kuru carved out a new kingdom, which was named after him as Kurukṣetra (i.e. the land of the Kuru), because he ploughed it. Thus, it was his cultivated territory. He also gave his name to Kurujāṅgala, a tract apparently less cultivated, which adjoined it on the east[434] and in which Hastināpur lay. The *Āraṇyaka Parva* of *Mahābhārata,* as well as the *Vāmana Purāṇa* contain very valuable references to the subject concerned. According to the *Āraṇyaka Parva*, Kurukṣetra was situated to the south of the Sarasvati and the north of the Dṛṣadvati.[435] The land between the rivers Sarasvati and Dṛṣadvati, popularly known as Kurukṣetra was also called Brahmāvarta. This can be confirmed by the *Vāmana Purāṇa*[436] as well as by the statement of Manu.[437] This region was also known as Brahmakṣetra[438] and Brahmavedi.[439] The countries of the Kurukṣetras, the Matsyas, the Pañcālas and the Śūrasenas, according to Manu, constitute Brahmarṣideśa that lies after Brahmāvarta.[440] The *Vāmana Purāṇa* also places Kurujāṅgala (the land on the west of Pañcāladeśa and sanctified by the penance of Kuru) between the rivers Sarasvati and Dṛṣadvati.[441] The importance of Kurukṣetra as a centre of *Vedic* culture has been sufficiently highlighted in the *Brāhmaṇas*.[442] It was one of the sacred places in ancient India, as we find both in the *Mahābhārata*[443] and the *Purāṇa*.[444] The region lying between the Sarasvati and Dṛṣadvati, formerly occupied by the Bhāratas (who later on merged in the Kurus), as reflected in the *Ṛgveda*,[445] was taken over by the Kurus. It appears that the *Mahābhārata* and the *Purāṇas* do not recognize everywhere the separate geographical entity of Kurukṣetra and Kurujāṅgala (the cultivated and uncultivated portions respectively). And hence, both portions, undoubtedly, formed the part of Kuru's territory. B.C. Law thinks that "The Kuru kingdom which extended from the Sarasvati to the Ganges consisted of these three parts : Kurujāṅgala, the Kuru-land proper and Kurukṣetra . . The Kurujāṅgala as its name implies was the jungle tract of the Kuru-land which extended as far as the Kāmyaka forest. There is a tradition to the effect that the kingdom of Uttarapañcāla was founded in this very part of Kuru in which case it must have stood on the left bank of the Bhagirathi Gaṅga".[446] The extent of Kurukṣetra varies from five to twenty *yojanas*.[447] According to Cunningham, it was an extensive land. It covered an area of thirty miles to the south of Ambala (Punjab) and forty miles to the north of Panipat.[448]

*Kurukṣetra*

A tract between the rivers Sarasvati (now Sarsuti, lost in the Rajputana desert) and Dṛṣadvati (Ghaggar), known as Brahmāvarta, Brahmakṣetra, etc., was nucleus of the Āryan culture in the *Vedic* age. This land is hallowed by its association with the Āryans who for the first time introduced the ploughing of the field here. V.S. Agrawala has correctly stated that the region stretching from the western coast of the Yamuna to the Sarasvati or Kurukṣetra was the centre of Āryan civilization in ancient times.[449]

Kuru's successors were called the Kurus or Kauravas after him, who represent the combination of Bhāratas and Pūrus. The Kurus became famous as rulers of their respective states. The territories occupied by them extended to the east far beyond the limits of Kurukṣetra. The *Mahābhārata*[450] specifically mentions that the Kurus like the descendants of Ikṣvāku, Yayāti, Yadu and Bhārata expanded over different parts of India.

After having compared and scrutinised the genealogies of Lunar kings in the line of Kuru as contained in the *Purāṇas*[451] and the *Mahābhārata*,[452] we find that Kuru's immediate successors were his three sons, Parikṣit I, the eldest, Jahnu and Sudhanvan. Kuru's grandson or Parikṣit's son was called Janamejaya II (Janamejaya I being one of the descendants of Pūru). Parikṣit as a king of the Kurus has been praised in the *Atharvaveda* (20, 127, 7-10) and his son Janamejaya has been simply mentioned in the *Śatapatha Brāhmaṇa* (13, 5, 4, 1), *Aitareya Brāhmaṇa* (7, 34; 8, 11, 21) and the *Sāṅkhyāyana Śrauta Sūtra* (16.8.27). It seems that Janamejaya II lost the throne, because it passed to a younger branch, Jahnu's son Suratha and his descendants, who continued the main

Paurava or Kuru line. The kingdom appears to have declined.

The bifurcation or segmentation of the line of Sudhavan (the youngest son of Kuru) into the Chedi and the Magadha branches, founded by his fourth successor Vasu, resulted in the formation of new dynasties and the setting up of new kingdoms, which have been described separately. Later, the Kurus again became eminent under Pratipa, who was blessed with three sons, Devāpi, Bāhlika and Śantanu. Devāpi and Śantanu also figure in the *Ṛgveda* (10, 98, 5-7) and *Nirukta* (2.10), but their progeny is different from that as provided in the epics and the *Purāṇas*. Bāhlika's seven sons became the rulers of Bāhlika (situated on the banks of Balkh, a branch of Vaṁkṣu or Oxus to the north-west of Hindukuśa) and they have been called "Saptavā-hliśvara", which can directly be confirmed by the *Purāṇic* evidence.[453] The name of Bāhlika as a Kuru prince also occurs in the *Śatapatha Brāhmaṇa* (XII, 9.3.8). H.H. Wilson, on the basis of evidence furnished in the *Purāṇas*, has established that "Bāhlika from whom the Bāhlikas sprang, is called the son of Pratipa, of the family of Kuru".[454] The *Mahābhārata* (*Karna Parva*, 30, 9-28) provides a detailed description of Bāhlika country (identified with Balkh in the extreme north of Afghanistan, as well as with Vāhika or Punjab), which is not for our use here.

Śantanu was succeeded by his son Bhiṣma (Devavrata), who prominently figures in the galaxy of Indian heroes. He was not only a great warrior, but also an able administrator. Further, among the descendants of Śantanu, the names of Dhṛtarāṣṭra and Pāndu are worth noting. Dhṛtarāṣṭra, the elder, being born blind, Pāndu was made a crowned king of Hastināpur. As a redoutable warrior, he vanquished the Daśarṇas, the kings of Mithila, Kāśi, Suhma and Pundra and thereby extended the frontiers of Kuru dominion. Dhṛtarāṣṭra had many sons, chief of whom were Duryodhana, Duhsāsana, etc., who as the elder branch were called the Kauravas. Pāndu had five sons, Yudhisṭhira, Bhima, Arjuna (from Kunti, daughter of Kuntibhoja), Nakula and Sahadeva (from Mādra, sister of Salya, the Vāhika king), who were known as the Pāṇḍavas. Pāndu's death was followed by an intense jealousy between the cousins.

*Kuru Kingdom*

The whole tract of land lying between the Ganga and the Yamuna and the region lying to the west of the Yamuna, known as Kurukṣetra (on the bank of the Sarasvati) or the upper portion of doāb, formed the part of the Kuru kingdom. This also relates to the expansion of the Āryans in the Ganga-Yamuna doāb during the later *Vedic* period. The Kurus gradually coalesced with the Pañcālas who occupied the middle portion of the *doāb*. According to the *Mahābhārata*, Pañcāla, Cedi, Matsya, Śūrasena, etc. were the neighbouring kingdoms of Kurus.[455] In *Vālmīki-Rāmāyaṇa* it is clearly stated that during the time of Daśaratha of Ayodhya, a messenger, while going to Kekaya-deśa (with its capital at Girivraja, i.e. Girjak of Jalalpur on the Jhelum) reached Hastināpur and therefrom proceeding further towards west passed through Pañcāla and Kurujāṅgala,[456] which shows their geographical proximity. This is why, in the *Jātaka* tradition (*Jātaka*, ii,

p. 214) Kuru, Pañcāla and Kekaya have been mentioned as three of the most powerful kingdoms in Jambudvipa.

Hastināpur (originally founded by Hastin, four generations upward, on the bank of the Ganga as stated earlier) has been distinctly mentioned in the *Mahābhārata* as the chief capital city of the Kauravas. It has been located in Kurujāṅgala. It is said to be the most magnificent of all the cities existing during the period concerned.[457] The *Mahābhārata* provides very positive evidence about the evolution of Hastināpur as a city in ancient times, which covers both the pre and post Bhārata war period.

Dhṛtarāṣṭra, because of being blind, was not accepted as *Rājā*; and consequently the younger brother Pāṇḍu was placed upon the throne.[458] But he did not care to rule as *Rājā*. Accordingly he left the *Rāj* in charge of Dhṛtarāṣṭra and went into the jungle and spent his days in hunting. Meantime Dhṛtarāṣṭra governed the *Rāj* inspite of his blindness. After the death of Pāndu, the five Pāṇḍavas returned to the old fort at Hastināpur with their mother Kunti and took up their abode. But the family rivalry soon sprang up between the Kauravas and the Pāṇḍavas and consequently they could not continue to dwell together much longer in the old ancestral home. Duryodhana and Yudhiṣṭhira put forth rival claims to the post of *Yuvaraja*, which conferred the right of succession to the *Rāj*. Dhṛtarāṣṭra ultimately appointed his own son Duryodhana to the post. The breach between the Kauravas and the Pāṇḍavas soon widened into an open quarrel. "The Pāṇḍavas after having resided at Pañcāla (Kāmpilya, the Southern Capital) along with their common wife Draupadi (daughter of King Drupada) for complete one year returned to Hastināpur"[459] and contended for their share of the Kaurava territory. But their hope turned into despair. Dhṛtarāṣṭra, in order to avoid the rivalry or conflict between the two branches of the family, divided the kingdom and gave half to the Pāṇḍavas assigning to them the small principality of Khāṇḍavaprastha, a part of Khāṇḍavavana on the bank of Yamuna and retaining Hastināpur proper with him to continue his rule over it.

The Pāṇḍavas led by Yudhiṣṭhira left Hastināpur for Khāṇḍavaprastha[460] with the view of establishing a new colony about sixty miles off on the bank of Yamuna, at a spot which was then covered with jungle, called Khāṇḍavavana. After clearing the jungle by setting it on fire and driving out the Nāga inhabitants (belonging to the old Nāga dynasty of the epic age), they established a colony, built a palace and made it their new capital, which became popularly known as the city of Indraprastha.[461] The new capital was set up in the vicinity of Delhi (or 2 miles South of Delhi), which is identified with modern Indrapat, near which the remains of famous Purana Quila do exist.

According to the *Mahābhārata*, Indraprastha, the capital city of the Pāṇḍavas, was splendid to look at.[462]

It will not be out of place to mention here that the ouster of Nāgas from their colony at Khāṇḍavaprastha in the wake of building the city of Indraprastha resulted in their future hostility with the Pauravas of the post-Bhārata war period. Khāṇḍavaprastha or Khāṇḍavavana and Kurukṣetra were the two chief strongholds of the Nāgas at that time.

The Pāṇḍavas wanted to exterminate them for the future prosperity of Indraprastha.[463] The colonization of Indraprastha by the Pāṇḍavas is a significant event in the *Vedic* Aryan tradition.

The Pāṇḍavas sometimes after their settlement subdued the rulers of different kingdoms in India and compelled them to acknowledge Yudhiṣṭhira as their overlord. Yudhiṣṭhira celebrated the *Rājasūya Yajña* at his new capital city, Indraprastha, and thereby confirmed his imperial position and asserted the right to the land or *Rāj*. They firmly established themselves and gradually consolidated their hold over the new territory. The coronation ceremony was attended by many neighbouring *Rājās*. It was an imperial assemblage.[464] The *Rājasūya* was regarded as a success and triumph; and it consequently reawakened the old jealousy of the Kauravas and kindled the spark of revenge in their breast. Accordingly, Duryodhana plotted with his brethren to humiliate the pride of the Pāṇḍavas by depriving them of their wife and land. In order to carry out the plots the Kauravas challenged the Pāṇḍavas to a gambling match or a game of dice, which was a part of conspiracy to oust them from their kingdom. The Pāṇḍavas were deprived of all their lands and possessions and were banished for thirteen years as the penalty of losing at dice, and at the end of that period when they re-claimed their kingdom, the Kauravas refused to consider their claim which eventually compelled the former to declare war against the latter.

The Pāṇḍavas were aided by the Vatsas, Matsyas, Cedis, Karusas, Kāsis, South Pañcālas, Western Magadhas (ruled by Jarasandha's son Sahadeva) and the South-western Yādavas from Gujarat and Sūrastra, including Yuyudhana and Satyaki of the Yādava family, etc., and the Kauravas were supported by eastern Magadha, Videha, Anga, Vanga and Kalinga, which were under Karna, Bhagadatta and Kirātas of Prāgjyotisha (Assam), Nila of Māhiṣmati, Vinda and Anuvinda of Avanti, Bhojas, Andhaka Vṛṣṇis, Vidarbha, the Punjab and the north-west comprising Jayadratha of Sindhu Sauvira, Sakuni of Gāndhāra, Susarma of Trigarta, Kekeya of Śibi, Salya of Madra, the Ambasthas, the Kambojas, etc. Actually the Madhyadeśa and Gujarat stood for the Pāṇḍavas, and the rest, viz. east, north-west and western India supported the Kauravas.[465] The battle between the two fought on the plain at Kurukṣetra continued for eighteen days and ultimately resulted in the victory of the Pāṇḍavas, the extinction of the Kauravas and annihilation of nearly all the kings and princes, who took part in it. Kriṣṇa played an important role in this battle to attain his goal, that was to maintain the political and cultural unity of India. This battle, no doubt, constitutes an epoch-making event in the annals of our country. The Pāṇḍavas proceeded in triumph to their old home at Hastināpur (instead of new one at Indraprastha) and took possession of the entire *Rāj*. The most noteworthy development of the post-Bhārata war period was the installation of Yudhiṣṭhira on the throne of Ḥastināpur. He became the new king of the Kurus and ruled over the kingdom for nearly thirty-six years.

The *Mahābhārata* provides a picturesque description of Hastināpur of Yudhiṣṭhira's time. The description of the settlement patterns of the dwellers of the city, the magnificant buildings on both sides of the road, the royal palace, gates, etc. gives us an impression that it was a grand city. It was decorated by the inhabitants on such a grand scale to receive their new king Yudhiṣṭhira that it wore a look of an urban centre.[466]

Thirty-six years after the Bhārata war the Yādavas (Andhaka-Vṛṣṇis, Bhojas, etc.) of Dvārakā in Gujarat entered into a fratricidal strife as a result of which many of them lost their lives. Thereafter, Arjuna at the instance of Kṛṣṇa came from Hastināpur to Dvārakā and took the bulk of the surviving population back to Indraprastha and placed Vajra, a Vṛṣṇi prince (son of Aniruddha or grandson of Kṛṣṇa) on the throne as a king.[467] The settlement of the Yādava population at Indraprashta was a significant event. Because the increase in population led to the growth of this city.

After some time Yudhiṣṭhira and his brothers abdicated and placed Arjuna's grandson Parikṣit II (son of Abhimanyu) on the throne of Hastināpur.[468] The accession of Parikṣit (after the death of Kṛṣṇa) marked the end of the Dvāpara Age and the beginning of the *Kāli* Age.

Hastināpur and Indraprastha on the banks of the Ganga and Yamuna respectively were two important urban centres during the later *Vedic* age.

We learn from the *Padma Purāṇa* that Indraprastha was situated on the banks of the river Yamuna. From east to west it was one *yojana* in extent. To the south its boundary is said to be four *yojanas.* It was also called Khāṇḍavaprastha.[469]

The epic-*Purāṇic* evidence can also be corroborated by the details provided in the Buddhist and Jaina literature and in other Indian and foreign sources.

According to the *Jātaka* tradition, the Kuru kingdom, which was three hundred leagues in extent, comprised several districts, towns and villages, and its capital Indapatta (*SK* Indraprastha) was seven leagues in circuit.[470] The ruling dynasty is said to have belonged to the Yudhiṭṭhilagotta (Yudhiṣṭhira-*gotra*).[471] It is further said that Ajjuna (Arjuna) of the stock of Yudhiṭṭhila reigned in the Kuru country when its capital was at Indapatta.[472] One of the *Jātakas* mentions Indapatta as one of the three chief cities of Jambudvipa, the other two being Uttarapañcāla and Kekaya.[473] Hastināpur (Pāli-Hatthipura) the earlier capital finds mention in *Apadāna.*[474] Hastināpur, the well-known chief city of the Kurus, has been frequently mentioned in the Sanskrit Buddhist text. The *Bodhisattvāvadāna-Kalpalatā* clearly states that it was the capital of the Kuru kings.[475] It is described in the *Divyāvadāna* as a rich, prosperous and populous city.[476] The *Lalitavistara* refers to Hastināpur as having been ruled by a king descended from the Pāṇḍava race. The king is said to be valiant and the most beautiful and glorious among conquerors.[477]

The *Mahāvastu-avadāna* refers to King Arjuna of Hastināpur.[478] In the Jain tradition Hastināpur (Hasthināpur or Gayapura) is included among ten capital cities of India.[479]

Pāṇini mentions the Kuru kingdom (IV. 1.172) as well as the town of Hastināpur (VI. 2.101), which was its capital.[480] The Kuru kingdom of the Āryāvarta and its capital

Hastināpur also find mention in *Patañjali's Mahābhāṣya* (1.4.51 and 11.1.16 respectively).[481]

The classical geographer Ptolemy, while referring to the kingdom and towns and cities of upper Gangetic region, clearly mentions Pandoouoi (Pāṇḍavas) and their capital cities, Hastināpur, on the bank of the Ganga and Indabara or Indabatta (Indraprastha of which the Prākrit form is Indrabattha) on the bank of the Yamuna in the neighbourhood of Delhi.[482]

The later *Vedic* Āryans definitely held the Valleys of the Ganga and Yamuna. In the beginning they formed rural settlements at Hastināpur and Delhi on the upper streams of the Ganga and Yamuna. But, in course of time, the increasing population, construction of forts, growing influence of iron-technology, etc. led to the transformation of the places concerned from rural to urban centres. Actually, there were several stages of their growth as two different cities. J. Talboys Wheeler observes : "The old domestic life at Hastināpur may be easily realized if the probable surroundings are first taken into consideration. A large village seems to have been constructed of mud and bamboos on the bank of the upper stream of the Ganges. This was known as the city of Hastināpur. It was probably inhabited by the cultivators of the neighbouring lands, and all the dependants and retainers of the colony; whilst the *Rāja*, with his family and immediate kinsmen, dwelt in a so-called palace or fort, which was most likely built in a rude square with a council-hall and inner quadrangle after the fashion of Hindu forts. The Aryan colony at Hastināpur was not, however, without its neighbours. Amongst others was a Naga people, who dwelt in cities, and had perhaps attained a certain stage of civilization . . ."[483]

About these two cities, Hastināpur and Indraprastha of the epic fame, B.C. Law has pointed out that the former was the earlier, as well as, the later capital of Kuru kingdom and it was one of the nineteen great cities of ancient India; while the latter was the capital of Pāṇḍavas or later capital of the Kuru kingdom founded by Pāṇḍavas on the banks of Yamuna, two miles south of modern Delhi.[484] Thus, the frontiers of Kuru kingdom in Madhyadeśa or Ganga-Yamuna *doāb* extended from Indraprastha to Hastināpur or from Delhi to Meerut.[485]

Hastināpur has been indentified with a ruined side (still called Hasti kā nagara) on the bank of the Ganga about fifty seven miles to the north-east of Delhi or twenty two miles to the North-East of Meerut (U.P.). The excavations were carried out in 1950-52 by Prof. B.B. Lal at the site near an old course of the upper Ganges. On the basis of the archaeological discovery of fragments of the ochre coloured ware or OC associated with copper hoards (Period I), Painted Grey Ware or PGW (well fired, greyish brown, dark in surface colour and surface painted with linear and dotted patterns, concentric circles, *swastikas*, etc. in matt black and red commonly represented by straight-sided bowls and dishes, etc.) together with remains of mud or mud-brick walls without any clear evidence of the use of baked bricks (Period II), over a hundred sherds of Northern Black Polished Ware or NBPW. (wheel made with a highly lustrous surface ranging from grey or brown to black and steel like in quality in the shapes of bows or convex-sided dishes), baked bricks alongside mud and mud brick, soakpits and ring wells, iron objects, copper coins both rectangular and round bearing symbols etc. (Period III), five coins of the rulers of Mathura-attributed to the second century B.C. (Period IV) and other objects (Period V), it has been conclusively proved that there were as many as five phases of occupation of the site (Hastināpur) with stratigraphical gap in between all of them. The Carbon-14 dates of the five occupational periods concerned are also given : Period I is ascribed to *c.* 1200 B.C. Period II, *c.* 1100-800 B.C.; Period III *c.* early sixth century B.C. to the third century B.C.; Period IV early second century B.C. to the end of the third century A.D. and Period V from the eleventh century to the fifteenth century A.D.[486]

Here we are concerned with only first two periods, archaeologically represented by OCP: Late Harappan and PGW generally ascribed to *c.* 2200-1700 B.C. and first half of the first millennium B.C. (based on C-14 dates) respectively. Because the period I is connected with the settlements of the Pauravas in Sarasvati and upper *doāb* and period II with the expansion of the Kurus in upper Sarasvati and Upper *doāb*. Their association, particularly, with PGW phase of cultures, whose diffusion took place at an extensive scale in the Gangetic valley, is absolutely justified, but it is very difficult to determine the antiquity, as various C-14 dates are available. It is quite obvious that the cities concerned came into existence much before the Bhārata war, whose dates also vary from scholar to scholar. Whatever may be the dates of PGW phase of cultures, but it definitely coincides with the emergence of kingdoms and urban centres in the Ganga-Yamuna *doāb* during the later *Vedic* period. These two periods here deserve our notice.

In the first phase of settlement at Hastināpur, those, who used crude ochre coloured pottery and copper-implements like arrow head, an antimony rod, etc. preceded the second phase of settlement of PGW period. It is generally inferred that the people representing copper-hoards were semi-nomadic food-gathering communities, capable of clearing patches of jungle and living by hunting, etc.[487] But on the basis of the distribution of ochre-coloured pottery in the upper Ganga valley and the excavation of some sites, the above statement is contradicted and it is further held that the OCP people were not nomads, but had a settled life.[488] The possibility of Pauravas' settlements at Hastināpur in the second millennium B.C. or much earlier to so-called period I (ascribed to c. 1200 B.C.) cannot be precluded. It has been rightly pointed out that "Āryans at the end of the second millennium B.C. may have found little previous occupation of a settled kind . . . they dropped their dominantly pastoral economy in favour of one based on agriculture in fertile river-side clearings. Here (the Ganga-Yamunā doāb) the territorial magnate began at no great interval to supersede the traditional tribal chieftain and to build the nations and kingdoms of the Indian epics of which this is the homeland. Here emerged the essential India with its imperial dynasties . . ."[489] B.B. Lal after having examined several samples from several sites in the upper Ganges, has postulated that OCP sites were abandoned because of long exposure to a dry climate or deluge in the Ganga-Yamuna valley after the seventeenth century B.C.[490]

All the distinguished archaeologists have unanimously accepted that the PGW period was a blooming period for the growth of urban centres in the Ganga-Yamuna *doāb*, but they seem to be divided in their opinion on the issues relating to its association with the towns and cities including Hastināpur, as mentioned in the epics and *Purāṇas*, and with the Āryans and its antiquity. There are contradictions in their statements, which raise various problems. Thus, there is an ample scope for fresh interpretation of the available data on the basis of their correct analysis.

The discovery of the PGW in the Ganga-Yamuna *doāb* (the Āryāvarta or Madhyadeśa of the *Upaniṣads*, the epics and the *Purāṇas*) constitues an archaeological evidence, which goes to substantiate the existence of towns and cities as mentioned in the epics and *Purāṇas*. It helps us determine their antiquity. It also fairly attests to the various phases of settlement of the people in remote past. Over and above it throws light on the evolution of urban cultures, which flourished in the entire Gangetic valley during the period concerned. In this connection the observation made by H.D. Sankalia is worth quoting. "For the first time the small and big places—towns and villages mentioned in the *Mahābhārata*—seemed to be truly living. Their antiquity was being established for the first time. But the archaeologists after probing the depths of Hastināpur and Ahichhatra said little about sociological background of the people, their houses, the layout of their settlement, habits, customs or manners and disposal of the dead. The Carbon-14 dates from Hastināpur and other sites proved the culture not older than seventh-eighth century B.C. The authors of the Painted Grey Ware cúlture whom the archaeologists associate with the *Mahābhārata* heroes—the Pāṇḍavas, Kauravas and Shri Krishna—should have lived only 2700 years ago and not 5000 years ago . . ."[491] On the basis of the discovery of pottery from each successive layers of deposits at Hastināpur and other identical pottery from the places mentioned in the *Mahābhārata* in connection with the quarrel between the Pāṇḍavas and the Kauravas, he does not consider the stories narrated in the epic as fiction and further associates the PGW phase of culture in the Ganga-Yamuna *doāb* with the early Āryans or the Kauravas and the Pāṇḍavas and their contemporaries in the region. First he took it 400 years older than the Buddha. But on the basis of the subsequent Carbon-14 dates of the PGW (*c*. Eighth to fourth Century B.C. and sixth to fifth century B.C. etc.) he takes it as contemporaneous with the dawn of historical period. But it seems that he does not totally accept its lower dating. He has also not discarded the value of the traditional accounts, as provided in the epics and *Purāṇas*. Traditionally, he seems to be inclined to place the epic details concerned anterior to the PGW period but archaeologically he does not consider the PGW phase of culture or the Gangetic culture older than the seventh or sixth century B.C.[492] In any case, Hastināpur of the *Mahābhārata* does not fall within the range of the later C-14 dates of the PGW. There is no perceptible link between the two.

Prof. B.B. Lal also connects the PGW sites with that mentioned in the *Mahābhārata* and thinks that it belonged to the early Āryans,[493] which, in particular, has been contradicted by H.D. Sankalia, who holds that "Traditionally the Āryans lived at much earlier period about 3000 B.C. . . ."[494]

The views expressed by Mortimer Wheeler are also worthy of our consideration. He observes that ". . . Civic life in recognizable form began at Hastinapur in the Painted Grey Ware level, that the culture represented by that ware was urban and that urban life began in the *doāb* in about 1000 B.C."[495] He frankly admits that Hastināpur was established before the *Mahābhārata* war for which he accepts the date *c.* 950 B.C., as suggested by others. But, on the other hand, he ascribed the PGW, (the earliest reputable pottery known to us from number of town sites), found at Hastināpur, to the eighth century B.C. The date *circa* 100 B.C. assigned to it by B.B. Lal is also not disputed by him.[496] But he is of the opinion that the remains of Hastināpur of the PGW period, "*c.* 800-500 B.C." show a developed township with an economy based on mixed farming, and with adequately constructed houses of which at present little is known.[497]

The archaeological findings of lumps of iron ore in the uppermost levels at Hastināpur and the occurrences of iron-slags at this site do attest to the familiarity of the *Vedic* Āryans with the use of the iron objects in the upper portion of the *doāb* in the first half of the first millennium B.C. But the exact period, which really marked the introduction of iron technology, is still a subject of dispute. Generally it is inferred that the iron weapons like iron axes, which were probably used by the Āryans for clearing the forests in the Upper Gangetic basin, did not come into use before *c.* 800 B.C. H.D. Sankalia himself admits that this date as given above is based on presumption.[498] Prof. R.S. Sharma, while connecting the PGW-Iron phase culture with the later *Vedic* Āryans and throwing light on the role of iron technology in accelerating the process of urbanization in the Ganga-Yamuna *doāb*, has also accepted the same date (given above), so far as the use of iron weapons is concerned.[499] Romila Thapar has identified the iron, which was used by the Āryans in the Gangetic valley, with "*Kṛṣṇayas*" (dark metal) referred to in the *Ṛgveda* (1.130.8; ix, 41.1 for *Kṛṣṇa* and V. 29, 10 for *'Anas'*), as quoted by her. She has ascribed it to the first millennium B.C.[500] But we find that the above references are not connected with *āyas*, i.e. iron. The identification is also not absolutely correct. Because, in the *Ṛgveda*[501] the iron has been clearly referred to as "*āyas*" and *āyas* only in four different places, which were used for building forts. The text even refers to an "iron-pot"[502] used for different purposes. Āyas can be easily distinguished from *Kṛṣṇa*. The Āryans of the period concerned were well equipped with the knowledge of iron technology much before the beginning of the first millennium B.C. with the help of which they became able to set up kingdoms, towns and cities in the valleys of the Ganga and Yamuna.

Indraprastha, now called Indrapat, is archaeologically identified with the ancient mound on which stands the Purānā Quila at Delhi and from where (on the eastern side) the Painted Grey Wares were obtained,[503] which is placed by Mortimer Wheeler in the first half of the first millennium B.C. (*c.* 1000-600 B.C.). He further states that this is the period, which witnessed the emergence of a comfortable and organised city life in the Yamuna-Ganga basin. "To this period belongs the earliest settled occupation known to us in the Delhi region : at the Purānā Qila or Indrapat . . . We may recognise in it the general urban background of the *Mahābhārata* . . ., a picture of the wealthy and jealous dynasties and politics, based upon a limitless and fertile soil and serviceable river communication . . ."[504] Hastināpur, Indraprastha, Ahicchatra, Kāmpilya and Mathura are those urban sites, which represent both PGW and NBPW phase of cultures.[505]

The archaeological data do testify to the existence of Hastināpur and Indraprastha—the two famous capital cities of the Kuru kingdom or the two important urban centres of the Later *Vedic* Āryans, as described in the *Mahābhārata* and the *Purāṇas*, but hardly provide any clue for determining their antiquity with greater amount of confidence. We cannot solely depend on the C-14 dates of the PGW phase of culture ranging sometimes from *c.* 1200 or 1100 to 800 B.C. and sometimes from *c.* 800-500 B.C. for the purpose of ascertaining the approximate period of the two cities concerned. As a matter of fact, both the cities came into existence much before the outbreak of the Bhārata war and remained in existence in post Bhārata war period too. So far as Hastināpur is concerned, it was ruled by both the Pauravas and Kauravas in the pre-war period and Pāṇḍavas in the post-war period. Yudhiṣṭhira alone ruled over it for more than 36 years—the period during which it had attained all paraphernalia of a prosperous city. Further, Parikṣit II ruled over it. The city remained in existence probably up to the sixth century B.C., and Parikṣit's successors ruled over it, which we have described in the next chapter. Likewise, Indraprastha developed as a city during the period concerned. We cannot draw here any plausible conclusion about their antiquity. So the matter is kept in abeyance till we decide upon the date of the Bhārata war. The whole problem has been subsequently discussed in detail. Here the period-III so called NBPW phase of culture, ascribed to the latter half of the second millennium B.C. (*c.* 500-200 B.C.), does not call for any description, because this phase is related to the next chapter.

**Cedi, Magadha, etc.**

The dynasties of Cedi, Magadha and the adjoining countries descended from Kuru's son Sudhanvan. We can, unhesitatingly, place our reliance on the evidence of the *Purāṇas* as well as the epics, so far as the dynastic and genealogical accounts are concerned. The Buddhist and Jain traditions also supplement the accounts to some extent.

One of the noteworthy developments during the period concerned was that Vasu (also known as *Uparicara Vasu*), the fourth in succession from Sudhanvan, conquered the Yādava kingdom of Cedi[506] and thereby obtained the title *Caidyoparicara*, 'the overcomer of the Caidyas'. His capital was Śuktimati on the river Śuktimati (the Ken). The kingdom of Cedi roughly corresponds to the country along the south bank of the Yamuna from the Chambal on the North West to Karwi on the South East Malava and the hills of Bundelkhand formed its southern limit. This kingdom represents the "mixed PGW and BRW cultures".[507] He extended his conquests eastwards as far as Magadha and annexed it along with the adjoining countries. He also conquered the Matsya country (probably occupied by the Yādava tribe), which adjoined Cedi on the North-West. And, hence, he was reckoned as a Cakravarti Samrat.

The genealogy of the Cedi or Ceti kings as given in the *Cetiya Jātaka* begins with the first king Mahāsammata. The tenth king Upacara or Apaçara is generally identified with the Puru king Vasu-Uparicara, as mentioned in the *Mahābhārata* and the *Purāṇas.* The Cetis or Cedis, known in the Buddhist tradition as Cetaputta, were one of the most ancient peoples of India whose territory lay midway between the kingdom of the Kurus and the Vaṁsas (i.e. Vatsas, the people of Kośāmbi).[508]

Vasu divided the territories among his five sons (by his wife Girika) known as Bṛhadratha, Pratyagraha, Kuśa or Kuśāmba called Maṇivāhana, Yadu (or Lalittha) and Mavella or Maruta or Matsya. His five sons carved out new kingdoms. The five different dynasties sprang from them. The countries and towns occupied by them were named after themselves.[509] Cedi and Magadha were two of those five kingdoms and other three kingdoms were Kauśāmbi, Karusa and Matsya.

The eldest son Bṛhadratha took Magadha with Girivraja as its capital, also named Bārhadrathapura after him, and founded the famous Bārhadratha dynasty there.[510] And, thus, Magadha for the first time occupied a prominent place in the traditional history. We learn from the *Rāmāyaṇa* that his father Vasu, the fourth son of Kusa (with three others being Kuśāmba, Kuśanābha and Asurtarajasa—all from his wife, the daughter of the king of Vidarbha) founded the city of Girivraja, which was also called Vasumati after him. There were five mountains around the city and the river Sumāgadhi (Sona) flowed by its side.[511] The foundation of the earliest capital city of the kingdom of Magadha is traditionally ascribed to Vasu. The capital Girivraja was well guarded by a cluster of five hills, which have been referred to in the *Mahābhārata* as Vaihāra, Vārāha, Vṛsabha, Ṛsigiri and Caityaka.[512] The royal city, being enclosed by hills on the sides, was impregnable, and was, thus, considered to be an ideal place for a capital of the Magadha kingdom. At present the hills are called Baibhargiri, Vipula-giri, Ratnagiri, Udayagiri and Sonagiri. The Pāli forms of the names of the hills as given in the *Majjhima Nikāya*[513] are Isigili, Vebhāra, Pāṇḍava, Vepulla and Gījjhakūta.

Bṛhadratha of Magadha was succeeded by Kuśāgra, Vṛsabha, Puṇyavāna (or Puspavāna) Satyahita (or Satyajita), Sudhanva, Urja Sambhava (Bṛhadratha II), Jarāsandha and his son Sahadeva (who was killed in Bhārata War) during the period concerned.[514] Bṛhadratha himself and nine of his successors are supposed to have reigned before the *Kāli* age.

During the time of Kuśāgra, the capital of the kingdom of Magadha was named after him as Kuśāgrapura. It appears that the new capital continued to exist till it was replaced by Rājagṛha. Fa Hien has clearly distinguished Kuśāgrapura from Rājagṛha.[515] Hiuen-Tsang has referred to Kiu-she-Kie-la-po-lo, which corresponds to Kuśāgrapura, "the city of the superior reed-grass. The city derived its name from the excellent fragrant reed-grass that grew there in abundance.[516] Cunningham has also mentioned Kuśāgrapura as the original capital of Magadha.[517] In the archaeological report it has been categorically stated that "The mighty ruins of the older city of Kusagrapura, the capital and centre of the great Magadha kingdom, go back to an antiquity of which no other monuments are left to us in India."[518] Kuśāgrapura has been referred to even in

*Mañjuśrimūlakalpa* and Jaina *Vividhatirthakala* of *Jinaprabha.*[519] One of the earliest and most famous king of Magadha was Jarāsandha of epic fame. The *Mahābhārata* speaks of Jarāsandha, son of king Bṛhadratha, as a very great and powerful king of Magadha, who reigned in the city of Girivraja.[520] His son Sahadeva, who became an ally of the Pāṇḍavas and was killed in the war, has been specifically mentioned therein.[521] In a Jaina text, Vasudevahindi of Dharmadasa,[522] Jarāsandha, has been mentioned as the son of Viyaddaha (Bṛhadratha) and as a powerful king of Rāyagiha (Rājagṛha).

The *Purāṇas* persistently described the Bārhadrathas as the royal dynasty that continued to rule the Magadha kingdom almost up to the sixth century B.C. The ancient capital of this kingdom had many names in the course of its long history. Here mention may be made of Vasumati, Bārhadrathapura, Girivraja, Kuśāgrapur, Magadha-pura and Rājagṛha (Rājagir). The capital became popularly known as Rājagṛha (the Royal palace situated at the foot of Girivraja, the fortress on the hill) from the sixth century B.C. onwards. It remained the capital of Magadha empire for centuries. Archaeologically Magadha is associated with BRW, and not PGW.

Kuśa or Kuśāmba is described in the epic tradition as the founder of the city of Kauśāmbi,[523] the capital of the kingdom called Vatsabhumi in the *Mahābhārata* and the *Purāṇas.* This is supported by Cunningham[524] and M. Wheeler.[525] Kauśāmbi has been identified with absolute certainty with the present village of Kosam on the right bank of the Yamuna—about fifty km. or thirty miles south-west of Allahabad.[526] The name Kosam is born by two adjacent villages Kosam Inam and Kosam Khiraj in the Allahabad District.[527] The above identification can also be confirmed by an epigraphic evidence-Kauśāmbi pillar, Edict of Aśoka on the Allahabad stone pillar.[528] The archaeological exploration undertaken by Prof. G.R. Sharma (the Department of Ancient History, Culture and Archaeology, Allahabad University) in the Central Ganga Valley extending from Kauśāmbi to Kakoria (in the Chakia sub-division of Varanasi district) has brought to light some new evidence about the antiquity of Kauśāmbi. On the basis of the study of the archaeological finds of the past few years including the pottery found at different levels of the site, Prof. Sharma has associated Kauśāmbi with Chalcolithic cultures of the late Harappan phase, which is ascribed to the second half of the second millennium B.C. The study of the material at the site has indicated that the Chalcolithic cultures were the precursor and progenitor of most of the pottery types of red ware, BRW and the PGW (the second cultural phase) found at Kauśāmbi, Hastināpur, Atranjikhera and other sites. Material found in the lowest levels of Kauśāmbi in the excavations of the defences and palace area has been identified as late Harappan.[529] The archaeological excavations carried out by Prof. Sharma at the site (Kauśāmbi) have also brought to light the pottery which at the earliest levels bears a close affinity with that of Navdatoli.[530] The earliest date (*c.* 1165 B.C. to *c.* 885 B.C.), as suggested by the excavator,[531] so far as the founding of Kauśāmbi is concerned, has been questioned by some archaeologists as too early.[532] As Kauśāmbi like Rājagir became famous as an urban centre or the capital city in the third phase of settlement in the latter half of the first millennium B.C. represented by NBPW, it is quite natural to debate the antiquity of

Kauśāmbi. However, its foundation in the pre-Bhārata war period cannot be doubted. The further details about Kauśāmbi and Rājagir have been provided in the next chapter. Kauśāmbi kingdom, as mentioned in an inscription taken from the gateway of the fort of Khara, is dated to Saṁvat 1092 or A.D. 1035.[533]

The other three sons of Vasu — Pratyagraha, Yadu and Matsya — were ruling the kingdoms of Cedi, Karusa and possibly Matsya. Karusa generally identified with the Shahabad District of Bihar is associated with BRW phase of culture and not PGW. The fifth kingdom Matsya, located in the Alwar-Jaipur region, belonged to the Matsyas. Here the evidence of mixed "BRW and PGW" has been found.[534]

In the *Cetiya Jātaka*, the five sons of Vasu Uparicara are said to have founded the cities of Hatthipura (in the Kuru realm), Assapura (in the kingdom of Aṅga), Sihapura (in the Punjab), Uttarapañcāla (in Pañcāla) and Daddarapura, the Giribbaja being excluded from the list.[535] But this cannot be corroborated by any evidence. Moreover, this is at variance with the epic and *Purāṇic* accounts, which are comparatively more reliable than the Buddhist accounts of the subject concerned.

As regards the collateral dynasties that reigned in the Pāṇḍavas' time, it can be asserted that Damaghosa, his son, Śiśupāla Sunitha, and his son Dhṛṣṭaketu were kings of Cedi, Vṛddhasarman and his son Dantavakra, kings of Karusa and Virāta, king of Matsya.

The historicity of Purāṇic accounts of the kingdoms and dynasties of Pre-Bhārata war period cannot be doubted. A.S. Altekar has rightly observed that "the various pre-Bhārata war dynasties mentioned in the *Purāṇas* are as historical and real as the dynasties of Mauryas, and Andhras . . ."[536] Sir William Jones' Statement, that the traditions of pre-*Kaliyuga* periods are purely mythological and that of *Kāli* Age is historical,[537] does not appear to be a balanced one, and hence, it can be disposed of.

## CHRONOLOGICAL RECONSTRUCTION IN THE LIGHT OF TRADITION AND ARCHAEOLOGY

### Preliminary Remarks

A chronological reconstruction of the subject under discussion appears to be an assiduous task because of manifold reasons some of which are stated below. There is a conspicuous absence of contemporary authentic records showing the chronological sequence of the events concerned. Nor do we find any particular set of acceptable dates obtained either from literature or archaeology. Different chronological systems followed in different ages in different traditions like the epic, *Purāṇic*, astronomical, Jain, Buddhist, classical (Greek and Roman), etc. appear to be so much irreconcilable that they can hardly be reconciled or harmonized. The historians and astronomers of different schools in the ancient past followed different systems for chronological computation, which give conflicting results. The adoption of different methods by different scholars for computing the regnal years of rulers of different dynasties and other numbers and figures concerned, the hypotheses advanced by them to substantiate their arguments, contradictions in their statements and the divergent interpretations of chronological data available in the *Purāṇas*, astronomical works and other sources, make the confusion worse confounded. The chronology worked out by some scholars in the past, because of being highly speculative and of contradictory nature, also does not help us much.

Further, different methods have been employed in the *Purāṇic* and astronomical texts for the purpose of astronomical calculations. The chronological statements in the *Purāṇas* are so discrepant that it becomes difficult to judge as to which one is more trustworthy than the other. That is why, the credibility of the traditional *Purāṇic* chronology is very often doubted. While commenting on the chronological system of the Hindus in 1788, Sir William Jones pointed out that there is no authentic system of Hindu chronology. "Even in the history of the present age (*Kali*) the generations of men and the reigns of kings are extended beyond the course of nature and beyond the average resulting from the accounts of the *Brāhmaṇs* themselves, for they assign to 142 modern reigns a period of 3,153 years". The highest probable antiquity assigned by him to three generations of men becomes almost equal to an average of hundred years. He has tried to show that the Hindus did not attain perfect accuracy in maintaining the systematic chronology.[538] The different chronological tables arranged by him for assigning dates to the kings of different dynasties, which we have used in proper context, are themselves very confusing, contradictory and anachronistic for which he has blamed the Hindus. He further states"... We have given a sketch of the Indian history through the longest period fairly assignable to it, and have traced the foundation of the Indian empire above 3,800 years from the present time; but on a subject in itself so obscure and so much clouded by the fictions of the *Brāhmaṇs*, who in order to aggrandise themselves, have designedly raised thair antiquity beyond the truth, we must be satisfied with probable conjecture and just reasoning from the best attainable data."[539]

John Bentley, while writing on the eras and dates of the ancient Hindus in 1796 also observed that "The confusion and darkness that pervade and overspread the Hindu chronology proceed from two different causes, the one owing to the fancy of their *Brāhmaṇs* and poets in disguising and embellishing their history with allegory and fiction, the other to the ignorance of modern Hindus, who not able to discern the difference between the several eras and modes of dating, which were made use of by their ancient historians, Brāhmaṇs and poets in recording past events, have blended the whole together into one mass of absurdity and contradiction. It is not easy to describe the meaning of all the different modes of dating formerly in use".[540] The above statements, undeniably, contain some substratum of truth.

The statement of F. Max Müller, that all the dates before Chandragupta are merely hypothetical"[541] also contains some elements of truth, which can be justified by the fact that the total lengths of reigns assigned to the kings of pre-Maurya dynasties, viz. Bṛhadratha, Pradyota, Śiśunaga and Nanda that (except Pradyota) ruled over Magadha in the post-Bhārata war period vary in such a way from 1,600 to 1,038 years that on the basis of their calculation it becomes difficult to fix the ancient Indian chronology upto the time of Chandragupta with absolute certainty and precision. However, it will not be reasonable to accept his view that everything in Indian chronology depends on the date of Chandragupta. Because the date of his accession is itself a subject of controversy among scholars. The probable dates are 322, 321, 315, 313 and 312 B.C. Max Müller has himself suggested 315 B.C. as the date of his accession to the throne of Magadha.[542] But the fact remains that his date of accession is 322 B.C.

The observation made by E.M. Elphinstone in 1839, that in ancient Indian history no date before the invasion of Alexander the Great (*c* B.C. 326-a sheet-anchor) can be fixed with any amount of confidence,[543] cannot be taken as tenable, as it runs contrary to the truth. V.A. Smith also for some time went on harping on the same tune.[544] But, later he himself admitted that "the researches of multitude of scholars and antiquarians have rendered it possible to fix the considerable number of dates in pre-Alexandrine period (extending from *c*. 600 B.C. to 326 B.C. from chronological point of view) with approximate accuracy as well as to reconstruct the obscure history of ancient India . . . with the help of literary tradition".[545] In the light of the above statement J.F. Fleet's view that no date before the invasion of Alexander has got any importance,[546] can also be disproved. A.A. Macdonell's remarks, that the Indian literature suffers from the "entire absence of exact chronology . . . the Brāhmaṇs . . . felt but little inclination to chronicle historical events. Such being the case definite dates do not begin to appear in the Indian history till about 500 A.D.",[547] can be dismissed as wholly unworthy of our credence.

The traditional evidence conflicts, to a greater extent, with archaeological one. Because, archaeologically (on the testimony of Carbon-14 dates) the whole subject, which is currently under our notice, falls within the range of second-first millennium B.C., but on the other hand, its antiquity on the basis of traditional dates goes back to the fifth or fourth millennium B.C. Such dichotomy between the traditional chronology and the chronology based on archaeological interpretations of the data makes our task more difficult. An obsession on the part of the traditionalists, on the one hand, and archaeologists, on the other, with their respective data further stands as a barrier in our way of chronological reconstruction of the subject concerned in its correct perspective. However, an humble attempt can be made to accomplish the task by striking a reasonable balance between varying propositions. In this direction, we shall, first of all, try to determine the date of the Bhārata war — a great landmark and an epoch-making event in traditional history, for fixing the chronology of rulers of both pre and post-war dynasties and some other important events, towns and cities, etc. The whole chronological reconstruction depends on the date of the war.

### Date of the Bhārata War

The evidences adduced in the *Mahābhārata, Purāṇic* texts, astronomical works of Āryabhatta, Vṛddha-Garga, Varāhamihira, Brahmagupta and Kālidāsa, epigraphic records, classical (Greek and Roman) literature, Kalhana's *Rājataraṅgini,* Persian chronicle, genealogical records and other reliable sources are decidedly of great help for determining the date of Great Bhārata war as well as for testing the accuracy of different dates, suggested by different scholars including orientalists, indologists and archaeologists, which generally range from *c.* B.C. 3,138 (based on astronomical tradition) to *c.* B.C. 1,000 or 950 (based on the lengths of reigns of eleven contemporaneous dynasties). If the date is put within the chronological framework followed by the archaeologists on the basis of the C-14 dates of PGW urban sites of the Gangetic *doāb* of the pre-war period, it may tentatively be placed between *c.* 1,000 and 800 B.C.

One hundred twenty dates ranging from *c.* 6,000 B.C. to *c.* 600 B.C. have been suggested so far by 120 scholars out of which sixty scholars follow the range, *c.* 3,300 - 3,000 B.C., forty of them support the dates which fall in between *c.* 1,500 B.C. and *c.* 1,000 B.C. and the rest twenty follow the remaining dates.[548]

It is, no doubt, very difficult to get an exact date of the war, because of the multiplicity of methods applied for chronological computations and interpretations, availability of different dates of Buddha, etc. However, an attempt can be made, as far as possible, to obtain an approximate date of the war, as well as, of the beginning of the *Kaliyuga* by getting all available evidences thoroughly examined.

Here, we shall first have to decide on the date of accession of Parikṣit II (which is marked by the commencement of *Kaliyuga*, thirty six years before which the battle took place) and the date of Coronation of Mahāpadma, the founder of the Nanda dynasty (by which the date of the former is fixed), with the help of the data available in the *Purāṇas*. The determination of the intervening period between the two is absolutely necessary for fixing accurately the chronology of ancient Indian history. According to the four important *Purāṇas* — *Vāyu, Matsya, Viṣṇu* and *Brahmāṇḍa* — a period of 1,050 years had elapsed between the birth of Parikṣit and the coronation of Mahāpadmananda, which can be testified to by the following verses :

महापद्माभिषेकात् तु यावज्जन्म परीक्षितः ।
एवं बर्षसहस्त्रं तु ज्ञेयं पञ्चाशदुत्तरम् ।।
— *Mats*; 273, 36.

महादेवाभिषेकात्तु जन्म यावत्परीक्षितः ।
एतद्वर्ष सहस्त्रं तु ज्ञेयं पञ्चाशदुत्तरम् ।।
— *Vy*; 99, 415.

यावत्परीक्षितं जन्म यावन्नन्दाभिषेचन्म ।
एतद्वर्ष सहस्त्रं तु ज्ञेयं पञ्चाशदुत्तरम ।।
— *Vṣṇ*; iv, 24, 104.

(or Mahāpadm-ābhiṣekāttu Yāvajjanma Parikṣitaḥ evaṁ varṣasahasraṁ tu jñeyaṃ

Pañcāśaduttaram)

In the *Brahmāṇḍa* (ii, 3, 74, 225-30) also we find the same period. H.H. Wilson in the translation of *Viṣṇu Purāṇa* reads it as 1,015 years.[549] In the *Bhāgavata* (XII, 2, 26-32) we find it 1,115 years. The intervening period between the two as shown in the *Purāṇas* has variant readings, viz. 1,050, 1,015, 1,115 and even 1,500 years, but on the weight of the evidence it is 1,050 years, which has been accepted by number of scholars.[550]

Some scholars in an attempt to prove the high antiquity of events take this intervening period as 1,500 years on the basis of the reading *"pancasatottaram"*, and show the total length of reigns of forty nine kings of pre-Nanda period, viz. 1,000 (for 32 Bārhadrathas) + 138 (for 5 Pradyotas) and + 362 (for 12 Śiśunagas) = 1500 years in support of their calculations, and while adding 422 B.C.the date of coronation of Mahāpadma Nanda to 1,500 (1,500 + 422) prove that 1922 B.C. was the date of birth of Parikṣit and the year of the Great war.[551] Others calculate it as 1,000 + 138 + 360 = 1,498 years and add 422 B.C. to it and thus (1498 + 422) = 1920 years B.C. is taken as the date of war.[552] While calculating 100 years (for Nanda dynasty) + 360 (for Śiśunagas) + 152 (for Pradyotas) + 1,000 (for Bārhadrathas) = 1,612 - 171 (the period of reigns of ten Bārhadrathas upto the time of Sahadeva, ruling over Magadha in pre-Parikṣit period, wrongly included in 1,000 years) = balance 1,441 years is obtained, which is further added to 322 B.C. — the date of accession of Chandragupta, which comes to 1,763 B.C., which is accepted as the year of the Great war.[553] Bṛhadratha ascended the throne of Magadha 161 years before war, so only ten years (161 + 10 = 171) will be too less for his nine successors to get any fruitful result. M. Krishnamachariar, while following the same line of enquiry on the basis of the acceptance of 1,500 years as the interval between Parikṣit and Mahāpadma also calculates in the same manner as shown above and accepts the same date i.e. 1,763 B.C. as the year of the war.[554]

None of the dates calculated on the basis of the interval 1,500 years is worthy of our acceptance because of very logical reasons, as stated below. Firstly, the reign periods of those ten Bārhadrathas, who ruled over Magadha before Parikṣit, has been added to the periods of another twenty-two of them (from Somādhi or Mārjari onwards), who ruled in the post-Parikṣit period, which comes to 1,000 years. The total lengths of those twenty-two rulers even vary from 940 to 723 or 638 years. The same is the case with the regnal years of other dynasties. Thus, the sum total of reign periods of rulers of all three dynasties, Bārhadrathas, Pradyotas and Śiśunagas according to different *Purāṇas* come to approximately, 1,512, 1,500, 1,514, 1,504, 1,498, 1,408, 1,412 and 938 years or so. Thus, no computation can be made from the one or other of them confidently. Nor can any positive conclusion be based on all of them combined together. That is why, Pargiter has discarded this method for determining the date of war.[555] H.H. Wilson also takes sixteen centuries as the longest *Purāṇic* interval between the two concerned and adding 300 years more (taking into consideration the time-gap of Chandragupta) finds that the nineteenth century B.C. marks the beginning of *Kaliyuga*, which he himself does not rely on. Depending absolutely on the intervening period concerned, as given in the *Puraṇas*, he suggests three possible dates, viz. B.C. 1,415 (1,015 + 400), B.C. 1,515 (1,115 + 400) and B.C. 1,450 (1,050 + 400), but does not draw any positive conclusion.[556] The utilization of the chronological data of the *Purāṇas* like that of astronomical data needs caution.

Accepting 1,050 years as the interval between Parikṣit and Mahāpadma (the earliest recorded *Purāṇic* evidence of the chronological sense of the ancient Indians, which may also be considered as a sheet-anchor in the realm of ancient Indian chronology), we shall proceed further to fix the date of accession of the latter in our attempt to determine the date of birth and accession of the former.

According to the *Matsya Purāṇa* (272, 18-22), Mahāpadma ruled for eighty-eight years and his eight sons for + 12 years = 100 years. The *Viṣṇu* (iv, 24, 20-28) also assigns 100 years to the rule of nine Nandas. But according to the *Vāyu* (99, 326-30), Mahāpadma ruled for twenty-eight years and his sons for +8 years = 36 years; and the last ruler ruled for 100 years, which is apparently wrong. This is perhaps misreading for total length of reigns. The Ceylonese chronicles, especially the *Mahāvaṁśa*, mentions twenty-two years as the total length of reigns of all the Nandas. According to the Jain tradition, it lasted for about 155 years, which is totally wrong. It is very difficult to ascertain as to which one of the remaining is the accurate period. If we accept 100 years, the date of accession of Mahāpadma will be *c.* 422 B.C. or 100 years before the end of the dynasty during the time of the last ruler Dhanananda (mentioned in the Buddhist literature and identified by the classical writers with Agrammes or Xandrames, who also happened to be the contemporary of Alexander) or before the accession of Chanragupta in about *c.* 322 B.C. (322 + 100 = 422). While adding 28 + 12 = 40 years to 322, it will be (322 + 40) = 362 years, 28 + 8 = 36 years to 322 it will be (322 + 36) = 358 years and twenty two years to 322 it will be (322 + 22) = 344 years. We have to find out as to which one is relatively more acceptable. R.S. Tripathi, while adding 22 years to the year 321 B.C. — the date of accession of Chandragupta, concludes that Mahāpadma overthrew the Śiśunaga dynasty in 343 B.C. or about the middle of the fourth century B.C.[557] S.N. Pradhan places Mahāpadma between *c.* 369 and 341 B.C.[558] Pargiter, while deducting twenty years (considering it as a period, which Mahāpadma took it to become ruler) from 100 (88 + 12) years rule of the Nanda, reduces it to eighty and adding that figure to 322 (322 + 80) takes it 402 B.C. as the date of accession of Mahāpadma.[559]

Thus Parikṣit was born either 422 or 362 or 344 years before the coronation of Mahāpadma. The three probable dates of his birth, which emerge after reckoning 1,050 + 422, 1,050 + 362 and 1,050 + 344 as = 1472, 1412 and 1394 years respectively, are coeval with the dates of war (-5 months, because he was born after 5 months of the war). There are positive evidences to show that Parikṣit succeeded Yudhiṣṭhira (who ten days after the close of the war being victorious ascended the throne of Hastināpur, which marked the introduction of a new era after him, called Yudhiṣṭhira era) thirty-six years after the war or one year later after the death of Lord Kṛṣṇa, which marked the commencement of *Kaliyuga*.[560] Thus, if we accept those three dates, as mentioned above, 1,436 or 1,376 or 1,358 B.C. will be the date of the beginning of *Kaliyuga*. According to these dates, Kṛṣṇa, who had spent 125 years up to that moment, may have probably born about either *c.* 1,561 (1,436 + 125) or 1,501 (1,376 + 125) or 1,483 (1,358 + 125) B.C. Yudhi ̣s ̣thira died (according to this chronology) in about *c.* 1,410 or 1,350 or 1,332 B.C., as he remained alive for sixty two years (1,472 - 62; 1,412 - 62; 1,394 - 62). It is believed that it was Yudhiṣṭhira who introduced the *Kaliyuga* (age of conflict) era in commemoration of the war.

D.C. Sircar, accepting the interval of 1,050 years between Parikṣit and Mahāpadma and adding 400 B.C. (the date of accession of the latter) to it, places the former in 1,450 B.C. and concludes that the war took place some time in the fifteenth century B.C.[561] Some scholars have assigned 1,472 B.C. (1,050 - 422) and 1,437 B.C. (1,015 - 422) to the birth of Parikṣit and the war.[562] S.B. Roy is in favour of the date 1,424 B.C. for the war.[563] A.D. Pusalker, on the basis of the calculation with the help of a period 1,015 or 1,050 years concludes that the war broke out either in *c.* 1,400 B.C. or in 1,000 B.C.[564] H.C. Raychaudhuri thinks that the birth of Parikṣit may be sometime in the fourteenth or fifteenth century.[565]

Capt. F. Wilford, on the basis of the study of the *Purāṇic* chronology as well as the astronomical data, has expressed the paradoxical views. On the one hand, he favours the date *c.* 1,370 B.C. (on the basis of calculation of 1,015 years — the intervening period + 40, the length of the reigns of the Nandas + 315 year B.C. — the date of accession of Chandragupta = 1,370 or 1,314 B.C. before Vikramāditya, i.e. 1,314 + 56 = 1,370), 1,078 B.C. or 1,219 B.C. for the beginning of the *Kaliyuga*,[566] and, on the other, he places Yudhiṣṭhira between *c.* 1,500 and 1,370 B.C. and states that he died in 1,332 or 38 years after the beginning of the *Kaliyuga.* On the astronomical ground he fixes the beginning of the *Kaliyuga* 3,044 years before Vikramāditya, that is *c.* 3,100 B.C. (3,044 + 56 = 3,100).[567]

A.S. Altekar, while supporting the chronological data of the *Purāṇas* relating to Parikṣit, etc., has accepted the date for the Bhārata war, which corresponds to *c.* 1,400 B.C.[568] K.P. Jayaswal also giving credence to the chronological statements in the *Purāṇas* and distrusting the astronomical statements (which according to him cannot have scientific precision) has suggested a date for the war, which falls in between *c.* 1,450 and 1,424 B.C.[569]

B.G. Tilak on the testimony of the astronomical data places the war in the Krittika period, which according to him "commences with the vernal equinox in the asterism of the Krittikas and extends up to the period recorded in the Vedanga Jyotisha, i.e. from 2,500 B.C. to 1,400 B.C." He synchronises the date 1,400 B.C. (or 1,181 or 1,269 B.C.) with the death of Bhiṣma and seems to be disposed to favour the date 1,400 B.C. for the outbreak of the war.[570] S.N. Pradhan, on the basis of the sum total of the reign-periods of the dynastic list of kings, has suggested three possible dates, i.e. 1,152 B.C. 1,151 B.C. and 1,149 B.C. of the great battle.[571] According to Velandi Aiyar, the battle took place on 14th October. 1,194 B.C.[572]

Duncker has calculated four different dates, i.e. 1,418, 1,390, 1,200 and 1,175 B.C. for the beginning of the *Kali* Age — approximately for the great battle.[573] But Pargiter, after getting his calculations revised by reckoning fifteen years average per reign, has lowered it to 1,100 B.C. On the basis of an assumption he also suggests the date 1,000 B.C. for the occurrence of the battle.[574] Pargiter later adopted another method for determining the date of war. Allowing a period of an average eighteen years for twenty-six kings (a mean of 257 kings of ten contemporary dynasties of Mahāpadma Nanda), that intervened between *king* Adhisīmakṛṣṇa, the sixth successor of Parikṣit, and Mahāpadma and fixing the time of latter in 382 B.C. (402 - 20 = 382, subtracting twenty years for the destruction of those kings of ten dynasties after his accession in 402 B.C.), he calculated it as such : 26 x 18 = 468 + 382=850 B.C. — the approximate mean date of Addhisīmakṛṣṇa and his contemporaries, the Aiksvāku king Divākara and the Bārhadratha Senajit. He further adds 100 years (giving average of twenty years for the reigns of a mean of five kings between Yudhiṣṭhira and Adhisīmakṛṣṇa, (20 x 5 = 100 years) to 850 (850 + 100) = 950 B.C., which he takes as an approximate date of the battle.[575] He finds the said *Purāṇic* intervals i.e. 1,050 or 1,015 years as discrepant and untrustworthy. Pargiter's method of computation distinctly suffers from anachronism. R. Morton Smith, a great follower of the former's line of enquiry, has fixed the date 975 B.C. of the battle.[576] A.K. Majumdar, out of the two dates, 1,389 B.C. (taking 1,015 year lunar = 983 solar years and adding Nanda's coronation period 405 to 983 = 1388) and 1,374 B.C. (adding 405 to 969 lunar), as calculated by him on the basis of the time-span between Parikṣit and Mahāpadma, as given in the *Purāṇas*, prefers the latter one for the war.[577]

Prof. S.R. Rao, on the basis of his archaeological findings at Bet-Dvārakā of Srikṛṣṇa, has placed the *Mahābhārata* period between *c.* 1,500 - 1,400 B.C.[578]

The information supplied by Sir William Jones is full of discrepancies. His study of the ancient chronology is mainly based on the *Bhāgavata Purāṇa* and the tentative inferences, which he drew on the basis of the wrong calculation of the data. He has placed Arjuna's son Abhimanyu (who was killed in the great Bhārata war) *c.* 2,029 years before Christ, and this is his date of the war, and, on the other hand, calculating from the twenty kings of Magadha and allowing 700 years instead of 1000 years between Arjuna and Pradyota, he has placed Abhimanyu about 2,368 B.C. His son Parikṣit has been ascribed to 1,017 B.C. On the authority of "*Bhāgavatāmṛta*", he fixes the beginning of the *Kaliyuga* about 1,000 years before Buddha, *c.* 1,027 B.C. He has also wrongly placed Nanda about 699 B.C. and 313 A.D. and Pradyota, 1,029 B.C. reckoning twenty or thirty generations 317-17 B.C.[579] He contradicts his statement by adding that "the Hindu astronomers agree that the first January 1,790 was in the year 4,891 of the *Kaliyuga*". He has also calculated the reign-periods of the post-war kings with the *Kali* era itself in 3102 or 3101 B.C. [580] We cannot draw any clear picture from his chronological tables, which he used to revive every now and then. There are some valuable astronomical data in the *Purānas* relating to the time of Parikṣit, which can be profitably used here. According to the *Purāṇas,* at the time of the birth of Parikṣit (or on the date of the coronation of Yudhiṣṭhira) when the Seven *Ṛisis* or *Saptarṣis* (the stars of the Constellation Great Bear) were in Magha Nakṣatra or asterism, the Kaliyuga comprising 1,200 divine years (a fraction of total 12,000 years of the four yugas — *Sata, Treta, Dvāpara* and *Kali*) and 4,32,000 human or common years (a fraction of 43,20,000 years of the four *yugas* combined together called *mahāyug*) began. The Seven *Ṛishis* are said to execute a cycle of twenty-seven centuries by staying for 100 years in each of the twenty-seven lunar asterisms of the ecliptic (100x27=2,700 human years = 67 Divine years, 360 human years = 1 Divine year). The *Saptarṣis*, who were in the *Magha* for one century, were at the time of the end of the Andhra dynasty in the twenty-fourth asterism after twenty-fourth centuries. It is also said that when they reached *Purvashadha*, the *Kali* Age attained its growth under the Nandas. From Mahāpadma Nanda to the Andhras there elapsed a period of 836 or 829 years.[581] The data concerned can be combined together for chronological computations and interpretations, and only in that case we may obtain some tentative result.

The *Saptarṣi Saṁvat*, also known as *Deva-Saṁvat, Nakṣatra-Saṁvat, Laukika-Saṁvat* and *Pahāḍi-Saṁvat*, was originally introduced in Kashmir sometime between *c.* 925-1025 A.D. The commencement of the era in the Hindu tradition is a very controversial subject. "The year 3,177 or 3,076 B.C.-(Lunar = 2,925 Solar)" is supported by those who favour the beginning of the *Kaliyuga* in 3,102 B.C.[582] According to the *Purāṇic* evidence, 3,030 years according to human calculation is equivalent to one *Saptarṣi* year.[583] The *Kaliyuga* epoch, 3,102 B.C.-Lunar is = 2,950 Solar.

Different modes of calculations can be adopted on the basis of this era. The interval between Parikṣit and the termination of Andhras (the last king Pulomavi) is 2,400 years and subtracting 836 we get 1564. Thus, the war took place 1,500 years before the Nandas or nineteen centuries before Christ (adding the date of the accession of Mahāpadma). The Andhra dynasty lasted for 460 years and the interval between Nanda and the commencement of the Andhra was = 836 - 460 = 876 years. Deducting 376 (instead of 836) from 1,400, we get 1,024 years as interval between Parikṣit and Nanda. According to this calculation, the war took place sometime in the fifteenth century B.C. Taking the interval between Andhra and Parikṣit as 2,400 years, if we deduct 460 years (length of reigns of the Andhras), we get = 1,940 year — the gap between Parikṣit and the rise of the Andhras in the first century B.C. (73 B.C.). This calculation also gives us roughly the nineteen century B.C. for the year of the war.[584] Parikṣit was born in 1,050 *Saptarsi Saṁvat* and ruled from 1,086 (1,050 + 36) to 1,146 (1,086 + 60) *Saptarṣi Saṁvat*. *Saptarṣis* were at the time of Parikṣit and Nanda. This period extends for 2,700 years. (1,000 *Saptarṣi Saṁvat* is considered to be an equivalent to 3,161 B.C.) Adding 422 years (the date of Nanda's coronation) to 2,700, we get 3,122 B.C., an approximate date of the war. According to the conventional explanation, the *Saptarṣis* entered the esterism *Magha* seventy-five years before the *Kaliyuga* that is (3,102 + 75) = 3,177 B.C. and stayed there for one century, thus it comes down to 3,077 B.C. When 2,400 years had passed after 3,177 B.C., the Andhra or Sātavāhana dynasty was set up. Thus, 3,177 - 2,400 = 777 B.C. marks the commencement of the dynasty and 477 B.C. (3,177 - 2,700) its end. We cannot rely on the data concerned, bacause the result does not concur with the accepted historical facts that the dynasty was set up sometime in the first century B.C. and came to an end probably in the second century A.D. Moreover, the *Purāṇas* record five different durations : 300, 411, 412, 456 and 460 for the dynasty, which bring down its starting point from the *Purāṇic* 802 B.C. to 391 or 390, 346, 342 B.C. Most of the *Purāṇas* assign a period of 100 years to Mahāpadma and his eight sons, who were followed immediately by Chandragupta Maurya. The interval between Chandragupta and Pulomavi, according to the Puranic chronology, will be 836 - 100 = 736 years, and as the former did not ascend the throne before 326 B.C., the latter (Sātavāhana king) according to the *Purāṇic* calculation cannot be placed earlier than 410 A.D. (326 + 410 = 736 ), which appears to be inconsistent with the date recorded in ancient Indian history.

The *Saptarṣi Saṁvat* 1,015 (or 1,050, 1,115, 1,500, 1,501 etc.) synchronising with the birth of Parikṣit, as recorded in the *Purāṇas,* is calculated and interpreted in different ways in terms of its corresponding years before Christ for getting an approximate date of the *Mahābhārata* war. It is generally believed that after five months of the war Parikṣit was born in 1,015 *Saptarṣi Saṁvat* (= 8,143 B.C.). Lord Krishna breathed his last in 1,051 *Saptarṣi Saṁvat* (= 3,111 B.C.). The *Saptarṣis* maintained their position in the *Magha Nakṣatra* till the end of the *Dvāpara Yuga* (or *Kali-Dvāpara Sandhi*, as mentioned in *Garga-Saṁhitā*). At that time the *Saptarṣi Saṁvat* was 1,061 (= 3,102 B.C.), which marked the termination of *Dvāpara.* The *Saptarṣi Saṁvat* 1,061 (= 3,101 B.C.) marked the beginning of the *Kaliyuga.* According to the data available in the *Mahābhārata,* the war began thirty six years before the beginning of the *Kaliyuga.* Thus, the date of the war on this basis (3,101 + 36) goes back to = 3,137 B.C. Parikṣit ascended the throne thirty six years after the war and ruled from 1,051 (1,015 + 36) to 1,111 *Saptarṣi Saṁvat* (or 01 + 33,111 - 3,051 B.C.) covering the period of sixty years. Pandit Bhagavaddatta in his work "*Bhāratavarasha kā Bṛhada Itihāsa* (Pt. II, p. 227) has associated Pariksit's reign with *Saptarṣi Saṁvat* 24. The *Saptarṣi Saṁvat* from 664 to 724 covered the span of sixty years, which is not in conformity with the *Purāṇic* tradition. Taking the *Saptarṣis* period in the *Magha* at the time of Parikṣit and Nanda, which extends for 2,700 years, and adding 430 years, the date of Nanda's coronation, to it, 3,130 B.C. is also taken as the probable date of the war. *Viṣṇupurāṇa* states that 1,500 years had elapsed between the birth of Parikṣit and coronation of Nanda. This gives the date of the birth of Parikṣit as 364 + 1,500 = 1864 B.C. Considering that his father Abhimanyu died in the Bhārata war itself, we do not get the date of the Bhārata war earlier than 1,965 B.C.

Wilford, depending on his result obtained both from the *Purāṇas* and astronomical works, states that according to the former the Seven *Ṛishis* had been in *Magha* at the time of the birth of Parikṣit, and in Purvashadha in the time of Nanda, but according to *Brahmasphuta-Siddhānta* "of Brahmagupta (550 Sakabda + 78 = 628 A.D.), they were in the *Sravana,* which makes a difference of fifteen Lunar Mansions or 1,500 years, according to which the *Kaliyuga* began 1,600 years B.C. Calculating the *Saptarṣi* era in his own way, he has drawn different conclusions. On the basis of their position in "Anuradhā", he has further suggested that the *Kaliyuga* began 1,400 years B.C.[585]

John Bentley, on the basis of astronomical calculations, has placed Yudhiṣṭhira and Sahadeva (Jarāsandha's son, who was killed in the war) in 2,825 years of the world (common years) and 1,920 years of the astronomical *Kaliyuga,* and Parikṣit in 2,835 years of the world and 1,925 years in astronomical era. According to him, the *Kaliyuga* commenced in Feburary in the 966th years of the world.[586] From another source it has come to our notice that Bentley is in favour of 575 B.C. — date of the Bhārata war,[587] which has been contradicted and assigned to the thirteenth or fourteenth century B.C.[588]

According to A. Cunningham, the Great war took place about 1,426 B.C.[589] M. Elphinstone ascribes the beginning of Yudhiṣṭhira *Saṁvat* to *c.* 1,450 B.C.[590]

A particular evidence of considerable historical importance, which has, probably, hitherto not been used by any scholar, as far as my knowledge goes, for determining the date of the war, is furnished below for the purpose of making calculation.

If the visit of Buddha to Hastināpur (the Kuru capital, then ruled by a king of the Pāṇḍava dynasty), as testified by two important Sanskrit Buddhist texts — *Divyāvadāna*[591] and *Lalitavistara*[592] and further confirmed by McCrindle[593], the shifting of capital from Hastināpur (after being washed away by the flooding of the Ganga) to Kauśāmbi during the time of Nicakṣu or Vivakṣu or Nirvaktra, the seventh successor of Parikṣit or the son of Adhisīmakṛṣṇa (ascribed by Pargiter to 850 B.C. by another mode of calculation already explained before), as evidenced by the *Purāṇas*,[594] and the Carbon-14 dates of the periods II (*c.* 1100 - 800 B.C.) and III (Sixth century B.C. to third century B.C.) at Hastināpur, as suggested by the excavator B.B. Lal, are correlated, a substantial result may possibly be obtained.

It is quite evident that Nicakṣu or Vivakṣu belonged to the Buddha's period, which extended approximately from his time to one of his lineal descendants, Udayan, ruler of Kausambi and contemporary of Buddha. Though the *Purāṇas* maintain a list of about sixteen kings in between, but except Udayana whose historicity is well proven fact, all are fictitious. Before we proceed further to arrive at any conclusion, here it must be made clear that the dates of Buddha as given in Chinese, Burmese and Tibetan accounts, Ceylonese chronicles and in other traditional Buddhist chronology inserted in different sources[595] generally vary from 2,422 B.C. to 483 or 482 B.C. (total 50 dates). But the traditional Buddhist chronology is hypothetical and full of absurdities. Only the Ceylonese chronicles contain a trustworthy and intelligible chronology. The dates given by *Mahāvaṁśa*[596] of Buddha (563 - 483 B.C.), who happened to be contemporary of both Bimbisara (*b.* 558, accession 543 B.C. - 491 B.C.) and Ajatasatru, (*c.* 491 - 459 B.C.), the rulers of Śiśunaga dynasty that ruled over Magadha, has been accepted by all the noted historians after carrying out lot of research on the subject.

From the analysis of the data concerned, we find that all the predecessors of Nicakṣu (sixth century B.C.) upward to the time of Parikṣit belonged to the period preceding Buddha. The maximum time period, that might have elapsed between the two for five or six kings, in any case cannot exceed three centuries. According to this calculation, we can place Parikṣit approximately sometime between *c.* 1,000 - 900 B.C., which goes in perfect harmony with archaeological evidence, based on C-14 dates of the PGW site-Hastināpur. The archaeologists are also unanimous on the point that Hastināpur was abandoned after the II period (*c.* 1,100 - 800 B.C.), which is followed by the III period (starting from the sixth century B.C.). This goes well in accord with that we have established on the basis of the evidence concerned. The two eminent archaeologists, B.B. Lal[597] and H.D. Sankalia[598] are also in favour of *c.* 1,000 B.C. as the date of the war. The former on the basis of C-14 dates has also placed it between the ninth and eighth century B.C. and the latter in preference over 1,400 B.C. accepts 1,000 B.C. This can also be corroborated by the statements of Romila Thapar. She has referred to the traditional date *c.* 3,102 B.C.,[599] as well as, to the early part of the first millennium B.C. or *c.* 900-800 B.C. (identifying the Kurus or the third phase of the Puru lineage with the PGW on the basis of the C-14 dates) as the approximate date of the war.[600] These two extreme propositions sometimes appear to be paradoxical. However, the emphasis is more on the latter date. E.J. Rapson on the basis of the dynastic lists of Hastināpur and Magadha as recorded in the *Purāṇic* tradition, has also demonstrably placed the Great war about 1,000 B.C.[601]

The gap between the traditional date *c.* 3,102 B.C. (the beginning of the *Kaliyuga* or +36= *c.* 3,138 B.C., the date of the war, based on astronomical speculation, as shown below) and the sixth century B.C. is too long to be bridged up. The seven kings from Parikṣit downward to Nicakṣu cannot be allotted such a long period; so far as their rule is concerned. If the traditional chronology is accepted, the entire chronological setting in ancient Indian history will undergo drastic change. The dates within the framework of traditional chronology in *Kali Saṁvat* will go like this : Śiśunagas (*c.* 1,962-1,602 or 1,635 B.C.), Buddha (*c.* 1,887-1,807 B.C. or 1,843-1,783 B.C.), Nandas (*c.* 1,602-1,502 B.C.), Mauryas (*c.* 1,502-1,365 B.C.), Chandragupta Maurya (*c.* 1,543-1,483 B.C. or 1,535 B.C.), etc. (as shown in the following two chapters through the comparative charts), which no sensible and unbiased historian will accept.

I am, therefore, not at all inclined to support the traditional date. On the basis of all the reliable evidences, I would rather like to support the view that the war took place sometime between *c.* 1,000-900 B.C. Any attempt to push back the antiquity of the ages concerned to vast figures will weaken the trustworthiness of the tradition.

A.K. Majumdar has rightly pointed out that "the *Kaliyuga* Epoch 3,102 B.C. is usually identified with the era of Yudhiṣṭhira and the date of the *Mahābhārata* war. This wrong notion has seriously disturbed the balance of our Hindu chronology."[602]

The conflicting views presented by different schools of Hindu astronomers, chronologists and historians, represented mainly by Āryabhatta, Vṛddha-Garga, Varāhamihira and Kalhana, also deserve our notice.

The famous Indian astronomer, Āryabhatta (499 A.D.), in his astronomical work, "*Āryabhattiyam*" (ch. "*Kālakriyāpādam*", tenth stanza) had calculated the beginning of the *Kali* era in 3,101 or 3,102 B.C. on the basis of the astronomical study of the movement of the heavenly bodies. He started the measuring of this *Kali* era in his life-time. He makes a reference to this time measure thus :

षष्ठ्यब्दानां षड्भिर्यदा व्यतीतास्त्रयश्च युगपादाः ।
त्र्यधिका विंशतिरब्द एतदेव मम जन्मनोऽतीताः ।।

It means that in the 360th (60x6) year the age of the author was twenty-three years. Actually, in the standard edition of the text the reading goes like this : "*Śaṣṭhyabdānām Saṣṭhiryadā*", which means that the author was in the 3,600 (60x60) years of *Kaliyuga*. Thus, taking the *Kali* era, 3,101 B.C. and adding 499 to it (3,101 + 499) it becomes equal to 3600 B.C. On the testimony of Āryabhatta *c.* 3,101 or 3,102 B.C. is taken to be the starting point of the so-called *Kaliyuga* era, thirty-six years before which the battle was fought. Thus, it comes to either *c.* 3,137 or 3,138 B.C. The same astronomical tradition was more or less followed by Varāhamihira, Brahmagupta and other Indian astronomers, and corroborated by the epigraphic records of the seventh century A.D. and the Sanskrit scholars of Akbar's time.

But J.F. Fleet, while criticising Āryabhatta's astronomical method of reckoning, observed that the *Kaliyuga* era-3,102 B.C. is invented one and it was not founded in *Vedic* times. It was, according to him, devised by Hindu astronomers for the purposes of their calculations some thirty-five centuries after the initial point, which they assigned to it. To quote him "Around *c.* 400 A.D. Indian astronomers realised the need to have a specified reckoning with a definite initial occasion. They found the required occasion in what a backward computation by them gave as a conjunction in 3,102 B.C. of the sun, the moon and the five then-known planets at the first point of the zodiacal sign *Mesha* (Aries). The reckoning thus devised was subsequently identified with the *Kaliyuga* of which the *Purāṇas* speak. The identification is first seen, though without the actual name, in the astronomer Aryabhatta in 400 A.D. By then the *Puraṇic puṇḍits* must have adjusted India's traditional history of the new date, fixed the time for the *Kaliyuga*'s close companion, the Bhārata war and constructed a whole long chronology. The acceptance of the new date must have become universal by 634 A.D. for in that year we have the public use of it in the Aihole Inscription of king Pulakesin II dating itself in the *Kaliyuga* era side by side with the *Saka* era and referring to the Bhārata war. But, as the former era is not a real historical one, the entire system of dates, the *Purāṇic puṇḍits* deduced from it and from the Bhārata war for events, is arbitrary. All the ages, they have assigned to the various dynasties of the past have no historical value."[603]

According to Varāhamihira, who flourished in the sixth century (A.D. 505-550) and quoted Vṛddha-Garga (154 B.C.) in his work, the Bhārata war took place 2,526 years before the *Śaka* era (78 A.D.), i.e. in B.C. 2,448 or 653 years after the beginning of *Kaliyuga*, i.e. (3,102–653=) in 2,449 B.C. The evidence furnished by Varāhamihira is quoted below :

आसन्मधासु मुनयः शासति पृथ्वीं युधिष्ठिरे नृपतौ ।
षड्द्विकपञ्चद्वियुतः शककालस्तस्य राक्षश्च ।।[604]

Thus, according to him, one can get the date of Yudhiṣṭhira (during whose time *Saptarṣis* were in *Magha Nakṣatra* or asterism) by adding 2,526 years to the *Śaka* years.

According to the said two conflicting traditions of the Gupta age, we find it very difficult to ascertain as to whether the battle took place near about 3,102 or 2,449-8 B.C. However, some writers[605] have made attempts in the past to reconcile the conflicting views put forth by the schools of Āryabhatta and Vṛddha-Garga by suggesting that the *Śaka-kāla* of Varāhamihira in *Śākya-kāla*, i.e. the era of the Buddha's *Nirvāna*. But this seems to be merely a conjecture, as it is not supported by any authentic evidence. Bhattotpala (*Śaka* 890), a commentator on the text, has also contradicted it by explaining *Śaka-Kāla* of the *Bṛhat Saṁhitā* passage as *Śaka-nṛpa-kāla*, i.e. an era of the Śaka king.[606] Varāhmihira himself refers to the "Śakendrakāla" or *Śaka-bhūpa-kāla*, i.e. the era of the Śaka king.[607] If *Yudhiṣṭhira Saṁvat*, i.e. 2,526 is deducted from 3,148 B.C. (the date of war =the *Saptaṛsi* era 1,015), we get 622. Thus 2,526+622=3,148 becomes the approximate date of the war. The data is interpreted in various ways.

The data provided by Garga and Varāhamihira is also interpreted in some different way. The *Śaka* year mentioned by them cannot be the year of the *Śaka* era currently in use, because Yudhiṣṭhira is said to have flourished before the *Śaka* era. The *Śaka Kāla* could only be the *Śākyakāla* i.e. the Buddha era, because Buddha was called Śākya. From the time of Yudhiṣṭhira to *Śākyakāla* or Buddha, 2,526 years had elapsed. Adding 2,526 to Buddha's date of *Nirvana*, i.e. 543 B.C. (as recorded in Ceylonese chronicle *Dipavamsa* and as current in Burma), we get 3,069 as the date of Yudhiṣṭhira. He is said to have ruled for thirty-six years after the *Mahābhārata* war. The date(3,069+36=3,105)we arrive at shows the difference of three years from 3,102 B.C.

Mr. P.C. Sen Gupta, a noted authority on the subject, accepts the dating of Vṛddha-Garga and Varāhamihira by supporting the tradition of astronomical calculation. He says that the *Purāṇic* or epic *Kaliyuga* began from the year 2,453 B.C. On the basis of his findings, he supports 2,449 B.C. as the year of the Bhārata battle. But, on the other hand, he points out that, according to the *Mahābhārata*, the battle was fought thirty six years before the year of Krishna's death, which was the true beginning of the *Kaliyuga*.[608] The discrepancies in his statements are quite apparent. There seems to be a need for making persistent attempt to search for the foundation, on which the chronological edifice of the subject can be built.

Kalhana, a Kashmiri historian of the twelfth century A.D., while following the Vṛddha-Garga-Varāhamihira tradition in the work "*Rājataraṅginī*" (so far as the subject under dicussion is concerned), has also placed the heroes of the Bhārata war 653 years after the beginning of the *Kaliyuga*, i.e. 2,449 B.C.(3,102-653) and 2,526 years before the *Śaka* era, i.e. in B.C. 2,448 (2,448+78), as it appears from the following verses of the text :

शतेषु षट्सु सार्धेषु त्र्यधिकेषुच भूतले ।
कलेर्गतेषु वर्षाणामभूवन् कुरुपाण्डवाः ।।

आसन्मधासु मुनयः शासति पृथ्वीं युधिष्ठिरे नृपतौ ।
षड्द्विकपंचद्वियुतः शककालस्तस्य राजस्य ।।

This can also be confirmed by the evidence furnished by H.H. Wilson[609] and Aurel Stein.[610] But the date of the Bhārata war—2,449-8 B.C. does not appear to be supported by genuine historical evidence and thus it demonstrates the unreliable character of the scheme of chronology followed by them.

Kālidāsa (first century B.C.) in his famous astronomical work—*Jyotirvidābharanā*'' has stated that after the expiry of 3,068 years of the *Kali* era (=33 B.C.) he wrote this work in V.E. 24 during the reign of Vikramaditya. Thus he is also pointing to 3,101 B.C. (3,101–33=3,068 ) as the beginning of the *Kaliyuga.*

In a Stone Inscription from a Jain temple at Aihole (Karnataka), ascribed to Ravikirti, panegyrist of Pulakesin II (the Chalukya ruler of Badama), dated *Śaka* 556 (expired) =A.D. 634, it is stated that at the time of its composition 3,735 years since the Bhārata war and 556 years of the *Śaka* era, i.e. 634 A.D. had elapsed, which can be confirmed by the following original text of the said inscription :

त्रिंशत्सु त्रिसहस्त्रेषु भारतादाहवादितः ।
सप्ताब्दशतयुक्तेषु श (ग) तेस्वब्देषु पञ्चसु ।।
पञ्चाशत्सु कलौ काले षट्सु पञ्चाशतासु च ।
समासु समतीतासु शकानामपि भूमुजाम ।।[611]

This shows that the *Kaliyuga,* which according to the *Mahābhārata* marked the end of the war, began in 3,101 B.C. (3,735–634=3,101 B.C.). This was widely used in the historical records including this inscription. The traditional date of the war, as recorded by Ravikirti in the Aihole stone insription, conforms to the tradition of Āryabhatta's time. However, the reliability of the higher antiquity is always open to doubt. In the Nidhānpur Copper Plate Inscription of Bhāskaravarman (*c.* 620-643 A.D.) of Kāmarūpa, who was contemporary of Harshavardhan, it is stated that "When the monarchs of his dynasty had spent three thousand years, then Pushyavarman became the lord of the world." In the descending order the genealogy of the family (much before Pushyavarman's time) starts with Naraka's son Bhagadatta followed by his son Vajradatta, who were contemporaries of Yudhiṣṭhira and also took part in the battle. Taking the year 3,101 B.C. into consideration just for rough calculation, "Bhagadatta is said to have ruled in the later half of the 31st century B.C. and Vajradatta in 3,000 B.C."[612] In the *Mahābhārata* (*Aśvamedha Parva,* 1977, 74, 1-2) also Vajradatta, son of Bhagadatta of Prāgjyotisha is said to have fought in the battle concerned.

The time of Yudhiṣṭhira in the beginning of *Kaliyuga,* as computed by the Sanskrit scholars at the initiative of Akbar and recorded by Abul Fazl in his *Ain-i-Akbari,* shows that in the fortieth years of Akbar or (1,555+40 ) in 1,595 4,696 years had elapsed since the time of Yudhiṣṭhira. Thus (4,696–1,595 ) =3,101 B.C. marked the commencement of the *Kali* era. It is further said that 3,044 years after Yudhiṣṭhira (or 3,044 years of the Kaliyuga had elapsed), Vikramaditya (57 B.C.) was crowned as a king. Thus, the *Kaliyuga* began in 3,101 B.C. (3,101–57=3,044 ).[613]

*Paṇḍit* Mādhavācārya also, on the basis of his astronomical research, recorded in "*Ṛājabali*," composed in V.E. 1,816, that from the beginning of *Kaliyuga* to Vikramaditya's time total 3,044 years had passed. Vikrama ascended the throne in 3,044 *Kaliyuga Saṁvat*, i.e. fifty-seven B.C. Thus, (3,044+57)=3101 B.C. was the starting point of the *Kali* era.[614]

As a matter of fact, the Bhārata war, Yudhiṣṭhira's reign and the *Kaligyua*—all are considered to be contemporaneous. According to the astronomical data, the *Kali* Era started in 3,101 B.C. The position of Vernal Equinox at this time (3101 B.C.) was in the middle of Rohini *Nakṣatra* at 46.20° on the ecliptic. Starting from the middle of Rohini the passage of time through each *Nakṣatra* is calculated approximately. The scholars having unshakable faith in the astronomical method of computation hold that the *Kaliyuga* began either in B.C. 3,101 or 3,102, thirty six years before which, i.e. in B.C. 3,137 or 3,138 the Great Bhārata battle was fought.

According to the astronomical tradition, it has been established that Yudhiṣṭhira was crowned as a king exactly ten days after the battle (B.C. 3,138) came to an end. The date of his accession marked the beginning of a new era, called "*Yudhiṣṭhira Śaka*". In the thirty-seventh year of his reign Lord Krishna left this world, which marked the end of the *Dvāpara* and the beginning of *Kaliyuga* and that was the eighteenth or twentieth February of B.C. 3,102. Krishna had spent 125 years till that date, which means that he was born on seventeenth or eighteenth July in 3,227 B.C. (3,102+125). Yudhiṣṭhira after having ruled for sixty two years departed this world in (3,138-62) B.C., 3076. It was after his death that a new era, called *Saptaṛsi Saṁvat* or *Laukika Yuga*, began, which synchronised with the birth of Parikṣit.[615]

The beginning of the *Kaliyuga* in 3,102 B.C. on astronomical ground is supported by William Jones, who writes that "Now the Hindu astronomers agree that the first January 1,790 was in the year 4,891 of the *Kaliyuga*".[616] Thus 3,102+1,790 is=4,892.. Capt. F. Wilford[617] and J. Bentley[618] refer to B.C. 3,100 or 3,100 as the beginning of the *Kali-Era*. P.C. Sengupta has strongly supported beginning of the *Kaliyuga* in 3,102 B.C. as declared by Āryabhatta, and which is different from the epic-*Purāṇic Kali* era.[619] Some prominent scholars have calculated the date of the war only on astronomical method.[620] Kota Venkatachalam refers to B.C. 3,138 as the date of the war.[621] D.S. Trivedi takes B.C. 3,137 as the date of war.[622] A good number of scholars on the basis of their researches have come out with a new date of the war, i.e. 3,067 B.C.[623] C.V. Vaidya has strongly pleaded in favour of 3,100 B.C. as the date of the *Mahābhārata* war.[624]

It is neither possible nor desirable to quote all the available dates, as suggested by individual scholars. However, before we draw any plausible conclusion on this debatable subject, it will be in the fitness of things to add the chronological data, as presented by the classical (Greek and Roman) scholars, to that of ancient Indian writers so as to notice the difference between the two styles of presenting the chronological tradition of India.

The Greek ambassador, Megasthenes, who visited the court of Chandragupta Maurya, has recorded the chronological belief, which prevailed in those days in India, according to his own interpretations of the data supplied to him by his Indian informants. He states that "From the time of Dionysos to Sandrakottos (Chandragupta Maurya) the Indians counted 153 kings, and a period of 6,042 years . . . The Indians also tell us that Dionysos was earlier than Heracles by fifteen generations."[625] Pliny (first century A.D.),[626] Arrian (second century A.D.)[627] and Solinus (third century A.D.)[628] have also quoted Megasthenes' statements as recorded in his Indika. Since the identity of Dionysos has not been firmly established, and the duration of 153 kings of India before Chandragupta extending over a period of "6,451" years, as pointed out by Pliny,[629] is at variance with regnal periods of the dynasties concerned, as reckoned in tune with the *Purāṇic* chronology, it is no use depending on this particular figure of Megasthenes. As the *Puraṇic* records contradict the Greek chronology, it is very difficult to judge their relative historical value. Wilford[630] also subscribes to the same view.

As a logical corollary to the fact that Dionysos was fifteen generations earlier than Heracles, it follows that Heracles (who has been, indisputably, identified with Hari or Shri Krishan and is said to be worshipped by the *Sourseni* Indian tribe, i.e. *Śurasenas,* possessing two large cities, Methora, i.e. Mathura and Cleisobora, i.e. Krishnapura) flourished (153-15)+138 generations before Chandragupta Maurya. Taking twenty years as the average for a generation we have an approximate period of (138x20)=2,760 years and adding to it Chandragupta's date of accession, B.C. 321, we get (2760+321)=3,081 B.C. as the approximate date of Shri Krishna, which nearly tallies with 3,101 B.C. (the beginning of *Kaliyuga*) or 3,137 B.C. (the date of the *Mahābhārata* war) as given by Indian astronomers. J.W. McCrindle, a noted authority on the classical treatises, has also admitted that "The commencement of his reign coincides with that of the *Kaliyuga,* which began 3,102 years B.C. or 2,785 before the accession of Chandragupta or Sandrokottos, who reigned while Meghasthenes was ambassador at his court in Palibothra (Pataliputra)".[631] If we add Chandragupta's date 312 B.C. (the date of his accession varies from B.C. 321 to 312) to 2,760 years, we get 3,072 B.C. as the approximate date of Krishna. The evidence, which we have adduced from the classical sources, is based upon the tradition prevalent in India in the fourth century B.C. The only possible way in which the tradition concerned may be impeached is by supposing that the Indians themselves had exaggerated the figures about their antiquity or Megasthenes himself had fabricated the data supplied to him.

The three different ranges of periods of war, which emerge from the computations, interpretations and analyses of basically three different types of data, astronomical, *Purāṇic* and archaeological, are *c.* 3,138-37 B.C., *c.* 1,472-1,370 B.C. and *c.* 1,000-800 B.C. respectively. The reasons for not accepting the first one have already been stated. In all probability, the war must have taken place sometime either in the fourteenth or fifteenth century B.C. or in the early first millennium B.C. The date of the war can tentatively be placed between *c.* 1,400-1,000 B.C. However, this is suggestive and not conclusive.

## TENTATIVE CHRONOLOGY OF THE PROMINENT RULERS OF THE SOLAR AND LUNAR DYNASTIES FROM THE TIME OF MANU TO THE BHĀRATA WAR PERIOD

The age of Manu Vaivasvata (*RV* X, 63.1), the originator of the human race and the first traditional king or Āryan patriarch from whom all the dynasties sprang, and who flourished according to the traditional or *Purāṇic* genealogies ninty-five generations before the Bhārata war, can be determined by taking average twenty years for one generation and keeping in view 1,400 B.C. as the date of war. Thus, (95x20+1400=) 3,300 B.C. can be taken as the approximate date of Manu. There is no unanimity among the scholars about the date concerned. A.K. Majumdar has placed him between *c.* 2,800-2,790 B.C.[632] A.D. Pusalker has ascribed him to *c.* B.C. 3,110-3,100.[633] Mr. Bentley suggests *c.* 1,736 B.C. as the date of seventh Manu,[634] which cannot be accepted. Ikṣvāku can be placed between 3,300 and 3,250 B.C. Pururavā (*RV* X, 95) flourished sometime between 3,250 and 3,200 B.C. Nahusa's period can be ascribed to 3,200-3,150 B.C. His son, Yayati (*RV* X, 63.1), who is fifth in descent from Manu, thus flourished (20x5=) 100 years after Manu or in (3,300-100=) 3,200 B.C. According to Pargiter, "Ayus, Nahusa and Yayati, who are alluded to in the *Ṛgveda,* would be placed later than twenty three centuries B.C. (2,300 B.C.).[635] However, the Yayati period can be placed between *c.* 3,200-2,900 B.C. Māndhātā of the Solar dynasty coming twenty generations after Manu can be placed in (3,300–20x20=) 2,900 B.C. The period of Arjuna Kārtavirya, Viśvāmitra, Jamadagni, Paraśurama and Hariśchandra can be placed between (3,300–31x20)=2,680 B.C. and (3,300–33x20=) 2,640 B.C. or roughly between 2,680 and 2,650 B.C. The Māndhāta period can be put between *c.* 2,900 and 2,650 B.C. The Paraśurāma period can be fixed between *c.* 2,650 and 2,450 B.C. Sagara of Ayodhyā and Dushyanta and Bhārata of Hastināpur flourished sometime between (3,300–41x20=) 2,480 B.C. and (3,300–44x20=) 2,420 B.C. or roughly between 2,450 and 2,400 B.C. The first twenty six kings of the Lunar dynaty had ruled from their capital at Pratishthāna. The twenty-seventh king Hasti, the founder of Hastināpur city, probably flourished sometime between 2,300 and 2,200 B.C. The Solar kings of Kosala ruled from 3,300 to 1,400 B.C. Rāma flourished sixty-five generations after Manu, i.e. in (3,300–65x20=) 2,000 B.C. The period of Rāma can be roughly placed between *c.* 2,400 and 2,000 B.C. The Krishna period can be tentatively fixed between 1,550 and 1,400 B.C. Brihadratha, the founder of Magadha dynasty, flourished 161 years before the outbreak of war, i.e. in (1,400+161=) 1,561 B.C. His son Jarasandha, who was a powerful monarch, flourished towards the close of the fifteenth century. The Pāṇḍava princes and Drupada of Pañcāla—all can be ascribed to the fifteenth century B.C. According to A.D. Pusalker[636] and H.D. Sankalia,[637] the period from Manu Vaivasvata to the Bhārata war extends from *c.* 3,102 (or 3,100) B.C. to 1,400 (or 1,000) B.C. A.K. Majumdar has fixed 2,000 years (*c.* 2,800-800 B.C.) for the events connected with the rulers of the Solar and Lunar dynasties of North India. According to his findings, from Manu to the Bhārata war the period covers *c.* 2,800-1,400 B.C.[638]

## Traditional Chronology and Carbon-14 Dates

The tradition and archaeology are, in fact, not as much correlative as complementary to each other. Their correlation can only partially be worked out. The correlation between the traditional data and archaeological data can best be examined in respect of colonization, technological and cultural advancement, the antiquity of peripheral sites in pre-PGW period and for a sequence of cultures as well as for calculating the chronological bracket of the PGW sites in the Ganga Valley. There can be no definite correlation between the two in case of PGW phase of archaeological cultures, because we don't find much parallelism between the traditional accounts, as given in the epic-*Purāṇic* texts, and the archaeological findings, so far as the urban centres of the Gangetic *doāb* associated with the Kuru and Pañcāla lineages are concerned. Moreover, the traditional chronology of the lineages concerned, as worked out on the basis of the data given in the texts, is not in perfect harmony with the available C-14 dates of the excavated PGW sites.

The distribution of the Yādava lineages in Arāvali, Gujarat, Malavā, Narmada Valley, Vidarbha, northern Deccan, the eastern Ganges valley and the middle Ganges valley may archaeologically be correlated with Chalcolithic BRW cultures which dates back to *c.* 2,000 B.C. (C-14 date). The early settlements of the Puru lineages in Sārasvati and Upper *doāb* are associated with Late Harappan and OCP cultures for which the suggested C-14 dates are *c.* 2,200-1,700 B.C.[639]

The PGW sites in the Ganga-Yamuna *doāb* are generally associated by the archaeologists with the sites depicted in the *Mahābhārata*. The archaeological findings absolutely based on the excavations of the sites concerned show that the PGW culture was essentially based on the rural culture. The authors of this culture were in the rudimentary stage of the cultural growth. They were agriculturists. They lived in the wattled structure and daub houses made of clay and mud bricks. Some fragments of baked bricks have also been found. They were familiar with the use of copper and iron. They were skilled in the art of making potteries. But, on the contrary, we find that Hastināpur, Indraprastha, Ahicchatra, Kampil and Mathura, as described in the *Mahābhārata*, were the flourishing urban centres. Their settlement and cultural patterns as portrayed in the text, are not consistent with the archaeological description of the same. The description tallies broadly with the type of culture, which the *Vedic* Āryans represented. Because they were, by and large, the dwellers of the rural areas. They were expert in making the mud forts. They were ignorant of the city life. The earliest reference to the baked bricks called "*Āmā*" occurs in the *Ṛgveda*. Their knowledge of iron technology can also be confirmed by the evidences adduced in the *Vedic Saṁhitās* (*RV* 10, 72.2; *AV* 3.5.6). The texts refer to the blacksmiths, who knew how to melt the iron in the furnace.

While making an attempt to correlate the traditional accounts—the epic and the *Purāṇic* with the archaeological discovery of the PGW sites in the Gangetic valley, and keeping in view the C-14 dates of the PGW ranging from *c.* 1,200 (of period-I) to *c.* 1,100-800 B.C. (of period II), H.D. Sankalia, on the authority of B.B. Lal, has associated the people representing the PGW culture with the Early Āryans or alternatively with the tribe or tribes to which the Kauravas and the Pāṇḍavas and their contemporaries in the region belonged.[640] He observes that "The Carbon-14 dates from Hastinapur and other sites proved the culture not older than seventh-eighth century B.C. The authors of the Painted Grey Ware culture, whom the archaeologists . . . associate with the *Mahābhārata* heroes—the Pāṇḍavas, Kauravas and Shri Krishna—should have lived only 2,700 years ago and not 5,000 years ago . . . Traditionally the Āryans lived at a much earlier period about 3,000 B.C. whereas some say in 1,200 B.C. . . . And the long gap, say of 500 or 700 years between 1,500 B.C. and 800 B.C. cannot be filled up by the Painted Grey Ware, for the simple reason that we know really little about it and secondly, it does not seem to go back beyond 800 B.C. at the most. Thus, the period between 1,500 B.C. and 800 B.C. is archaeologically unknown in northern India" (the Indo-Gangetic plains).[641] The PGW culture, according to him, also raises lot of vexed problems relating to the *Mahābhārata* and the Āryans. He takes the *Purāṇic* accounts and all the early accounts purporting to go back to 3,000 B.C. as imaginary. It is a fact to reckon with that nothing positive can be established about the antiquity of a particular phase of culture represented by a particular group of people exclusively on the basis of C-14 dates of PGW. However, it cannot be denied that in northern India the beginning of the said phase of culture goes as far back as *c.* 2,000 B.C. In all likelihood, the Āryans of Puru lineage might have established their kingdom in Hastināpur more than 3,000 years ago.

H.D. Sankalia has aptly remarked that "Whether we find the traces of earlier culture or not the present evidence indicates that the Sarasvati-Drishadvati valley was inhabited by at least 2,500 B.C. . . . If we accept this, what would be the significance of C-14 dates around 1,500 B.C."[642]

Keeping in view the long gap between the traditional dates and C-14 dates concerned, it is really very difficult to determine the exact antiquity of those kingdoms, towns and cities of the Gangetic valley, which flourished in the pre-Bhārata war period after the emergence of the Kuru lineage and found place in the epic-*Purāṇic* accounts and archaeologically represent the PGW sites. The C-14 dates are, no doubt, relatively more reliable than the traditional one. But one basic difficulty, which we are baset with, is regarding the ascertainment of the antiquity of samples (collected from the PGW deposits), which are put to test in the laboratories through C-14 method for obtaining the approximate dates. The possibility of mistakes at the time of testing, because of natural, human and other factors, has been widely accepted by the archaeologists. The mistakes become apparent after getting the result in the form of different dates for the same site and sometimes even for the same layer. Moreover, it is very difficult to decide as to which particular phase of human settlements do they represent ? Over and above, no uniformity is found in C-14 dates, which have been obtained from different laboratories in India (notably, Tata Institute of Fundamental Research, Bombay and later physical Research laboratory, Ahmedabad), U.S.A. (University of Pennsylvania) and other foreign countries. This is evident from the Chart of C-14 test) dates collected by different archaeologists.[643] Further, the radiocarbon dating readjusted with "MASCA Correction" (a corrective factor evolved by the Museum Applied Science Centre for Archaeology, University of Pennsylvania, and generally applied for the C-14 give rise to doubts in our mind about their Correctness and application. These are the reasons because of which the reliability of C-14 dates have become questionable and their validity has become a subject of controversy among the archaeologists themselves.[644] Thus, they cannot be absolutely relied upon either.

## References and Notes

1. See *Mats.* (Gorakhpur, 1985), 11, 40-41; *Vy.* (text with Hindi tr. by R.P. Tripathi Śāstri, Prayaga, 1987), 64, 29-30; 85, 3-4; also D.K. Rājārām Patil, *cultural History from the Vāyu Purāṇa* (Poona, 1946, reptd, Delhi, 1973), pp. 6-13; *Vṣṇ.* (Gorakhpur, 9th edn. V.E. 2041), iv, 1, 7 refers to ten sons; see also *Vṣṇ.* (Eng. tr. H.H. Wilson, Calcutta, 1961), *Bk.* IV, ch. 1, pp. 277-78; *Agn.* (text with Hindi tr. by Tārinisha Jha and Ghanashyam Tripathi, Allahabad, 1986), 272, 5-7; *Mkd.* (text with Hindi tr. by Dharmendra Śāstri, Meerut, 1983), 108, 4-5 (only seven sons); *Br.* (text with HIndi tr. by Tārinisha Jha, Prayag, 1976), 7, 1-2; *Bhāg.* (Gorakhpur, 8th edn. V.E. 2040), ix, 1.7-12; *Krm.* (text with Hindi tr. by Shree Chaudhury Shree Narayan Singh and ed. by Ananda Swarupa Gupta, Varanasi, 1972), i, 19, vv. 1-27; *HV* (with Hindi tr. and Comm., Gorakhpur, *Samv.* 2044, 4th edn.), *Harivaṁśa Parva*, 10, 1-2; *Bmd.* (Venkatesvara Press, Bombay, 1906), iii, 60, 2-3; 2, 38, 30-32; *Mbh. Ādi Parva* (1968), 70, 11-45 (ten sons); see also F.E. Pargiter, *AIHT* (Ist Edn. London, 1922, reptd., Delhi, 1972), p. 255; R. Morton Smith, *DDEI* (Delhi, 1973), Pt. 1, pp. 10 ff; A.D. Pusalker; "Traditional history from the Earliest Time to the Accession of Parikshit" in R.C. Majumdar (ed.): *HCIP, The Vedic Age* (Bombay, 1965), p. 276; Romila Thapar (*A History of India*, Middlesex, 1966, vol. 1, p. 28), also refers to his nine sons.
   There is no uniformity in the *Purāṇic* and Epic list of names of Manu's sons. There is also some discrepancy about their number which varies from nine to ten. In some of the *Purāṇas* ten names are enumerated, but their number figures as nine in the original verses. Some of the *Purāṇas* include even his daughter Ila as one of his ten sons. That is why, the texts have been collated and it has been found that in actuality he had nine sons and one daughter named Ila, which have been generally accepted by all the authorities concerned.
2. *Mats.*, 12, 19; *Br.*, 7, 20; *Bmd.*, iii, 60, 20; *Lg.* (Venkatesvara Press, Bombay, 1927), i, 65, 28; *Vāl. Rām.*, *Bāla Kāṇḍa* (tr. by Pt. Yudhiṣṭhira Mimāṁasak and ed. by Pt. Akhilananda, Amritasar, V.E. 2025), 70, 21-22.
3. *Vy.*, 88, 5-7; *Vṣṇ.*, iv, 2, 5-10; *Vṣ,179.*, (tr. H.H. Wilson), *Bk.* IV, ch. ii, pp. 286-87.
4. Morton Smith, *op. cit.*, p. 13.
5. *Vy.*, 88, 4-5; *Vṣṇ.*, iv, 2,4; *Vṣṇ.* (tr. H.H. Wilson), *Bk.* IV, Ch. ii, p. 286, *Bmd.*, iii, 63, 4-5; *Br.*, 7, 25; *Agn.*, 272, 11; *Bhāg.*, ix, 2, 17 refers to them as *Brāhmaṇs*, but *Gar.* (Bombay, 1906), 1, 138, 15 says that these *Kṣatriyas* became degraded as *Vaiśyas*.
6. See *Mkd.*, Eng. tr. by F.E. Pargiter (*BIS, ASB*, Calcutta, 1904), Vol. II, Pt. II, p. 311.
7. *Shiv Purāṇa*, VII, 60, 20.
8. *Mats.*, 12, 21-22; *Vy.*, 86, 24-27; *Vṣṇ.*, 4, 1, 62-64 & 91; *Vṣṇ.* (tr. H.H. Wilson), *Bk.* IV, Ch. 11, pp. 284-85; *Agn.* 273, 12; *Br.*, 7, 28-29, *Bhāg.*, ix, 3 see also *Vmn.*, (text with tr. ed. by Anandaswarup Gupta, Varanasi, 1968), 12, 51 (for Kuśasthalipur) and *Krm.*, 1, 18, 20-2; 1, 25, 33, 35; 1.26.5 (for Dvārakāpuri and Dvāravatipuri).
9. Junagarh Rock Inscription of Rudradāman, A.D. 150 in D.C. Sircar (ed.) : *SI*, (Calcutta, 1965), Vol. 1, Line-11, p. 178.
10. See *Vy.*, 86, 3-17; *Vṣṇ.*, iv, 1.19-49; *Vṣṇ.* (tr. H.H. Wilson) *Bk.*, IV, Ch. 1, p. 283; Ch. 11, p. 281; *Bmd.*, iii,

61, 3-18 and 8, 35-7; *Lg.*, 1, 66, 53; *Gar.*, 1, 138, 5-13; *Bhāg.*, ix, 2, 23-36; *Mkd.*, 113 to 136 and 109 to 110; *PK*, p. 481; Pargiter, *AIHT*, pp. 96-97, 256, 268 and 273; *Vāl. Rām.*, *Bāla Kāṇḍa*, 47, 11-12; *JRAS*, 1902, pp. 267 f.

11. *Agn.*, 272, 10; *Br.*, 7, 24; *Śiv.*, vii 60, 19; Morton Smith, *op. cit.*, p. 12.
12. *Br*,. 7. 27; *Bmd.*, III, 61, 8.
13. *Vṣṇ.*, iv, 1, 18; *Vy.*, 86, 2; *Mats.*, 12.24.
14. *Mkd.*, tr. Pargiter, p. 341.
15. *Vṣṇ.* tr. H.H. Wilson, *Bk.* iv. Ch. 11, p. 281.
16. *Mats.*, 12, 24½; *Vy.*, 86, 1-2; *Vṣṇ.*, iv, 1, 17; *Br.*, 7, 43; *Lg.*, 1, 66, 52; *Śiv.*, vii, 60, 32; *Agn.*, 272, 18; *Gar.*, i, 138, 4; *Pdm.* (Ananda Srama Skt. Series, Poona, 1894), V, 8, 130.
17. Purūravas Aila was born out of union of Manu's daughter Ilā and Budha, son of Soma. In Manu's genealogy, which is partly legendary and partly historical, he seems to have descended from Ilā, who was later transformed into a Kimpurusha and named Sudyumna. There is no positive historical evidence to substantiate such fabulous pedigrees. However, the *Purāṇic* accounts of the kingdoms and dynasties established by their descendants are, to some extent, reliable. For details see *Mkd.*, 108, 13-15; *Vy.*, 85, 5-24; *Mats.*, 12, 1-16; *Hv.* 1, 10-17; *Vṣṇ., iv, 1-8-16; RV* (Bareilly, 1974), 10, 95; *Śat. Br.* (Varanasi, 1984), XI, 5,1.1.
18. *Mats.*, 12, 18; *Vṣṇ.*, IV, 1, 16; D.K. Rājārām Patil, *op. cit.*, pp. 6-13; *PK*, pp. 315 and 331; *Vāl. Rām.*, 7, 56, 26; 7, 90, 23; *Mbh.*, *Ādi Parva*, 90, 7-9.
19. *Vy.*, 85, 21-23; *Vṣṇ.*, IV, 1, 16; *Agn.*, 273, 10-11; *Mkd.*, 108, 18; *Bmd.*, iii, 60, 21-2; *Lg.*, i, 65, 29-31; *Hv.*, 1, 10; *PK*, p. 331.
20. See *Mats.*, 12; 17-18; *Vy.*, 85, 18-19; *Vṣ*, iv, 1, 14; *Agn.*, 273, 7-11; *Br.*, 7, 18½; *Pdm.*, V, 8, 123; *Vṣṇ.*, (Tr. H.H. Wilson), *Bk.*, IV, Ch. 11, p. 280; *Mkd.*, 108, 15-16.
21. *Vy.*, 85, 19; *Agn.*, 273, 7-8.
22. *Vṣṇ.* tr. H.H. Wilson, *Bk.* IV, Ch. 11, p. 280.
23. *AIHT*, p. 288.
24. *PPIP* (Poona, 1974), p. 556.
25. For details see his "Archaeology and Tradition" in S.P. Gupta and K.S. Ramachandran (eds.); *AIHA* (Delhi, 1977), pp. 277-81 and "Prehistoric Colonization in India : Archaeological and Literary Evidences" in *ibid.*, pp. 298-311.
26. *AIHT*, p. 289.
27. *Vy.*, 88, 20-21; *Br.*, 7, 46; *Hv.*, 1, 11; also D.K. Rājārām Patil, *op. cit.*, pp. 6-13; *Vāl. Rām.*, *Bāla Kāṇḍa*, 70, 21-23.
28. See, *Vy.*, 88, 9-11; *Vṣṇ.*, IV, 2, 12-14; *Mats.*, 12.26-28; 113, 19-21 and 30; *Vṣṇ.*, (tr. H.H. Wilson), IV. ii, p. 287. *Pdm.*, V, 8, 130-3; *Lg.*, i, 65, 31-2; *Krm.*, I, 20, 10-11. See also P. Gupta, *GAII* (Delhi, 1977), p. 127.
29. *Mats.*, 12, 29-30; *Vy.*, 88, 24-27; *Vṣṇ.*, iv.2, 36-37; *Vṣṇ.* (tr. H.H. Wilson), iv, ii, p. 289; *Hv.*, 1, 11; see also *JRAS*, 1909, pp. 1066 f.
30. *AIHT*, pp. 257-8.
31. *Mbh.*, VII, 79,12-20.
32. *Sabhā Parva* (1981-82), 3, 3-6.
33. *Vy.*, 89, 1-6; *Vṣṇ.*, IV, 5, 1, 21-23; *Bhāg.*, ix, 13, 1, 11-27.
34. *AIHT*, pp. 257, fn. 6.
35. *Bhāg.*, ix, 6, 4-12.
36. For details see *SPHI* (Delhi, 1971), pp. 110-16.
37. *Vāl. Rām.*, 87, 3 and 7; 88, 9-24; 89, 2-23; 90, 7, 10, 17-19, 21-23½.
38. *Mat.*, 115, 6-8, 10-11, 12-19.

39. *PHAI* (Calcutta, 1953), p. 25, fn. 17.
40. See *Vāl. Rām. Ko.*, pp. 179 and 184.
41. *RV*, 10, 95.
42. *Ādi Parva*, 90, 7-9.
43. India in the *Vedic* Age (Lucknow, 1956), p. 25.
44. *Ibid.*, pp. 66 f.
45. *AIHT*, pp. 295-96.
46. *Imp. Gaz. of India* (1907), I, pp. 357-58.
47. *AIHT*, p. 298; *JRAS*, 1919, pp. 358-61. See also M.A. Stein, *JRAS*, 1917, pp. 91 f.
48. *Mkd.* (tr.), p. 311.
49. *AIHT*, p. 302.
50. *Imp. Gaz. of India* (1907), I, p. 358.
51. *AIHT*, p. 296.
52. *Ibid.*, pp. 297-98, 300 and 302. See also Keith, *JRAS*, 1913, pp. 412 f. See *Vy.*, 91, 5-8 and *Vsn.*, iv, 6, 1-87 for legend concerned.
53. *PPIP*, p. 557; *AIHA*, pp. 308 and 310; *Prehistory of India* (Delhi, 1977), p. 179.
54. *AIHA*, p. 308.
55. *Ibid.*, p. 310.
56. *Ibid.*, p. 279.
57. *AIHT*, pp. 295-96.
58. *Ibid.* (based on the linguistic evidence of Grierson, *Imp. Gaz. of India*, 1907, I, p. 359.
59. *Ibid.*, p. 295.
60. *Imp. Gaz. of India*, I, pp. 386-7; *JRAS*, 1907, p. 188.
61. *AIHT*, p. 297.
62. *Vāl. Rām.*, *Bāla Kāṇḍa*, 5, 1-3; B.B. Lal, "Ayodhya of the *Vālmīki Rāmāyaṇa* . . . its identification" in *Purātattva*, No. 16, 1985-86, pp. 79-84; *Pdm.*, *Pātālakhaṇḍa*, 28.49; *Pdm.*, *Uttarakhaṇḍa*, 242, 41-42; *Bhāg.*, ix, 8.17-19; *Vṣṇ. Dh.* (Venkatesvara Press, Bombay, *Śaka*, 1834), 1, Ch. 240, 2; 1, Ch. 13, 1-12; *PK*, p. 29; see also *AV*, X, 1, 2, 31; *Tai. Ar.*, 1, 27, 2-3; Thomas Watters, *YCTI* (*RAS*, London, 1904-5, Delhi, 1973), Vol. 1, p. 354.
63. *Vāl. Rām.*; *Bāla Kāṇḍa*, 5, 6.
64. *Ibid.*, 5, 7.
65. *Bmd.*, 4, 40, 91.
66. *Vāl. Rām.*, *Bāla Kāṇḍa*, 70, 21-22; *Ayodhya Kāṇḍa* (ed. and tr. by Pt. Akhilananda, Amritasar, *VE* 2019), 49, 13; *Mats.*, 12, 19; *Br.*, 7, 20; *Bmd.*, 3, 60, 20; *Mbh.*, *Sabhā Parva*, 13, 3-6.
67. *Ṛgv.*, 10, 5, 60, 4.
68. See *Vy.*, 88, 3-183; *Bhv.* (Bareilly, 1978), Vol. 1, vv. 3-61, pp. 277-86; vv. 3-7, p. 287.
69. *Vāl. Rām.*, *Bāla Kāṇḍa*, 70, 22-24.
70. *Vy.*, 88, 67-70; *Vṣṇ.* iv, 2, 63,-66; *Vṣṇ.* (tr. H.H. Wilson), iv, 11, p. 289. See also *Mats.*, 12, 34-35. The *Go. Br.*, (1.2.10) also refers to *Māndhātṛ Yuvanāśva.*
71. See *AIHT*, pp. 261-2 and Bhagavadadattas̄ *Bhāratavarsha kā Brihat Itihāsa* (Delhi, Samv. 2008), pp. 66-68.
72. *Vy.*, 88, 71-72; *Mats.*, 12, 34-35. Purukutsa is referred to both in the *RV* (1.11.63.7) and in the *Śat. Br.* (XIII, 5.4.5). He along with his son Trsadasyu finds mention in the *RV* (IV. 4, 42.8). Some other Aikṣvākus also figure in the *Pan. Br.*, XIII, 3.12.
73. See *Vy.*, 94, 5-7, 28; *Bmd.*, iii, 69, 28; *Br.*, 13, 176-8; *Pdm.*, V, 12, 130-2; *Mats.*, 43, 29-31; H.D. Sankalia, *PPIP*, p. 557.

74. *Vy.*, 88, 115-17, *Bmd.*, iii, 63, 115; *Br.*, 8.24; *Hv.*, 1, 13; *Lg.*, 1, 66, 10.
75. *Vy.*, 88, 117-19; *Hv.*, 1, 13, Hariścandra and his son Rohita are also alluded to in the *Ait. Br.*, VII, 13.16; VII, 14 and styled as Aikṣvākus. See also *Mats.*, 12, 25-42½.
76. N.L. Dey, *GDAMI* (Calcutta, 1927), p. 170.
77. *Vy.*, 88, 122-43; *Vṣ*, iv, 3, 40-49; *Vṣn.* (tr. H.H. Wilson), iv, iii, p. 299-300; *Br.*, 8, 28-32, 35-51; *Bmd.*, iii, 63, 120-41; also *Bmd.* (Bareli 1988) Vol. I, vv. 25-26, pp. 437-38; *Hv.*, 1, 13; *Pdm.* (*Svargakhaṇḍa*, ed. by Aśoka Chatterjee Śāstri, Varanasi, 1972), 15, 41-57; D.K. Rājārām Patil, *op. cit.*, p. 279; Raj Kumar Arora, *Historical and Cultural Data from the Bhaviṣya Purāṇa* (Delhi, 1972), p. 37. see also *JRAS*, 1910, pp. 9-10, 1914, pp. 279-81; 1919, pp. 353-61, From *Vāl. Rām.* (*Bāla Kāṇḍa*, 70, 28-29) it appears that Haihayas and Tālajanghas had hostilities with Aikṣvākus even before the time of Sagara.
78. P. Carnegy, *NRPO* (Lucknow, 1868), p. 2.
79. *Vṣn.*, IV, 3. 25-46; *Pdm.*, *Uttarakhaṇḍa*, 2. 188 ff.
80. For rulers of the post-Sagara period down to Daśaratha see *Vy.*, 88, 144-83; *Vṣn.* (tr. H.H. Wilson), iv, iv, pp. 301-7; *Mats.* 12, 25-42; *Bhv.* Supra, vv. 31-56, pp. 282-85; vv. 4-7, p. 287; *Vāl. Rām. Bāla Kāṇḍa*, 70, 38-43.
81. See *Vāl. Rām.*, *Bāla Kāṇḍa*, 5, 7-23; S.C. De, *HRIAS* (Delhi, 1976), p. 157.
82. *CAGI*, pp. 341-2.
83. Carto, xiii, Śloka, 79; Canto xiv, Śloka 13.
84. *Bmd.*, 3, 54, 54.
85. *PDKA* (Varanasi, 1962), p. 53.
86. *CAGI*, p. 341; *CASR*, 1, p. 318.
87. *As. Res.*, vol. XX, p. 442.
88. *Abhidhānacintāmani* (Ahmedabad, Samv. 2013), p. 222.
89. A Fuhrer, *MAINWO* (1891), p. 275. *cf.* T.W. Rhys Davids, *BI* (Delhi, 1971), p. 39.
90. Thomas Watters, *YCTI*, Vol. i, pp. 354-55.
91. *Mahāvastu*, Senart's Ed., Vol. 1, p. 348; *Bodhisattvāvadāna Kalpalatā* (3rd, p. 2) *cf.* B.C. Law, *GAGI* (Varanasi, 1976), p. 23, fn. 1; *Jātaka*, 3, 270.
92. See J.C. Jain, *LAIJC* (Delhi, 1984), p. 337.
93. Ed. by Muni Jina Vijaya, Gujarat Purātattva Mandir, Ahmedabad), p. 32.
94. *BI*, p. 39.
95. *Ṛgveda* 1.19, 126, 4; X, 8, 93, 14 (respectively).
96. *Vāl. Rām. Ayodhya Kāṇḍa*, Chs. 68-71; vii (*Uttarakāṇḍa*), 113-14. For details see A.K. Chatterjee, "The Kekayas in Ancient India", *JIH*, Vol. LVI, 1978, Pt. II, pp. 197-202.
97. *JASB*, 1895, 250 ff. See also V.S. Agrawala, *IP* (Lucknow, 1963), p. 53; B.N. Puri, *ITP* (Bombay, 1968), p. 69; B.C. Law, *GAGI*, p. 143.
98. J.W. McCrindle, *AIMA* (Calcutta, 1926), pp. 163 f, 196; *Ind. Ant.*, Vol. V, p. 332.
99. *Vy.*, 88, 188-91; *Vṣn.* iv, 4, 104; *Vṣn.* (tr. H.H. Wilson), iv, iv, p. 308; *Bmd.* iii, 63, 188-91; *Vṣn. Dh.* I, ch. 269, 12.
100. *Vāl. Rām.*, vii, 100, 16; 101, 10-15; *Vāl. Rām.*Ko. p. 181.
101. *CAGI*, pp. 41-42; *CAI* (Varanasi, 1971), p. 32; *CASR*, II, pp. 111-35; III, p. 35; V, 66, 75.
102. McCrindle, *AIT* (Calcutta, 1927), Notes, p. 362.
103. Periplus (London, 1912), p. 238.
104. *IP*, p. 50.
105. Periplus, pp. 183-84; *CAGI*, p. 42; A Foucher, *NAGG* (Varanasi, 1974), p. 11.
106. *CAGI*, p. 88; A Foucher, *op. cit*, p. 38; N.L. Dey, *GDAMI* (Delhi, 1971), p. 200.

107. *Vy.*, 88, 184-190; *Vṣṇ.*, IV, 4, 104; *Vṣṇ.* (tr. H.H. Wilson), iv, iv, p. 308; *Bmd.*, iii, 63, 188-91; *Pdm.*, V, 35, 23-24; vi, 271, 10-12.
108. *Vāl. Rām. Uttarakāṇḍa*, 102, 9.
109. *Vy.*, 88, 184-87; *Vṣṇ.*, iv, 4, 100-1, 104; *Vāl. Rām.*; *Uttarakāṇḍa*, 70, 5-14; *Bmd.*, iii, 63, 186, 188-91; 4.40.19; *Vṣṇ.* (tr. H.H. Wilson), iv, iv, p. 308; *Pdm.*, V, 35, 23-24; VI, 10-12; *Bhāg.*, ix, 11, 14.
110. *YCTI*, p. 301.
111. McCrindle, *AIT*, Notes, pp. 366-68.
112. *GEB*, (Varanasi, 1973), p. 20, fn. 1.
113. *GAGI*, p. 26. See also B.C. Law "Mathura in Ancient India" in *JASB*; Vol. 13 (1947), pp. 21-30.
114. McCrindle, *AIMA* (London, 1877), pp. 201-3; R.C. Majumdar, The Classical Accounts of India (Calcutta, 1960), p. 206; E.J. Rapson (ed.) : *CHI* (Delhi, 1962), Vol. I, *Ancient India*, p. 367; *CAGI*, pp. 315-16; D.C. Sircar, *SGAMI* (Delhi, 1971), p. 109; see also B.C. Law, *GAGI*, p. 134; *GEB*, p. 20.
115. J.C. Jain, *op. cit.*
116. *IAR*, 1954-55, p. 15.
117. *Vy.*, 88, 198-200; *Bmd.*, 2, 16, 41, 64; 3, 53, 199; 74, 197; 3, 63, 188-91; *Vṣṇ.*, iv, 4, 104; *Mats.*, 12, 40-44; *Vmn.*, 16, 32, 38, 19; *Pdm.*, vi, 208, 46-47; vi, 271, 10-12; *Vṣṇ.*, (tr. H.H. Wilson), p. 308; *PK*, pp. 121, 133.
118. *Vāl. Rām. Uttarakāṇḍa*, 107, 17; 108, 4; also 10, 17; *Vāl. Rām. Ko.*, p. 73.
119. G.P. Malalasekera, *DPPN*, (London 1937-38), VoL. I, p. 653; Vol. II, 454; also *SBE*, II, p. 248.
120. *DPPN*, Vol. I, p. 653.
121. *Raghu.* Cantos, XIII, 79, XVI, 25-42.
122. *CAGI*, pp. 335-37.
123. CF. *YCTI*, Vol.II, p. 339.
124. *Vy.*, 88, 199-200; *Vāl. Rām. Uttarakāṇḍa*, 107, 5, 17. See also *YCTI*, Vol. II, pp. 200-1; *RBK*, (by H.A. Giles, Cambridge, 1923, Varanasi, 1972), pp. 30-31; *Vṣṇ.* (tr. H.H. Wilson), p. 308.
125. *Raghu.* VI, 71 and XI, 1.
126. *CAGI*, pp. 343-46.
127. Cf. *YCTI*, Vol. II, p. 339.
128. B.C. Law, "Countries and Peoples of India", (Epic and *Purāṇic* Sources") in *ABORI*, Vol. XVII, 1935-36, Pt. III, p. 225 and *GAGI*, p. 130; *GEB*, p. 5; "The Kosalas in Ancient India" in *IHQ*, Vol. I, Nos., 1-2 (Delhi, 1979), pp. 139-65; also his article on Ayodhya in *JGRI*, Vol. L, pp. 423-43; S.M. Ali, *GP* (Delhi, 1983), p. 135; E.J. Rapson, *Ancient India from the Earliest Times to the First Century* A.D. (Varanasi, 1981), p. 82.
129. *IAR*, 1958-59, p. 48.
130. *Vṣṇ.*, iv, 4, 105-12; *Mats.*, 12, 42-57; *Vy.*, 88, 201-7; *Bhv.*, Supra, vv. 8-23, pp. 287-90.
131. *Vṣṇ.*, iv. 4, 112; *Vy.*, 88, 208-12; *Bhv.* Supra, V. 23, p. 290.
132. *Udyoga Parva* (1969), 163, 18.
133. *AIHA*, p. 304.
134. *Vy.*, 89, 1-3; *Vṣṇ.*, iv, 51, see also up to 14; *Bhāg.*, IX, 13.1; *Bmd.*, iii, 64, 1-4; *Gar.*, i, 138, 44 f; I, 139, 1; *Vāl. Rām. Bāla Kāṇḍa*, 71, 3.
135. *Vāl. Rām.*; *Uttarakāṇḍa*, 55, 4-21.
136. *Vy.*, 89, 1-3.
137. *Vy.*, 89, 3-6; *Vṣṇ.*, iv, 5, 20-23; *Vṣṇ.* (tr. H.H. Wilson), iv, v. pp. 310-11; *Bmd.*, iii, 64, 4-6; *Bhāg.* ix, 13, 13; See also *Br.* 17, 19 and 28 (for Mithilāpuri); S.C. De, *op. cit.*, p. 38.
138. *Bālakāṇḍa*, 71, 3-4; see also 13, 21 and 48, 9-10 (for Janaka of Mithila and the Capital city).
139. *Vy.*, 89, 6-18; *Vṣṇ.*, iv, 5, 24-31; *Vṣṇ.* (tr. H.H. Wilson), iv, v, 311-12; *Bmd.*, iii, 64, 1-24; *Bhāg.* ix, 13, 1-27; *Gar.* i, 138, 44-58.

140. *Bāla Kāṇḍa*, 71, 4-20.
141. *Ibid.*, 70, 2-8; 71, 14-19; *Vy.*, 89, 18; *Vṣṇ*, iv, 5, 32-33; *Vṣṇ.* (tr. H.H. Wilson), p. 312. *Bmd.*, iii, 64, 18-19; *Vāl. Rām. Ko.*, p. 34.
142. Thomas Watters, *YCTI*, Vol. I, pp. 333-35; V.S. Smith, *cf. Ibid.*, Vol. II, p. 338; *CAGI*, pp. 311-14 and 484; E.B. Cowell, "The Chinese Buddhist Pilgrims in India"—a reprint from M. Elphinstone's The History of India, 9th ed. 1911 and pub. in *Ancient India* (by M. Elphinstone, E.B. Cowell and others, Delhi, 1983), Ch. VIII, p., 72, fn. 10, V.S. Agrawala, *IP*, p. 73.
143. *Mbh.*, 105, 11-12.
144. *Mbh.*, 26, 4-6; 27, 10-13.
145. *Vy.*, 89, 18-23; *Vṣṇ.*, iv, 5, 29-34; *Vṣ,179.* (tr. H.H. Wilson), p. 312; *Bmd.*, iii, 19-24.
146. *Śat. Br.*, 1.4.1.10;; *SBE*, XII, Intro. XLII.
147. *Abhidhānacintāmani*, p. 222.
148. "Ancient Countries in Eastern India" in *JASB*, Vol. LXVI (1897), Pt. I, p. 89. See also *CASR*, XVI, 34.
149. *Jātaka*, ed. by Fausboll (London, 1877-97) and tr. by various hands under the editorship of E.B. Cowell (Cambridge, 1895-1913) Vols. V-VI; also *DPPN*, Vol. II, p. 879.
150. *Mahāvastu* (ed. by E. Senart, Paris, 1882-97), Vol. III, p. 172.
151. *Divyāvadāna* (ed. E.B. Cowell and R.A. Neil, Cambridge 1886), p. 424.
152. *Lalita-Vistara* (ed. Rajendralal Mitra, Calcutta, 1877), Ch. III.
153. J.C. Jain, *op. cit.*
154. 119, 20-21; 120, 17-20.
155. *Vṣṇ.* (tr.), iv, 1, pp. 283-84.
156. See his tr. of the *Meghadūta of Kālidāsa* (Delhi, 1969), Purva, note 28, p. 53.
157. *Vy.*, 86, 3-14; *Vṣṇ.*, iv, 1, 19, 29-36; *Vṣṇ.* (tr. H.H. Wilson), iv, 11, p. 281; *Bmd.*, iii, 61, 3-12; *Mkd.*, Ch. 119-121; *Bhāg.*, ix, 2, 23-33; *Gar.*, i, 138, 5-13; *Lg.*, i, 66, 53.
158. For details see *Mkd.*, 119, 1-2, 20-21; 120, 1-20; 121, 1-50; *PK*, p. 481.
159. Pargiter, *AIHT*, p. 268.
160. Br., 7, 27; *Bmd.*, iii, 61, 8.
161. *Vy.*, 86, 14-17; *Vṣṇ.*, iv, 1, 43-49; *Vṣṇ.*, (tr. H.H. Wilson), iv, 11, p. 283; *Bmd.*, iii, 61, 12-13; *Bhāg.* ix, 2, 33-34; *Gar.*, i, 138, 10-13; *PK.*, p. 481.
162. *Vāl. Rām. Bāla Kāṇḍa*, 47, 11-12; *Vāl. Rām. Ko.*, p. 35.
163. *Vāl. Rām.*, VII, 2; VII, 14.
164. *Bāla Kāṇḍa*, 45, 8-12 and 13 ff; 47, 17-22; also S.C. De, *op. cit.*, p. 38.
165. *CAGI*, pp. 373-74.
166. *YCTI*, Vol. II, p. 63.
167. *RBK* (Oxford, 1886, Delhi, 1972), Ch. XXIV, pp. 70-71.
168. *The Life of Hiuen-Tsang* (London, 1884, Delhi enlarged, 1973), p. 230.
169. *Ancient India*, p. 85.
170. *GAGI*, p. 17. See also *JRAS*, 1902, p. 267.
171. *Vy.*, 86, 17-21; *Vṣṇ.*, iv, 1, 50-60; *Bmd.*, iii, 61, 12-17; *Bhāg.*, ix, 2, 33-36; *Bāla Kāṇḍa.*, 47, 13-17.
172. *Vy.*, 86.22; *Vṣṇ.*, IV, 1, 61; *Bāla Kāṇḍa*, 47, 18.
173. *AIHT*, p. 97; The *Vedic Age*, p. 296.
174. *Vy.*, 86, 22-28; *Vṣṇ.*, iv, 1, 62-65 and 91-94; *Mats.*, 12, 21-24; *Br.*, 7, 27-41; *Agn.*, 273, 12-16; *Bhāg.*, ix, 3,1-2, 27-36; *Bmd.*, iii, 61, 18-24; 63, 1-4; *Lg.*, i, 66, 47-9; *Pdm.*, V, 8, 126-09; *Vmn.*, 12.51; *Krm.*, 1, 18, 20-2; 1, 25, 33-35; 1, 26.5; *Bbh.*, *Sabhā Parva*, 13, 49, 51; *Mbh. Ko.*, p. 100; *PK*, p. 44-45, 121.

175. *Vy.*, 91, 1-2, 5-8 and 51; 92, 1-7; *Vṣṇ.*, iv, 1, 8-64; *Br.*, Chs. 9-11; *Bhāg.*, ix, 14, 1 ff; ix, 15.1; 17.1; *Bmd.*, 1.1.89; 2.14; 3, 65, 45-6; 3, 66, 1-2, 19-22; *Bhv.* (Supra), Vol. 1, vv. 43-47, pp. 292-3; H.H. Wilson, *op. cit.*, vi, vii and viii, pp. 318-19, 324-5; D.K. Rājārām Patil, *op. cit.*, pp. 6-13. *Vāl. Rām.*, *Bāla Kāṇḍa*, 70, 42-43; *Uttarakāṇḍa*, 56, 26-28; *Mbh.*, *Ādi Parva*, 70, 11-45; 90, 7-9 (all for Purūravas Dynasty).
176. *Vy.*, 91.5.
177. *Vy.*, 91, 51-96, 103; *Br.*, 10, 13-60, 68; *Bmd.*, iii, 66, 22-68, 75; *Vṣṇ.*, iv, 7, 2-17; *Bhāg.*, ix, 15, 3-16, 36; *Gar.*, i, 139, 2-7.
178. *YCTI*, Vol. I, p. 340; See also *CAGI*, pp. 317-18.
179. VI, Vol. II, p. 116 fn.
180. *AV*, 4, 7.1.
181. Ed. by E. Senart (Paris, 1882-97), Vol. III, p. 402.
182. *Śat. Br.*, xiii, 5, 4, 19-21; *Go. Br.* Purva, ii, 9.
183. *Vāl. Rām*, *Bāla Kāṇḍa*, 13, 23; *Ayodhyā Kāṇḍa*, 10, 37; *Uttarakāṇḍa*, 38, 17-19.
184. *Uttara*, 56, 25,
185. *Anuśāsana Parva*, 31, 10-26.
186. *Vy.*, 92, 3-9, 18-26, 28, 59-75; *Vṣṇ.*, iv, 8, 1-21; *Br.*, 11, 35-45; 13, 66-74½; *Bmd.*, iii, 67, 1-79; *Gar.*, i, 139, 8-14; *Bhāg.*, ix, 17, 2-10; *HV.*, 1, 29, 25-72; ch. 1, 32, 20 ff; See also *ABORI*, Vol. XVII (1936), Pt. III, pp. 224-25.
187. *RV.*, 1. 130, 7.
188. *Ibid.*, 1, 130, 10.
189. *Ibid.*, 4, 30, 20.
190. *Ibid.*, 6, 26, 8.
191. *Vāl. Rām.*, *Uttarakāṇḍa*, 38, 15, 19-20.
192. S.N. Pradhan, *Chro-Anc. Ind.* (Varanasi, 1979), p. 30.
193. *CAGI*, p. 369.
194. Banaras, *City of Light* (London, 1983), p. 25.
195. *Vāl. Rām.*, *Uttarakāṇḍa*, 59, 19.
196. *Ādi Parva*, 90, 33-34.
197. *Udyoga Parva*, 170, 9-11; See also 171, 2; 172, 17-19; 173, 1; 174, 11 (for Kāśi-*rāja*).
198. *Mahābhārata*, *Sabhā Parva*, 27, 6-7.
199. B.C. Law, *IETBJ*, p. 129; *Śat, Br.*, (XIII, 5, 4.19) also mentions Dhṛtarāṣṭra, as a king of Kāśi.
200. *Jātaka*, iv, 15, 119-20.
201. *Jāt.*, VI, p. 160.
202. *Vṣṇ.*, V, 34, 14, 21-40; *Bmd.*, iii, 67, 26-62.
203. *Jāt.*, IV, pp. 119-20.
204. McCrindle, *AIT*, p. 228.
205. J.C. Jain *op. cit.*, pp. 337-38.
206. *Vy.*, 93, 87-92; *Agn.*, 274, 1-23; *Vṣṇ.*, iv, 10, 30-32; *Br.*, 12, 18-19; *Mats.*, 36, 5; *Bmd.*, iii, 68, 90-92; *Krm.*, i, 21, 9-11; *Lg.*, i, 67, 11-12; H.H. Wilson, *op. cit.*; iv, X, pp. 331-32; *Hv.* (*Harivaṁśa Parva*), 30, 1-2, 5, 17-18. See also S. Chattopadhyaya, *RAENIT* (Delhi, 1973), pp. 66-67.
207. *Ṛgveda*, 1. 108.8 (for all five sons of Yayāti mentioned together); 7.18.6, 12-14; 10.62.10 (mentioned separately); See also 1.122.8; 9.91.2 (for Nahuṣa); A.A. Macdonell and A.B. Keith, VI. (1st end. London, 1912, 3rd. edn. Indian Texts Series, 1967), Vol. 1. pp. 466-67; Vol. II, pp. 1113; R.C. Jain, *EAB.* (Varanasi, 1970), pp. 70-92. See also Hopkins *JAOS*, 15, 260.
208. *Vāl. Rām.*, *Uttarakāṇḍa*, 58, 8-13.
209. *Ādi Parva*; 70, 11-45; 80, 26; 82, 5; 89, 10-12; 90, 8-14.

210. *AIHT*, p. 259.
211. *Bhv.* (Supra), Vol. I, vv. 48-49, pp. 293-94; *Ādi Parva*, 80, 26; 82, 5;
212. 99, 462.
213. *Vy.*, 94, 1-5; *Vṣṇ.*, iv, 11, 5-7; H.H. Wilson, *op. cit.*, IV, XI, pp. 333-34; *Mats.*, 43, 7-8; *Br.*, 13, 154-60; *Agn.*, 275, 1-11; *Bmd.*, iii, 69, 3-5 (See also *Bmd.*, Bareli edn. 1988; Vol. I, p. 465); *Bhāg.*, xi, 23, 19-21; *Krm.*, 1, 21, 1-20; *Pdm.*, V, 12, 110-15 (See also *Pdm.*, Bareli edn. 1986, Vol. 1, pp. 103-6); *Lg.*, 1, 68, 3-5; *Gar.*, 1, 139, 19-20.
214. *Vy.*, 94, 3-54; *Vṣṇ.*, iv, 11, 8-30; H.H. Wison, *op. cit.*, Iv, XI, pp. 333-35; *Mats.*, 43, 8-52; *Pdm.*, V, 12, 110-49; *Krm.*, 1, 22, 1-21; 23, 1-13; *Bmd.*, iii, 69, 3-55; *Br.*, 13, 154-207; *Agn.*, 275, 1-51; *Br.*, 13, 154-207; *Agn.*, 275, 1-51; *Lg.*, 1, 68, 3-20; *Gar.* 1, 139, 19-24; *Bhāg.*, xi, 23, 21-30.
215. *Vṣṇ.*, iv, II, 8-9; *Pdm.*, Vi (*Uttarakāṇḍa*) 115, 4; 220, 17; V (*Sṛṣṭikhaṇḍa*) 8, 39-40; 17, 206; also Bhūmikhaṇḍa, 92, 33; *Hv.*, 33, 4-5; See also *Vmn.*, 39, 137 (for Māhismati) and *Vy.* , 945 (for Māhismāna).
216. *Vy.*, 94, 6; *Mats.*, 43, 9-11; *Vṣṇ.*, iv, II, 10.
217. *Vy.*, 94, 8-25; *Vṣṇ.*, iv, 11, 10-11; *Mats.*, 43, 11-28; *Agn.*, 275, 4-8; *Br.*, 13, 160-75; *Bmd.*, III, 69, 5-15; *Pdm.*, V, 12, 115-25.
218. *Vy.*, 94, 26; *Vṣṇ.*, iv, 11, 19; *Mats.*, 43, 29; *Br.*, 13, 176-78, also 184-85; *Hv.*, 33, 25-26; 38, 14-20; *Pdm.*, VI, 115, 4; 242, 2. See also *PK*; p. 102.
219. *Vāl. Rām.*, *Uttarakāṇḍa*, 31, 7-10, 32, 1-7; *Vāl. Rām. Ko.*, p. 28; S.C. De, *HRIAS*, p. 116.
220. *Anuśāsana Parva* (1978), 152, 3-4, See also *Ādi Parva*, 31, 5-8, 98, 1 (for Karkotak and Haihaya); *Udyoga Parva* (1969), 19, 22-23, 163, 4 (for Māhismatipur and its ruler Nila); *Mbh. Ko.*, p. 33 (for Kṛtavirya Arjuna), Sorensen, *INM* (london, 1904), Vol. I, p. 458, Vol. II, p. 457, and *Sabhā Parva*, 28, 17 and 24 (for Māhismatipur).
221. *PPIP*, p. 557.
222. *DDEI*, pp. 343-44.
223. See Jamna Das Akhtar's Notes, cf. *CAGI*, XXI, B.C. Law, *IETBJ* (Delhi, 1980), pp. 104-5.
224. See his "Archaeological and Tradition" and "Mahismati and Maheswar" in *AIHA* pp. 280 & 215 respectively.
225. H.D. Sankalia "Excavations at Maheshwar and Nevasa and their possible bearing on *Purāṇic* History" in *JBBRAS*, Vols. 33-32 (1959), pp. 229-39, "Traditional Chronology and C-14 Dates of Excavated Sites" in *JIH*, Vol. XLII (1964), pp. 635-50; *PPIP*, p. 434. See also H.D. Sankalia, B. Subba Rao and S.B. Deo "Excavations at Maheshwar and Navdatoli" 1952-53, Poona-Baroda, 1958, pp. 37-41.
226. See his "Prehistoric Colonization in India : Archaeological and Literary Evidence" in *AIHA*, pp. 303 and 306.
227. *AIHA*, pp. 226-27.
228. *SI*, Vol. 1, line, 11, p. 178, See also his *SGAMI*, p. 97.
229. *JRAS*, 1910, 444-47, *Ep. Ind.*, Vol. 19, p. 261.
230. *JNSI*, Vol. XVII, 1955, p. 95.
231. See B.C. Law, *GAGI*, p. 157; *ABORI*, Vol. XVII, 1935-36, Pt. III, pp. 225 ff.; *HGAI* (Paris, 1954), p. 174; *IETBJ* (Delhi, 1980), pp. 34, 77 and 104; *CAGI*, p. 411-12; *CASR*, Vol. VII, pp. 103-6; S.B. Chaudhuri, *ESAI* (Calcutta, 1955), p. 67; Pargiter (tr.) : *Mkd.*, Vol. II, Pt. II, p. 333; Dashratha Sharma, *JOIB*, Vol. X, (1960-61), pp. 306-7; Wilford, *As. Res.*, Vol. 9 (1809), p. 105; Mirashi, *JRAS*, 1910, pp. 440-44; Sleeman, *JASB*, 1837, p. 622; *JAOS*, Vol. 58, pp. 262 ff.; Pandya, *JGRS*, Vol. VIII (1940), pp. 135-38; S.K. Dikshit, *PIHC* (Calcutta, 1939), pp.131 ff. 141 ff; D.B. Diskalkar Maheshwar through the Ages in *PIHC* (Patna Session 1946), pp. 61 ff; P.V. Kane, *JBBRAS*, Vol. 27 (1951), p. 38.
232. Thomas Watters, *YCTI*, Vol. II, pp. 251-52; *CAGI*, pp. 412.
233. *Sabhā Parva*, 28, 1-15, 37-43.
234. *Digha Nikāya*, Ed. T.W. Rhys Davids and J.E. Carpenter (PTS. London, 1890-1911), ii, pp. 220 and 236.

235. Ch. 43, vv. 24-35, See also Vasudeva Sharana Agrawala, "Brahma Purāṇa Men Ujjayini" in *Itihāsa Darśana* (Collection of papers, collected and ed. by P.K. Agrawala, Varanasi, 1978), pp. 157-60 and D.R. Bhandarkar, Carmichael Lectures, 1918, p. 54 (for two capitals of Avanti Kingdom).
236. *Bmd.*, IV, 40, 91.
237. *Vṣṇ*, iv, 11, 20; *Mats.*, 43, 30-44; *Vāl. Rām. Bāla Kāṇḍa*, 75, 23-27. See also C. Chakraberti, *CSARM* (Delhi, 1979), p. 21.
238. See *Vṣṇ.*, IV 11, 22-24; *Mats*; 43, 45-46.
239. *Br.*, 13, 199-200½.
240. *Vy.*, 94, 49-50.
241. For an overall impression see *Mats.*, 43, 45-49; *Vy.*, 94, 48-53; *Vṣṇ.*, IV, 11, 22-24; *Agn.*, 275, 5-11; *Br.*, 13, 201-5; See also *Bhāg.*, IX, 23, 28 (where Tālajanghas have been called Kṣatriyas); *Bmd.*, iii, 69, 52; 74, 265.
242. *Vṣṇ.*, iv, 11, 24-30; *Br.*, 13, 206-7; *Mats.*, 43, 49-52; *Bhāg.*, IX, 23, 29-30.
243. See Pargiter (tr.) : *Mkd.*, pp. 344-5, 371; also his "The Earliest Indian Traditional History" in *JRAS*, 1914, p. 274 and *JRAS*, 1910, p. 867, note.
244. *AIHT*, pp. 270-71.
245. McCrindle, *AIT*, p. 166.
246. *Vy.*, 95, 14-47; *Bmd.*, iii, 70, 14-48; *Vṣṇ.*, iv, 12, 2-45; *Mats.*, 44, 14-47; *Br.*, chs. 14 and 15, 1-30; *Pdm.*, v. 13, 1-30; *Lg.*, i, 68, 21-49; *Krm.*, i, 24, 1-32; *Agn.*, 275, 12-23; *Gar.*, i, 139, 25-35; *Bhāg.*, ix, 23, 30 to 46; ix, 24, 1-11 (for Vidarbha dynasty); *Hv.*, ch. 37; H.H. Wilson, *op. cit.*, iv, XII, pp. 336-39.
247. *Vy.*, 95, 14-19; *Vṣṇ.*, iv, 12, 2-3; H.H. Wilson, *op. cit.*, iv, xii, p. 336; *Bmd.*, iii, 70, 19; *Agn.*, 275, 13.
248. H.H. Wilson, *op. cit.* ch. XII, p. 337; Pargiter, *AIHT*, p. 269, fn. 3 and 4. See also *PK*, p. 420; Motichandra, Sārthavāha (Patna, 1966), pp. 76-77 and J.C. Jain, *op. cit.*, p. 342 for identification of Mṛttikavati.
249. *Br.*, 15, 15.
250. *Mkd.*, (tr.), p. 359; *JASB*, 1895, p. 255.
251. *Āśvamedha Parva* (1977), 84. 1-6.; *Mbh. Ko.*, p. 29.
252. See *Vy.*, 95, 34-36; *Mats.*, 44, 36; *Hv.*, *Viṣṇu Parva*, 60; H.H. Wilson, *op. cit.*, ch. XII, 337-38; Pargiter, *AIHT*, p. 269, fn. 5; *Mkd.*, (Eng. tr.), p. 335; B.C. Law, *GAGI*, p. 159; *Mbh. Sabhā Parva*, 28, 37-43 (for Bhojakata of Rukmin); *Ind. Ant.*, Vol. III, pp. 262-63 (for identification of its two capitals Kundina and Bhojakota).
253. *Sṛṣṭikhaṇḍa*, 34, 157.
254. A.D. Pusalker, *op. cit.*, p. 288.
255. Pargiter, *JASB*, 1895, p. 253; N.L. Dey, *GDAMI* (2nd edn. London, 1927), p. 48; B.C. Law, *GAGI*, p. 25.
256. *Vy.*, 96, 1-160; *Vṣṇ.*, iv, 13, 1-6, 8-10, 19-20, 35-70, 108-61; iv, 14, 1-45; iv, 15, 11f; *Mats.* 44, 45-85; 45, 1-34; 46, 1-29; *Bhāg.*, ix, 24, 6-45; *Br.*, 14, 14-25; 15, 30-45, 16, 9-49; *Agn.*, 275, 24-49; *Bmd.*, iii, 71, 1-144; *Pdm.*, V, 13, 31-117; *Lg.*, i, 69, 1-45; *Harivaṁśa Parva*, ch. 34; *Krm.*, i, 24, 35-70; *Gar.*, i, 139, 36-55; *Bhv.* (Supra), Vol. 1, p. 305, V. 50, *PK.*, pp. 5, 113, 393, 476, 496 and 499.
257. 1. 138; 210, 15-19; 211, 2; 212, 12; 213, 1, 23-29, 34-35,, 52-53; *Mbh. Ko.*, p. 34. See also *Āraṇyaka Parva*, 13.1; *Udyoga Parva*, 28, 11-12.
258. *Mahābhārata*, 13, 24-25, 51; 14, 4.
259. *Mahābhārata Shānti Parva*, 82, 8-17, 25-26 and 29.
260. *Hindu Polity* (Bangalore, 1981), *APP.*-A, p. 335, also *Bh. Sv.*, Vol. 3, pp. 259-60.
261. Cf. J.C. Jain, *op. cit.*, pp. 448, 459-60.
262. Cf. B.C. Law, *IETBJ*, pp. 99-103.
263. V.S. Agrawala, *IP*, p. 454.
264. Ed. with Hindi tr. by V. Gairola (Varanasi, 1984), XI, 1, p. 669.
265. A Cunningham, *CAI* (London, 1891), p. 70; J Allan, *CCBM* (London, 1936), pp. Clvi-Clvii, 281.
266. *Bh. Sv.*, Vol. 3, pp. 259-60.

267. D.C. Sircar, *SI*, Vol. I, lines 11 and 12, p. 178, also *Ep. Ind.*, Vol. 8, pp. 44 and 60.
268. *GESM* (Lucknow, 1945), p. 64.
269. 13, 4-7.
270. *Vy.*, 96, 1-2; *Vṣṇ*, iv, 13, 1; *Bmd.*, iii, 71, 1-2; *Br.*, 15, 30-31; *Mats.*, 44, 47-8; *Pdm.*, V, 13, 31-2; *Lg.*, i, 69, 1-2.
271. IV, 13.7; H.H. Wilson, *op. cit.*, p. 339; *PK*, pp. 385 and 420.
272. See V.S. Agrawala, *IP*, pp. 56-57 (for identification of Śālva country).
273. *GDAMI* (2nd edn. London, 1927), p. 132.
274. *AIHT*, p. 279.
275. *GAGI*, p. 133.
276. *Āraṇyaka Parva* (1969), 15, 1-22; 16, 2-4, 13-23; 17, 1-33; 18, 1-24 and chs. 19-21; *Mbh. Ko.*, p. 100.
277. *Bh. Sv.*, Vol. I, pp. 206-9.
278. *GAGI*, p. 133.
279. *Mats.*, 44, 36, 66, 70; *Vy.*, 95, 35-36; *Bmd.*, iii, 71, 128; *Pdm.*, V, 13, 56; *Br.*, 15, 54,; B.C. Law, *IETBJ*, 105-6; *GAGI*, p. 159; *ABORI*, XVII (1936), Pt. III, pp. 230 ff; N.L. Dey, *op. cit.*, p. 132; B.C. Law, *GEB*, p. 62.
280. J.C. Jain, *op. cit.*, 342.
281. *Vy.*, 96, 6-18; *Mats.*, 44, 51-60; also 46, 1-29 (for Bhoja dynasty with full of confusion); *Bmd.*, iii, 71, 6-18; *Br.*, 15, 35-45; *Pdm.*, V, 13, 35-45; *Lg.*, i, 69, 4-9; *Krm.*, 1, 24, 35-38; *Vṣṇ.*, IV, 13, 3-6; *Agn.*, 275, 25-27; *Gar.*, i, 139, 38; *Bhāg.*, ix, 24, 9-11.
282. *AIHT*, p. 279.
283. *Mbh. Sabhā Parva*, 28, 1-15, 37-43.
284. *AIHT*, p. 280.
285. *Vy.*, 45, 132, 86, 28; *Bmd.*, 2, 16, 64; *Mats.*, 113, 52; *Pdm. Svargakhaṇḍa*, 6.35; B.C. Law *IETBJ*, p. 108; *GAGI*, p. 167; "Some Ancient Indian Tribes" in *Indian Culture*, Calcutta, Vol. I, No. 3, pp. 384-86; *GEB*, p. 62.
286. See J.F. Fleet, *JRAS*, 1910, pp. 824 f; K.P. Jayaswal, *JBORS*, Vol. III, pp. 425 f, Vol. XIII, pp. 221 f; Vol. VI, pp. 364 f; K.P. Jayaswal and R.D. Banerji, *Ep. Ind.*, Vol. XX, pp. 72 ff; R.C. Majumdar, *Ind. Ant.*, Vol. XLVII, pp. 223 f, Vol. XLVIII, pp. 187 f, note; D.C. Sircar, *SI*, Vol. I, pp. 220 f; Rajbali Pandeya, *HLI* (The Chowkhamba Sanskrit Series), Vol. XXIII, p. 46.
287. B.C. Law, *IETBJ*, pp. 106-7, also p. 44.
288. E. Hultzsch, *CII* (Oxford, 1925), Vol. I, (inscriptions of Aśoka by A. Cunningham), p. 48; D.C. Sircar, *SI*, Vol. I, pp. 17-38; D.R. Bhandarkar, Aśoka, Calcutta, 1932 (the Carmichael Lectures, 1923), pp. 29 ff; Janardan Bhatt, *Aśoka Ke Dharmalekha* (Delhi, 1957), pp. 30, 45, 55 and 74; B.C. Law, *HGAI* (Paris, 1954), p. 114.
289. *IETBJ*, pp. 106-7; *GEB*, p. 62.
290. See *Ep. Ind.* Vol. I, p. 187 and *JRAS*, 1908, p. 132.
291. *Sṛṣṭikhaṇḍa*, 47, 163.
292. See *Karna Parva* (1973).
293. *Ep. Ind.*, Vol. IV, pp. 158 ff.
294. 96. 57-61, 62-66.
295. *Sabhā Parva*, 13, 24-25.
296. Cf. B.C. Law, *IETBJ*, p. 107.
297. *SBE*, Vol. XLV, pp. 71 and 118.
298. *Jātaka*, i (ed. by V. Fausboll, London, 1877-97), p. 45.
299. Eds. L. Feer and Mrs. Rhys Davids (*PTS* London, 1884-1904), Vol. I, pp. 61-62.
300. *IETBJ*, pp. 106-7; *GEB*, p. 62.
301. *Mats.*, 47. 17-29.

302. *Ādi Parva*, 210, 15-20; 213, 23-29, 34-38, 52-55; *Sabhā Parva*, 13, 5-17, 24-45, 49-55; 18, 1; *Āraṇyaka Parva*, 16, 5-18; also 13, 31 (only for Dvārakā city); *Mausala Parva* (1977), 2, 1-20; 3, 1-22; 4, 33, 36 and 41, ch. 5, 6, 1-15, 7, 9-22, 8, 4-11, 32-47, 58-74; *Āśvamedha Parva* (1977), 84, 13-16; *Mahāprasthānika Parva* (1977), 1, 7-9 (for Parikshit's accession to Hastināpur and Yādava prince Vajra's to Indraprastha) and 1, 43 (for Sunken Dvārakā city in the Sea as beheld by the Pāṇḍavas with their own eyes), See also *Bh. Sv.*, Vol. I, pp. 143-44; Vol. 3, pp. 221-23; *Mbh. Ko.*, p. 100.

303. *Bhāg.*, 1, 10, 7-10, 34-35; 1, 11, 8-14; ix, 3, 1-2, 27-36; X, 50, 7-19, 21-23, 34-57; X, 52, 5 f; X, 53, 5-22; X, 58, 12; X, 80, 8-12; XI, 30, 4-25, 30-48; XI, 31, 23-25, See also *Srimad Bhāgavata Mahāpurāṇa* (text with tr. by C.L. Goswami, 2nd edn. Gorakhpur, 1982), Pt. 11 (Bks. ix-12), X, 50, 1-20, 46-55; XI, 30, 10-48; XI, 31, 46-48; also ix, 3, 27-36; *Hv.* (*Viṣṇu Parva*), 34, 1-22; 35, 1-111; 36, 1-40; 39, 10-32; 56, 7-35, 58, 3-56; *Vṣṇ*, V, 23, 9-15; V, 24, 5-7, V, 37, 22-39, 42-63; V, 38, 34-35; also iv, 1, 62-65, 91-94; *Br.*, 14, 53-56; 195, 1-12; 196, 5-15; 210, 56-58; 212, 9; also 7, 29-32; *Vy.*, 96, 46, 57-61, 62-66, 83-93, 111-42, see upto 258, also 86, 24-28; *Bmv.* (*Uttarakhāṇḍa*, tr. and ed. by T. Jha, Allahabad, 1985 A.D.), 103, 7-33 and 80; *Pdm.*, VI, 200, 66, 246, 40-45; ch. 272; 279, 56 ff, also V, 23, 10; *Bhv.* (Bombay, 1910), iv, 129, 44 f; also *Kṛṣṇajanmakhaṇḍa* (*Uttara.*) ch. 103; Skd. (Ānandāshrama Skt. Series, Poona, 1893) *Prabhāsa-Khaṇḍa* (44 chs. on Dvārakā); also 4.52; see also *Mats.*, 12, 21-22, 69, 9; *Agn.*, 273, 12; *Bmd.*, iii, 61, 18-23; iii, 71, 48, 62 and 85; *V h*, 149, 7-8; *PK*, pp. 121, 242 & 393.

304. *Bh. Sv.*, Vol. 1, pp. 206-7.

305. Cf. J.C. Jain, *op. cit.*, p. 460.

306. *SBE*, Vol. 45, p. 115.

307. V. Fausboll (ed.); The *Jātaka* (London, 1877), Vol. IV, pp. 82-85.

308. *IHQ*, Vol. X, pp. 541-50.

309. *ASI*, Vol. XLV (Imperial Series), Introd., p. 1.

310. *Bombay Gazetteers*, Vol. VIII, pp. 518-20, 552, also Hathibhai Shāstri, *POC*, Vol. VIII, pp. 1171-73.

311. "Report on the Antiquities of Kathiawad and Kacch" (London, 1876), p. 13.

312. See his tr. of *Mkd.*, p. 289, note.

313. "Ancient Towns and Cities in Gujarat" in *Ind. Ant.*, Vol. 54 (1925), p. 25 as a supplement to "Towns and Cities in Gujarat and Kathiawar" *Ind. Ant.*, 1924.

314. "Dvārakā" in B.C. Law Volume 1 (Calcutta, 1945), pp. 218-24.

315. "Antiquity of Modern Dwarka or Dwarka in Literature and Archaeology" in *AIHA*, pp. 191-201.

316. "Archaeology and Tradition" in *ibid.*, p. 280.

317. For fuller details see *Indian Express* (Sunday Edn.) March 6, 1988, see also *The Hindu* (Gurgaon), Sunday, Feb., 7, 1988; Gunakar Mule, "Kahāṅthi Shri Kṛṣṇa Ki Dvārakā" in *Gaganāncal* (ed. G.K. Mathur, Bharatiya Śāṁskṛtika Sambandha Pariṣada, Delhi, 1987), 10, 3, pp. 8-15.

318. *Mahābhārata*, 16, 19.

319. 80, 83. See also G.P. Singh, "A Fresh Literary Discovery of the seals of Dvārakā in the Epic Age as a supplement to Archaeological Discovery by S.R. Rao" (Paper presented in the Ancient India Section of Indian History Congress held at Calcutta University, Dec. 1990); see *PIHC*, Calcutta Session, 1990, p. 161.

320. See Romila Thapar "Purāṇic Lineages and Archaeological Cultures" in *Purātattva*, Vol. 8, 1975, pp. 87-92 and *AISH* (Hyderabad, 1984), pp. 242-52; H.D. Sankalia, "Archaeology and Tradition" in *op. cit.*, pp. 278-79.

321. D.P. Agrawal "Protohistoric Chronology and Technology and Ecological factors . . ." in *Purātattva*, 1967-68, No. 1, pp. 17-23; D.P. Agrawal and Sheela Kusumgar, Prehistoric Chronology and Radio-Carbon Dating in India (Delhi, 1974), pp. 103-13.

322. See *Mats.*, 48, 1-5; *Vy.*, 99, 1-6; *Agn.*, 277, 1-4; *Br.*, 13, 141-50; *Bmd.*, iii, 74, 1-6; *Gar.*, i, 139, 63-65; *Bhāg.*, ix, 23, 16-18; *Pdm.*, vi, 250, 1-2. (In *Br.*, 13, 147½-151—Pāṇḍya, Kerala, Cola and Kulya are said to have sprung from Athāhrida, son of Karuroma of Puru dynasty). It is very difficult to ascertain the truth about them.

323. *Mats.*, 48, 6-9; also 114, 40-41; *Vy.*, 99, 6-12; *Vṣṇ.*, iv, 17, 1-5; *Agn.*, 277, 4-5; *Bmd.*, iii, 74, 7-12; *Br.*, 13, 148-53; *Gar.*, 1; 139, 64-5; *Bhāg.*, ix, 23, 14-16; H.H. Wilson, *op. cit.*, iv, XVII, pp. 353-54.
324. H.H. Wilson, *Ar. Ant.* (Delhi, 1971), p. 131, note, 5; B.C. Law, *IETBJ*, pp. 86-87; J. Das Akhtars notes in *CAGI*, xxii-xxiii.
325. B.C. Law, *HPL* (Delhi, 1983), Vol. II, p. 434.
326. *RV*, 1, 126-7. They also find mention in the *AV*, V, 22, 14.
327. Mortimer Wheeler, Charasada (Oxford, 1962), Summary facing, p. 1.
328. *Karna Parva* (1973), 30, 26-28, 35-47; *Bh. Sv.*, Vol. 2, pp. 266-67, See also H.H. Wilson, *HHK* (Calcutta, 1960), pp. 105-7; D.C. Sircar, *SGAMI*, pp. 238-39.
329. W.H. Schoff, *Periplus*, p. 183.
330. See *Mats.*, 48, 13-21; *Vy.*, 99, 15-24; *Vṣṇ.*, iv, 18, 5-10; *Br.*, 13, 23-26½; *Bmd.*, iii, 74, 15-20; *Agn.*, 277, 5-10; *Gar.*, 139, 65-70, *Bhāg.*, ix, 23, 16-20; *Vmn.*, 38, 12; *PK*, pp. 495-96 (for Śivis), H.H. Wilson (tr.) *Vṣṇ.*, vi, XVIII, pp. 354-55; *Hv.*, 1, 31, 27-30.
331. *Vṣṇ. Dh.*, 1, 156, 24-28.
332. B.C. Law, *IETBJ*, pp. 88-92; also *Jātaka*, VI, p. 137.
333. *Ind. Ant.*, 1891, p. 375. See also A.K. Chatterjee, "The Kekayas in Ancient India" in *JIH*, Vol. LVI (1978), Pt. II, pp. 198-202.
334. *RV*; VII, 18.7; *Ait. Br.*, VIII, 23, 10; 38.3; *Go. Br.* II, 9; VI, Vol. 1, p. 103.
335. *Ādi Parva*, 88, 6, 17-19; also ch. 1, 172-75; *Drona Parva* (1975), 6, 2-7; *Sabhā Parva*, 29, 5-6; *Bhiṣma Parva*, 10.7.
336. *Ar. Ant.*, p. 199.
337. "On the Ancient Indian tribes" in *ZFKDM*, Vol. III, p. 183, ref. to in *ibid.*, fn. 2.
338. V.S. Agrawala, *IP*, pp. 9, 37 and 54.
339. B.N. Puri, *ITP*, p. 72.
340. *Op. cit.*, p. 54.
341. *Br. Sam.* (Bombay, 1952), iv, 24; V, 67; XI, 59-60; XVII, 19.
342. B.C. Law, *HPL*, (Delhi, 1983), Vol. I, p. 292; Vol. II, p. 661; *IETBJ*, pp. 91-92; *GEB*, pp. 51-52; also Fausboll, *Jātaka*, iv, pp. 401-12.
343. M.L. Feer, A Study of the *Jātakas* (tr. by G.M. Foulkes from the French article in the *JA*), Delhi, 1984, p. 22.
344. Cf. B.C. Law, *GAGI*, p. 31.
345. Sylvain Levi, *JA*, 1915, pp. 37 and 70; also *JUPHS*, XV, 2, pp. 27 and 36.
346. McCrincle, *AIMA* (London, 1877), p. 111, note; Arrian's India (Leipzig, 1867), 1st part, chs. 1-XVII cf. *ibid.*, p. 196; R.C. Jain, McCrindle's *AIMA* (Delhi, 1972), p. XV; McCrindle, *The Invasion of India by Alexander the Great* (Edinburg, 1892), p. 366, note; also McCrindle, *AIT*, pp. 285-92.
347. *GDAMI* (London, 1927), p. 202.
348. *Ep. Ind.*, XVI, 1921, p. 16.
349. *CAGI*, pp. 17, 1-74.
350. *HGAI* (Paris, 1954, Delhi, 1976), pp. 66, 127-28; *IETBJ*, pp. 92.
351. *Bh. Sv.*, Vol. 1, pp. 158-59.
352. See *CASR*, VI, p. 200-4; Prinsep's Essays on Indian Antiquities (London, 1858), pp. 112-14, Pl. VIII, 2-3 (for Carllyle's and Stacy's description respectively); *ASIAR*, 1915-16, Pt. I, p. 15 (for Coins found by Bhandarkar); *JASB*, 1887, p. 14; *JNSI*, Vol. IX, p. 83, Pl. V; John Allan, *CCBM* (London, 1936), p. cxxiii; V.A. Smith, *CCIM* (Oxford, 1906), 1, p. 180, Pl. XXI, 12; E.J. Rapson, *Indian Coins* (Varanasi, 1969), p. 14.
353. *Mats.*, 48, 22-29; *Vy.*, 99, 25-28; *Vṣṇ.*, iv, 18, 11-14; *Agn.*, 277, 11; *Br.*, 13, 36; *Bhāg.*, ix, 23, 5-6; *Bmd.*, iii, 74, 24-35; *Gar.*, i, 139, 68-74; Pargiter (tr.) *Mkd.*, p. 324-9, 334; *Mbh.*, *Ādi Parva*, 207, 9-10. See also H.C.

Chakaladar, *AOEI* (Calcutta, 1962), pp. 63-64.

354. *Mats.*, 48, 97; *Vy.*, 99, 104-6; *Vṣṇ.*, iv, 18, 19-20; *Agn.*, 277, 13-14; *Br.*, 13, 42-43; *Mbh. Ko.*, pp. 14-15; H.H. Wilson (tr.), *Vṣṇ*, iv, xviii, pp. 355-56. See also *JS*, p. 50; *Bmd.*, iii, 74, 197; *PK*, p. 166.

355. James Legge, *RBK* (Oxford, 1886, 2nd edn. Delhi, 1972), ch. XXXVII, p. 100; also H.A. Giles, *RBK* (Cambridge, 1st Pub. 1923, Varanasi, 1972), p. 65.

356. *YCTI*, Vol. II, pp. 181-82.

357. *CAGI*, p. 402.

358. D.P. Agrawal and Sheela Kusumgar, *op. cit.*, pp. 103 ff.

359. B.B. Lal, "The Copper Hoard Culture of the Ganga Valley" in *Antiquity*, Vol. XLVI, 1972, pp. 282-87.

360. H.D. Sankalia, *PPIP*, pp. 397-98.

361. B.B. Lal, "The Ochre-coloured Pottery—A Geochronological Study" in *Purātattva*, 1971-72, No. 5, pp. 49-58; "A Deluge", *American Anthropologist*, Vol. LXX, 1968, pp. 857-63; "The Copper-Hoard Culture of the Ganga Valley" in *Antiquity*, Vol. XLVI, 1972, p. 286.

362. *Vy.*, 99, 119-165; *Vṣṇ*, iv, 19, 1-10; *Mats.*, 49, 1-42; *Agn.*, 278, 1-9, 15; *Br.*, 13, 2-8, 50-63; *Gar.*, i, 140, 1-8; *Bhāg.*, ix, 20, 1-39; 21, 1, 20-1; *Hv.*, 1, 32, 1-22; H.H. Wilson, (tr.), *Vṣṇ.*, iv, XIX, pp. 356-59.

363. *Mbh.*, *Ādi Parva*, 89, 5-25; 90, 10-38.

364. *Mats.*, 49, 10-11; *Vy.*, 99, 133-34; *Agn.*, 278, 7; *Br.*, 13, 56-57; *Vṣṇ.*, iv, 19, 10-11; *Bhv.* (Supra), I, pp. 302-3, vv. 33-36; *Mbh.*, *Ādi Parva*, 89, 16; 90, 29-30 and 33; *Hv.*, 1, 32, 9; also *Pdm.* (*Svargakhaṇḍa* by A.C. Śāstri, Varanasi, 1972, 6, 8-12).

365. *Ādi Parva*, 69, 49.

366. Pargiter, *AIHT*, pp. 272-73.

367. H.D. Sankalia, *PPIP*, p. 557.

368. *Mats.*, 49, 42; *Vy.*, 99, 165; *Vṣṇ.*, iv, 19, 27-28; *Bhāg.*, ix, 21, 20; *Bhv.* (Supra), 1, pp. 303-4, vv. 45-47; *Vmn.*, 63.2. (for Hastināpur); *PK*, p. 550; H.H. Wilson (tr.); *Vṣṇ.*, iv, XIX, pp. 360-61; *Mbh.*, *Ādi Parva*, 90, 36; *Mbh. Ko.*, p. 737; *Bh. SV*, Vol. 1, p. 84.

369. *Bhv.* (Supra), V. 46, pp. 303-4.

370. Pargiter, *op. cit.*, p. 137. See also A Ghosh, The City in Early Historical India (Simla, 1973), pp. 43 ff.

371. *Mats.*, 49, 43-44; *Vṣṇ.*, iv, 19, 29-30; *Vy.*, 99, 165-66.

372. *Ādi Parva*, 89, 26; also 90, 37-38 (only Ajamidha).

373. *Vy.*, 99, 166-214; *Vṣṇ.*, iv, 19, 30-75; *Mats.*, 49, 44-79; 50, 1-5, 17-22; *Br.*, 13, 102-7; *Agn.*, 278, 25-27; *Bhāg.*, ix, 21 and 22; *Gar.*, i, 140, 24-5; H.H. Wilson, *op. cit.*, pp. 361-63; *Hv.* 1, 32, 23-47.

374. *Ādi Parva*, 89, 26-41; 90, 38-41.

375. *Mats.*, 91, 43-47; *Vy.*, 99, 167-70; *Vṣṇ.*, iv, 19, 30-32. See also *RV*, 8, 55,4; *Bhāg.*, XII, 1.49 and *Mats.*, 191, 26 for Kānvāyana Brāhmaṇas.

376. *Vy.*, 99, 170-82; *Vṣṇ.*, iv, 19, 33-47; *Mats.*, 49, 48-50.

377. *Mats.*, 49, 48-59.

378. *Mats.*, 50, 1-4; *Vy.*, 99, 194-96, *Vṣṇ.*, iv, 19, 56.

379. *Mats.*, 50, 19-20; *Vy.*, 99, 214; *Vṣṇ.*, iv, 19, 74-75.

380. *Ādi Parva*, 89, 27-29.

381. *Vy.*, 99, 215-22, 229-49; *Mats.*, 50, 19-57; *Vṣṇ.*, iv, 19, 75-84; 20, 3-9, 31-53; *Br.*, 13, 108-23; *Agn.*, 278, 27, 31-41; *Gar.*, i, 140, 25, 30-40; *Bhāg.*, ix, 22, 4, 9-33; *Hv.*, 1, ch. 32, vv. 47-78.

382. *Ādi Parva*, 89, 42-55; 90, 40-96.

383. *Vy.*, 99, 184-93; *Vṣṇ.*, iv, 19, 48-55; *Bhāg.*, ix, 21, 27-30; *Gar.*, i, 140, 14-16.

384. *Mats.*, 49, 70-79.

385. *RV*, 4, 4, 43 and 44.

386. *Vy.*, 99; 196-99; *Hv.*, 1, 32, 26-29; *Mats.*, 50, 2-4; *Vṣṇ.*, iv, 19, 57-59; *Bhāg.*, ixz, 21, 27-35. See also *Vmn.*, 37, 26; 63, 13. (for Pañcāla); *PK*, p. 287 and Gustav Oppert, *OIB* (Delhi, 1972), pp. 608-9. H.C. Raychaudhuri (*PHAI*, 6th edn. Calcutta, 1953, p. 71) thinks that the Pañcālas (the federation of five peoples) "consisted of five clans—the Krivis, the Turvaśas, the Kesins, the Sriñjayas and the Somakas". See also R.C. Jain, *EAB.* (Varanasi, 1970), p. 127.
This does not tally with that of the *Purāṇic* accounts, and, moreover, we do not find any historical basis to support such views.
387. For details see Pargiter, "The North Pañcāla Dynasty", *JRAS*, 1918; B.C. Law, "The Pañcāla and their capital Ahicchatra" in *MASI*, No. 67, Delhi, 1942; *CAGI*, p. 303; A. Cunningham, *CAI* (Varanasi, 1971), p. 79; N.L. Dey, *GDAMI* (Delhi, 1971), pp. 2, 145.
388. *Bh. Sv.*, Vol. 1, p. 85; Pargiter, *AIHT*, p. 113.
389. *Vy.*, 99, 194-212; *Hv.*, 1, 32, 36-42; *Bhāg.*, ix, 22, 1-2; *Mats.*, 50, 1-16; *Br.*, 13, 93-101; *Vṣṇ.*, iv, 19, 15-18; *Agn.*, 278, 18-25; *Gar.*, i, 140, 17-24.
390. *Mbh. Ādi Parva*, 89, 33-35. See also *Bh. Sv.*, Vol. I, pp. 84-85.
391. *Divyāvadāna*, p. 435.
392. Pargiter, *AIHT*, p. 281; *JRAS*, 1910, pp. 49-50; 1918, pp. 246-8.
393. *Vy.*, 99, 183 and 191-92; *Mats.*, 49, 78; *Vṣṇ.*, iv, 19, 53-54.
394. *Vy.*, 99, 170-82; *Mats.*, 49, 47-59, *Hv.*, 1, 23, 28 and ch. 24; *Vṣṇ.*, iv, 19, 11-13; *Bhāg.*, ix, 21, 22-26; *Gar.*, i, 140, 10-13.
395. *Vāl. Rām.*, *Bāla Kāṇḍa*, 33, 19; also *Vāl. Rām. Ko.*, p. 57.
396. *Hv.*, 1, ch. 23, V, 28; ch. 24.
397. *Mbh. Ādi Parva* (Gorakhpur, *Samv.*, 2044, 5th edn.), ch. 137, vv. 3, 5-7, 9-61, 63-69, 70-76; see also *CAGI*, p. 303.
398. *Ādi Parva*, 175, 5; 176, 1; *Udyoga Parva*, 1, 4; 19, 32.
399. *Vy.*, 99, 211-12; *Hv.*, 1, 32, 42; *Mbh.*, *Āraṇyaka Parva*, 13, 2; *Udyoga Parva*, 168, 8-9; *Ādi Parva*, 175, 7-9.
400. *Sabhā Parva*, 48, 42; *Udyoga Parva*, 217, 17.
401. *Ādi Parva* (Gorakhpur edn.), 137, 76; *Udyoga Parva*, 19, 30.
402. *Ādi Parva* (Ibid), 137, 73-74.
403. *Vāl. Rām.*, *Ayodhyā Kāṇḍa*, 68, 13.
404. *Ibid.*, *Bāla Kāṇḍa*, 33, 19.
405. *Sṛṣṭikhaṇḍa*, 34. 38; *Pātālakhuṇḍa*, 12, 40-41.
406. 1. 23, 28.
407. *Yajurveda*, VI., Vol. 1, p. 149; also *Tai. Sam.*, 7, 4, 19, 1— (for Kāmpilya)
408. Malalasekera, *DPPN*; ii, p. 108.
409. *Ibid.*, 1, p. 525.
410. B.C. Law, *IETBJ*, p. 97; *GEB*, pp. 18-19.
411. Law, *GEB*, pp. 18-19.
412. B.C. Law, *IETBJ*, p. 97.
413. J.C. Jain, *LAIJC*, pp. 337, 340-41.
414. *SBE*, Vol. XLV, pp. 56-57, 80-81.
415. McCrindle, *AIMA* (Calcutta, 1960), pp. 139-40.
416. McCrindle, *AIT*, pp. 131-33, 161, 164-66.
417. D.C. Sircar, *SI*, Vol. 1, p. 97.
418. *Ibid.*, p. 265, Line 21, note 2.
419. *AI*, No. 1, 1946, pp. 37-40; *AI*, No. 8, 1952, pp. 33-34; Mortimer Wheeler, *EIP* (London, 1968), pp. 131-32;

A Ghosh, *op. cit.*, pp. 60-72; see also V.A. Smith in *YCTI*, Vol. II, p. 338.

420. *AI*, No. 1, 1946, pp. 55-58; Mortimer Wheeler, *op. cit.*, pp. 26-35; H.D. Sankalia, *PPIP*, App. II, Table 6, p. 566. See also *Purātattva*, No. 5, 1971-72, pp. 65-83 (on *OCP* and *NBPW*).

421. *AI*, No. 10-11, p. 140.

422. *CASR*, Vol. XI, p. 12.

423. "*Rigveda Brāhmaṇas : The Aitareya and Kauṣītakī Brāhmaṇas*", tr. by A.B. Keith and ed. by C.R. Lanman (Harvard Oriental Series, 1st edn. 1920, first Indian Reprint, Delhi, 1971), Vol. XXV, *Ait. Br.*, VIII, 14, p. 45; see also "Aitareya Brāhmaṇan of the Rigveda" by Martin Haug Vol. 1 (Varanasi, 1976) text, VIII, 14, pp. 203-4; Vol. II (1977); tr. pp. 518; A.A. Macdonell and A.B. Keith, VI, Vol. I, pp. 154-55, 165 f, 190, 468-69; Vol. II, p. 126; see also *Ait. Br.*, 38.3.

424 *Śat. Br.*, iii, 2,3,15; V, 5,2,3,5; V, 7,2,8; also *Śat. Br.* (tr. J. Eggeling's), *SBE*; Vol. XII, pp. XLI-XLIII; *Tai. Br.*, 1.8.4; *Go. Br*; 1.2.9; 2.10; See also *Vājasaneyi Saṁht* (Kanva recension), XI, 3,3; 6.3.

425. *Kauṣītakī Upaniṣad*, iv, 1; see also *Bṛhadāraṇyaka Upaniṣad*, III, I, I; iii, 9, 19-20; VI, 2.1; *Chāndogya Upaniṣad*, V. 3.1; *Jaiminiya Upaniṣad Brāhmaṇa*, III, 7.6; iv, 7.2; iii, 6, 1.30; 6, 1.1.2; 6.3.9; iii, 30, 6; IV, 6.2. in the *Upaniṣadic* age the importance of the Kuru-Pañcālas increased because of the frequent visits of their *Brāhmaṇas* to Videha of Janaka to attend sacrifices.

426. *Vedic* India (tr. from the French by Philip Spratt), *Classical India*, Vol. 3, Delhi, 1971, pp. 126-27.

427. *Ādi Parva*, 3, 20-23, 176, 5-9, 27; *Sabhā Parva*, 26, 1-3; *Karna Parva* (1973), 30-73; *Udyoga Parva*, 162, 22, 168, 1-5.

428. *Karna Parva*, 30, 60, 30, 79; *Mats.*, 114, 34; *Vy.*, 45, 109, *Vṣṇ.*, 2, 3, 15; *Bmd.*, 2, 16, 40; *Agn.*, 118, 8.

429. *Op. cit.*, p. 615.

430. *Vy.*, 9, 214; *Mats.*, 50, 19-21; *Vṣṇ.*, iv, 19, 75-76; *Agn.*, 278, 24-25; *Br.*, 13, 106; *Bhāg.*, ix, 22, 3-4; *Hv.*, 1, 32-47.

431. *Ādi Parva*, 89, 42; 90, 39-40.

432. *RV*, 10, 32, 9; 10, 33, 4; also *VI*, Vol. I, pp. 165-67.

433. A.D. Pusalker, *Studies in Epics and Purāṇas of India* (Bombay, 1955), pp. 42-48.

434. *Vy.*, 99, 214-15; *Mats.*, 50, 20-22; *Vṣṇ.*, iv, 19, 75-77; *Agn.*, 278, 24-26; *Br.*, 13, 106; *Bhāg.*, ix, 22, 3-4; *Vmn.*, 22, 59, 60; *Ādi Parva*, 89, 43; *Udyoga Parva*, 19, 29 (for Kurujangala); *Bh. Sv.*, Vol. 1; pp. 84-85, 99, 255, Vol. 2, p. 143; *PK*, pp. 118-119; *Mbh. Ko.*, pp. 199-200.

435. 81, 175.

436. 23, 12, 9.

437. *Manusmṛti* (Varanasi, 1970), 2, 17.

438. *Āraṇyaka Parva*, 81, 1-7.

439. *Ibid.*, 81, 177; *Vmn.*, 23, 12, 15.

440. *Manu.*, 2, 19.

441. 23, 1, 1.

442. *Śat. Br.*, 4.1.5.13; *Tai. Br.*, 5.1.1.

443. *Āraṇyaka Parva*, 81, 1-7, 20, 125, 175-78.

444. *Vmn.*, 23, 11, 23, 11, 1-4, 23, 12, 1-16, 23, 13, 3-8, 23, 21, 17-25.

445. *RV*, 3, 23.4; also *Śat. Br.*, 5.4.2.1.

446. *IETBJ*, pp. 34-35; *ABORI*, XVII, 1936, Pt. III, p. 226.

447. *Vmn.*, 22 and 23; *Bhv.* (Supra), vv. 66-67, pp. 307-8.

448. *CASR*, XIV, pp. 86-106.

449. *Bh. Sv.*, Vol. I, p. 255.

450. *Ādi Parva*, 1, 44-45.

451. *Vy.*, 99, 215-20, 229-50; *Mats.*, 50, 23-26; 34-57; *Vṣṇ.*, iv, 19, 78-80; iv, 20, 1-53; *Agn.*, 278, 27-41; *Br.*, 13, 1 7-25; *Agn.*, 278, 27-41; *Br.*, 13, 107-25; *Bhāg.*, ix, 22, 4-18, 22-39; *Hv.*, i, 32, 49-52; H.H. Wilson, *op. cit.*, pp.

365-67.

452. *Ādi Parva*, 89, 44-55, 90, 40-46. See also Lassen, *Ind. Ait.* (Leipzig, 2nd edn. 1867-73), Vol. 1, pp. 734-38.
453. *Mats.*, 50, 37-39; *Vy.*, 99, 234-35.
454. *Ar. Ant.*, p. 125.
455. *Virāta Parva* (1969), 1, 9-14.
456. *Ayodhyā Kāṇḍa*, 68, 13.
457. *Ādi Parva*, 94, 10, 102, 22; *Mbh. Ko.*, p. 737.
458. *Ibid.*, 105, 17-22.
459. *Ibid.*, 55, 22.
460. *Ibid.*, 55, 23-25.
461. *Ibid.*, 213, 13, 22-24, 35; *Bh. Sv.*, Vol. 1, p. 129.
462. *Ibid.*, 213. 22.
463. *Ibid.*, 3, 144-46; also 219, 1-2; *Bh. Sv.*, Vol. 1,pp. 128-29.
464. *Sabhā Parva*, chs. 23-31.
465. *Mbh. Udyoga Parva*, 19, 7-32; *Drona Parva* (1975), 6, 2-7, also 19, 7-35.
466. *Śānti Parva*, 38, 37-38, 43, 45-49; 39, 1-10; *Udyoga Parva* (173, 2) also refers to Hastināpur.
467. *Mbh. Ādi Parva*, 213, 29, 34, 38, 52-55; *Mausala Parva*, 8, 10-11, 32-47, 68-70, 73-74; *Vṣṇ.*, V, 38, 34-35; *Bhāg.*, 10, 58, 1-12; 11, 30, 48; 11, 31, 25; *Pdm.*, VI, 279, 56f.
468. *Ādi Parva*, 37, 9.
469. *VI*, 196, 5; *VI*, 200, 5, 75-77; See also *Vṣṇ. Dh.*, 1, 80, 14.
470. *Jātaka*, V. pp. 57, 484; *VI*, p. 255.
471. *Ibid.*, 111, p. 400; iv, p. 361.
472. *Ibid.*, V, p. 57 f; VI, p. 255.
473. *Ibid.*, 11, pp. 213-14. Indapatta also finds mention in *Jātaka*, 11, pp. 365 f. According to M.L. Feer (*op. cit.*, p . 22), altogether seven *Jātakas* refer to Indraprastha.
474. II, p. 359.
475. 3rd Pallava, p. 116; 64th, p. 9; also 64th, p. 62.
476. *Divyāvadāna*, p. 435.
477. Chap. III.
478. III, p. 361.
479. J.C. Jain, *op. cit.*, p. 340.
480. V.S. Agrawala, *op. cit.*, pp. 55 and 73.
481. B.N. Puri, *op. cit.*, pp. 75 and 79.
482. McCrindle, *AIT*, pp. 121-23, 129-35; Lassen, *Ind. Ait.*, Vol. III, p. 151 cf. *Ibid.*
483. *India from the Earliest Ages* (Hindu, Buddhist and Brāhmanical Revival, Vol. III of the History of India, Delhi, 1973), p. 29.
484. "Hastinapur and Indraprastha in Ancient India" in *Journal of the Asiatic Society of Bombay*, Vol. 30, 1955, Pt. 1, pp. 9-16.
485. *Bh. Sv.*, Vol. 2, p. 143.
486. B.B. Lal, "Excavations at Hastināpur and other Explorations in the Upper Ganga and Sutlej Basins (1950-52)" in *AI*, Nos. 10-11, 1954-55, pp. 5-151; Mortimer Wheeler, *op. cit.*, pp. 129-31, also 26 f, 30 f, 117, 120; *IAR*, 1963-69.
487. M. Wheeler, *op. cit.*, pp. 117, 124, 126, 129; B.B. Lal, "The Copper Hoard Culture of the Ganga Valley" in Antiquity, Vol. XLVI, 1972, pp. 282-87; "Further Copper Hoards from the Gangetic Basin and a Review of the Problem" in *AI*, no. 7, 1951, pp. 20-39; H.D. Sankalia, *PPIP*, pp. 397-98.

488. H.D. Sankalia, *op. cit.*, pp. 399-400.
489. M. Wheeler, *op. cit.*, pp. 122-23.
490. "A Deluge ? which Deluge ? . . ." *American Anthropologist*, VOl. LXX, 1968, pp. 857-63; *Antiquity*, XLVI, 1972, p. 286. "The Ochre-coloured Pottery—A Geochronological Study" in *Purātattva*, 1971-72, No. 5, pp. 49-58.
491. *PPIP*, pp. 400-1.
492. See *ibid.*, p. 403, App. 11 (Table 6), p. 566; *AIHA*, pp. 277, 308.
493. "Excavations at Hastināpur", *op. cit.*
494. *PPIP*, p. 403.
495. *Civilisation of the Indus Valley and Beyond* (London, 1966), p. 98.
496. *EIP*, p. 26 f.
497. *Ibid.*, p. 130.
498. *PPIP*, p. 403.
499. See R.S. Sharma, "The Later *Vedic* Phase and the painted Grey Ware" in *PIHC* (35th Session), Jadavpur, 1974; "Iron and Urbanisation in the Gangetic Basin" in *IHR*, Vol. 1, 1974, pp. 99-102. See also Bridget and F.R. Allchin, *The Birth of Indian Civilisation : India and Pakistan before c.* 500 B.C.; (Harmondsworth, London, 1968), pp. 144 ff.
500. *The Past and Prejudice* (Delhi, 1975), p. 27.
501. *RV*, 2.20.8, 4.27.1, 7.15.14, 10, 101.8.
502. *Ṛgveda*, 10, 101, 8.
503. Purana Qila, New Delhi, *IAR*, 1954-55, p. 17; *AI*, Nos. 10 and 11, 1954-55, p. 140.
504. *Op. cit.*, p. 132.
505. Wheeler, *op. cit.*, pp. 30 ff.
506. See *Vy.*, 93, 26-27, 99, 219-20; *Mats.*, 50, 26; *Vṣṇ.*, iv, 19, 79-80; *Hv.*, 1, 32, 32, 53; *Bṃd.*, iii, 68, 27; *Br.*, 12, 15-16; *Agn.*, 278, 27; *Gar.*, i, 140, 25-30; *Bhāg.*, ix, 22, 4-6; *Mbh.*, *Ādi Parva.*, 57, 1-2, 7-9, 12 and 27; *Bh. Sv.*, Vol. I, p. 57; *PK*, p. 175-76.
507. *IAR*, 1958-59, p. 26; *IAR*, 1961-62, p. 98.
508. *Cetiya Jātaka* (E.B. Cowell's edn., *Cambridge, 1895-1813)*, Vol. III; *Bk.* VIII, no. 422.
For fuller details see B.C. Law, *Ancient Mid-Indian Kṣatriya Tribes* (Calcutta, 1924), Vol. 1, Ch. V.
509. There is no uniformity in the epic and *Purāṇic* accounts with regard to the number and names of the sons of Vasu. The *Purāṇas* invariably refer to his six or seven sons, whereas the *Mahābhārata* mentions only five sons. See *Mats.*, 50, 26-28; *Vy.*, 99, 220-22; *Vṣṇ.*, iv, 19, 80-81; H.H. Wilson, (tr.), *Vṣṇ.*, IV, XIX, p. 364. *Bhāg.*, IX, 22, 6-7; *Hv.*, 1, 32, 54; *Mbh.*, *Ādiparva*, 57, 28-30; *Bh. Sv.*, Vol. 1, p. 59.
510. *Sabhā Parva*, 17, 4; *Mbh. Ko.*, *p. 503.*
511. *Vāl. Rām.*, *Bāla Kāṇḍa*, 32, 1-4, 7-9; also *Vāl. Rām. Ko.*, pp. 71, 103, 315.
512. *Sabhā Parva*. 19, 1-3; also Lassen, *Ind. Ait.*, Vol. I, p. 604; Vol. II, p. 79.
513. III, pp. 68 f.
514. *Vy.*, 99, 222-28; *Mats.*, 50, 28-33; *Vṣṇ.*, iv, 19, 82-84; *Agn.*, 278, 28-31; *Hv.*, 1, 32, 55-60; H.H. Wilson, *op. cit.*, p. 365.
515. Legge, *RBK*. Ch. XXVIII, p. 81.
516. Samuel Beal, The life of Hiuen Tsang (London, 1884, Delhi, 1973), p. 113; also *BRWW* (London, 1884, 1906), Vol. ii, pp. 149-50; Thomas Watters, *YCTI*, Vol. II, p. 148; E.B. Cowell, "The Chinese Buddhist Pilgrims in India" in *Ancient India* (Delhi, 1983), p. 76.
517. *CAGI*, p. 390.
518. *ASIAR*, 1905-6, p. 58.
519. B.C. Law, Rājagṛha in Ancient Literature . . . in *MASI* (Delhi, 1938), No. 58, p. 1.

520. *Sabhā Parva*, 17, 5-9, 21-23; 18, 21-30; 19, 1-3, 4-13, 14-18; 22, 42; *Bh. Sv.*, Vol. 1, pp. 143, 146-47.
521. *Sabhā Parva*, 13, 29-32.
522. (Pub. Bhavnagar, 1930), 247, 16 f.
523. *Vāl. Rām. Bāla Kāṇḍa*, 32, 6.
524. *CAGI*, pp. 330 f.
525. *Op. cit.*, pp. 127-28.
526. *CAGI*, p. 332.
527. E.J. Rapson, *Ancient India* (Varanasi, 1981), p. 86.
528. D.C. Sircar (ed.), *SI*, Vol. 1, p. 70, note 2.
529. "New Light on Chalcolithic cultures of Uttar Pradesh" in *The Statesman*, October 13, 1978.
530. G.R. Sharma, *The Excavation at Kausambi*, 1957-59 (Allahabad, 1960), pp. 6-7.
531. *Ibid.*, p. 22.
532. K.K. Sinha, "Stratigraphy and Chronology of Early Kausambi—A Reappraisal" in *Radiocarbon and Indian Archaeology*, eds. D.P. Agrawal and A Ghosh (Bombay, 1973), pp. 231-38; A Ghosh, *op. cit.*, pp. 11, 62, 80-81.
533. *As. Res.*, Vol. ix, p. 433.
534. *IAR*, 1958-59, p. 45.
535. *Jātaka*, Vol. III, pp. 454, 460-61.
536. "Can we Reconstruct Pre-Bhārata war History" ? in *JBHU*, Vol. IV, pp. 183-223.
537. "On the Chronology of the Hindus" in *As. Res.* (Delhi, 1979), Vol. 2, p. 111.
538. *Ibid.*, pp. 111-12; also Lord Teignmouth, The works of Sir William Jones (London, 1807), Vol. IV, p. 42.
539. Lord Teignmouth, *op. cit.*, pp. 42 f.
540. "On the Principal Eras and Dates of the Ancient Hindus" in *As. Res.*, Vol. 5 (Delhi, 1979), p. 315.
541. *HASL* (Varanasi, 1968), p. 268.
542. *Ibid.*, p. 267.
543. *The History of India*, ed. by E.B. Cowell (9th edn. London, 1911), p. 11.
544. *EHI* (4th revised edn. by S.M. Edwards, Oxford, 1967), p. 1.
545. *Ibid.*, pp. 4, 10-11.
546. *IGI*, Vol. II, "Epigraphy in Indian Empire", pp. 3-6.
547. *HSL* (3rd edn. Delhi, 1972), p. 10.
548. For details see Shri Ram Sathe, *Search for the year of Bhārata war*, Hyderabad, 1983.
549. *Vṣṇ.*, p. 389. In other versions of (iv. 24.32) it is also 1,015 years.
550. For details see H.H. Wilson (tr.), *Vṣṇ.*, p. 389; The *Matsya Purāṇam* (ed. by J.D. Akhtar and notes by B.C. Majumdar, S.C. Vasu, H.H. Wilson, Bentley, Wilford and others, *SBA*, Delhi, 1972), Vol. 1, *APP*, ii, xiii-xxvi; *APP*, iii, xxxviii-xl, xlvi-xlviii,; A.K. Majumdar, *EHIDS* (Delhi, 1981), Vol. 1, pp. 59-60; *Mats.* (Gorakhpur, 1985), note, p. 1053; F.E. Pargiter, *PDKA* (London, 1913), pp. 58, 74-76; H.C. Raychaudhuri, *PHAI* (6th edn. Calcutta, 1953), p. 29; A.D. Pusalker, cf. *The Vedic Age*, p. 273; S.N. Pradhan, Chro, *Anc. Ind.* (Varanasi, 1979), p. 248; also "Intervening Age between Parikshit and Nanda" in *JIH*, Vol. XIX, pp. 1-16.
551. The *Matsya Purāṇa*, cf. *SBA*, App. III, xxxviii-xl.
552. *Ibid.*, App. iii, Xlviii (according to Sridhara Svāmin).
553. *Ibid.*, App. ii, Xiii-xxvi.
554. *HCSL* (3rd edn. Delhi, 1974), Intr; LXXVI (*Purāṇic Chronology*).
555. *PDKA*, pp. 13-22, 67-9; *AIHT*, p. 180. See also Kota Venkatachalam, *The Plot in Indian Chronology* (Vajayawasa, 1953), pp. 23 f, 38 f, 81 f; *Chronology of Ancient Hindu History* (Vijayawada, 1957), Pt. 1, pp.

34f, 95-100, 281 f.

556. *Op. cit.*, p. 389.

557. *HAI*, (Delhi, 1985), pp. 109, 112 and 149.

558. *Op. cit.*, p. 245.

559. *PDKA*, pp. 25-6, 69-70; *AIHT*, p. 179.

560. *Mbh.*, *Mausala Parva*, 2, 2,10 and ch. 8; *Mahāprasthānika Parva*, 1,7-9; *Bhāg.*, XII, 2, 33; *Vṣṇ.*, iv, 24, 110-11.

561. *The Bhārata War and Purāṇic Genealogies* (Calcutta, 1969), pp. 19 ff.

562. The *Matsya*, *SBA*, App. ii, XIII-XXVI.

563. *Date of Mahābhārata Battle*, a monograph of the Institute of Chronology, (Gurgaon, 1976), pp. 39-40. See also his *Ancient India*, a Chronological Study, 1500-400 B.C.

564. *Op. cit.*, pp. 273, 304, 316,; see also *Studies in Epics and Purāṇas of India* (Bombay, 1955).

565. *Op. cit.*, p. 30.

566. "An Essay on the Sacred Isles in the West with other Essays connected with that work"—Essay : III—"Of the kings of Magadha : their Chronology" in *As. Res.*, Vol. IX (Delhi; 1979), pp. 87-89; Essay IV—Vikramāditya and Śālivahana : their respective Eras, *ibid.*, pp. 208-10.

567. *As. Res.*, Vol. IX (Ibid), pp. 86-88, 118, 161, 208-10.

568. Presidential address to the "Archaic and Early cultural History" Section (1) of the Indian History Congress, *Proceedings of the Third Session* (Calcutta, 15-17 Dec. 1939), pp. 68-77.

569. *JBORS*, Vol. I, pp. 67 f, iii, pp. 346 f, iv, pp. 26-35.

570. *Orion* (or Research into the antiquities of the Vedas; Bombay, 1893), pp. 207, also 34-37.

571. *Op. cit.*, pp. 268-69.

572. *The Chronology of Ancient India* (Madras, 1901).

573. *HA.*, Vol. IV, pp. 74-7, ref. to in F.E. Partiger's "Ancient Indian Genealogies and Chronology", *JRAS*, 1910, p. 56.

574. *Ibid.*

575. *AIHT*; pp. 179-182; *PDKA*, pp. 58, 74.

576. *DDEI*, pp. 344 ff, 359 f; "The Ancient Chronology of India" in *JAOS*, Vol. 77, No. 2, April-June, 1957 and No. 4, Dec., 1957.

577. *Op. cit.*, pp. 59-60.

578. Gunakar Mule, *op. cit.*, pp. 8-15; *The Hindu*, Gurgaon, Sunday, Feb. 7, 1988.

579. 'On the Chronology of the Hindus" (written in 1788) in *As. Res.* (Delhi, 1979) Vol. 2, p. 113; also Lord Teignmouth, *op. cit.*, pp. 42-46.

580. Lord Teignmouth, *op. cit.*, p. 52.

581. *Mats.*, 273, 37-45; also Ch. 9, 1-3 and Ch. 142, Ch. 165; *Vy.*, 99, 416-23; *Vṣṇ.* iv, 24, 105-7, 112; also VI, 1,1-6; *Bmd.*, 11, 24, 234; 111, 74, 225-36; *Bhāg.*, XII, 2, 26-32; H.H. Wilson, *op. cit.*, *Hindu concept of Time*, pp. 467 f; J. Bentley, "On the Hindu System of Astronomy, and their connection with History in Ancient and Modern Times" in *As. Res.* (1st Pub. 1809, Delhi, 1979), Vol. VIII, pp. 195-244; Capt. F. Wilford, "Chronology of the Hindus" in *As. Res.* (Delhi, 1979), Vol. V, pp. 241-46. Colebrooke, "The Saptarsi Era" in *As. Res.* (1st Pub. 1811, Delhi, 1979), Vol. ix, pp. 323-76; Hindu Chronology in *EB.*, London (1st Pub. 1768), 1071, Vol. 5, p. 722; see also D.R. Mankad's papers on "Manvantaras" in *IHQ.* Vol. XVIII, pp. 208-30 and on "Yugas" in Bhārtiya Vidya Bhavan, Bombay, Vol. VI, pp. 6-10.

582. A. K. Majumdar, *op. cit.*, pp. 55-56, 114; *EB*, Vol. 5, p. 722.

583. *Mats.*, Ch. 142.

584. See also *Matsya*, *SBA*, App. iii, -XL-Xliii, Xlvi-Xlviii; App. ii-Xiii-xxvi."The date of the Mahābhārata War" by Sris Chandra Vidyarnava.

585. *As. Res.*, Vol. ix, pp. 84-87.

586. "On the Principal Eras and the Dates of the Ancient Hindus" in *As. Res.*, Vol. V, (Chronological Table of Ancient Eras), pp. 318-38.

587. "Historical view of Hindu Astronomy", p. 67 cf. H.H. Wilson, *op. cit.*, p. 390.

588. *Ibid.*

589. CAGI, p. 390.

590. *The History of India* (1866), pp. 257 f, 272 f.

591. Eds. E.B. Cowell and R.A. Neil (Cambridge, 1886, repted, 1970) pp. 72 and 435.

592. *Memoirs of the early life of Śakya-Siṁha* (ed. R.L. Mitra, Calcutta, 1877), ch. III.

593. *AIT*, note, pp. 121-23.

594. Mats., 50, 78-79; *Vy.*, 99, 270-71; *Vṣṇ.*, iv, 21, 6-8; *Bhv.*, (Supra), pp. 309-10.

595. F. Max Müller, *HASL*, pp. 235-45, 267-68; *Csoma*, Tibetan Grammar, pp. 199-201 (dates from 2422-546 B.C.) *cf.* Max Müller, *op. cit.*, p. 237; Lassen, Indian Antiquities, Vol. II, pp. 58 f.*cf.* Max Müller, *op. cit.*, p. 236; Wilford, *As. Res.*, Vol. ix, pp. 88-89 (1367); *As. Res.*, Vol. 5, pp. 241 ff; William Jones, *As. Res.*, Vol. 2, p. 113 (1,027 B.C.); J. Bentley, *As. Res.*, Vol. 5, pp. 318-20 (from 1,002, 1,043, 1,101 B.C.); S.H. *li.*, The Life of Hiuen-Tsang, translated by S. Beal (London, 1914), p. 98; *The Mahāvaṁśa*, (tr. into English by W. Geiger, *PTS*, London, 1912), Introd., pp. *Xl-Xlvi*; *The Dipavaṁśa*, ed. and tr. by H. Oldenberg, (London, 1879, Delhi, 1982); J.F. Fleet, *JRAS*, 1904, pp. 5-20; 1909, pp. 5-30, 325-44; *Ind. Ant.*, Vol. X (1881), pp. 153 f (for Buddhist Chronology); Max Müller, *Ind. Ant.* (1884), pp. 148-51; J. Burgess, *Ind. Ant.* (1884), pp. 117 f; P.C. Mukherjee, *Ind. Ant.* (1903), pp. 227-33 (for Hindu view of Buddhist Chronology); D.S. Triveda, Roads to Indian History (Varanasi, 1978), pp. 22, 29 (*c.* 1873-1793 B.C.); see also his *Bhārat kā Nayā Itihāsa* (Pune), pp. 10-15.

596. W. Geiger, *op. cit.*

597. See his excavation report of Hastināpur in *op. cit.*, also S.P. Gupta and K.S. Ramachandran (eds.) : *Mahābhārata*—Myth and Reality—Differing Views (Delhi, 1976)—a collection of views of about 40 scholars.

598. *AIHA*, pp. 299 and 306.

599. See *History of India*, p. 28; *AISH*, pp. 285-86.

600. *Ibid.*, p. 31; *ibid.*, pp. 255, 334.

601. *CHI* (Delhi, 1962), Vol. 1, *Ancient India*, p. 273.

602. *Op. cit.*, pp. 55-56.

603. See his articles, "The Kaliyuga Era" in *JRAS*, 1911, pp. 476 ff, also 479 ff, 675 f; "Hindu Chronology" in *EB.*, 11th edition, Vol. XII, p. 497.

604. *Br. Sam.* (text with tr. by Pt. Baldeva, Pt. Mishra, Bombay, 1952), XIII, 3. See also *Garga-Yuga Purāṇam*, a Chapter from the *Garga Saṁhitā*, ed. D.R. Mankad, Vallabhvidyanagar, Gujarat, 1951; K.P. Jayaswal, "Historical data in the Garga Saṁhitā and the Brāhmin Empire", in *JBORS*, 1928, Vol. XIV, pp. 397-421.

605. *IHQ*, 1932, pp., 85 f; *Modern Review*, June, 1932, pp. 650 ff.

606. *The Bṛhat-Saṁhitā by Varāhamihira with the commentary of Bhaṭṭotpāla* (ed. by Sudhakara Dvivedi, B.H.U.), p. 281.

607. *Br. Sam.*, VIII, pp. 20-21.

608. "Bhārata Battle Traditions" *JRABS*, Vol. IV, 1938, No. 3 (Sept. 1939), pp. 393-413.

609. *HHK* (Calcutta, 1960), *APP*, IV, p. 96.

610. *Rājataraṅgini* (tr.), 2nd edn. Delhi, 1960, 1, 49-56.

611. Fleet, *Ind. Ant.*, V, pp. 67 ff, VIII, pp. 237 ff; Kielhorn, *Ep. Ind.*, VI, pp. 11, 12; D.C. Sircar (ed.) : *SI*, Vol. II (Delhi, 1983), pp. 443, 444-48.

612. For details see *Kāmarūpa Śāsanāvali* (ed. by D. Sarma, Gauhati, 1981), Pt. II—text, line 7, p. 21, Pt. III, tr., p. 161, note 4, p. 162; M.M. Sharma, *Inscriptions of Ancient Asam* (Gauhati, 1978), text-line 7, p. 41, tr., p. 50.

613. See "Era of the Hindu" in *Āin-i-Akbarī* by Abūl-Fazl Allami (tr. into English by Col. H.S. Jarrett and annotated by Sir J. N. Sarkar, Delhi, 1988), Vol. 2, pp. 15-16; also *Āin-i-Akbarī* (Calcutta, 1867), p. 269.
614. See *Harishcandra Candrikā* (Aug. A.D. 1874), pp. 87-90.
615. See Buhler's view in *Ind. Ant.*, Vol. VI, pp. 264-68.
616. Lord Teignmouth, *The Works of Sir William Jones* (London, 1807), Vol. IV, p. 52.
617. "An Essay on the Sacred Isles in the West . . " in *As. Res.* Vol. IX (Delhi, 1979), Essay—III, p. 86; Essay IV, pp. 118, 161 and 208.
618. "On the Principal Eras and Dates of the Ancient Hindus" in *As. Res.*, Vol. 5 (Delhi, 1979), pp. 318 f; "On the Hindu System of Astronomy, and their connection with History in Ancient and Modern Times" in *As. Res.*, Vol. 8 (Delhi, 1979), pp. 225 ff.
619. See his *Ancient Indian Chronology*, Calcutta, 1947.
620. For details see K.S. Raghavan, *The Date of Mahābhārata War and Kali-Yugadi*, Madras, 1969; V.B. Ketkar, "On the use of Astronomical Phenomena in fixing the Chronological periods in Indian History" in *POC*, 1st Session, Pune, 1919; "The Date and Time of Mahābhārata War—Approach on Astronomical Considerations" in *ABORI*, Pune, 1944, Vol. XXV.
621. See his *The Plot in Indian Chronology and Chronology of Ancient Hindu History.*
622. "Five thousand years ago—the Mahābhārata War" in *JIH*, Vol., XVI (1931) pp. 239 ff; See also his Indian Chronology, Bhāratiya Vidya Bhavan, Bombay, 1963.
623. See "Mythology to History through Astronomy (ed. N. Mahalingam), Madras, 1980 and "*A Peep into the Past History* (ed. V.G. Ramachandran), Madras, 1982. (Both the above works are the proceedings Vols. containing the reasearch papers presented in the Seminars held at Madras in 1979 and 1981 respectively).
624. *The Mahābhārata : A Criticism* (Delhi, 1966), pp. 56-61.
625. J.W. McCrindle, *AIMA* (London, 1877), (Indika's Fragments, 23-24), p. 208; also pp. 201 and 204.
626. *Natural History* (New York, 1962), VI, XXI, 4-5.
627. *Indica* (Teubner's edn; Leipzig; 1867), Pt. 1, IX; also tr. of *Arrian*'s Indica, 1st Part, chs. 1-XVII, *cf. AIMA*, p. 208.
628. 52.5.
629. *Cf.*, J.W. McCrindle, *AICL* (Westminster, 1901, repted., Delhi, 1984), p. 108.
630. "Chronology of the Hindus", *Purāṇic Chronology, As. Res.*, Vol. 5 (Delhi 1979), pp. 291-2.
631. *AICL*, note, 1, p. 108.
632. *EHIDS* (Dacca, 1920, Delhi, 1981), 2 Vols., Vol. 1, pp. 58-60, 232.
633. *The Vedic Age*, pp. 273-75.
634. *As. Res.*, Vol. 8, p. 228.
635. "Ancient Indian Genealogies and Chronology" in *JRAS*, 1910, p. 56.
636. *Op. cit.*, pp. 273 ff.
637. *AIHA*, pp. 301-6.
638. *Op. cit.*, Vol. 1, pp. 229-55, Vol. II, pp. 354-416.
639. D.P. Agrawal and Sheela Kusumgar, *Prehistoric Chronology and Radio-Carbon Dating in India* (Delhi, 1974), pp. 103 ff.
640. "Archaeology and Tradition" in *AIHA*, p. 277; "Prehistoric Colonization; Archaeological and Literary Evidences" in *op. cit.*, p. 308; *PPIP*, p. 403.
641. *PPIP*, pp. 400-1, 403-4; *AIHA*, pp. 277, 308-9.
642. "Radio-carbon Dates in India . . ." in *Radiocarbon and Indian Archaeology*, eds. D.P. Agrawal and A. Ghosh (Bombay, 1973), p. 219.
643. See H.D. Sankalia, *PPIP*, Appendix II, Table 6, pp. 564-66; "Traditional Indian Chronology and Carbon-14

Dates of Excavated Sites" in V.N. Mishra and M.S. Mate (eds.) : *Indian Prehistory*, 1964 (Poona, 1966), pp. 219-35; "Radiocarbon Dates in India,, their consistency and cultural implications" in D.P. Agrawal and A. Ghosh, *op. cit.*, pp. 211-21; "Traditional Chronology and C-14 Dates of Excavated Sites" in *JIH*, Vol. 42, (1964), pp. 635-50; D.P. Agrawal, S. Guzder and S. Kusumgar, "Radiocarbon Chronology in Indian Prehistoric Archaeology" in *JIH* (Golden Jubilee Vol.), 1973, pp. 1-20; See also D. Mandal, *Radiocarbon Dates and Indian Archaeology* (Allahabad, 1972); Bridget and F.R. Allchin, *The Birth of Indian Civilization : India and Pakistan before 500* B.C. (Baltimore, 1968), pp. 334-38.

644. See *Antiquity*, Vol. LII, 178, p. 117; *East and West*, Vol. 25, pp. 111-145; *American Antiquity*, Vol. 43 (1978), pp. 231-44.

# 3

# The Dynasties and Kingdoms of the Post- Bhārata War Period

## (from the accession of Parīkshit to the end of the Bārhadratha Dynasty)

THE dynasties and kingdoms of the post-Bhārata war period extending from the accession of Parīkṣit II or the beginning of *Kali-yuga* down to the sixth or fifth century B.C., notably, the Kurus (Pauravas) of Hastināpur and Vatsa (Kauśāmbī), Ikṣvākus of Kośala and Bārhadrathas of Magadha are well recorded in the *Purāṇas.* The dynastic genealogies as given therein are also of considerable historical importance. The *Purāṇic* list of the noteworthy kingdoms that continued to exist even after the Bhārata war comprise states in the eastern part of North India, Ayodhya, Kāśi, Videha, Magadha, Aṅga and Kalinga, the middle states of the Vitihotras, Haihayas and Aśmakas; and those that bounded these along their west side, North Pañcāla, the Kurus (the combined Kuru-Pañcālas), Śūrasena and Avanti. The *Purāṇas* specifically refer to the Kurus, Aikṣvākus, Pañcālas, Kaśis, Haihayas, Kalingas, Aśmakas, Maithilas, Śūrasenas and Vitihotras, who reigned contemporaneously in ten different kingdoms during the period following the great Bhārata War. They continued to maintain their existence till Mahāpadma Nanda absorbed all their kingdoms in his Nanda empire of Magadha and brought all their territories under his political sway about the middle of the fourth century B.C. The subject matter concerned has been discussed in detail in proper place. The *Purāṇas,* no doubt, provide the detailed accounts of the Pauravas, Aikṣvākus and the Bārhadrathas, but in case of other ten contemporary dynasties as mentioned above they transmit very meagre information, which do not go beyond the number of kings, etc.

The resurgence of the *Kṣatriyas* of both Solar and Lunar race after their annihilation at the hands of Paraśurama and their further expansion and rule over different kingdoms have been clearly mentioned in some of the *Purāṇas.* The *Purāṇas* refer to their 100 families, who belonged to the Ikṣvaku dynasty. The kings of the *Kṣatriya* dynasty of the

Lunar race consist of 200 Bhojas, 100 Kurus, 100 Pañcālas, 100 Dhārtarāṣtras (Pali Dhataraṭṭhas) and 100 Brahmadattas, who were no other than the Kāśi kings of the line of Bhārata, 80 Janmejayas, 100 Nāgas, 100 Hahayas, 100 Pratibindhyas (the descendants of Yudhiṣṭhira from Dropadi), 100 Kāśis and 2,000 Nipas and Śaśabindus or Śatabindus.[1]

### The Pauravas

One of the most illustrious kings of the Paurava line of the post-Bhārata War period was Parīkṣit II (son of Abhimanyu and grandson of Arjuna),[2] who ascended the throne of Hastināpur, the ancient capital of the Kuru princes, after thirty-six years of Yudhiṣṭhira's rule over it. He ruled for about twenty-four years and died at the age of sixty. Traditionally, he is placed between *c.* 3101-3041 B.C. But, on the other hand, some scholars on the basis of the *Purāṇic* chronology place him between *c.* 1884-1824 B.C. calculating the date of the Bhārata War in 1920 B.C.[3] Sometimes he is ascribed to the fifteenth century B.C. on the basis of the same chronology as discussed in the preceding chapter. But, scientifically he can be placed around *c.* 1,000 B.C. However, it is a proven fact that his reign constituted a glorious epoch in the history of the Pauravas. According to the epic and *Purāṇic* tradition, the Kuru kingdom over which he ruled roughly corresponded to modern Thanesvar, Delhi and the upper Gangetic *doāb*. The age-old hostility between the Nāgas and the Kurus resulted in his death at the hands of one of the Nāga kings Takṣaka (who has been mythologized as a king of the Snakes), son of Kadru of the Nāga dynasty. From the *Mahābhārata* it distinctly appears that Khandavaprastha and Kurukṣetra (along the banks of the Ikṣumati river) were the two chief habitats of the Nāgas.[4] It appears that they, after having lost their former two principalities on the Sarasvati and at Indraprastha, moved towards the north-west and established themselves at Takṣaśilā. Taking advantage of the unstable condition of the Pauravas following the Bhārata war the Nāgas led by Takṣaka subsequently marched towards Hastināpur and assailed the kingdom and king Parīkṣit probably died in his encounter with them or in his attempt to repulse them.

Parīkṣit was succeeded by his son Janamejaya III, the celebrated king of Hastināpur.[5] From the *Mahābhārata* we learn that in order to avenge his father's death he invaded Nāgas' capital, Takṣaśila and after having uprooted the Nāgas and conquered their capital he returned to Hastināpur.[6] Further, he is credited with having conquered the whole Sindhu region.[7] The conquest of Taxila in the extreme north-west indicates that the intervening Madra or Central Punjab might have fallen under the control of Janmejaya and the rulers of Kekaya territory lying to the east of Gāndhāra also might have acknowledged his suzerainty. The *Aitareya Brāhmaṇa* (VIII. 21) also refers to him as a great conqueror and performer of horse-sacrifice. In the *Purāṇas* he is said to have performed *Aśvamedha* and *Vājasaneya yajñas*. It was during his time that the *Brāhmaṇas* secured a honourable place in the society.[8]

The *Pañcaviṁśa Brāhmaṇa* (XIV. 1. 12; XXV. 3.6) affords a testimony to the fact that Janamejaya's brother Kakṣasena established a separate kingdom. We are told that Dṛti, apparently a priest of *king* Ābhipratarina, son of Kakṣasena performed a sacrifice in Khaṇḍava, where the epic locates Indraprastha, the ancient stately capital city of the Pāṇḍu princes.

After getting the evidence of the *Vedic* texts and that of the *Purāṇas* reconciled, we may safely assume that after the death of Janamejaya the Kuru Kingdom was split up into several parts. One part, which had its capital at Hastināpur, was ruled by the direct descendants of Janamejaya himself. Another part was ruled by the descendants of his borther Kakṣasena. The junior branch probably resided at Indraprastha, which continued to be the seat of kings claiming to belong to the Yudhiṭṭhilagotra (Yudhiṣṭhira's *gotra* or clan). The Kuru kings at Indraprastha continued to rule there long after the destruction of their principal metropolis, Hastināpur, and the migration of the elder line of Kuru kings to Kauśāmbi.

Janamejaya was succeeded by his son Śatānika I (contemporary of Ugrasena Janaka or Videha), whose son was Aśvamedhadatta, who was succeeded by his son Adhisīmakṛṣṇa, a king of repute, during whose reign *yajñas* were performed for three years in Puskara region and for two years on the bank of Dṛṣadvati in Kurukṣetra.[9]

It is said that the Paurava king Adhisīmakṛṣṇa, the Ikṣvāku king Divakara of Kosala and the Bārhadratha Senajit of Magadha were reigning contemporaneously. The approximate mean date of the beginning of their reigns has been fixed *c.* 850 B.C.[10] Hastināpur remained the outpost of the Hindu Kingdom of North India up to the time of Adhisīmakṛṣṇa. It was Nicakṣu (also called Vivakṣu, Nirvaktra, Nemicakra, etc.), the sixth in descent from Parīkṣit II or the son and successor of Adhisīmakṛṣṇa, who abandoned Hastināpur after being carried away by the Ganges and shifted his capital from there to Kauśāmbi (modern Kosam village on the Yamuna about 31 miles from south-west of Allahabad) as stated in the *Purāṇas*.[11] In fact, the Pauravas led by Nicakṣu settled in Vatsa bhumi with Kauśāmbi as their capital. The *Purāṇic* evidence can also be confirmed by the statements of Cunningham : "The city of Kośāmbi was one of the most celebrated places in ancient India and its name was famous amongst *Brāhmaṇs*, as well as Buddhists. The city is said to have been founded by Kusamba, the tenth indescent from Purūravas; but its fame begins only with the regin of Chakra (Nemicakra), the eighth in descent from Arjuna Pandu, who made Kośāmbi his capital after Hastināpur had been swept away by the Ganges".[12]

It is, indeed, a difficult task to determine the exact period of shifting of capital from Hastināpur to Kauśāmbi during the reign of Adhisīmakṛṣṇa's son, Nicakṣu. Pargiter has ascribed his migration from the northern part of the Ganga-Yamuna *doāb* to Kauśāmbi to *c.* 820 B.C.[13] But, from the Sanskrit Buddhist text (*Divyavadāna*, pp. 72, 435) it appears that Buddha (*c.* 563-483 B.C.) in course of his visit to Hastināpur found the city rich, prosperous and populous. The *Lalitavistara* (ch. III) also refers to Hastināpur as ruled by a king, who descended from the Pāṇḍava race, and was valiant and glorious among conquerers.[14] J.W. McCrindle also supports the statement and observes that "From a passage in the Lalitavistara we learn that at the time of birth of Śakyamuni (Buddha), a Pandava dynasty reigned at Hastinãpur, a city on the upper Ganges about 60 miles to the north-east of Delhi."[15] In the Jain sources also it is recorded that Hathinãpura (Hastinãpur), one of the ten capital cities of India, was visited by Mahavira (*c.* 599-527 B.C.).[16] If there is any element of truth in the Buddhist and Jain accounts, it implies that Hastinãpur must have been deserted sometime in the sixth-century B.C. after the visits of Buddha and Mahavira.

The *Purāṇic* evidence relating to the subject-matter concerned can reasonably be correlated to the archaeological data. The excavations carried out by Prof. B.B. Lal at Hastinãpur during 1950-52 have revealed that there were as many as five occupational periods at the site concerned with a definite break in between all of them. The first three periods have been dated as follows :

Period I to 1200 B.C.
Period II *c.* 1100 B.C. to *c.* 800 B.C.
Period III *c.* early sixth century B.C. to third century B.C.

The excavation has shown that the city was abandoned after being washed away in the flooding of the river Ganga sometimes after the second period, i.e. *c.* 800 B.C.[17] The transfer of the capital from here to Kauśāmbi archaeologically, might have taken place some time between *c.* 800 B.C. and *c.* 600 B.C.

The history of the Paurava kings of Kauśāmbi is still shrouded in obscurity. A list of twenty-three kings, who succeeded Nicakṣu one after another, as given in the *Purāṇas* include Uṣṇa (or Ukta, Bhuri), Citraratha, Śuciratha, Bṛṣṇimant, Susena, Sunitha (or Sutirtha) Ruca, Nṛcakṣu (or Tricakṣu) Sukhivala, Paripluta (or Pariṣṇava), Sunaya (or Sutapas), Medhāvin, Nṛpañjaya (or Purañjaya; Durva (or Urva), Tigma, Bṛhadratha, Vasudāman (or Sahasrānika), Śatānika II, Udayana, Vahirara (or Budhi, Naravahana), Daṇḍapāni, Niramitra and Kṣemaka.[18] Among the above mentioned rulers Śatānika and his son Udayana are important. The details are available only about them, which leave some room for doubt about the historicity of rest of them. Śatānika II, also styled as Parantapa, became the King of the Vatsa Kingdom with its capital at Kauśāmbi. According to Jain sources, when Mahavir visited Kauṣāmbi, the King of that place was Sayāṇiya or Sasānika (Śatānika).[19] Pradyota (called Pajjoya) of Avanti is said to have waged war against Sayāniya, father of Udayana of Kauśāmbi. When Pajjoya reached Kauśāmbi, Sayāniya transferred his forces from South bank of the Yamuna to the north bank to obstruct the movement of the enemy. In the meantime Sayāniya's forces achieved success in defeating the soldiers of Pajjoya. Pajjoya after being defeated fled in panic.[20] After Śatānika's death his son Udayana governed the kingdom. There was also a combat between him and Pajjoya. Udayana marched against Pajjoya of Ujjeni. In the fight Pajjoya suffered a humiliating defeat.[21]

From the Buddhist literature, it distinctly appears that in Buddha's time Udayana or Udena (*c.* 513-490 B.C.) of the Vatsa country with its capital at Kauśāmbi was a very powerful king. His father's name was Parantapa and his son's name was

Bodhikumara.[22] In the *Lalitavistara* Udayana is said to have been born on the same day as Buddha.[23] The same statement has been recorded in Hiuen-Tsang's accounts.[24] But, it does not contain substratum of truth. He was, of course, contemporary of Buddha. He was also known to Tibetans as the king of Kauśāmbi.[25] Tradition has preserved a long story of his love, adventures and war. We have it in two recensions, in Pali, the *Udena-Vatthu*[26] and in Sanskrit, the *Mākandika-avadāna.*[27] We are informed that he after being captured in a war by Pajjota (Pradyota) of Avanti cleverly eloped with his rival's daughter, Vāsuladattā, or Vāsavadattā and married her in his capital. The tradition recorded in Somadeva's *Kathāsaritasāgra* (ed. Bomb. 1889, 26-89; *Tarangas,* 11-16, IX, 29, 39, 69, 71) also confirms that Udayana of Kauśāmbi was married to Vāsavadattā, daughter of Pradyota of Ujjayini. Kauśāmbi[28] has been referred to as Vatsapattanam. The text wrongly refers to Śatānika's son Sahasrānika as the father of Udayana. As a matter of fact, Sahasrānika was his grandfather. Actually, he entered into matrimonial alliances with the ruling houses of Avanti, Magadha and Aṅga. He was at war with some of his contemporaries, kings of Kosala and Avanti. His victory over Kalinga is also supported by the tradition. Udayana of Vatsa or Kauśāmbi is described in Bhāsa's *Svapnavāsavadattā*[29] as a king of Bhārata dynasty. He is said to have married Padmavati, sister of king Udayibhadda or Udayin of Magadha. Kālidāsa in his *Meghadūta* (*Purvamegha,* V. 31) also refers to Udayana as the king of the Vatsa country (Vatsarāja) with its capital at Kauśāmbi.

The kingdom of Kauśāmbi seems to have been annexed to Avanti by Pālaka, son of Pradyota. From the dynastic list of the kings in the *Purāṇas* it appears that Udayana of Vatsa, Pradyota of Avanti and Prasenajita of Kosala were succeeded each by four or five kings after which their dynasties came to an end. The synchronism among the rulers as established in the *Purāṇic* and Buddhist tradition shows that Udayana of Kauśāmbi was not only contemporaneous with the Buddha, but also with Pradyota of Avanti and Ajātaśatru of Magadha.

The Purus with their capitals (Hastināpur, Indraprastha and Kauśāmbi) in the north, east and west, evidently ruled over a large area extending from the Delhi-Meerut region on the north to the Benares Division on the south-east. Ptolemy (*AIT,* p. 72) also refers to Kauśāmbi, the Puru's capital.

The archaeological excavations systematically carried out by Prof. G.R. Sharma at the site Kauśāmbi during 1949-1959 have brought to light 25 structural periods out of which the four periods are dated as follows :

I. *c.* 1165-885 B.C.
II. *c.* 885-605 B.C.
III. *c.* 605-45 B.C.
IV. *c.* 45 B.C.-*c.* 580 A.D.

The archaeological discovery included the rampart walls (mud rampart).[30] The rule of Udayana over Kauśāmbi can be connected with the early phase of third period, which is associated with NBPW phase of culture, dating back to the latter half of the first millennium B.C. The date suggested by the excavator with regard to the founding of Kauśāmbi has been questioned by some archaeologists.[31] The kingdom of Kosambi (the capital of Vatsa Raja) mentioned in an inscription taken from the gateway of the fort of Khara is dated in *Samvat* 1092 or A.D. 1035 (*As. Res.* IX, 433; *JASB*, V, 731), which shows its antiquity. Whatever may be the truth, the settlements of the Pauravas at Kauśāmbi in the sixth century B.C. cannot be doubted. It can rather be archaeologically confirmed. According to H.D. Sankalia, the beginnings of Kauśāmbi city "go back to the 8th century B.C., but with its moat and encircling protection wall over 3½ miles (5.7 km.) in length and provided with bastions and watch towers, will give idea of a city (state) in the Ganga Valley from the sixth century B.C. to second century B.C. . . . These indicate the kind of civic life people had at this period. In the earliest phase (*c.* 700 B.C.), as well as in the first five phases of period II, which is associated with the NBP, the houses had mud-walls. Around 400 B.C. appears the first brick structures"[32] Further, "If the capital of the Vatsa had such a grand and strong wall to protect it; that of Pradyota, Ujjayini, also boasted of a very thick and broad rampart from the earliest period (*c.* 700-500 B.C.) of the city's foundation."[33] Mortimer Wheeler has clearly stated that before and after the time of the Buddha (*c.* 500 B.C.) Kauśāmbi with a circuit of some four miles was the capital of the Vatsa kingdom of the *Purāṇas.* "The ramparts over thirty feet high and armed at regular intervals by bastions were built of mud revetted externally with a battered facing of baked bricks, which as excavated presents an imposing frontage. They were built before the introduction of NBP ware but overlapped the arrival of this fabric and a central date in the sixth century B.C. provisionally meets the evidence."[34] Cunningham, while referring to the city, the capital of the later Pandu princess, observes: "The present ruins of Kosambi consist of an immense fortress formed of earthen ramparts and bastions, with a circuit of . . . exactly four miles and three furlongs. The ramparts have a general height of from thirty to thirty five feet above the fields, but the bastions are considerably higher, those on the north face rising to upwards of fifty feet, while those of the south-west and south-east angles are more than sixty feet."[35]

The Puru dynasty of the Lunar race with twenty nine rulers comprising both *Brāhmaṇas* and *Kṣatriyas* came to an end with Kṣemaka, the last in the line.[36] According to the "*Sanskrit Rājāvali*" 1, 812 years of *Kali-yuga* had passed up to his time.

**The Kosalas**

The *Purāṇas*[37] provide a list of thirty kings of the Ikṣvāku-dynasty (of the Solar race) of Kosala as the lineal descendants of Bṛhadbala (the descendant of Lava of the Sravasti line), who was killed in the Bhārata war by Abhimanyu. The list is as follows :

1. Bṛhatkṣana-Bṛhatkṣaya-Bṛhatkṣatra
2. Urukṣaya-Tatakṣaya

3. Vatsavyūha
4. Prativyūha-Prativyoma
5. Divākara
6. Sahadeva
7. Bṛhadaśva
8. Bhānuratha
9. Pratītāśva
10. Supratika
11. Marudeva
12. Sunakṣattra
13. Kinnara-Puṣkara
14. Antarikṣa
15. Suṣena-Suparna
16. Amitrajit-Sumitra I
17. Bṛhadrāja-Bharadvāja
18. Dharmi
19. Kṛtañjaya-Dhananjaya
20. Ranañjaya
21. Sanjaya
22. Śākya
23. Śuddhodana
24. Siddhārtha i.e. Gotama
25. Rahula
26. Prasenajit
27. Kṣudraka-Vidudabha
28. Kṣulika
29. Suratha
30. Sumitra II

The next important king of Ayodhya after Bṛhadbala was Divākara, sixth in descent from him and a contemporary of the Paurava king Adhisīmakṛṣna. The old kingdom of Ayodhya gradually disintegrated, each faction of it being ruled by a king of the same dynasty but founding a new sub-dynasty. The Śākyas and the Licchavis were branches of the same people—Ikṣavākus (or Okkaku of Pāli canon). Later it became difficult for the dismembered parts of the Kosala empire to resist the onslaughts of the enemies, and, therefore it was thought desirable to form confederations of a number of kingdoms for ensuring better resisting power. One such confederation was formed in the time of Śākya, the grandfather of Buddha. Śākya, the twenty-second king of the Ikṣvāku dynasty of the post-Bhārata war period, became the ruler of the north-western portion of Kosala kingdom lying at the foot of the Himalaya mountain adjoining Nepal with its capital at Kapilavastu, whose ruins have been discovered from Piprahavā village in the north of Basti (U.P.), about 100 kms. away from Gorakhpur.

The historical credibility of the *Purāṇic* genealogy of the Ikṣvāku kings of Kosala with references to Śākya, Suddhodana, his son Siddhartha and the latter's offspring Rahula, immediately preceding Prasenajita, is beyond dispute. The *Purāṇic* evidence, that Lord Buddha, the son of Suddhodana (the twenty third king of the Ikṣvāku dynasty) belonged to the Śākya family of Kosala[38] can be confirmed by the Buddhist sources.[39] Aśvaghosha, a celebrated Buddhist scholar, who adorned the court of Kanishka (78-125 A.D.), in his famous work "*Saundarananda*" (1.24) has also supported the *Purāṇic* statement. The *Kalki Purāṇa* (one of the up-*Purāṇas*) also provides the brief life-sketch of Gautama Buddha.[40]

In Buddha's time Kosala was the predominant kingdom in Northern India, but it was being eclipsed by the growing power of Magadha. The *Purāṇic* accounts of the Kosala kings succeeding Buddha being incomplete can be supplemented by the Buddhist accounts of the subject concerned. From the Buddhist literature it appears that in Buddha's time Ayodhyā (Pāli Ayojjhā), the earliest capital of Kosala kingdom had sunk into insignificance and Sāketa and Srāvasti (Pāli Sāvatthi) rose into prominence as its two important capitals. Srāvasti, the last and the third capital, has been identified with Sahet-Mahet on the south bank of the Rapti on the borders of the Gonda and Bahraich districts (U.P.). The archaeological excavations at Srāvasti have brought to light its mud rampart and brick wall. The culture that flourished here in the sixth century B.C. is associated with NBPW phase.[41]

The Buddhist accounts give us the impression that there were frequent wars between the neighbouring kingdoms of Kosala and Kāśi for establishing supremacy over each other. Kāśi ultimately became subordinate to Kosala during the Kosala king Mahākosala. He was, in fact, the sovereign of both Kāśi and Kosala. At the time of the rise of Buddhism, Prasenjita (Pāli-Pasenadi), the son and successor of Mahākosala and contemporary of Buddha was king of Kosala with its capital at Srāvasti. His accession dates back to *c.* 533 B.C. The throne of Kosala was usurped by Prasenjita's son called Vidūdabha in the *Purāṇas* and Virūdhaka in the Buddhist literature.[42]

The Ikṣvāku dynasty of *Kṣatriya* rulers came to an end with Sumitra II. It is traditionally believed that thirty kings of this dynasty altogether reigned for 1504 years during the period *c.* 3138-1634 B.C. Their reginal years, on the other hand, in contrary to above, can reasonably be placed between the first millennium B.C. and the fifth century B.C.

### The Bārhadrathas of Magadha

As already stated earlier, Bṛhadratha, the eldest son of Uparicara Vasu in the time of Kuru of the Lunar race took Magadha with Girivraja (the fortress on the hill) as its capital, also known as Bārhadrathapur, and founded the famous Bārhadratha dynasty there about 161 years before the Bhārata war. He himself as well as nine of his successors are stated to have reigned before the *Kali* Age. Jarāsandha, the first great and peaceful emperor of Magadha before that war was succeeded by his son Sahadeva, who was killed in the war. After Sahadeva, his son Somadhi became the king of Girivraja, at the foot of which Rājagṛha, the famous ancient capital of Magadha, grew up. Twenty two rulers of the Bārhadratha dynasty, who successively ruled over Magadha in the post war period, are given below with their names and reign-periods as recorded in the *Purāṇas.*[43]

| | Accepted reign-periods | Reign-periods as given in the Pur¯a ṇas | | |
|---|---|---|---|---|
| | | *Mats.* | *Vy.* | *Bmd.* |
| 1. Somādhi-Somāpi-Mārjari | 50 years | 58 | 58 | 58 |
| 2. Śrutaśravas | 6 years | 64 | 64 | 64 |
| 3. Ayutāyus-Apratīpi | 26 years | 36 | 26 | 26 |
| 4. Niramitra | 40 years | 40 | 100 | 40 |
| 5. Sukṣattra-Sukṛtta | 50 years | 56 | 56 | 56 |
| 6. Bṛhatkarman | 23 years | 23 | 23 | 23 |
| 7. Senajit | 23 years | 50 | 23 | 23 |
| 8. Srutañjayr | 35 years | 40 | 40 | 40 |
| 9. Mahāvāhu-Bibhu-Vipra | 28 years | 28 | 33 | 28 |
| 10. Suci | 6 years | 64 | 58 | 58 |
| 11. Kṣema | 28 years | 28 | 28 | 58 |
| 12. Subrata-Bhubata-Anubrata | 24 years | 64 | 64 | 64 |
| 13. Dharmakṣetra-Sumetra | 5 years | 25 | 5 | 5 |
| 14. Nivṛti-Nṛpati | 58 years | 58 | 58 | 58 |
| 15. Suśrama-Trinetra-Subrata | 28 years | 28 | 38 | 28 |
| 16. Dṛahasena-Dyumat-Sena | 8 years | 48 | 58 | 48 |
| 17. Mahinetra-Sumati | 33 years | 33 | 33 | 33 |
| 18. Sucala-Acala | 22 years | 32 | 22 | 22 |
| 19. Sunetra | 40 years | 40 | 40 | 40 |
| 20. Satyajit | 30 years | 30 | 83 | 30 |
| 21. Visvajit | 25 years | 25 | 35 | 35 |
| 22. Ripuñjaya | 50 years | 50 | 50 | 50 |
| Total | 638 years | | | |

Senajit, the sixth in succession from Somādhi was a contemporary of the Aikṣvāku King Divākara of Kosala and the Paurava King Adhisīmakṛṣṇa. He has been ascribed by Pargiter to *c.* 850 B.C.[44] The Bārhadratha dynasty in Magadha came to an end with the killing of Ripuñjaya, at the hands of his own minister Pulika (or Pulaka, Punika) who then installed his son Pradyota on the throne. The Bārhadrathas were supplanted by the Pradyotas, who figure separately in the following chapter.

Ripuñjaya, the last ruler of the Bārhadratha dynasty, and the contemporary of

Bimbisāra probably ascended the throne in *c.* 563 B.C. and after a long reign of fifty years was murdered by his minister in (563-50=) *c.* 513 B.C. The twenty two successive kings of the said dynasty might have ruled probably sometime between (513+638=) *c.* 1151 B.C. and 513 B.C. We find some discrepancies in the *Purāṇic* chronology, so far as the total length of reigns of twenty two Bārhadrathas is concerned. It varies from 1,000 to 1,006 years, which is, in fact, an exaggerated figure. It is not very clear whether the total reign-periods are for twenty-two rulers of the post-war period only or altogether for thirty-two rulers including 10 (22+10) of the pre-war period. According to the traditional dates, the regnal years of twenty-two Bārhadrathas extends from *c.* 3138 B.C. to 2132 B.C. The basis of such calculation is that Somādhi began to rule 36 years before the beginning of the *Kali-yuga.* Thus, (1006-36=) *Kali* era 970 or (3138-1006=) 2132 B.C. marked the end of Ripuñjaya's rule over Magadha. Some scholars[45] believe that twenty-two Magadhan kings of the post-war period ruled from *c.* 1920 B.C. to 920 B.C. However, these are all tentative chronology.

## Other Kingdoms

In addition to three important kingdoms of Vatsa (Kauśāmbi) Kosala and Magadha, as mentioned above, there were several others, which flourished during the period concerned, but we have very meagre information about their histories. The Pañcāla kingdom, according to the *Purāṇas,* was ruled by twenty-seven rulers, whose names are not mentioned.

The kingdom of Śurasena with its capital at Mathura on the Yamuna was under the occupation of the scions of the Yadu family in the pre-Bhārata war period. The *Purāṇas* mention twenty three Śurasenas, who ruled over the kingdom in the post-Bhārata war period up to Mahapadma Nanda, but no dynastic lists are available.

The kingdom of Avanti in the Western Mālwā with its capital at Ujjain (Ujjayini) on the Sipra, a tributary of the Chambal (Charmaṇavati) fell under the rules of twenty eight Haihayas, twenty five Asmarkas and twenty Vitihotras, who like the Śurasenas belonged to the great family of the descendants of Yadu. They also occupied the countries of the river Chambal in the north and the river Narbada in the south. They continued to rule over the Avanti kingdom till the establishment of the Nanda dynasty. About five centuries later than the Bhārata war Avanti also came under the rule of the Pradyotas.

The *Purāṇic* and Buddhist accounts of the kingdom of Kāśi of the post-war period are equally important. They are in fact, supplementary to each other. The *Purāṇas* mention twenty-four kings, who ruled over the kingdom of Kāśi down to the time of Mahāpadma Nanda. According to the *Purāṇic* account, at different periods of history Kāśi came under the political sway of the three successive sovereign powers of Northern India—the Pauravas of Vatsa, the Ikṣvākus of Kosala and the kings of Magadha, but it seems to have enjoyed its independence in the interval between the decline of Vatsa and the rise of Kosala, when its famous king Brāhmadatta conquered Kosala possibly about a century-and-a-half before the Buddha's time. The administration of the kingdom of Kāśi for sometime fell to the share of Dhataraṭṭhas, who are represented as kings of the line of Bhārata. The Bhārata line of the Kāśi kings appears to have been supplanted by a new line of Brāhmadattas, who were probably of the Videhan origin.

The *Matsya Purāṇa,* in particular, refers to the 100 kings of Brāhmadatta family as ruling over Kāśi with its capital at Vārānasi.[46] Some of the *Jātakas* also testify to the dynastic rule of the Brāhmadattas of Kāśi.[47] D.R. Bhandarkar has also pointed out that some of the Kāśi kings in the *Jātakas* find mention also in the *Purāṇas.*[48]

The Buddhist literature speaks of the frequent struggle for supremacy between the kings of Kāśi and Kosala. The series of struggles ended finally in the permanent annexation of the kingdom of Kāśi to that of Kosala.[49] During the reign of Prasenjit or Pasenadi Kāśi formed a part of Kosalan empire.

The Kāsis, one of the most ancient people in the *Brāhmanical* mid India or of Northern India, founded a kingdom named Kāśi after them, which was 300 leagues in extent with its capital at Vārānasi, which was known by other names in the past ages.[50] The city of Vārānasi, which stood on the left bank of the Ganges, was encompassed by the walls that were twelve leagues in circuit. According to the *Mahāgovinda Suttanta,* Kāśi with Vārānasi as its capital is included in the list of seven sub-kingdoms.

The ancient city of Vārānasi was situated on the place, where we find the fort of Rājghat. Excavations of the site were carried out in 1957-58.[51] Further, A.K. Narain and T.N. Roy (B.H.U.) resumed the excavation at Rājghat in 1960-61. The archaeological discovery includes an enormous clay rampart, which dates back to the earliest occupation of the site in the first quarter of the first millennium B.C. The dates assigned to the first period are as followes :

a. *c.* 800-600 B.C.
b. c. 600-400 B.C.[52]

The reigns of the *Purāṇic* rulers in Kāśi during the period following the great Bhārata war can archaeologically be connected with the above mentioned periods. D.L. Eck, while referring to the archaeological excavations carried out at Rājghat in 1940 and in mid 1960's, also supports the earliest occupation of the Rājghat, one of the important urban centres, in the ninth century B.C.[53]

The *Purāṇas* mention twenty-eight Maithilas, who ruled over the kingdom of Videha after the Bhārata war. The Maithilas take their names from Mithila, the capital of the Videhas. According to the *Purāṇas,* the Āryan kings of the Videhas were a branch of the Puru family. In Buddha's time, the Videhas together with the Licchavis of Vaiśāli and other powerful clans formed a confederation, known collectively as the Vṛjjis (Vajjis). The frequent struggle between Kāśi and Videha led to the overthrow of the Videha monarchy at the hands of the Kāśi people. One of the branches of the royal family of Kāśi possibly established itself in Videha. The gradual decline of their power marks an epoch in the expansion of the kingdom of Magadha. To the east of Magadha the kingdom of Aṅga with its capital at Champa existed during the period concerned. The frequent eruption of hostility between Aṅga and its neighbouring kingdom, Magadha, ultimately, proved to be disastrous for the former, though at one point of time some parts of Magadha formed the part of Aṅga. The sovereignty of Aṅga is evident from the victory of its king, Brāhmadatta, over king Bhattiya of Magadha. But, the Aṅga kingdom soon lost its independence. Because, we find that Bimbisara, son of Bhattiya, killed king Brāhmadatta of Aṅga, annexed the capital Champa to his empire, and continued to rule over there as Viceroy till he left for Rājagṛha on his father's death. Bimbisara later converted Aṅga into a separate province and appointed his son Ajātaśatru as its governor with headquarters at Champa.

The *Purāṇas* refer to thirty-two rulers of Kalinga, but do not furnish any details of them. The existence of many other kingdoms during the period cannot be denied. But, unfortunately, we do not have anything at our disposal to throw light on them.

The foregoing accounts make it conspicuous that Northern India was parcelled out into a large number of states, and there was no paramount power during the long period of six or five centuries following the Bhārata war to exercise its supremacy over all of them. The struggles among various powers for supremacy and their repeated attempts to pursue the ideal of imperialism stood as barriers in the way of the political unification of India.

## References and Notes

1. *Mats.*, 273, 65-72; *Vy.*, 99, 448-55.
2. *Mats.*, 50, 57; *Vy.*, 99, 249-50; *Vṣṇ.*, IV, 21, 2; *Bhāg.*, IX, 22, 33-35; *Mbh.*, *Ādi Parva*, 37, 9.
3. *Mats.*, *SBA*, (ed. by J. Das Akhtar and notes by B.C. Majumdar, S.C. Vasu, H.H. Wilson, Bentley, Wilford and others, Delhi, 1972), Vol. 1, App. Section, Table IV.
4. *Ādi Parva*, 3, 144-46; See also *Bh. Sv.*, Vol. I, pp. 128-29.
5. *Mbh.*, *Ādi Parva*, 3, 10-17, 40, 6-8; *Mats.*, 50, 57; *Vy.*, 99, 249-50; *Vṣṇ.*, IV, 21, 2; *Vṣṇ.* (tr.) H.H. Wilson, ch. XXI, p. 368; *Bhāg.*, IX, 22, 35-38; *Bhv.* (Bareli, 1978) Vol. 1, p. 309, *VV* 82-83. According to *Vṣṇ.* and *Bhāg.*, Parīkṣit was blessed with four sons, Janmejaya, Shrutasena, Ugrasena and Bhimsena, but other *Purāṇas* do not maintain the same list. But they figure in *Śat. Br.*, XIII, 5, 4, 3.
6. *Ādi Parva*, 3, 18, 3, 179-80; *Mbh.*, *ko.*, p. 293; *Bh. Sv.*, Vol. 1, p. 53.
7. *Virāta Parva* (1969), 5, 21.
8. *Vy.*, 99, 249-55; *Mats.*, 50, 58-65.
9. *Vy.*, 99, 255-69; *Mats.*, 50, 65-67; *Vṣṇ.*, IV, 21, 3-6; *Bhv.* (Supra), p. 309, *vv.*, 83-84.
10. Pargiter, *AIHT*, p. 182, also *PDKA*, pp. 4, 24, note 16.
11. *Vy.*, 99, 270-71; *Mats.*, 50, 78-79; *Vṣṇ.*, IV. 21, 6-8; *Vṣṇ.*, (tr.); H.H. Wilson, ch. XXI, p. 368; *Bhāg.*, IX, 22, 39-40; Pargiter, *PDKA*, p. 5.
12. *CAGI*, p. 330. Secaso H.A. Giles. Ṭhe travels of Fa-hien or RBK. (Varanasi, 1972), pp. 61-62.
13. *AIHT*, p. 285.
14. *Cf.* B.C. Law, *Geographical Essays*, p. 29.
15. *Cf.* *AIT*, pp. 121-23, note.
16. J.C. Jain, *LAIJC*, p. 340.

17. AI, Nos. 10 and 11 (1954-5), pp. 5 ff.
18. *Mats.*, 50, 79-89; Vy., 99, 272-79; *Vṣṇ..*, IV, 21, 9-18; *Vṣṇ.*, (tr.); H.H. Wilson, Ch. XXI, pp. 308-69; *Bhv.* (Supra), pp. 309-11, *VV* 84-95.
19. See *Vinayavijayaganin's subōdhikā commentary on Kalpasūtra* (of Bhadravāhu), VI. 118; J.C. Jain., *op. cit.*, p. 341.
20. *Āvaśyaka Cūrni*, pp. 88 f, 167 f, *cf.* J.C. Jain, *op. cit.*, p. 467.
21. *Āvaśyaka Cūrni*, pp. 400 f; *Uttarādhyayana Tikā*, 18 pp. 253 ff. *cf.* J.C. Jain, *op. cit.*, pp. 467-68.
22. *Udāna* (ed. p. Steinthal, *PTS* London, 1885 and tr. D.M. Strong, London, 1902), VII, 10; *Saṁyutta Nikāya*, (ed. L. Feer and Mrs. Rhys Davids, PTS, London, 1854-1904), IV, 110-13; *Mahāvastu* (ed. E. Senart, Paris, 1882-97), Vol. II, pp. 2 f; *Lalitavistara* (ed. R.L. Mitra, BIS, Calcutta, 1877) p. 27; Bodhisattvādāna Kalpalatā 35th, pp. 3 f); Vinaya (ed. H. Oldenberg, London, 1902), 11, 127; IV, 198; *Majjhima Nikāya* (ed. V. Trenckner and R. Chalmers, PTS, London, 1888-99), 11, 97; *Jātaka* (ed. V, Fausboll, London, 1877-97) and tr. by various authors under the editorship of E.B. Cowell, Cambridge 1895-1913), III, 157; Peta-Vatthu commentary (ed. E.E. Hardy, PTS, London, 1901), 140; see also B.C. Law, Geographical Essays, pp. 25-26; *IETBJ*, p. 133; "Kausambi in Ancient Literature" in *MASI*, No. 60, Delhi, 1939; Pargiter, *JRAS*, 1910, pp. 26-29; *PDKA*, pp. 7, 66.
23. *CAGI*, p. 331.
24. See *YCTI*, Vol. 1, p. 368.
25. Csoma de Kőros in *As. Res.*, Vol. XX, p. 299.
26. *Dhammapada commentary* (ed. H.C. Norman, PTS, London, 1906-14), 1, 161-230.
27. *Divyāvadāna* (ed. E.B. Cowell and R.A. Neil, Cambridge, 1886, reptd. 1970), 515-544, see also H.K. Deb, *Udayana Vatsarāja* (Calcutta, 1919), pp. 4 f.
28. *PK*, p. 59.
29. Ed. Ganapati Sastri (Trivandrum Series), Act. 1, pp. 4-5, also p. 140, Act. 11; Act IV.
30. See G.R. Sharma, The Excavations at Kausambi (1957-59), Allahabad, 1960, pp. 6-22; see also *IAR*, 1953-54, p. 9; 1954-55, p. 16; 1955-56, p. 20; 1956-57, p. 28; 1957-58, p. 47; *MASI*, 74, 1969, pp. 24-26.
31. K.K. Sinha, "Stratigraphy and chronology of Early Kausambi: A Reappraisal" in D.P. Agrawal and A. Ghosh (Eds.): *Radiocarbon and Indian Archaeology* (Bombay, 1973), pp. 231-39; A. Ghosh, *The City in Early Historical India* (Simla, 1973), pp. 11, 62, 80-81.
32. *AIHA*, p. 240.
33. *Ibid.*, p. 251, also *IAR*, 1956-57, p. 20; 1957-58, p. 34, Fig. 9, pl. XLIA.
34. *EIP* (London, 1968), pp. 127-29.
35. *CAGI*, p. 334.
36. *Vy.*, 99, 276-79, also 432 (the text refers to only 25 rulers); *Vṣṇ.*, IV. 21, 17-18; *Mats.*, 50, 88-89.
37. *Mats.*, 271, 4-18; 273, 52-53; *Vy.*, 99, 280-93 also 431; *Vṣṇ.*, IV, 22, 1-13; *Bmd.*, 3, 74, 104 f; *Bhv.* (supra), VV, 36-40, pp. 333-34; H.H. Wilson (tr.), *Vṣṇ.*, ch. XXII, pp. 369-70; *Mats.*, *SBA*, Pt. II, ch. CCLXXI, pp. 331-32; Pargiter, *PDKA*, pp. 10-11,66-67.
38. *Mats.*, 271, 12-15; *Vy.*, 99, 288-90; *Vṣṇ.*, IV, 22, 5-10; *Bhv.* (Supra), *Vv.*, 36-38, pp. 333-34; *PDKA*, pp. 11, 67.
39. *Majjhima Nikāya*, 2-124; *Digha Nikāya* (ed. T.W. Rhys Davids and J.E. Carpenter, PTS, London, 1890-1911), 2-8, also 2-52; *Sumaṅgala-Vilāsini* (commentary on the Digha, ed. Rhys Davids, PTS, London 1886), 1, pp. 258-60; *Sutta Nipāta* (ed. D. Andersen and H. Smith, PTS, London, 1913), Verse-422; *Mahāvaṁsa* (ed. W. Geiger, PTS, London, 1908, tr. W. Geiger, PTS, London, 1912), 11, 17-22; *Pabbajjāsutta, Sutta Nipāta*, pp. 72-74 *cf.* B.C. Law, *HPL*, Vol. 1, p. 248; *Dhammacetiya* Sutta, Majhima, 11, p. 118 *cf.* B.C. Law; *IETBJ*, p. 131; B.C. Law, *Kshatriya Clans in Buddhist India* (Calcutta, 1922), pp. 1 ff; Ancient Indian tribes (London, 1934), ch. 11, see also *YCTI*, Vol. II, p. 34; Attha-Śālini (Buddhaghosa's comm. on Dhammasaṇgani, ed. E. Müller, PTS, London, 1897), p. 305.
40. See *Purāṇa Kathā*, Kalyāna Series (Gorakhpur, April, 1989), No. 1, p. 340.

41. See *IAR*, 1958-59, p. 48; K.K. Sinha, *Excavations at Srāvasti* (1959), Varanasi, 1967.
42. *The Kosala Saṁyutta, Sutta Nipāta*, 1, pp. 68-102; *Bodhisattvāvadāna Kalpalatā*, 100th, p. 2; *Jātaka*, II, p. 237; IV, pp. 342 ff; B.C. Law, *HPL*, Vol. 1, p. 162; *IETBJ*, pp. 43-44, 131-32; *GEB*, p. 5; *Geographical Essays*, pp. 22-23; The Kosalas in Ancient India" in *IHQ*, Vol. 1, Nos. 1-2 (Delhi, 1979), pp. 137-65; "Countries and Peoples of India, Epic and Puranic Sources" in *ABORI*, Vol. XVII, 1935-36 (Poona, 1936), Pt. III, p. 225; "Sravasti in Ancient Indian Literature" in *MASI*, No. 50, Delhi, 1935; H.A. Giles, *RBK*, pp. 30-31; *YCTI*, Vol. I, p. 377; *CAGI*, p. 346.
43. *Vy.*, 99, 294-308; *Mats.*, 271, 18-30; *Mats.*, *SBA*; pp. 332-33; *Vṣn.*, IV, 23, 1-13; H.H. Wilson (tr.); *Vṣn.*, XXIII, pp. 371-72, *Bmd.*, 3, 74, 107-21; *Bhāg.*, IX, 22, 46-49; *Hv.*, 1, 32, 63-78; Pargiter, *PDKA*, pp. 13-22; K.P. Jayaswal, Brihadratha Chronology, *JBORS*, Sept. 1915, IV, 1, pp. 26-35.
44. *PDKA*, p. 15.
45. *Mats.*, *SBA*, Table No. V.
46. 273, 72-73.
47. *Dhummedha Jātaka*, 1, p. 259 f; *Gaṅgamāla Jātaka*, No. 421 cf. B.C. Law, *IETBJ*, pp. 129-30; *Kosiya Jātaka* (Fausboll), Vol. 1, p. 463; see also B.C. Law, Historical Gleanings (Delhi, 1976), p. 3; *DPPN*, Vol. II, p. 332.
48. *Carmichael Lectures on the Ancient History of India*, 1918 (Calcutta, 1919), p. 57.
49. *Vinaya*, *SBE*, Vol. XIII, 294-99; *Kaṇāla Jātaka*, No. 636; *Kośāmbi Jātaka* No. 428.
50. *Jātaka*, iv, 15, 119-20.
51. *IAR*, 1957-58, p. 86.
52. *Ibid.*, 1960-61, pp. 35-37.
53. *Banaras : City of Light* (London, 1983), p. 46.

# 4

# The Pradyota Dynasty

## (*c.* 513-411 B.C.)

THE *Purāṇic* chroniclers have not properly maintained the sequence of dynasties ruling over Magadha in the post-Ripuñjaya period from Pradyota to Śiśunāga. We, therefore, cannot absolutely depend only on the *Purāṇic* evidence. In order to get a clearer picture of the subject, we shall have to place our reliance on the combined testimonies of the *Purāṇas*, some other Sanskrit, Buddhist and Jain sources, etc.

According to the *Purāṇic* tradition, Punika (or Pulika, Pulaka, Sunika, etc.) after having assassinated his sovereign Ripuñjaya, the last king of the Bārhadratha dynasty of Magadha, anointed his own son Pradyota in his stead. But we have no positive evidence to show that there was ever any Pradyota dynasty of Magadha. As a matter of fact, Pradyota was installed on the throne of Avanti (Western Malawa) with its capital at Ujjain (Ujjayini) after Vitihotras rule over the kingdom came to an end. He subdued all neighbouring kings and made all his *sāmants* or vassals loyal to him within no time through the charisma of his personality. The fact stated above can be testified to by the statement recorded, particularly, in the *Matsya Purāṇa*.[1] Pradyota was also known as *Mahāsena* on account of his large army.[2] The identification of the Pradyota dynasty with the Paunika family mentioned in Bāna's *Harṣacarita*[3] can, undoubtedly, be established.

Caṇḍa Pajjota (Pradyota) was, no doubt, a powerful king of Avanti. His clash with Udayana of Kauśāmbi has already been referred to. According to the Buddhist tradition, his power grew to such an extent that even Ajatasattu or Ajatasatru (*c.* 491-459 B.C.) had to fortify his capital, Rājagaha (Rājagṛha), shortly before the Buddha's death in anticipation of an invasion of his territory by Pajjota of Avanti.[4] According to R. Morton Smith, this dates back to *c.* 488-7 B.C.[5] It was, probably, because of the death of Caṇḍa Pradyota towards the earlier parts of the reign of Ajatasatru that the invasion of Magadha, as contemplated by him, could not be materialized. In the Jain tradition also Caṇḍa Pajjoya (Pradyota), the lord of Avanti, is said to have fought many battles. It is stated that Abhayakumar foiled his attempt to attack Rāyagiha (Rājagṛha).[6] Kumarasena was the younger brother of Caṇḍa Pradyota-Mahāsena and not his son, as erroneously supposed by K.P. Jayaswal.[7] When he tried to abolish the age-old practice of selling human flesh on the occasion of the feast of Mahākāla of Ujjayini, he was killed by Tālajangha.

According to the information supplied by Somadeva in his *Kathāsaritsāgara,* after the death of Pradyota-Mahāsena, Udayana, his son-in-law, asked his elder brother-in-law, Gopala, to go to Avanti and take charge of the kingdom. But Gopala, the eldest son of Pradyota, abdicated the throne in favour of his younger brother Pālaka and went to Kauśāmbi, where he used to live with his affectionate sister Vāsavadatta.[8] Pālaka appears to have annexed Kauśāmbi to his realm. He was overthrown by Ajaka (or Āryaka), the son of his elder brother, Gopala. Pālaka, because of having imprisoned Ajaka, was ousted by Śarvilaka, who organised a rebellion and installed Ajaka on the throne of Avanti.[9] Pālaka was thus succeeded by Ajaka. After Pālaka was deposed, his son Viśākhayūpa, probably, established a principality in some adjacent district and ruled for quite some time. His brother Avantivardhana, however, succeeded Ajaka to the throne of Avanti and continued to rule over there till he was ousted by Śiśunāga. The pedigree and progeny of king Pradyota of Avanti are given in different sources. His genealogy, as given in the *Purāṇas,* shows that he was succeeded by his son Pālaka (or Bālaka). His son was Viśākhayūpa, who was succeeded by his son Ajaka (or Janaka, Sūryaka, Rajaka). Ajaka's son was Nandivardhana (= Avantivardhana).[10] The *Purāṇic* genealogy of Pradyotas seems to be discrepant. Because we find that Viśākhayūpa and Avantivardhana were the two sons of Pālaka and Ajaka was the son of Gopala or the grandson of Pradyota-Mahāsena. According to the Jaina chronology, Gopala and Pālaka were the two sons of Pajjoya. Palaka's sons were Avanti-Vardhana and Rāṣṭravardhana, and Avantisena and Maniprabha were the two sons of the latter.[11] The *Purāṇic* genealogy is in complete agreement with all other chronologies, so far as the Pālaka's succession to his father Pradyota is concerned. The length of reigns of the five kings of the Pradyota dynasty of Avanti, as given in different *Purāṇas,*[12] are given below :

1. Pradyota . . . 23 years, *Mats., Vy.*
2. Pālaka ...24 years, *Mats.,-24, Vy., Bmd.*
3. Ajaka . . . 21 years, *Mats.,-31, Vy.*
4. Viśākhayūpa . . . 50 years, *Mats., Vy.*
5. Avantivardhana (or Nandivardhana) . . . 30 years, *Mats.,-20, Vy.*

The total of the reign - periods of the said five kings has been wrongly mentioned in the *Matsya Purāṇa* as fifty two years. The calculation of the figures as given therein brings it to 152 years. But according to the evidence of other *Purāṇas* (*Vṣṇ., Vy., Bhāg.* and *Bmd.*) they actually ruled for 138 years. Their chronology can accordingly be determined.

Caṇḍa Pradyota ascended the throne of Avanti in 513 B.C. and ruled for 23 years. He, thus, reigned up to (513-13=) 490 B.C. In fact, he ruled from 513 to 488 B.C. He was as such contemporary of Bimbisāra and Ajatasatru (the fifth and sixth in the *Purāṇic* list of the kings of so-called Śaiśunāga dynasty, mistakenly separated by more than 150 years from Pradyota and the first and second kings according to the *Mahāvaṁśa*) of Magadha, the Puru king Udayana of Vatsa, the Ikṣvāku king, Prasenajit of Kosala, and Buddha. Pālaka ruled for twenty four years. He may be placed either between 490 B.C. and 466 B.C. or between 488 B.C. and 464 B.C. Ajaka ruled for twenty one years. He ruled from 466 or 464 B.C. to 445 or 443 B.C. The accession of Viśākhyūpa, the son of Pālaka, took place in 466 B.C. (=490-24) or 464 B.C. He reigned for 50 or 53 years. Hence his reign ended sometime between 415 B.C. and 411 B.C. Avantivardhana succeeded to the throne of Avanti in 445 or 443 or 441 B.C. and ruled for full 30 years. He, thus, continued up to either 415 or 413 or 411 B.C., i.e. about the same year of the accession of Śiśunāga (= Nandivardhana). It appears that the duration of the reigns of the five kings of Pradyota dynasty was probably 100 or 102 years. Their reign periods fall in between *c.* 513 B.C. and 413 or 411 B.C.[13]

The following genealogical tables: (a) based on the *Purāṇic* and other Sanskrit sources and (b) based on the Jain tradition show the succession and reign-periods of the Pradyota kings :

**(a)**

Punika (Pulika)

Pradyota-Mahāsena
*c.* 513-488 B.C.

*Kumārasena*

Gopāla

Pālaka
488-464 B.C.

Ajaka
*c.* 464-443 B.C.

Viśākhyūpa *c.* 464-411 B.C. (He took over the charge of the govt. of Māhiśmati in the same year in which the accession of Ajaka of Avanti took place)

Avantivardhana *c.* 443-411 B.C. (he directly succeeded Ajaka and ruled till he was ousted by Śiśunāga sometime between 415 B.C. and 411 B.C.)

**(b)**

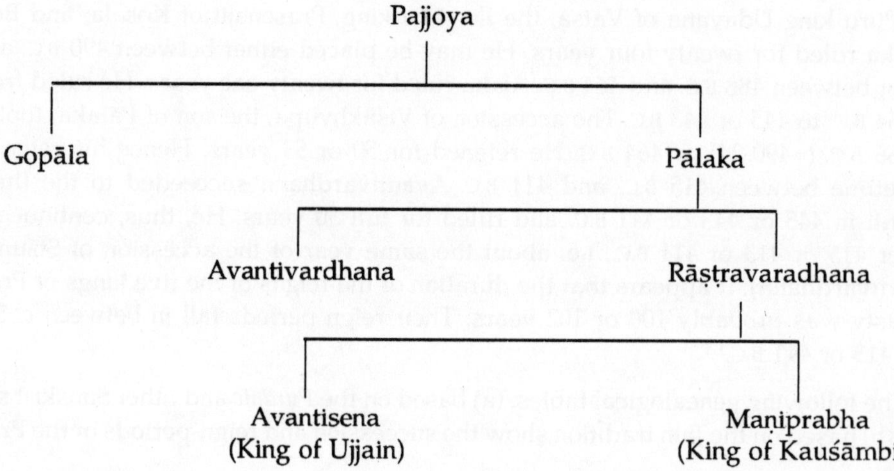


According to the Jaina sources, the date of the Nirvāna of Mahāvira, i.e. 477 B.C. (and not *c.* 527 B.C.—the conventional date, which is based on the period of interval between the Vira-Nirvāna and *Vikrama-Saṁvat*, as given in the *Vicāra-Śreni* of Merutunga, as 470 years, i.e. 470+57=527) coincided with the succession of Pālaka, the son of Caṇḍa Pradyota, to the throne of Avanti, and he ruled for about sixty or sixty-four years,[14] which is at variance with the *Purāṇic* data. Moreover, it is not corroborated by any other source.

A.K. Majumdar's statement (based on the authority of Pandit Kāliprasanna Vidyāratna, who in his translation of the *Viṣṇu Purāṇa* has fixed 128 years as reign-periods of the Pradyotas), that (655 + 124 solar years =128 Lunar) 779 B.C. witnessed the end of the Bārhadratha dynasty and the beginning of the Pradyota, which ruled up to 655 B.C.,[15] seems to be absurd. Some scholars believe that the Pradyotas reigned from 920 B.C. to 782 B.C.[16] According to Pargiter, the Pradyotas' rule began sometime between 627 and 619 B.C. He assigns a reign of fifty-two years to five kings (average, 10½ years).[17] According to the traditional dates, the Pradyotas ruled from *c.* 2132 B.C. to 1,994 B.C. Their rule covering a period of 138 years came to an end in *Kali*-era (970+138=) 1108 or in ( 2,132-138=) 1,994 B.C.

The two noted dynasties, the Pradyotas and Śiśunāgas, were almost contemporary. The fame of the Pradyotas, according to the *Purāṇas*, was destroyed by Śiśunāga (who flourished four or five generations after Pradyota, the founder of the dynasty and the contemporary of Bimbisara) most probably in a war between the houses of Magadha and Avanti. It was Avantivardhana, the last king of the dynasty, who was ousted by Śiśunāga sometime between 415 B.C. and 411 B.C. It has been rightly observed by B.C. Law that "within a century and-a-half from the death of Pajjota, the country of the

Avantis became merged in the Mauryan empire."[18] The Pradyota dynasty was supplanted by Śiśunāga, the founder of the so-called Śaiśunāga dynasty, the details of which follow in the next chapter.

## References and Notes

1. 272, 1-2. The *Vy.* (99, 308-11) also provides some clues to the Pradyota's installation as the king of Avanti. Kota Venkatachalam's statement that Pradyota dynasty ruled over Magadha (Chronology of Ancient Hindu History, Pt. 1, pp. 34, 281), cannot be accepted.
2. Bhāsa's *Svapnavāsavadatta*, V. 20.
3. Tr. by Cowell and Thomas (London, 1897), p. 193.
4. *Majjhima Nikāya*, III, 7.
5. *DDEI*, pp. 344-46.
6. J.C. Jain, *LAIJC*, p. 466.
7. *JBORS*, Sept., 1915, p. 106.
8. *Kat. Sar. Sag.* (ed. Bombay, 1889, tr. by C.H. Tawney, *BIS*, 1880-87), III, 60-63.
9. Śūdraka's *Mṛcchakatikā* (ed. by J. Vidyāsāgara, Calcutta, 1886), IV, 24, X, 46, 51.
10. *Mats.*, 272, 1-5; *Vy.*, 99, 308-14; *Vṣṇ*, IV, 24, 1-8; *Vṣṇ.*, tr. H.H. Wilson, ch. XXIV, p. 372; *Bhāg.*, XII, 1, 2-4; *Bmd.*, 3, 74, 121-25; *Bhv.* (Supra), pp. 311-12; Pargiter, *PDKA*, pp. 18-21, 68-9; See also M. Krishnamachariar, *HCSL*, Introduction.
11. J.C. Jain, *op. cit.*, p. 466.
12. *Mats.*, 272, 2-5; *Mats.*, *SBA*, ch. CCLXXII, pp. 334-35; *Vy.*, 99, 311-14; *Bmd.*, 3, 74, 125; Pargiter. *PDKA*, p. 68; F. Max Müller, *HASL* (Varanasi, 1968), p. 265.
13. See also S.N. Pradhan, *Chro. Anc. Ind.* (Varanasi, 1979), pp. 244-45.
14. Yativṛsabha's *Tiloyapaṇṇati* or *Trailokya-Prajñapti* (ed. by A.N. Upādhyāya and H.L. Jain Solapur, 1951), *vv.* 95-99; Jinasena's *Harivaṁśa Purāṇa*, (Bombay, 1930), Sarga, 60, *vv.* 487-92, 551 f; *Pattāvali Samuccaya* (ed. Muni Darsanavijaya, 2 Vols. Viramgam, 1933), *Titthogāli Painna*, p. 197; The *Tirthoddhāra-Prakarana* and the *Tapāgaccha-Pattāvali* cf. *Pattāvali Samuccaya*; see also "*Gurjara-deśa-Bhupavali*" of *Rangavijaya* (V.E. 1886).
15. *EHIDS* (Dacca, 1920, Delhi, 1981), Vol. 1, p. 59; Vol. II, pp. 494-95.
16. *Mats.*, *SBA*, Tables.
17. *AIHT*, p. 287.
18. *IETBJ*, p. 105.

# 5

# Magadhan Dynasties of The Pre-Maurya Period

## (from Bimbisāra to the end of the Nanda Dynasty *c.* 543-321 B.C.)

### The Dynasties of Bimbisāra and Śiśunāga (c. 543-343 B.C.)

IN order to make a scientific, systematic and comparative historical study of the two separate dynasties, founded first by Bimbisāra and then by Śiśunāga, collectively, called as the Śaiśunāga dynasty in the *Purāṇas,* we shall have to go for analyses and interpretations of the data contained in the *Purāṇic* texts, the Pāli Canon, chronicles and commentaries, the Sanskrit texts of the Buddhists and the Canonical and non-Canonical texts of the Jainas. But before we proceed to do so, we would first like to compare the different dynastic or genealogical lists of the successive kings, as given in the *Purāṇas,*[1] the *Mahāvaṁśa*[2] and the *Dipavaṁśa,*[3] the two Buddhist chronicles of Ceylon, and the *Samantapāsādikā* (a commentary on the *Vinaya Piṭaka*)[4] with the length of their reigns. It is worthy of note that the list contained in the *Dipavaṁśa* is incomplete, but identical with that of the *Mahāvaṁśa,* so far as the reign periods of some of the kings are concerned. The *Samantapāsādikā* contains more or less a similar list, but the regnal years of few rulers do not tally with what we find in the *Mahāvaṁśa.* The lists are given on the following page.

Before arranging the genealogy of the kings in a chronological order and fixing their total reign-periods, accordingly, by placing our reliance on those figures, which are relatively more reliable, and other available evidences, we will critically examine the historical authenticity of the lists keeping in view the order of the succession of kings and one basic question as to whether Bimbisāra and Śiśunāga belonged to the same dynasty or were the founders of the two separate dynasties!

The first eight kings in the *Purāṇic* genealogy seem to have been arranged into two groups, the first headed by Śiśunāga and the second by Bimbisāra. This arrangement is reversed in the Buddhist lists, while Śiśunāga's group is omitted altogether in the Jain tradition. The Jaina scholars have recognised only three kings, Bimbisāra, (Sreṇika), Ajātaśatru (Kūṇika) and Udāyin.[5] It is really difficult to reconcile the three traditions, the *Purāṇic*, Buddhist and Jain. However, an attempt can be made in this direction.

## (a) The Purāṇic List

| No. | Name | Length of Reign |
|---|---|---|
| 1. | Śiśunāga | 40 years (*Vy., Mats.*) |
| 2. | Kākavarṇa | 26 years (*Mats.*), 36 (*Vy.*) |
| 3. | Kṣemadharman | 20 years (*Vy.*), 36 (*Mats.*) |
| 4. | Kṣemajit or Kṣatraujas | 24 years (*Mats.*), 40 (*Vy.*) |
| 5. | Bimbisāra | 28 years (*Vy., Mats., Bmd.*), (*Bmd.*, 28 or 38) |
| 6. | Ajātaśatru | 25 years (*Vy., Bmd.*), (*Mats.*, 25 or 27) |
| 7. | Darśaka | 24 years (*Mats.* 24 or 35), 25 (*Vy., Bmd.*) |
| 8. | Udāyin | 33 years (*Vy., Mats. Bmd.*) |
| 9. | Nandivardhana | 40 years (*Mats., Bmd.*), 42 (*Vy.*). |
| 10. | Mahānandin | 43 years (*Mats., Bmd.*), (*Vy.* 43 or 45) |
| | Total | 303 Years (or 360, 362 years) |

## (b) The Buddhist List

| No. | Name | Rengal Years | |
|---|---|---|---|
| | | **Mahāvaṁsa, Samantapāsādikā** | |
| 1. | Bimbisāra | 52 years (Same in the Dipavaṁśa) | |
| 2. | Ajātaśatru | 32 years | 24 years |
| 3. | Udāyi-bhadda | 16 years (same in the Dip.) | 16 years |
| 4. | Anuruddha and his son | 8 years (Joint reign-periods) | 18 years |
| 5. | Muṇḍa | | |
| 6. | Nāgadāsaka | 24 years | 24 years |
| 7. | Śuśunāga (Śiśunāga) | 18 year | 18 year |
| 8. | Kālāśoka (*Purāṇic* Kākavarṇa, called Kākavarnin in the *Divyāvadāna*, XXVI, p. 369) and | 28 year | 28 year |
| 9. | His ten sons (The most prominent among whom was Nandivardhana. They ruled simultaneously) | 22 years (Same in the Dip.) | 22 years |
| | Total | 200 years. | |

The *Purāṇic* and Buddhist lists, as shown above, are manifestly not in agreement with one another. They are rather too contradictory to present a clear picture of the subject, so far as the succession of kings and their regnal years are concerned. However, both can be collated for obtaining satisfactory result.

In the *Purāṇic* list, Śiśunāga has been placed at the top as the founder of the so-called Śaiśunāga dynasty and as a progenitor of the family of Bimbisāra, who is said to have been the fifth in succession from him. But this is contradicted not only by the testimony of other Sanskrit and Buddhist sources, but by the *Purāṇas* themselves. The *Purāṇists* have, no doubt, distorted history to a certain extent. They have not maintained, at all, the chronological sequence of the kings. Whereas, on the other hand, we find that the Buddhist scholars have presented more faithful accounts of the subject than the *Purānakāras.* In contrast with the discrepancy as discernible in the *Purāṇic* genealogy, the Buddhist genealogy preserved in the *Mahāvaṁśa,* ascribed to Mahānāman, is more consistent. From the Pāli accounts, which is comparatively more trustworthy than the *Purānic* ones from the historical point of view, it distinctly appears that Śiśunāga flourished four or five generations after Pradyota and his contemporary Bimbisāra, and the dynasty, which he founded, succeeded that of Bimbisāra. We have also seen in the preceding chapter that according to the *Purāṇas* themselves, the glory of the Pradyotas was eclipsed by Śiśunāga. We are told that the last king of the Pradyota dynasty, Avantivardhana, who was ousted by him, was one of the descendants of Caṇḍa Pradyota, the first king of this dynasty. Thus, there can hardly be any doubt about the posteriority of Śiśunāga to Bimbisāra. The *Purāṇas* are, of course, self-contradictory. Because it is said that Śiśunāga after placing his son Kākavarna on the throne of Kāśi established himself aṭ Girivraja (or Rājagṛha), the earlier capital of Magadha. That Varanasi was included within Śiśunāga's dominions also testifies to the fact that he became the ruler of Magadha after Bimbisāra and Ajātaśatru, who were the first two kings to establish the political supremacy of Magadha over Kāśi. As a matter of fact, Śiśunāga, before founding the new royal dynasty and seizing power, was only a chieftain (or an *amātya*) of Benares. The statement recorded in the Mālālaṃkāravatthu[6] that Rājagṛha lost its rank as a royal city from the time of Śiśunāga also goes to show that Śiśunāga came to power after the flourishing days of Rājagṛha, i.e. the period of Bimbisāra and Ajātaśatru. Śiśunāga probably chose the old capital Rājagṛha as his headquarters to repulse the attacks of Avanti's rulers on that part of Magadha. The *Purāṇic* evidence, that Bimbisāra and Ajātaśatru belonged to the line of Śiśunāga, not being corroborated by other sources can be disapproved of. If we accept the *Purāṇic* evidence that Śiśunāga was the ancestor of Bimbisāra, we will be led to believe that the Śaiśunāga dynasty was established before 600 B.C. But the fact remains that Bimbisāra, who ascended the throne of Magadha in 543 B.C. was the first to found the dynasty that ruled over this kingdom. This can further be supported by the statements of D.R. Bhandarkar and V.A. Smith. According to the former, Bimbisāra, the founder of a dynasty, carved out a kingdom for himself at the expense of the Vajjis,[7] and in the latter's view, . . . Bimbisāra may be regarded as the real founder of the Magadhan imperial power".[8] S.N. Pradhan strongly supports the view that Bimbisāra was the first king to rule over Magadha and Śiśunāga succeeded him 132 (=52+32+16+8+24) years later and Ajātaśatru after 80 (=32+16+8+24) years as stated in the *Mahāvaṁśa.*[9] In both the cases Śiśunāga's accession took place in (543-132 or 491-80=) 411 B.C. But Mr. Pradhan accepting 495 B.C. as the date of accession of Ajātaśatru ascribes Śiśunāga's accession to (495-80=) 415 B.C.

H.C. Raychaudhuri also refers to the "Bimbisārian (of the "Haryanka-kula" in the Pāli version) and Śaiśunāga dynasties" as two separate dynasties,[10] which is also supported by R.S. Tripathi.[11] But we are unable to understand the justification of the use of the term "Haryanka". For entering into further details into a systematic manner the *Purāṇic* and the Buddhist genealogies have been combined together and arranged into a chronological order, which follows :

Bimbisāra of the so-called Haryanka dynasty was the son of a petty chieftain Bhaṭṭiya (who was defeated by Brahmadatta, a king of Aṅga), and was also known as Srenika or Seniya (being the possessor of a large army). He was born in *c.* 558 B.C. He was fifteen years old when he was anointed king by his father. Thus, he ascended the throne of Magadha in 543 B.C. He was the first powerful sovereign of this kingdom. He is said to have built the new capital, Rājagṛha (Pāli Rājagaha), i.e. 'the king's house' or the royal palace to the north of the old capital at Girivraja (Pāli Giribbaja), 'the Hill fort', about which we will enter into details little later, because there are contradictory evidences as regards to the foundation of the city of Rājagṛha. Bimbisāra consolidated his position or extended his political influence by adopting a policy of matrimonial alliances. He married Kośaladevi, daughter of Mahākośala, the father of Prasenajit, the king of Kośala, Cellanā, a daughter of Cetaka, the Licchavi chief of Vaisali, and Kṣema, a daughter of the king of Madra in Central Punjab. These marriages paved the way for the expansion of Magadha both westward and northward. He also enlarged his kingdom by following a policy of conquest and annexation. After defeating Brahmadatta, he annexed Aṅga to his kingdom. Aṅga was small kingdom to the east corresponding with the modern Monghyr and Bhagalpur districts (Bihar). His eldest son, Ajātaśatru, imprisoned him and starved him to death. There are different accounts in the Pāli literature[12] about the circumstances, which resulted in his murder at the hands of his own son. The details may or may not be true, but this is a historical fact that he was put to death in 491 B.C. by Ajātaśatru exactly eight years before the death of the Buddha. According to the *Mahāvaṁśa* and the *Dipavaṁśa*, Bimbisāra ruled for fifty-two years, but according to the *Purāṇas*, either for twenty-eight or thirty-eight years. His historicity needs no further examination.

Bimbisāra was succeeded by his son Ajātaśatru about the year 491 B.C. He has been referred to as Vedehi-putto-Aajātaśattu in the canonical Pāli texts (being the son of the princess of Videha) and as Kunika in the Jaina canon. During the lifetime of his father he acted as Viceroy at Campa, the capital of Aṅga, which formed part of the kingdom of Magadha. Later he became an independent ruler of Magadha with its capital at Rājagṛha.

After Bimbisāra's death Queen Kosaladevi died of grief. Ajātaśatru then began to enjoy the revenues of the Kāśi village, dowry of his mother. But Pasenadi (or Prasenjita) of Kośala immediately confiscated the revenues of the Kāśi estate, which resulted in hostilities between him and Ajātaśatru. At last, the Magadhan monarch not only got the disputed township of Kāśi, but also the hand of Prasenjita's daughter, Vajira. Thus, Kāśi once again came under the sway of Ajātaśatru and the two kingdoms of Magadha and Kośala were once more closely united by matrimonial alliance.

Ajātaśatru afterwards succeeded not only in permanently annexing Kāśi to his kingdom, but also in absorbing the land of the Licchavis. According to the Pāli commentatorial tradition, Ajātaśatru being jealous of the Vrji-Licchavis (Vajjian confederacy) of Vaiśāli on account of their national solidarity and numerical strength declared war against them for uprooting their power. The sanguinary and protracted war, which took place between the two kingdoms, ultimately resulted in victory for Ajātaśatru. Consequently, the Licchavi territories were absorbed into the kingdom of Magadha. From the Pāli literature it appears that Ajātaśatru employed two of his ministers, Sunidha and Varsakāra, to build a fortress at the village of Pātali (called Pātaligāma or Pātaligrāma) opposite to Kotigāma on the other side of the Ganges (which formed the boundary between the two kingdoms) as a bulwark to repel attacks of the Licchavis on Magadha or as a protection against the Vajjian confederacy of Licchavis, Videhas and other clans of North Bihar.[13] The *Mahāparinibbāna Suttanta* (Digha II) states that Buddha, while going from Nālandā to Vaiśāli, visited Pātaligāma, where the two ministers of Ajātaśatru had built a fort to crush the Vajjians.

The annexation of Aṅga, Kāśi, Vaiśāli and other adjacent territories made Magadha the mightiest kingdom in Northern India. The Magadhan empire, no doubt, reached its height of glory during the reign of Ajātaśatru. It naturally aroused the jealousy of Pradyota of Avanti, who conceived of a plan of attacking Magadha. And, thus, Ajātaśatru began the fortification of his capital, Rājagṛha.[14] The remains of the wall can still be seen. The proposed invasion, however, did not materialize. The *Mahāvaṁśa* assigns a reign of thirty-two years of Ajātaśatru, while *Samantapāsādikā* gives twenty four years only as its duration. The *Purāṇic* tradition indicates that he reigned for twenty five or twenty-seven years. According to the *Mahāvaṁśa*,[15] he suffered the same miserable fate as his father, being put to death by his son Udāyi-Bhadda or Udāyibhadra in 459 B.C.

Here it is necessary to throw some light on the controversy, which centres round the building of the new city Rājagṛha, the ancient capital of Magadha, which had many names in the course of its long history. Its foundation is ascribed to both Bimbisāra and Ajātaśatru. According to the *Vinaya Pitaka*, "on account of the frequent night attacks on the old capital, Kuśāgrapura (the city of the "superior reed-grass" named after the *king* Kuśāgra of the Bārhadratha dynasty of the Pre-Bhārata war period), and the houses of citizens therein being set on fire at night by the Licchavis, Bimbisāra built the new capital, Rājagṛha (the outer town) to the north of Giribraja to check their invasions". Hiuen-Tsang in his account of Magadha has also clearly stated that "king Bimbisāra had his capital at Kuśāgrapura, which was constantly afflicted by disastrous fires. . . . When a fire broke out in the palace he made his heir king, and went to live in the cemetary. Hearing this the king of Vaiśāli proceeded to invade Magadha, whereaupon the new city Rājagṛha ('the king's abode') was built and all the inhabitants of Kuśāgrapura were removed to the site." Another story ascribes the building of the new city to Ajātaśatru. He as well as his successors made it their capital. He also refers to the outer wall of Rājagṛha city, which was utterly destroyed, but the "foundation of the inner wall stood out prominently and were twenty *li* in circuit with one gate".[16] Cunningham also supports the view that the new town of Rājagṛha was built by Bimbisāra, but his statement that its foundation cannot be placed later than "560 B.C. according to Buddhist chronology"[17] is not beyond dispute. Fa-Hien also refers to the old city of Bimbisāra and the new fortified city of Ajātaśatru. He attributes the foundation of new city Rājagṛha to Ajātaśatru.[18] According to the Chinese pilgrims' accounts, high mountains surrounded it on every side and formed its external ramparts as it were. The town was about 150 *li* in circuit. The remaining foundations of the wall of the inner city were about thirty *li* in circuit.[19] The Jain canonical texts also attest to the fact that the old city of Kuśāggpura of Bimbisāra's time was a "frequent prey to fires".[20] The old city is also mentioned in the non-canonical text.[21] Rājagiha (Rājagṛha) is mentioned also as Magadhapura.[22] In the Jain tradition Rājagiha, the capital city of Magadha, was one of the twenty-five and-a-half Aryan countries. It was included among ten prominent capitals of ancient India.[23] One of the very important non-canonical Jain text describes Rājagṛha as the residence of Bimbisāra (Srenika) and his sons and Ajātaśatru (Kunika). The city contained 36,000 houses of merchants including both Buddhists and Jainas.[24] In the Sanskrit Buddhist texts too the city finds mention. It is referred to in one of the texts as Mahānagara or a great capital city of Magadha. The city of Rājagṛha has been described as Magadhapura.[25] It was a rich, prosperous and populous city at the time of Bimbisāra and Ajātaśatru. It was also an important centre of inland trade, where the merchants flocked from different quarters.[26] According to Buddhaghosa, the inner and outer areas of Rājagaha city contained each nine crores of people. The city had thirty-two gates and sixty-four posterns.[27]

During the reigns of Bimbisāra and Ajātaśatru, the city of Rājagṛha was at the height of its prosperity. The city must have lost its glory with the removal of the capital to Pātaliputra or Kusumapura by Udayibhadda, some twenty-eight years after the Buddha's demise.[28] The ruins of both the old and the new capitals are still extant. The stone walls or the cyclopean walls of the old capital Giribraja are probably the oldest identified remains in India. According to Rhys Davids (BI; Delhi, 1971, pp. 37-38), the fortification of both old town, Giribbaja (a hill fortress, laid out by Mahā Govinda) and new town, Rājagaha or Rājagir (built by Bimbisāra at the foot of the hills) are "still extant, 4½ and three miles respectively in circumference; the most southerly point of the walls of Giribbaja . . . being one mile north of the most northerly point of the walls of the new town of Rājagaha, the "King's House". The stone walls of Giribbaja are the oldest extant stone buildings in India." The archaeological findings at the site—Rājagir include fortification forty kms. in circuit, citadel, brickwalls, the earthen rampart of the post-Buddhist period with deposits of NBPW, which dates back to 265+105 B.C. according to C-14 method of dating, etc.[29] Sir Mortimer Wheeler also points out that the earliest stone-structures in India are the remnants of the great defences of old Rājagir, twenty-five miles in length enclosing the site of the city, which was associated in the sixth century B.C. with the Buddha and Mahavir.[30]

According to the genealogical lists given in the *Purāṇas*, Ajātaśatru was succeeded by Darśaka, whose historicity can also be established on the basis of the evidence recorded in the Sanskrit literature. It is said that he was the king of Magadha and brother of Padmāvati, who was married to Udayana of Kośāmbi.[31] Actually, he was not the immediate successor of Ajātaśatru. He can be identified with Nāga Dāsaka, as mentioned in the Ceylonese chronicles. The Buddhist[32] and Jaina sources[33] confirm that Udāyi-Bhadda was the son and immediate successor of Ajātaśatru.

Udāyi or Udāyi-Bhadda, who succeeded his father about 459 B.C., is known to all the three traditions, the *Brāhmaṇic*, Buddhist and Jain. The *Purāṇas* bear testimony to the fact that Udaya or Udāyin founded the city of Kusumapura (=Pātaliputra) on the south bank of the Ganges in the fourth year of his reign and made it his new capital.[34] This agrees fairly well with the Jain tradition, according to which he transferred his capital from Campā (where he was acting as his father's viceroy) to Pātaliputra.[35] The new city of Kusumapura, which was either identical with the later Pātaliputra or its immediate neighbourhood, was built by Udāyi near the fortress, which his father had established at the village of Pātali. Pātaliputra, originally a village of Magadha and known as Pātaligāma, subsequently emerged as one of the greatest capitals in Gangetic India. The *Purāṇic* evidence can also be confirmed by the statements of Max Müller,[36] Lassen (German scholar)[37] and Greek writers.[38] But Lassen's statement that he ascended the throne of Magadha in 519 B.C. or twenty-four years after the *Nirvāna* of Buddha,[39] is partly wrong. The year of his accession was (483-24) 459 B.C. The Buddhist tradition ascribes the foundation of Pātaliputra to Kālaśoka, but it is not supported by other traditions. The date of his accession, i.e. 453 B.C., as recorded in the Greek source,[40] is not correct at all. According to the *Mahāvaṁśa*, Udāyin reigned for sixteen years, but the *Purāṇas* unanimously assign thirty-three years to him.

According to the *Purāṇas*, the successors of Udāyin were Nandivardhana and his son Mahānandin. The *Purāṇic* account does not tally with the *Mahāvaṁśa* and *Samantapāsādikā*, because these two sources mention Anuruddha, Muṇḍa and Nāga-dāsaka as the lineal descendants of Udāyi-Bhadda. Anuruddha and his son Muṇḍa jointly ruled for eight years and not eighteen years. The existence of Muṇḍa as the king of Magadha can fairly be attested by the testimony of *Divyā-vadāna*[41] and *Aṅguttara Nikāya*.[42] The latter by mentioning Pātaliputra as the capital of Muṇḍa confirms the tradition regarding the transfer of the Magadhan metropolis from Rājagṛha to Kusumapura or Pātaliputra before his reign.

According to the *Mahāvaṁśa*,[43] each of the five kings from Ajātaśatru to Nāgadāsaka killed his father and predecessor within a period of fifty-six years. The citizens because of being disgusted with the 'dynasty of patricides' deposed Nāgadāsaka, the last king of Bimbisāra's line, who had ruled for twenty-four years, and anointed the minister Śiśunāga as king in his stead. And, thus, a new dynasty known after him as Śiśunāga was founded. We cannot discard his evidence as wholly incredible.

Śiśunāga before becoming the king of Magadha was a mere *amātya* (minister) at Vārānasi. The *Purāṇas* also record that after placing his son on the throne of Kāśi, he occupied Girivraja,[44] the old capital of Magadha. The accession of Śiśunāga (Nandivardhana), according to the *Mahāvaṁśa*, took place eighty years (32+16+8+24) after the accession of Ajātaśatru, which falls in 411 B.C. According to the *Mahāvaṁśa*, he reigned for eighteen years, but the *Purāṇas* assign a reign-period of forty years to him. According to the Buddhist sources, he being the son of a Licchavi king of Vaiśāli had also his royal residence there. He later transferred his capital from Rājagṛha to Vaiśāli and thereafter Rājagṛha lost her rank of royal city.[45] The most noteworthy achievement of Śiśunāga was the destruction of the power and prestige of the Pradyotas.

Śiśunāga was succeeded by his son Kālāśoka (or Kākavarna), who reigned for twenty-six or twenty-eight years. He is said to have transferred his capital to Pātaliputta (Pātaliputra).[46] Chronologically, Kālāśoka, Kākavarna and Mahāṅandi are identified with each other.[47] The *Mahāvaṁśa* allots 22 years to the sons of Kālāśoka (V. 14) and twenty-two years to the nine Nandas (V. 15). Thus forty-four years elapsed between the death of Kālāśoka and the accession of Chandragupta (321 B.C.). This shows that Kālāśoka (Kākavarna-Mahānandi) died in (321+44=) 365 B.C.

The ten sons of Kālāśoka : Bhardrasena, Koraṇḍavarna, Mangura, Sarbañjaha, Jālika, Ubhaka, Sañjaya, Korabya, Nandivardhana and Pañcamaka (*Mahābhōdhivaṁśa*, p. 98) ruled simultaneously for twenty-two years perhpas under the guardianship of Mahāpadma Nanda by whom they were later murdered. Nandivardhana need not be identified with the *Purāṇic* Nandivardhana, as suggested by D.R. Bhandarkar.[48] The Śiśunāga dynasty was overthrown by Mahāpadma about the middle of the fourth century B.C. According to the *Purāṇas*, ten Śiśunāga kings ruled for 360[49] or 362 years.[50] According to the traditional dates, their rule began in 1,994 B.C. and ended in (1,994-360=) 1,634 B.C. or *Kali*-era (1108+360=) 1468.[51] According to some scholars, they reigned from 782 B.C. to 422 B.C.[52] A.K. Majumdar suggests their reign-periods as 655-405 B.C.[53] R. Morton Smith by fixing the date of Bimbisāra (521-493) on the basis of the *Purāṇic* figures has also followed wrong chronology.[54] According to the chronology arranged by F.E. Pargiter, their rule began in 575 B.C. or 567 B.C. and they ruled for (10 x average 16½ years) 165 years or 163 years.[55] However, the above dates are not acceptable to us.

In order to determine the chronology of the Śiśunāga kings, we have accepted their reign-periods given in the *Mahāvaṁśa* as correct in preference to those given in the *Purāṇas* and other sources, knowing it fully well that it may also be questioned, but it affords the best working hypothesis, which has yet been discovered. The chronology may be arranged thus :

1. Bimbisāra *c*. 543-491 B.C. — Contemporary with the Buddha c. 563-483 B.C.
2. Ajātaśatru *c*. 491-459 B.C.
3. Udāyi-bhadda *c*. 459-443 B.C.
4. Anuruddha and
5. Muṇḍa *c*. 443-435 B.C.
6. Nāgadāsaka or Darśaka *c*. 435-411 B.C.
7. Śiśunāga (=Nandivardhana) *c*. 411-393 B.C.
8. Kālāśoka (Kākavarna-Mahānandi) *c*. 393-365 B.C.
9. His ten sons *c*. 365-343 B.C.

This is a tentative chronological arrangement and there is always some scope for further adjustment.

The approximate dates of accession of the kings, as suggested by H.C. Raychaudhuri[56] in his chronological table, are as follows :

1. Bimbisāra 545-44 B.C.
2. Ajātaśatru 493 B.C.
3. Udāyibhadra 461 B.C. (foundation of Kusumapura or Pāṭaliputra in 457 B.C.)
4. Anuruddha and
5. Muṇḍa 445 B.C.
6. Nāga-Dāsaka 437 B.C.
7. Śiśunāga 413 B.C.
8. Kālāśoka (Kakavarna) 395 B.C.
9. Sons of Kālāśoka 376 B.C.

End of the Śaiśunāga dynasty 345 B.C.

The chronology arranged by S.N. Pradhan,[57] as given below, is primarily based on the dates modified in a Jain work, *Sthavirāvalicarta* of Hemacandra :

Bimbisāra 547 B.C.-495 B.C.
Ajātaśatru 495 B.C.-463 B.C.
Udāyin 463 B.C.-447 B.C.
Aniruddha-Muṇḍa 447 B.C.-439 B.C.
Nāga-Dāsa 439 B.C.-415 B.C.
Nandivardhana-Śiśunāga 415 B.C.-397 B.C.
Kākavarna-Mahānandi=397 B.C.-369 B.C.

Mr. Pradhan has not calculated the reign-period (22 years) of 10 sons of Kālāśoka assuming that Mahāpadma Nanda ruled during that period in their name. But this can fairly be disputed.

It is true that the *Purāṇas* knew no break of political continuity between the Śiśunāgas and the Nandas, but it is not impossible to distinguish them and to draw a demarcation line between the end of one dynasty and the beginning of other. It was probably 343 B.C. which marked the end of the Śaiśunāga dynasty. R.S. Tripathi[58] has also accepted exactly the same date.

### The Nanda Dynasty (*c.* 343-321 B.C.)

According to the *Purāṇas*, the founder and first kings of the Nanda dynasty (which was basically a Śudra dynasty) was Mahāpadma Nanda, son of Mahānandin by a woman of Śudra or servile class. After having exterminated the *Kṣatriyas* comprising twenty-four Aikṣvākus, twenty-seven or twnety-five Pañcalas, twenty-four Kāśis, thirty-six or twenty-six Kurus, twenty-eight or twenty-four Haihayas, thirty-two Kalingas, twenty-five Aśmakas, twenty-eight Maithilas, twenty-three Śurasenas and twenty Vitihotras (who were ruling contemporaneously over ten different kingdoms during the reign-periods of the Śiśunāga kings) and brought their territories under his political hegemony, he extended the influence and the limits of the Magadha kingdom, which made him sovereign ruler (ekarāt) and, thereafter, established Śudra rule in Magadha. He has rightly been compared with Paraśurama, who was the first to destroy the *Kṣatriya* race. Mahāpadma was succeeded by his eight sons, including Sumalya (or Sukalpa, Sumati, etc.), who also ruled over Magadha[59] for considerable period of time, which has been discussed in detail later.

According to the *Bhaviṣya Purāṇa*, the successors of Mahāpadma were Prananda, Parananda, Samananda, Priyananda, Devānanda, Yajñananda, Mauryananda and Mahānanda.[60] This is not fully worthy of credence, because of inclusion of Mauryananda (the founder of the Maurya dynasty) in the list. The more credible list is provided in the *Mahābōdhivaṁśa* (p. 98), according to which the nine Nandas were : Ugrasena, Paṇḍuka, Paṇḍugati, Bhūtapāla, Rāṣṭrapāla, Gōvisāṇaka, Dasasidhaka, Kevaṭṭa and Dhanananda. The last reigning Nanda king, called Dhanananda in the Buddhist literature and Agrammes or Xandrammes in the classical (Greek and Roman) literature, was the contemporary of Alexander (326 B.C.). According to Curtius, he maintained a stupendous army, consisting of 200,000 infantry, 20,000 cavalry, 2,000 chariots and 4,000 elephants and possessed immense wealth. Within a few years of Alexander's retirement from India the Nanda dynasty was overthrown by Candragupta Maurya with the help of his astute minister, Kautilya or Cāṇakya, and the suzerainty passed from the Nandas to the Mauryas. According to the *Mahāvaṁśa*, Dhanananda was put to death by Cāṇakya.[61] The *Purāṇic*,[62] Buddhist[63] and Jain[64] traditions confirm that the Nanda were uprooted by Kauṭilya, who installed Candragupta Maurya on the throne of Magadha about 322-21 B.C. This fact can also be attested to by *Kauṭilya*'s *Arthaśāstra*, *Kāmandaka's Nītisāra* and *Viśākhadatta's Mudrārākṣasa.*

The duration of the Nanda dynasty consisting of two generations—Mahāpadma and his eight sons, according to the *Matsya* (88+12 years respectively)[65], the *Vayu* (which mentions twenty-eight years for the former and 100 years for all)[66] and the *Viṣṇu Purānas*

(100 years for all)[67], was 100 years. The long reign of eighty-eight years assigned to Mahapadma in the *Matsya* is obviously an error for twenty-eight. At best, (28+12=) 40 years can be assigned to them according to the *Purāṇas*. According to traditional dates, their rule began in 1,634 B.C. and came to an end in (1,634–100=) 1,534 B.C. or 1568 (1468+100) *Kali*-era.[68] Some scholars suggest that they ruled from 422 B.C. to 322 B.C.[69] R. Morton Smith by assigning eighty-eight years to Mahāpadma has erroneously placed him between 422 B.C. and 334 B.C.[70] A.K. Majumdar has also wrongly assigned to them ninty-two years. According to him, they ruled from 405 to 313 B.C.[71] S.N. Pradhan by assigning twenty-eight years to Mahāpadma and sixteen years to his sons (believing that Kauṭilya took sixteen years to uproot them) has allotted total (28+16=) 44 years to them. And, accordingly, Mahāpadma ruled from 369 B.C. to 341 B.C. and his sons 341 B.C. to 325 B.C.[72] Wilford accepting the *Purāṇic* figures—40 years (=28+12)—has fixed their period as *c.* 355-315 B.C.[73] Pargiter does not take the *Purāṇic* figures (88+12=) 100 years as unreasonable. But, on the other hand, by reducing it to eighty years he has reckoned their reign-periods as 402-322 B.C.[74] According to V.A. Smith, Mahāpadma usurped the throne of Magadha in or about 413 B.C.[75] Prof. Lassen in order to attach an historical importance to the conventional date (543 B.C.) of Buddha's death, adds sixty-six years to twenty-two years of the reign of the Nandas and he quotes in support of this the authority of the *Purāṇas*, which assign eighty-eight years to the first Nanda.[76]

According to the Jain chronology, the first Nanda became king sixty years after the death of Mahavira, which comes to (477–60=) 417 B.C. Nanda and his descendants continued to rule Magadha till the last king was deposed by Cāṇakya 155 years after the death of Mahāvira. It is equivalent to (477-155=) 322 B.C. Thus, they ruled from 417 B.C. to 322 B.C., which covers a period of 95 years=(417-322 or 155-60).[77] This is in approximation to the *Purāṇic* figure, i.e. 100 years. A lot of confusion abounds in the Jaina works. Thus, they also cannot be accepted in toto. The Pāli chronicle[78] and commentary[79] assign altogether twenty-two years to all the Nandas as the length of their reigns. The Buddhist chronology is definitely more reliable than the other chronologies. Hence, the Nanda dynasty, probably, came to an end in (343-22=) 321 B.C.

## References and Notes

1. *Vy.*, 99, 314-21; *Mats.*, 272, 5-13; *Mats.*, (*SBA*) ch. CCLXXII, pp. 334-35, also Tab; *Vṣṇ.*, IV, 24, 9-19; *Vṣṇ.*, tr. H.H. Wilson, ch. XXIV, pp. 372-75; *Bmd.*, 3, 74, 127-33; *Bhāg.*, XII, 1, 4-7; *Bhv.*, (Supra), Vol. 1, pp. 332-33, *vv.* 26-31; See also Pargiter, *PDKA*, pp. 21-6, 67-9; F. Max Muller, *HASL*, pp. 365-6; R.S. Tripathi, *HAI* (Delhi, 1985), pp. 113-14; S.N. Pardhan, *Chro. Anc. Ind.*, p. 228. For the regnal years the *Vy.*, *Mats.* and *Bmd.* are important. The *Bhaviṣya Purāṇa* gives *bombastic* figures, which have not been used.
2. Ed. W. Geiger (PTS, London, 1908), ch. 11, *vv.*, 28-32; IV, 1-7; V. 14; also pp. 12 and 15; tr. W. Geiger (PTS, London, 1912), Intr. pp. XI-XIVI, ch. VII, pp. 163 f, 168 f.
3. Ed. and trans. H. Oldenberg (London, 1879), III, 50-60, 97; ch. v. The source is of limited value.
4. Ed. J. Takakusu and M. Nagai (PTS, London, 1924), Vol. 1, pp. 72-73.
5. *Āvaśyaka Cūrni*, II, pp. 158, 165-7, 179 f; *Paramaṭṭhadipani* Comm. on the Udāna, p. 104; *Uttarādhyayana Sūtra*, 20, 58; Udāyibhadda is mentioned in the Vinayavastu of the Mūlasarvāstivāda, pp. 42 f. *cf.* J.C. Jain, *LAIJC*, pp. 449-52, 462, 472-73; also Pattāvali-Samuccaya, p. 17.
6. cf. *SBE*, XI, p. 16.

7. Carmichael Lectures, 1918.
8. *EHI* (4th ed., Oxford, 1924), pp. 31-32.
9. *Op. cit.*, pp. 244-45.
10. *PHAI* (6th edn. Calcutta, 1953), pp. 205, 210, 225.
11. *Op. cit.*, pp. 93, 109, 114.
12. *Vinaya* (ed. H. Oldenberg, London, 1879-83), II, 190; *Digha-Nikāya*, (*Sāmaññapaphala-Sūtta*), I, 86; *Sumangala-Vilāsini*, I, 133-36.
13. *Digha Nikāya*, II, 87; *Sumangalavilāsini*, II, pp. 516-17; *Mahā-parinibbāna Suttanta* (ed. S.G. Prajñānanda, Lucknow, 1981), pp. 33-37; *Vinaya Texts, SBE*, II, p. 101, *cf.* B.C. Law, *HPL*, Vol. II, pp. 648, 650.
14. *Majjhima Nikāya*, III, 7.
15. Ch. IV, v. 1.
16. Thomas Watters, *YCTI* (Delhi, 1973), Vol. II, pp. 162, also pp. 148, 151; See also S. Beal, *The Life of Hiuen-Tsang* or *BRWW* (Delhi, 1973), p. 113.
17. *CAGI*, p. 394.
18. Giles, *RBK*, pp. 48-49; Legge, *RBK*, ch. XXVIII, p. 81.
19. S. Beal, *op. cit.*, p. 113.
20. *Āvaṛyaka Cūrni*, II, p. 158 *cf.* J.C. Jain, *op. cit.*, p. 449.
21. *Vasudevahiṇḍi* (Bhavnagar, 1930-1), p. 74, 7 *cf.* J.C. Jain, *op. cit.*, p. 482; see also J.C. Jain, *The Vasudevahiṇḍi* (Ahmedabad, 1977).
22. Ibid., 2, 16; 16, 4, 20, 5; *Āvaṛyaka Cūrni*, p. 459; *Commentary on Uttarādhyayana*, 13, p. 192 *cf.* J.C. Jain; *LAIJC*, p. 389.
23. J.C. Jain, *op. cit.*, p. 407.
24. *Jinaprabhasūri, Vividhatirthakalpa* (ed. by Jinavijaya, Bombay, 1934), p. 22.
25. *Lalitavistara*, pp. 239, 243, 246.
26. *Divyāvadāna*, pp. 307, 545.
27. S. Hardy, Manual of Buddhism, p. 323.
28. B.C. Law, "Rājagṛha in Ancient Literature" in *MASI*, No. 58, Delhi, 1938.
29. See A. Ghosh, Rājagir-1950, AI; No. 7, pp. 66 ff; also his The City in Early Historical India (Simla, 1973), pp. 60-72.
30. *EIP* (London, 1968), p. 173.
31. *Bhāsa's Svapnavāsavdatta*, Act. 1 (ed. Trivandrum SK. Series, p. 4, 5).
32. *Dipavaṁśa*, v. 97; *Mahāvaṁśa*, IV.1; *Digha Nikāya (Sāmaññaphala-Sutta)*, I, p. 50; *Sumangalavilāsini*, Vol. I, pp. 153-4; *Samantapāsādikā*, Vol. I. p. 72.
33. *Hemacandra's Pariṛiṣṭaparvan* (ed. H. Jacobi, *BIS*, Calcutta, 2nd ed. 1932), p. 42.
34. *Vy.*, 99, 319-20; *Mats.*, 272, 8-11, *Hv.*, 32, 61. See also *PK*, pp. 22-23, 122.
35. *Parisiṣṭaparvan*, IV, 34; 175-80, also pp. 42-43; Hemacandra's *Sthavirā-Valicarita* (ed. H. Jacobi, *ASB*, Calcutta, 1891), VI, 22-188; J.C. Jain, *op. cit.*, p. 472.
36. *Op. cit.*, p.. 265, note 4.
37. *Ind. Alt.*, Vol. II, p. 63.
38. McCrindle, *AIMA* (London, 1877), pp. 211-12.
39. *Op. cit.*
40. *AIMA*, p. 211.
41. Ed. E.B. Cowell and R.A Neil (Cambridge, 1886), XXVI, 369.
42. Ed. R. Morris and E. Hardy (PTS, London, 1885-1990), III, pp. 57 ff.

43. Text, IV, 3, 7, tr. ch. VII, pp. 168 f; See also *Samantapāsādikā*, Vol. I, pp. 72-73 *cf.* B.C. Law, *HPL*, p. 407.
44. *Bmd.*, III, 74, 127-8; *Vy.*, 99, 314-15; *Mats.*, 272, 5-6.
45. T.W. Rhys Davids, *BI* (Delhi, 1971), p. 37; *Mahāvaṁśatikā*, Turnour's tr. of *Mahāvaṁśa*, XXXVII.
46. Rhys. Davids, *BI*, p. 37.
47. K.P. Jayaswal (*JBORS*, 1915, Sept. p. 77) has wrongly identified Kākavarna Śaiśunāgi with Nandivardhana, the successor of Udāyi.
48. Carm. lec. 1918, p. 83.
49. *Mats.*, 272, 12-13; *Bhāg.*, XII, 1, 4-6.
50. *Vy.*, 99, 321; *Vṣṇ.*, IV, 24, 18-19.
51. M. Krishnamachariar (*HCSL*, Intr.) has fixed their reign-periods as 1,995-1,635 B.C.
52. *Mats.*, *SBA*, Tables.
53. *EHIDS*, Vol. II, pp. 396-502.
54. *DDEI*, pp. 346-58.
55. *AIHT*, p. 287; PDKA; 21-22, 67-9.
56. *PHAI*, p. 228.
57. *Op. cit.*, p. 245.
58. *Op. cit.*, p. 149.
59. *Vy.*, 99, 321-28; *Mats.*, 272, 14-21; *Mats.*, *SBA*, p. 335; *Vṣṇ*, IV. 24, 20-24; *Vṣṇ.*, tr. H.H. Wilson, ch. XXIV, p. 374; *Bhāg.*, XII, 1, 9-12; *Bmd.*, 3, 74, 139-44; Pargiter, *PDKA*, pp. 23-4, 69; Max Muller, *HASL*, p. 266.
60. Supra, Vol. I, pp. 333, *vv.* 31-35.
61. pp. 15 and 21.
62. *Vṣṇ.*, IV, 24, 25-28; *Vy.*, 99, 329-31; *Mats.*, 272, 21-22.
63. *Mhv.*, pp. 15 and 21.
64. J.C. Jain, *op. cit.*, pp. 453-54.
65. *Mats.*, 272, 18-22.
66. *Vy.*, 99, 326-30.
67. *Viṣṇu Purāṇa*, IV, 24, 25-26.
68. See also *HCSL*, Intr. XLIX-XLVIII (where it is 1,635-1,535 B.C.)
69. *Mats.*, SBA, p. 335 and Tables.
70. *DDEI*, pp. 359-61.
71. *EHIDS*, Vol. II, pp. 502-3.
72. Op. cit., pp. 227, 245.
73. *As. Res.*, Vol. IX, pp. 91-116.
74. *PDKA*, pp. 25-6, 69-70; *AIHT*; p. 287.
75. *EHI*, (4th edn.), p. 41.
76. *cf.* Max Muller, op. cit., p. 268.
77. *Pariśiṣṭaparvan*, VI, 243; VIII, 339; *Sthavirāvali-carita*, VI, 231-43; VIII, 339.
78. *Mhv.*, V. 15.
79. *Samantapāsādikā*, Vol. I, p. 72, *cf. Mhv.*, ch. IV.

# 6

# The Maurya and the post-Maurya Dynasties down to the Sātavāhanas

### (*c.* 321 B.C.—225 A.D.)

## The Maurya Dynasty (*c.* 321-184 B.C.)

THE *Purāṇic*, Buddhist and Jain traditions confirm that Candragupta was the founder of the Imperial Maurya dynasty of Magadha. Traditions differ regarding his antecedents. According to the *Brāhmaṇic* tradition, he was the son of the last Nanda Monarch by his *śudra* wife (or concubine), named Mura after whom he and his descendants were styled as Mauryas.[1] The Jain tradition represents him (Candagutta) as the son of a daughter of the chief of a village of peacock-tamers (*mayura-posaka*), which belonged to the Nandas.[2] The Buddhist tradition testifies to the fact that he was the son of the chief queen of the king of *Kṣatriya* or Moriya clan (a branch of the Śākyas) then ruling over Pipphalivana,[3] a tribal republic situated between Rummindei in the Nepalese Tarai and Kasia in the Gorakhpur district (U.P.). The three traditions seem to be irreconcilable. Like his origin, the date of his accession is also a controversial subject. Historians and other scholars are divided in their opinions about any conclusive date, the reasons for which may precisely be attributed to different methods of calculation of the duration of reign of each individual king and total reign-periods of all the kings of the Bimbisārian, Śaiśunāga and Nanda dynasties, as given in the *Purāṇic* and Buddhist literature, and that of the date of *Nirvānas* of Buddha and Mahāvira. The determination of the date of his accession principally depends on dates of the end of latter two dynasties mentioned above, as they are closely interlinked. According to our calculation (that the Śaiśunāga dynasty ended in 343 B.C. and the Nandas reigned for twenty-two years only, vide the preceding chapter), he ascended the throne of Magadha in 321 B.C., (343-22)which goes in accord with the date suggested by the Ceylonese Buddhist chronicles. According to them, Candragupta ascended the throne 162 years after the death of

Buddha in 483 B.C. (given in the *Mahāvaṁśa*), which comes to 321 B.C. (483-162) The Buddhist tradition of Ceylon is far more reliable than any other tradition in this regard.

S.N. Pradhan, accepting 487 B.C. as the date of the death of Buddha, has suggested 325 B.C. (487-162) as the probable date for the accession of Candragupta.[4] Further, in confirmation of this date he, on the basis of his calculation, suggests that 369 B.C. marked the end of the Śiśunāga dynasty and the Nandas ruled from 369 B.C. to 325 B.C., which covers a period of 44 years.[5] Max Muller, by placing his reliance on the Buddhist and Greek chronology, has inferred that Candragupta became king about 315 B.C. According to him, he ascended the throne 162 years after the death of Buddha in 477 B.C., which comes to 315 B.C. (477-162). Justin's (XV. 4) account, that Sandrocottus (Candragupta) had seized the throne of Magadha after the prefects of Alexander had been murdered in 317 B.C., has also led him to believe that his accession might have taken place in 315 B.C.[6] The date is purely based on his own supposition.

The Jaina tradition recorded in Hemacandra's *Pariśiṣṭaparvan*[7] proves that Candragupta became king 155 years after the death of Mahāvira. This gives us 322 B.C. (=477-155) as the date of his accession. Another Jaina tradition recorded in Merutunga's *Vicāra-śreni* places his accession 255 years before Vikrama. Hence, his accession dates back to 312 B.C. (255+57). It is on the strength of the Jaina traditions that A.K. Majumdar[8] and N.K. Bhattasali[9] have accepted 312 B.C. and 313 B.C. respectively as the date of his accession.

Wilford, by assigning 355 B.C. to the beginning of Nanda dynasty and allotting total forty years to the Nandas' rule over Magadha, has accepted 315 B.C. (355-40) as the date of Candragupta's accession.[10] Some scholars blindly accepting 100 years duration of the Nanda dynasty, as given in the *Purāṇas*, place the Nandas between 422 and 322 B.C. and accept the latter as the date of his accession. The available dates of his accession altogether vary from 325 to 312 B.C. I am unable to agree with scholars who suggest 325 B.C. or whose dates range from 315 to 312 B.C., so far as the date of his accession is concerned. At best, either 322 or 321 B.C. can be accepted. These are the two dates which have received maximum support from the historians.

Candragupta was succeeded by another eight or nine kings. We find some variations in the dynastic lists of the Mauryan kings given in the *Purāṇic* texts, and the Pali chronicles and commentaries and the Sanksrit texts of the Buddhists. The lists containing the names of kings and the length of their reigns are given below.

The following list (a) is based on the comparative and critical study of the *Purāṇas* (texts, translations and commentaries).[11]

## (a) Purāṇic List

| No. | Name | Length of reign | Remarks |
|---|---|---|---|
| 1. | Candragupta | 24 years (*Vy., Bmd.*) | |
| 2. | Bindusāra (Bhadrasāra) | 25 years (*Vy., Bmd.*) | |
| 3. | Aśoka | 36 years (*Bmd.*, 26 or 36 ; *Vy.*) | The interval of 4 years, falling in between his accession and coronation, have not been added to 36 in the *Purāṇas*. Actually, he ruled for 40 years, which is historically authenticated. |
| 4. | Kunāla (or Suyaśa) | 8 years (*Vy., Bmd.*) | |
| 5. | Daśaratha (Bandhupālita) | 8 years (*Vy., Bmd., Mats.*) | |
| 6. | Indrapālita (or Samprati, Sangata, etc.) | 10 years (*Vy., Bmd.*) (or 9 years) | |
| 7. | *Śāliśuka* | | The name of Śāliśuka has been omitted from the lists of all the *Purāṇas* except the *Vṣṇ.*, where he has been mentioned without regnal year. But in some annotated versions, he has been assigned a reign of 13 years, which can be set aside on the authorities of the *Vy.* and *Bmd.*, which clearly state that the successors of Daśaratha or Bandhupālita excluding Śāliśuka reigned for ten years. The name of Śāliśuka appears only in certain recensions of the *Purāṇic* list. |
| 8. | Devavarman (or Somaśarman) | 7 years (*Vy., Bmd.*) | |
| 9. | Satadhanvan (or Satadhara, Satadhanus) | 8 years (*Vy., Bmd.*) 6 (*Mats.*) | |
| 10. | Bṛhadratha (or Bṛhadasva) | 7 years (*Vy. Bmd.*) (*Mats.* 70, which is an error for 7) | |
| | Total | 133 + the said 4 years = 137 years. | |

The *Purāṇas* are unanimos so far as 137 years duration of the reigns of nine or ten Mauryas are concerned.[12] The *Viṣṇu Purāṇa* is the exception, where the total of the reign-periods has been inadvertently mentioned as 173 years.[13] The kings of the Maurya dynasty according to the *Purāṇas* ruled over Magadha for 137 years, which is absolutely the correct figure. The historical validity of the said *Purāṇic* duration will be further examined by the genealoy and chronology of this chapter. Here some other dynastic lists are given, so as to judge the historicity of the *Purāṇic* list as well as to have a comparative view of all the lists concerned :

## (b) Pargiter's List[14]

| No | Name | Length of reign | Remarks |
|---|---|---|---|
| 1. | Kunāla or Suyaśas | 8 years | There are some discrepancies in his list. He has wrongly mentioned Daona as a son of n. 3 and Daśaratha as a son of n. 4. Daona does not figure in the original *Puraṇas.* Samprati was not the son of no. 5. The fact remains that Daśaratha or Bandhupālita and Samprati or Indrapalita were the two sons of Kunāla. |
| 2. | Bandhupālita, son of Kunāla | 8 years | |
| 3. | Indrapālita | | |
| 4. | Daona, son of 3 | 7 years | |
| 5. | Daśaratha, son of 4 | 8 years | |
| 6. | Samprati or Saṅgata, son of 5 | 9 years | |
| 7. | Śāliśuka, son of 6 | 13 years | |
| 8. | Devadharman or Devavarman. Somasarman, son of 7 | 7 years | |
| 9. | Satadhanvan or Sasadharman, son of 8 | 8 years | |
| 10. | Bṛhadratha | 7 years | |

### (c) List based on the Buddhist Sources

| | *Mahāvaṁśa*[15] | *Samantapāsādikā*[16] |
|---|---|---|
| Candragupta | reigned for 34 years (which is mistake for 24) | 24 (the same in the Dip.) (*c.* 321-297 B.C. |
| Bindusara | 28 years (In the Burmese tradition 27) | 28 (*c.* 297-269 B.C.) |

***Aśoka***

According to the Buddhist tradition of Ceylon, his coronation took place 218 years after the death of Buddha.[17] Thus, it was 265 B.C. (483-218). Since he was crowned four years after his accession,[18] the actual beginning of his reign, according to this chronology will go back to 269 B.C., which is not acceptable. There is another evidence to show that his coronation did not take place until 269 B.C.[19] which means that he ascended the throne in 273 B.C. On the assumption that he ruled for thrity-six or thirty-seven years, as the *Purāṇas* and Pāli sources affirm, it is believed that he either reigned from 274-3 B.C. to 237-6 B.C. or from 269 B.C. to 232 B.C.[20] In fact, he ruled from 272 to 232 B.C., which covers a period of forty years. According to V.A. Smith, Candragupta abdicated or died in 298-13 B.C.,[21] Bindusāra's reign terminated about 273 B.C. and Aśoka's reign began in 272 B.C.[22] The Buddhist chronology is not at much variance with the *Purāṇic* chhronology from Candragupta's time onwards.

## (d) According to Divyāvadāna[23]

1. Candragupta
2. Bindusāra
3. Aśoka
4. Kunāla
5. Sampadi, son of 4 (Samprati or Indrapālita)
6. Vrihaspati, son of 5 (Śāliśuka)
7. Vrishasena, son of 6 (Devavarman)
8. Pushyadharman, son of 7 (Satadhanven)
9. Pushyamitra (Commander-in-chief of the last ruler, Brihadratha)

Chronology is not given.

The *Purāṇas* do not provide the details of achievements of any one of the Mauryan kings listed above. However, it is significant to note that in one particular *Purāṇa* it is incidentally mentioned that Candragupta was married to the daughter of Suluva (Seleucus),[24] a general of Alexander, following the peace treaty, which was concluded in 305 B.C. or sometime between 303 and 302 B.C. It is needless to enter into details about the first three kings, since much has already been written about them and their historicity is well-established.

The existence of some of Aśoka's successors (or the later Mauryas), as mentioned in the *Purāṇas*, can, or course, be proved with the help of some available historical and archaeological evidence.

There are contradictory accounts about the immediate successor of Aśoka, who died in or about 232 B.C. after a long reign of forty years. According to the *Vāyu* and *Brahmāṇḍa Purāṇas*, Aśoka was succeeded by one of his sons, Kunāla (Suyaśa), who ruled for eight years. But his accession to the imperial throne is doubted on account of his blindness. The possibility of his being the virtual ruler cannot be precluded. The *Vāyu*, *Brahmāṇḍa* and *Matsya Purāṇas* testify to the fact that he was succeeded by his son Daśaratha (Bandhupālita), who also ruled for eight years. The existence of Daśaratha can be proved by the 'Nāgārjuni Cave Inscriptions'.[25] According to Buhler, the said inscriptions date back to *c.* 232 B.C.,[26] which constitutes the basis for deduction that he might have been the immediate successor of Aśoka. The succession of Indrapālita (Samprati), another son of Kunāla, immediately after Daśaratha can also be substantiated by the *Purāṇas*. He ruled either for nine or ten years. But Jain and Buddhist writers hold that Aśoka was immediately succeeded by his grandson, Samprati,[27] which is not tenable. V.A. Smith's view, that after Aśoka there was a partition of the Maurya Empire between his two grandsons, Daśaratha and Samprati, the former got the eastern part and the latter the western,[28] appears to be conjectural. Actually, this partition occurred after the death of Kunāla. The existence of Śāliśuka is proved not only by the testimony of the *Viṣṇu Purāṇa*, but also by the *Yuga Purāṇa* Section of the *Gārgi Saṁhitā*.[29] The successors of Samprati, as mentioned in the lists concerned, were weak and incompetent, which gradually led to the decline of the Maurya power. According to the Purāṇas, Bṛhadratha, the last king of the Maurya dynasty, was treacherously murdered by his own commander-in-chief, Puṣyamitra Śuṅga, who established himself upon the throne of his master and set up the Śuṅga dynasty.[30] This can also be supported by the evidence furnished in *Bāṇa's Harṣa-Carita*.[31]

**Genealogy of the Mauryas with Chronology**
**(based on the *Purāṇic* list)**

Candragupta Maurya (*c.* 321-297 B.C.)

Bindusāra (*c.* 297-272 B.C.)

Aśoka (*c.* 272-232 B.C.)

Kunāla (Suyaśa) (c. 232-224 B.C.)

Daśaratha (Bandhupālita) (*c.* 224-216 B.C.)

Samprati (Indrapālita)
Śāliśuka
*c.* 216-206 B.C.

Devavarman or Somaśarman (*c.* 206-199 B.C.)

Satadhanvan or Sasadharman (*c.* 199-191 B.C.)

Bṛhadratha (*c.* 191-184 B.C.)

It appears that the Mauryas ruled from 321 B.C. to 184 B.C., which covers a period of exactly 137 years. This proves the validity of the *Purāṇic* chronology. The traditional belief that the duration of this dynasty was 316 years and the Mauryas ruled from 1,534 B.C. to (1,534-316=) 1,218 B.C. (in *Kali* era=1,884=1,568+316),[32] can be disposed of.

**The Śuṅga Dynasty (*c.* 184-72 B.C.)**

Puṣyamitra, the founder of the Śuṅga dynasty, ruled over Magadha with its capital at Pātaliputra for thirty-six years from 184 to 148 B.C. The *Divyāvadāna* (p. 434) affirms that the emperor continued to reside in Pātaliputra. He was followed by nine kings, who altogether ruled for seventy-six years.

The dynastic list of ten Śuṅga kings, as given in the *Purāṇas*,[33] is furnished below :

| No. | Name | Length of reign | Remarks |
|---|---|---|---|
| 1. | Puṣyamitra | 36 years (*Mats.*), 60 (*Vy.*, *Bmd.*) (184-148 B.C.) | Sixty years is manifestly due to textual corruption. |
| 2. | Agnimitra | 8 years (*Mats.*) (reigned during the period of his father) | The *Vy.* and *Bmd.* do not mention him at all. He was the viceroy at Vidisa during the life-time of his father. |
| 3. | Vasujyeṣṭha or Sujyeṣṭha | 7 years (*Vy.*, *Bmd.*, *Mats.*) (148-141 B.C.) | |
| 4. | Vasumitra | 10 years (*Vy.*, *Bmd.*, *Mats.*) (141-131 B.C.) | |
| 5. | Odraka (or Andhraka, Udaka, etc.) | 2 years (*Vy.*, *Bmd.*, *Mats.*) (131-129 B.C.) | |
| 6. | Pulindaka | 3 years (*Vy.*, *Bmd.*, *Mats.*) (129-126 B.C.) | |
| 7. | Ghosa (or Ghosavasu) | 3 years (*Vy.*, *Bmd.*) (126-123 B.C.) | |
| 8. | Vajramitra | 9 years (*Mats.*, 9 or 14), 7 (*Bmd.*) 3 (*Vy.*), (123-114 B.C.) | 9 years is correct figure. |
| 9. | Bhagavata | 32 years (*Vy.*, *Bmd.*, *Mats.*), (114-82 B.C.) | |
| 10. | Devabhuti or (Devabhumi) | 10 years (*Vy.*, *Bmd.*, *Mats.*), (82-72 B.C.) | |
| | Total | 120-8 = 112 years | |

The aggregate of the figures as shown above amounts to 120 years. But the total duration of the reigns of ten Śuṅga kings (who appear to have been Brāhmaṇs) as mentioned in some *Purāṇas*,[34] is 112 years, which seems to be absolutely correct, because Agnimitra's reign-period of 8 years is not included in 120 years. Thus, they ruled exactly for (120-8=) 112 years from 184 B.C. to 72 B.C. and not for "300 years", as wrongly mentioned in the *Matsya Purāṇa*.[35] It will not be correct to say that they ruled from 1,218 B.C. to (1,218-300 =) 918 B.C. (or *Kali* era 2,184=1,884+300).[36]

Puṣyamitra and Agnimitra of Vidisa (their Western capital) and Vasumitra have also been mentioned in the *Mālavikāgnimitra*[37] of Kālidāsa. Agnimitra's successor Vasujyeṣṭha mentioned in the *Purāṇas* is identical with Jethamitra of the coins.[38] The name of Vasumitra or Sumitra is also mentioned in Bāna's *Harṣacarita*.[39] K.P. Jayaswal has identified Odraka or Udaka of the *Purāṇic* list with Ordaka of Pabhosā (the ancient kingdom of Kauśāmbi) inscription (no. 904).[40] He has identified the *Purāṇic* list of Śuṅga kings like Ghosavasu and Sujyeṣṭha with those found in the coins and inscriptions.[41] The last king, but one, *Bhāgavata* of the *Purāṇas*, is identified with Bhāgabhadra mentioned in a Garuda pillar Inscription found in the Old City of Vidisa or Besnagar. The inscription was engraved, when the king was reigning in his twelfth year. In the fourteenth year of his reign, the Besnagar column was erected by Heliodrous, son of Dion, the Yavana ambassador, who had come to the court of Vidisa from Antialcidas, king of Takṣaśilā.[42] Devabhuti, the last monarch of the Śuṅga family, was killed by his minister, Vasudeva, a Kāṇva *Brāhman*, who founded the Kāṇva dynasty.[43] The Śuṅga dynasty probably came to an end about 73-2 B.C.

According to E.J. Rapson, "... the Śuṅgas were military power, and that they became puppets in the hands of their *Brāhmaṇ* counsellors. They ruled originally as feudatories of the Mauryas at Vidisa, the modern Besnagar on the Vetravati near Bhilsa and about 120 miles east of Ujjain".[44]

**The Kāṅva Dynasty (*c.* 72-27 B.C.)**

According to the Purāṇas,[45] this dynasty comprised four kings, who ruled in Magadha for forty-five years only. The details are given below :

| No. | Name of king | Length of reign |
|---|---|---|
| 1. | Vasudeva | 9 years (*Mats., Vy.*) (*c.* 72-63 B.C.) |
| 2. | Bhūmitra | 14 years (*Mats.*, 24 (*Vy.* an error for 14) (*c.* 63-49 B.C.) |
| 3. | Nārāyana | 12 years (*Mats.*, Vy.) (*c.* 49-37 B.C.) |
| 4. | Suśarman | 10 years (*Mats., Vy.*) (*c.* 37-27 B.C.) |
| | Total | 45 years |

The *Purāṇas* have correctly assigned a duration of 45 years to the four Kāṇva or Kāṇvayana Brāhmaṇ kings.[46] Thus, they reigned from 72 B.C. to 27 B.C. R.G. Bhandarkar[47] and R.S. Tripathi[48] have supported the Purāṇic duration of their rule. According to H.C. Raychaudhuri, their rule extended from *c.* 75 B.C. to 30 B.C.,[49] which is not worthy of acceptance. Rajabali Pandey, while supporting the Purāṇic list of the Śuṅga kings, has ascribed to them a period extending from *c.* 73 B.C. to 29 B.C.[50] The traditional scheme of chronology, according to which they are said to have ruled for 85 years from 918 B.C. to (918-85=) 833 B.C. (=or *Kali* era—2,269=2,184+85),[51] cannot be accepted. The details about the rulers of this dynasty are not available. The *Purāṇas* hint at the fact that the Kāṇvas enjoyed the allegiance of their feudatories, but we do not have any evidence to substantiate it. The *Purāṇas* clearly state that Simuka or Sisuka, a royal servant, murdered the last king of the dynasty, Suśarman, usurped the throne and founded the Andhra dynasty. Simuka not only uprooted the Kānvas, but also destroyed the power of Śuṅgas.[52] R.G. Bhandarkar supports the *Purāṇic* evidence.[53] But his view that the Kānvas ruled contemporaneously with the later Śuṅgas, is not tenable. The Kāṇvas are referred to in the *Purāṇas* as "*Śuṅgabhṛtyas*", i.e. servants of the Śuṅgas. H.C. Raychaudhuri observes, "It, therefore appears likely that when the princes of the Śuṅga family became weak, the Kāṇvas usurped the whole power and ruled like the Peshwas in modern times, not uprooting the dynasty of their masters but reducing them to the character of nominal sovereigns . . ."[54]

**The Andhra (or Sātavāhana) Dynasty (c. 27 B.C.-225 A.D.)**

According to the *Purāṇas*, it was Simuka (or Śiśuka, Sindhuka, Sipraka, etc.), who after overthrowing Śuśarman, the last of the Kāṇvas, founded the Andhra (or Sātavāhana) dynasty. The exact date of the beginning of this dynasty has always been a subject of controversy among historians. Some scholars, relying on the *Purāṇic* testimony that the Andhras ruled for about four centuries and-a-half, postulate that their rule might have possibly begun in the second quarter of the third century B.C. and came to an end towards the close of the first quarter of the third century A.D. According to V.A. Smith, their rule extended from about 240 or 230 B.C. ("long before the suppression of the Kāṇvas about 28 B.C.") to 225 A.D.[55] E.J. Rapson has placed Simuka's accession between *c.* 244 B.C. and *c.* 202 B.C.[56] R.G. Bhandarkar[57] and H.C. Raychaudhuri[58] assign the beginning of their rule to the first century B.C. But Dr. Bhandarkar's date 73-72 B.C. is not beyond dispute. Dr. Raychaudhuri, on the one hand, describes Simuka ("*c.* 60-37 B.C.") as the contemporary of Śuśarman (40-30 B.C.) and, on the other, suggests that the former may have ascended the throne several years before 40-30 B.C., which appears to be contradictory. According to our calculation, Simuka flourished after 45 years of the Kāṇvas' rule, i.e. (72 B.C.-45 years=) in 27 B.C. That the dynasty was founded by him in the first century B.C., can also be testified to by the epigraphic evidence.[59] However, the possibility of the beginning of his rule sometime about the middle of the 1st century B.C. cannot be precluded. The genealogy and chronology of this dynasty have also generated a lot of debate among scholars.

There is no uniformity in the dynastic lists of the *Purāṇas*[60] with regard to the number of kings and their names, order of succession, regnal years and total duration of their rule. The number of kings varies from 17 to 30 or 31. It is only the *Matsya Purāṇa* which provides the full list of twenty nine kings, but in the end refers to thirty or thirty one kings. The *Vāyu* refers to 23 kings, but, actually, only 14 of them have been enumerated therein. The *Viṣṇu, Brahmāṇḍa* and *Bhāgavata Purāṇas* refer to thirty kings, but their actual number, as mentioned therein, appears to be 24, 17 (or 19) and 23 respectively. However, an attempt has been made to put them in proper order by maintaining synchronism. The list is given below:

| No. | Name | Length of reign | Remarks |
|---|---|---|---|
| 1. | Simuka | 23 years (*Mats., Vy.*) | |
| 2. | Kṛṣṇa | 18 years (*Mats., Vy.*) | |
| 3. | Srī-Śātakarṇi I | 10 years (*Mats.*) | |

| No. | Name | Length of reign | Remarks |
|---|---|---|---|
| 4. | Purnotsanga | 18 years (*Mats.*) | (In *Vy.* king Āpādabaddha reigned for 10+24+6 years |
| 5. | Skandhastambhi | 18 years (*Mats.*) | |
| 6. | Śātakarṇi II | 56 years (*Mats., Vy.*) | |
| 7. | Lambodara | 18 years (*Mats.*) | |
| 8. | Apilaka | 12 years (*Mats.*) | |
| 9. | Meghasvati | 18 years (*Mats.*) | |
| 10. | Svāti | 18 years (*Mats.*) | |
| 11. | Skandasvati | 7 years (*Mats.*) | |
| 12. | Mṛgendra Svātikarna | 3 years (*Mats.*) | |
| 13. | Kuntala Svātikarna | 8 years (*Mats.*) | |
| 14. | Svātivarna | 1 years (*Mats.*) | |
| 15. | Pulomāvi or Pulumayi I | 36 years (Pargiter's list) (24 *Bmd.*) | |
| 16. | Ariktavarna or Nemikṛṣna | 25 years (*Mats.* and *Vy.* respectively) | |
| 17. | Hala | 5 years (*Mats.*), 1 year (*Vy., Bmd.*) | According to the *Vy.* there were 5 or 7 great kings in the line of Hala. Names are not given. |
| 18. | Mantalaka | 5 years (*Mats.*) | |
| 19. | Purindrasena or Purikasena | 21 years (*Vy.*) | |
| 20. | Sundara Śātakarṇi | 1 years (*Mats.*) | |
| 21. | Chakora-Svātikarna (or Śātkarṇi) | 6 months (*Mats.*) | According to *Vy.* Śātakarṇi reigned for 1 year and 6 months. |
| 22. | Sivasvāti | 28 years (*Mats., Vy.*) | |
| 23. | Gautamiputra Sātakarṇi | 21 years (*Mats., Vy.*) | |
| 24. | Vāsiṣṭhiputra Srī Pulamāvi or Pulumayi II | 28 years (*Mats.*) | |
| 25. | Śiva-Srī Pulumayi III | 7 years (*Mats.*) | |
| 26. | Śivaskandha-Śātakarṇi | 29 years (*Mats.*) | |
| 27. | Yajña-Srī Śātakarṇi | 29 years (*Mats.*), 19 (*Vy., Bmd.*) | |
| 28. | Vijaya-Srī | 6 years (*Mats., Vy.*) | |
| 29. | Caṇḍasri or daṇḍa Srī Śātakarṇi | 10 years (*Mats.*), 3 (*Vy., Bmd.*) | |
| 30. | Pulumayi IV | 7 years (*Mats., Vy.*) | |

These thirty kings reigned for 456 years according to the *Viṣṇu, Bhāgavata* and *Brahmāṇḍa Purāṇas* and 460 years according to the *Matsya.* Whereas the *Vāyu Purāṇa* assigns a duration of 411 years altogether to twenty-three kings. The *Purāṇic* duration is, of course, longer than the actual one. Because we find that all the kings listed above do not have the historical identity. Only few of them were virtually the rulers. The final picture about the duration of their rule will emerge at the end of the discussion.

Meanwhile, the historicity of some of the early and later kings, who established themselves in the Western India and the Deccan, can be examined with the help of the epigraphic and numismatic evidence.

The Cave inscriptions of Nānaghāt (nos. 1112-20) not only prove the historicity of Simuka, the founder of the dynasty, and of his son or nephew Sātakarṇi I, but also confirm that they held the Nana pass, which leads from Junar in the Deccan to the Konkan, the coastal region of Western India.[61] Simuka's brother Krisṇa has been identified with Kānhā ("Rājā of the Sātavāhana-kula"), mentioned in a Nasik inscription.[62] They all belonged to the first century B.C. In place of Purnotsanga and Skandhastambhi, two successors of Sātakarṇi I, the names of Vedisiri and Ṣatisiri figure in the Nānaghāt inscription.

The authenticity of the *Purāṇic* list in respect of the eighth king, Apilaka, has been proved with the help of a copper coin of the king. K.N. Dikshit reads the legend as *"rano-Śiva-Siri-Apilakasa."*[63] The next important king of this dynasty was Hala, the seventeenth in the *Purāṇic* list. He belonged to the first century A.D. He is well-known as an author of the Prākrit work, *"Gāthā-Saptaśati* (or *Saptaśataka*).

The early Sātavāhana kings including the successors of Sātakarṇi must have been in possession of the greater part of Maharashtra (where most of their inscriptions have been found) till the later part of the first century of the Christian era, when the Śakas established their power. The Sātavāhanas were dispossessed of their dominions by the Śakas. But Gautamiputra Sātakarṇi, (the twenty-third king in the list) restored the fallen fortunes of the Sātavāhanas by driving out the Śakas from the country. He brought under his political hegemony Malava, Berar, North Konkan, Kathiawar (Gujarat) and the region around Poona and Nasik.

The Nasik cave inscription bears testimony to the fact that Gautamiputra Sātakarṇi ruled for twenty-four years from 106 A.D. to 130 A.D.[64] The date of his accession can also be confirmed by the coins.[65] From the Nasik inscription it appears that he was true champion of *Brāhmaṇism*.[66]

Gautamiputra's immediate successor was his son Vāsiṣṭhiputra Srī Pulumayi (*c.* 130-158 A.D.). He extended the Sātavāhana sway over Andhradeśa. He set up his capital at Pratiṣṭhāna, the modern Paithan on the north bank of the Godāvari in Aurangabad district. He also figures in inscriptions found in the Nasik and Karli caves.[67] Pulumayi or Pulamāvi is identical with Sātakarṇi, lord of Dakṣināpatha, mentioned in the Junagadh Rock inscription as having been defeated by Rudradāman I (*c.* 130-150 A.D.)[68] the Śaka ruler of Saurastra (Kathiawar). Pulumayi has been also identified with Vāsiṣṭhiputra Sri Sātakarṇi mentioned in a Kanheri (Thana) inscription. He was succeeded by Śiva-Srī Pulumayi, who ruled for seven years from 158 to 165 A.D. Yajña Srī Sātakarṇi (*c.* 165-194

A.D.) was the great monarch of the dynasty. An inscription discovered at Chinna in the Krişņa district is in full accord with the *Purāņic* evidence, so far as his reign-period (29 years) is concerned. His coins have also been found in Andhra, Maharastra, Madhya Pradesh and Gujarat. In one of the coins he has been represented as "rana Samasa Siri Yāña Satakanasa".[69] He was succeeded by Vijaya Srī, who ruled for six years from 194 to 200 A.D. His successor Caņḍasrī-Sātakarņi ruled from 200 to 210 A.D. with the accession of Pulumayi IV (*c.* 210-17 A.D.), the last ruler of the dynasty, the process of disintegration of the Sātavāhana empire began. According to the *Vāyu-Purāņa*, it was divided into five minor dynasties.[70] The Abhiras seized Maharastra (Western Deccan), the Ikṣvākus and the Pallavas established their rule in the Southern Deccan, the Chutus occupied the eastern portion, etc. Thus, the great Sātavāhana dynasty came to end about A.D. 220 or 225.

According to the *Purāņic* tradition, the period of 836 years intervened between Mahāpadma Nanda and the last Andhra (Śātavāhana) king, Pulumayi, which is evidenced by the following verses from the texts :

पौलोमास्तु तथान्ध्रास्तु महापदमान्तरे पुनः ।
अनन्तरं शतान्यस्टौ षट्त्रिंशत् तु समास्तथा ।।[71]
प्रमाणं वै तथा चोक्तं महापदमान्तरं च यत ।
अनन्तरं तच्छतान्यस्टौ षट्त्रिंशच्य समाः स्मृताः ।।
एव्कालान्तरं भाष्या अन्ध्रान्ता ये प्रकीर्तिताः ।
भविस्यैस्त्र संख्याताः पुराणज्ञैः श्रुतर्षिभिः ।[72]

Thus, the Andhras' rule began 376 years after the Nanda and lasted for 460 years (376+460=836 years). The end of the Andhra or Sātavāhana dynasty is assigned roughly to 436 A.D. But the fact remains that the successors of the Sātavāhanas, such as the Ikṣvākus of Southern Deccan, the Abhiras of Western Deccan (whose era started in 248 A.D.) and the Vākāṭakas of Northern Deccan--all began to rule independently in the third century A.D. Thus, the Sātavāhana power must have collapsed about two centuries before the traditional date recorded in the *Purāņas*. Keeping in view the fact that the rule of the Śatakarņis survived in Kuntala till the rise of the Kadambas, the little longer duration of their rule cannot be doubted. According to Wilford 975 years (648+327 or 836+139) elapsed between Mahāpadma and the Andhras,[73] which is totally based on his miscalculation.

The duration of this dynasty may roughly be estimated as (27 B.C.-225 A.D.) 252 years. The traditional evidence, that the Andhras ruled for 506 years and their rule began in 833 B.C. and came to end about (833-506=) 327 B.C. (or in *Kali* era 2,774=2,268+506,[74] cannot be accepted.

## References and Notes


1. *Vṣṇ.* (text with tr. by Shree Munilala Gupta, 9th edn.; Gorakhpur, Samv. 2041) IV, 24, 26-28 (with comments). The information is also based on the authority of the commentator on the *Vṣṇ.*, tr. H.H. Wilson, p. 375; The *Vy.*, (99, 336) unequivocally states that the Mauryas belonged to the Nanda dynasty; see also The *Mudrārākṣasa* of Visākha Dutta (ed. with Sanskrit and Hindi commentaries by Satyavrata Singh, Varanasi, 1973), Act. II and IV.
2. *Pariśiṣṭaparvan*, pp. 56; VIII, 229 f; J.C. Jain, *LAIJC*, p. 453.
3. *Mhv.* (Geiger's tr.), p. 27; The commentary on the *Mhv.* (ed. Turnour), Intr. pp. XXXVIII-XIII; *Mahāparinibbāna Sutta*, cf. *SBE*, XI, p. 134-35.
4. *Chro. Anc. Ind.*, pp. 238-39.
5. *Ibid.*, p. 245.
6. *HASL*, pp. 267-68.
7. *Pariśiṣṭa parvam*, VIII, 339.
8. *EHIDS*, Vol. II, pp. 504 f, 511 f.
9. *JRAS*, 1932, pp. 273-88.
10. *As. Res.*, Vol. IX, pp. 90-91.
11. *Vy.*, 99, 331-36; *Mats.*, 272, 22-26; *Mats.*, *SBA*, pp. 335, App. VI, IXXII; *Vṣṇ.*, IV, 24, 28-32; *Vṣṇ.*, tr. H.H. Wilson, pp.74-76; *Bmd.*, 3, 74, 145-49; *Bhāg.*, XII, 1, 12-15; *Bhv.* (Supra), Vol. I, pp. 334-35, vv. 43-44; Wilford, *As. Res.*, Vol. IX, pp. 90-91; Max Muller, *HASL*, p. 266; R. Morton Smith, *DDEI*, pp. 363-64; M. Krishnamachariar, *HCSL*, Int., XLix f.
    It is only the *Viṣṇu Purāṇa* in which names of all the ten kings of the dynasty have been mentioned, but their regnal years are not given. The list inserted in the *Mats.* is incomplete, but the text refers to ten kings. Some other *Purāṇas* mention only nine kings. The *Vy.*, *Bmd.* and *Mats.* are important for the length of reigns of the kings.
12. *Vy.*, 99. 336; *Mats.*, 272, 25-26; *Bmd.*, 3, 74, 149; *Bhāg.*, XII, 1, 15.
13. *Vṣṇ.*, IV, 24, 31-32.
14. *PDKA*, pp. 28-30.
15. *Mahavaṁsa*, p. lii
16. *Samantapāsādikā*, Vol. I, pp. 72-73.
17. *Dip.*, VI, 1.; *Bhv.*, V, 21; *Mhv.* (Geiger's tr.), Intr., pp. XXXI f.
18. *Samantapāsādikā*, Vol. I, p. 41.
19. *Mhv.* (Geiger's tr.), p. 28.
20. For details see E.J. Rapson (ed.); *CHI*, Vol. I, *Ancient India* (Delhi, 1962), p. 453; *JRAS*, 1906, p. 179 f, 669 f, 983 f; M. Senart, *Ind. Ant.*, XX, p. 229; Buhler, *Ind. Ant.*, Vol. VI, p. 149.
21. *EHI* (4th edn.), p. 126.
22. *Aśoka* (3rd edn.), pp. 73 f, 232 f; *EHI*, pp. 171-72.
23. *Divyāvadāna*, pp. 370-71, 409, 433.
24. *Bhv.* (Supra), pp. 334-35, v. 43.
25. *Ep. Ind.*, Vol. XX, p. 364; also E. Hultzsch, CII, Vol. I (Oxford, 1925), pp. 103-4, 134-5.
26. *Ep. Ind.*, Vol. XX, p. 364.
27. Aśokāvadāna, cf. *Divyāvadāna*, XXIX; Jinaprabhasuri's Pātaliputrakalpa, cf. *Pariśiṣṭaparvan*, ix, 51-53; XI, 65.
28. *EHI*, (4th ed.), p. 203; Aśoka (3rd ed.), p. 70; also Lassen, *Ind. Alt.*, Vol. II, pp. 283 ff.
29. *Yuga Purāṇam* : A chapter from the *Garga Saṁhitā* (ed. D.R. Mankad, Vallabhvidyanagar, 1951), p. 32; also cf. H. Kern, *Br. Sam.* (*BIS*, Calcutta, 1865), p. 37.
30. *Vy.*, 99, 336-37; *Mats.*, 272, 26-27; *Vṣṇ.*, IV, 24, 34.

31. Tr. (Cowell and Thomas), p. 193.
32. *HCSL*, Intr. XLIX-XLVIII (1,535-1,219 B.C.).
33. *Vy.*, 99, 336-342½; *Mats.*, 27, 26-33; *Mats., SBA*, p. 336, also App. VI, LXXII; *Vṣṇ.*, IV, 24, 33-37; *Vṣṇ.*, tr. H.H. Wilson, pp. 376-77; *Bhāg.*, XII, 1, 16-20; *Bmd.*, 3, 74, 150-55; see also Pargiter, *PDKA*, pp. 30-32, 70; Wilford (*As. Res.* Vol. IX, pp. 91-115) has not provided the correct figures.
34. *Vy.*, 99, 341-42½; *Vṣṇ.*, IV, 24, 37.
35. *Matsya Purāṇa*, 272, 32.
36. See *HCSL*, Intr. XLIX-XLVIII (1,219-919 B.C.).
37. Text with tr. by M.R. Kale (revd. by J.L. Dave and A.S. Upadhyaya, Delhi, 1985), Act-V, pp. 191 f; see also K.P. Jayaswal, "Historical Data in the Gargisaṁhitā and the Brāhmin Empire" in *JBORS*, Vol. XIV, 1928, pp. 397 ff.
38. Cunningham, *CAI*, p. 74.
39. Trans. (Cowell and Thomas), p. 192.
40. *JBORS*, Dec. 1917, pp. 473-5; also Further, Ep. Ind., II, pp. 240-3.
41. *JBORS*, 1917, p. 479; 1934, pp. 7 ff.
42. For details see *ASIAR*, 1908-9, p. 126; D.R. Bhandarkar, *ASIAR*, 1913-4, p. 190; R.P. Chanda *JRAS*, 1919, p. 396; *MASI*, 1920 (no. 5), p. 152.
43. *Mats.*, 272, 32-33; *Vṣṇ.*, IV, 24, 39., *Harṣacarita* (tr. Cowell and Thomas), p. 193; Bombay, edn., 1925, Ch. VI, p. 199; Pargiter, *PDKA*, pp. 34-71.
44. *CHI*, Vol. I, p. 471.
45. *Vy.*, 99, 343-47; *Mats.*, 272, 32-37; *Mats., SBA*, p. 337, also Table V, IIXXIII; *Vṣṇ.*, IV, 24, 38-42; *Vṣṇ.*, tr. H.H. Wilson, p. 377; *Bhāg.*, XII, 1, 21 f; *Bmd.*, 3, 74, 155-60; Pargiter, *PDKA*, pp. 33-38, 71. The regnal years of the kings given by Wilford (*As. Res.*, Vol. IX, pp. 92-115) are not absolutely correct.
46. *Vy.*, 99, 346-47; *Mats.*, 272, 35-37; *Vṣṇ.*, IV, 24, 42.
47. A peep into the Early History of India (322 B.C.-*Circa* 500 A.C., Varanasi, 1978, p. 20. The duration of reigns of the Śuṅgas and the Kāṇvas, as given in the *Purāṇas*, have been supported by him. See also his *EHD*, (Delhi, 1979), p. 23.
48. *HAI*, pp. 189-91.
49. *PHAI*, p. 400.
50. *Bhāratiya Itihāsa Kā Paricaya* (Varanasi, 1963), pp. 69-70.
51. See *HCSL*, Intr. XLIX-XLVIII (919-834 B.C.).
52. *Vy.*, 99, 347-48; *Mats.*, 273, 1-3.
53. *EHD*, p. 23.
54. Op. cit., p. 399.
55. *EHI* (4th revd. edn. by S.M. Edward, London, 1967), pp. 216-17, 220.
56. *CHI*, Vol. I, p. 477, fn. 3.
57. *EHD*, pp. 15-23; A Peep into the Early History of India, pp. 36-37.
58. *PHAI*, pp. 403-405, 406, fn. 1, 414. See also A.D. Pusalker's article on R.G. Bhandarkar for views of other scholars too, in *Historians and Historiography on Modern India* (ed. S.P. Sen, Calcutta, 1973), pp. 32-34.
59. Nānaghāt Inscription, cf. Buhler's Report, *Arch. Surv. of West India*, Vol. V, pp. 60-71.
60. *Vy.*, 99, 348-58; *Mats.*, 273, 1-17; *Mats, SBA*, pp. 337-39 and Table V, IXXIII; *Vṣṇ.*, IV, 24, 43-50; *Vṣṇ.*, tr. H.H. Wilson, pp. 378-80; *Bmd.*, 3, 74, 160-70; *Bhāg.*, XII, 1, 22-28; Pargiter, *PDKA*, pp. 36-43, 71; See also Wilford, *As. Res.*, Vol. IX, p. 116; R. Morton Smith, *DDEI*, pp. 382-86; Daṇḍin's Avantisundari (Trivandrum Skt. Series, No. 172), pp. 184-85 (A List of 26 kings is given in the text); R.G. Bhandarkar, *EHD*, p. 23; *JIH*, Vol. LVI, 1978, pt. I, pp. 48-49, 52-53.
61. Buhler, *Arch. Surv. of West Ind.*, Vol. V, pp. 60-71; See also Luder's *A List of Brāhmi Inscriptions from the*

*Earliest times to about* A.D. *400*, Pub. as an App. to *Ep. Ind.*, Vol. X, 1910, p. 160, No. 1113 (for Simuka).

62. Buhler, *Arch. Surv. of West Ind.*, Vol. IV, p. 98; also Luder's List--Nos. 1114, 1144.
63. *JIH*, Vol. LVI, 1978, Pt. I, p. 53.
64. D.C. Sircar, *SI*, Vol. I (Calcutta, 1965), pp. 197-201; also *Ep. Ind.*, Vol. VIII, No. 5, pp. 73, 74; E.J. Rapson, *Coins of the Andhra Dynasty*, Etc., 1908, p. XXX.
65. E.J. Rapson, British Museum Catalogue, *Coins of the Andhra Dynasty*, etc., 1908, p. XXX.
66. *Ep. Ind.*, Vol. VIII, pp. 60, 61, 1. 5, 7; K.P. Jayaswal, *JBORS*, Vol. XVI, Pts. III and IV, pp. 265-66.
67. Buhler, *Arch. Surv. of West. Ind.*, Vol. IV, p. 110.
68. *EP. Ind.*, Vol. VIII, pp. 36-49; D.C. Sircar, *SI*, Vol. I, pp. 176-80.
69. *JNSI*, Vol. III, June, 1941, Pt. 1, pp. 43-45.
70. *Vy.*, 99, 357-58.
71. *Mats.*, 273, 37.
72. *Vy.*, 99, 416-17; See also *Vṣṇ.*, iv, 24, 105-7, also 12; *Bmd.*, 3, 74, 225-36; *Bhāg.*, XII, 2, 26-32. (According to the *Purāṇic* calculation, the beginning of the Andhra dynasty can be assigned to the period falling 376 years after the Nanda. The beginning was 2,700 years after 3,076 during which the Saptarsis were in Magha Nakṣatra. Thus, 3076-2700=376). See *Vy.*, 99, 418-23; *Mats.*, 273, 38-45.
73. *As. Res.*, Vol. IX, p. 87.
74. *HCSL*, Intr., XLIX-LVIII.

# 7

## The Nāga Dynasties

### (from the Second Century B.C. to the Fourth Century A.D.)

THE Nāgas occupy very important place among the non-Āryan tribes of ancient India. The *Purāṇas* do contain some useful information about the rule of the Nāga dynasties at Vidiśā (the capital of eastern Mālavā), Padmāvatī (modern Padam Pawaya near Narwar in the Gwalior state, M.P.), Kāntipuri (Kuntipuri or Kamantalapuri, twenty five miles north of Gwalior), Campāvati or Campāpuri (near Bhagalpur, Bihar) and Mathura between the second century B.C. and the fourth century A.D. But there are some vacuums in the *Purāṇic* accounts of the subject concerned, which, of course, can be filled in with the help of the epigraphic, numismatic and other collateral evidence. The *Purāṇic* style of presentation of the subject-matter is completely different from what we find in other sources. However, from the twilight of the *Purāṇic* history it appears that the Nāgas (mostly serpent-worshippers) had spread far and wide in Central, Northern and Eastern India. Some Nāga rulers became powerful during the times of the later Kuṣānas in the second century A.D. and some of them re-established themselves after the expulsion of the Kuṣānas from some parts of Northern India in the early third century A.D. Some Nāga chiefs ruling in the Yamuna valley and Central India were exterminated by the Gupta ruler about the middle of the fourth century A.D.

We shall begin with the Nāga dynasty of Vidiśā, which has been divided into two parts in the *Purāṇas.* To the first part belonged those kings who flourished before the end of the Śuṅgas and to the second part belonged those, who ruled in the post-Śuṅga period. The *Purāṇas* mention the names of Śeṣanaga, Bhogin, Rāmacandra, Sadācandra, Dharmavarma, Candrāmsa, Vinsaja or Vangara (who ruled during the Śuṅga and Kāṇva period), Bhutinandi, Madhunandi, Śiśunandi, Nandiyaś as (or Yaso Nandi) and his descendants, Dauhitra and Sisuka, Śivanandi, etc. (who ruled in the post-Kāṇva period).[1]

According to the *Bhaviṣya Purāṇa*, Bhutanandi of the Nāga dynasty became the king of Kilkilapuri and ruled over there for fifty years. He was succeeded by Śiśunandi, who popularised the cult of serpent-worship. His younger brother, Yasonandi, ruled either for twenty or twenty-five years. His son Praviraka ruled for eleven years. He is said to have defeated the *Mlecchas* of Bāhlika.[2]

The Nāgas of Vidiśā (Nos. 1 to 8) have been chronologically arranged by K.P. Jayaswal[3] in the following manner.

1. Śeṣa Nāga (110-90 B.C.)
2. Bhogin (90-80 B.C.)
3. Rāmachandra (80-50 B.C.)
4. Dharma-Varman (50-40 B.C.)
5. Vangara (40-31 B.C.)
6. Bhutanandi (*c.* 20 B.C.-10 B.C.)
7. Śiśu Nandi (*c.* 10 B.C.-25 A.D.)
8. Yasah Nandi (*c.* 25 A.D.-30 A.D.)
9. Puruṣadata.
10. Uttamadatta.
11. Kamadata.
12. Bhavadata.
13. Śiva Nandi.

It has been stated by Dr. Jayaswal that the last five kings (Nos. nine to thirteen who belonged to the dynasty of Mathura) are known only from inscriptions and coins, and their order of succession can also not be satisfactorily determined. However, all the thirteen Nāga kings, as mentioned above, are stated to have ruled for a period of 200 years extending from *c.* 110 B.C. to *c.* 78 A.D. "Those around Vidiśā were worshippers of Nāgas from early times, as the republican coins of Era prove".[4]

Some Nāga rulers belonged to the family of the Bhāraśivas, who rose in prominence after the fall of the Kuṣāna empire. One of the prominent rulers of this family was Virasena (*c.* 175-210 A.D.), who "re-established Hindu sovereignty" at Mathura, formerly a centre of the Kuṣāna power. His coins have been found in different parts of Northern India, particularly, at Mathura. He is said to have ousted the Kuṣānas from Mathura and the Ganga-Yamuna *doāb*. One of the Bhāraśiva Nāga kings was Bhava-nāga, who ruled from about 290 to 315 A.D. His daughter was married to Gautamiputra, the son of the Vākāṭaka prince, Pravarasena. Padmāvati was one of the centres of the Bhāraśiva government during his time.[5]

The *Purāṇas* refer to nine Nāga kings of Padmāvati and Campāvati. Kāntipuri was also one of the chief seats of their power. Compāvati is said to be one of their capitals. It appears to be the subordinate seat of their power.[6] The names of the Nāga rulers of the places concerned have not been mentioned in the *Purāṇas*.

The names of nine kings of the Nāga dynasty of Padmāvati (as referred to in the *Purāṇas*) occur on the coins discovered by E.J. Rapson,[7] V.A. Smith[8] and Cunningham.[9] The said Nāga kings were known as Bhava Nāga, Ganapati Nāga, Nāgasena, Bhimanāga, Skandanāga, Bṛhaspatināga, Devanāga, Vibhanāga and Vyaghranāga.

According to Rapson, closely connected with these coins were some other coins bearing the inscription "Acyu". Acyuta may have been one of the Nāga princes.[10] The Allahabad pillar inscription bears an eloquent and glowing testimony to the fact that Ganapatināga and Nāgasena—the two kings of the Nāga dynasty of Padmāvatī were among those nine monarchs of Āryāvarta, who were extirpated by Samudragupta (*c.* 335-380 A.D.). Nandin and Acyuta (a king of Ahicchatra or modern Rāmnagar, Bareilly Dist.), who were also crushed by the said Gupta emperor, belonged to the Nāga families. Some of them were reduced to the status of tributary kings.[11] Nāgasena of Padmāvat has also been mentioned in Bāna's Harṣacarita as a scion of the Nāga-Kula (Nāga family).

The *Purāṇas* also refer to the seven Nāga kings, who ruled at Mathura[12] after the Kuṣānas. The seven Nāgas from Mathura continued to rule over *doāb* for 383 years, which can also be proved on the testimony of the *Purāṇas.*[13] The coins discovered from Mathura bear the names of the Naga kings as Puruṣadatta, Uttamadatta, Ramadatta, Kamadatta, Śeṣadatta, Bhavdatta and Balabhuti. They were probably the vassals of the Kuṣānas.

Pargiter has correctly stated that the Nāga families ruled from more than one place, viz. Vidiśā, Padmāvatī and Mathura.[14]

K.P. Jayaswal, while throwing light on the Hindu republics in the Nāga period (150 A.D.-284 A.D.), has opined that the Nāgas of Mālavā and Padmāvatī were, by and large, republican communities.[15]

The Nāgas, no doubt, played conspicuous role in driving out the Kuṣānas from India. They set many new traditions in the arena of the growth of Hinduism and art and culture, which were further revived by the Vākāṭakas and the Guptas.

## References and Notes

1. *Vy.*, 99, 366-70; *Vṣṇ.*, IV, 24, 56; *Vṣṇ.* (tr.) : H.H. Wilson, pp. 382-83.
2. *Bhv.* (Supra), Vol. 2; pp. 284-85, vv. 1-14.
3. *History of India*, 150 A.D. to 350 A.D. (Lahore, 1933), pp. 3-15.
4. *Hindu Polity* (Bangalore, 1981), p. 154.
5. K.P. Jayaswal, *History of India* (*c.* 150-350 A.D.) pp. 19-24; *JBORS*, March-June, 1933, pp. 3 f; also CII; Vol. III, pp. 237, 241, 245, 248 (only for Bhāraśivas).
6. *Vy.*, 99, 382-83; *Vṣṇ.*, IV, 24, 63; *Vṣṇ.* (tr.) : H.H. Wilson, p. 385; *Bmd.*, 3, 74, 194, 197; *PK*, p. 267.
7. *Ind. Co.* (Varanasi, 1969), pp. 13, 28 and Plate V.
8. *JRAS.*, 1897, p. 643 (coins of the 4th century A.D.); *CCIM* (Oxford, 1906), Vol. I, pp. 176-77 (some Nāga coins of Padmāvatī belong to the second century A.D.).
9. *JASB*, 1865, p. 115; *CMI* (London, 1893), p. 20, Pl. 11, 13-25, p. 21; *ASR*, 11, p. 307; VI, p. 178 cf. Rapson, *op. cit.*, p. 28.
10. *Op. cit.*, p. 28; *JRAS*, 1897, p. 420.
11. Fleet, *CII*, Vol. III, no. 1, pp. 1-17, Lines 20-21.
12. *Vy.*, 99, 382-83; H.H. Wilson, *op. cit.*, p. 385.
13. *Bmd.*, 2, 74, 194-95, 267; *Vy.*, 99, 453, cf. *PK*, p. 267.
14. *PDKA*, p. 49.
15. *History of India* (*c.* 150-350 A.D.), pp. 53-54; Hindu Polity, pp. 154-55.

# 8

# The Vākāṭakas and the Guptas

## (from the Third to the Sixth Century A.D.)

### The Vākāṭakas

ONE of the most powerful, glorious and illustrious dynasties of the Deccan was that of the Vākāṭakas, who ruled contemporaneously with the Guptas from the middle of the third century A.D. to the second quarter of the sixth century A.D.

The founder and first king of the Vākāṭaka dynasty was Vindhyaśakti, who flourished about the middle of the third century A.D. His name occurs in the *Purāṇas.* He is said to have ruled for ninty six years. He was succeeded by his son, Pravira, who ruled for sixty years. Kāṇcanapuri was the capital of his kingdom. Being an ambitious ruler, he carried his arms to the Narmada in the North and succeeded in annexing the kingdom of Purika, which was being ruled by a king named Śisuka. He is said to have performed Vājapeya sacrifices after assuming the title of Samrāt. Pravira had four sons[1], but all of them did not become rulers. The information contained in the *Purāṇas* about the dynasty does not go beyond what has been mentioned above.

The historicity of the *Purāṇic* accounts can be examined by the epigraphic evidence and the statements of some noted authorities on the subject concerned.

A good deal of controversy has arisen among the scholars over the original home of the Vākāṭaka rulers concerned. The position assigned to them in the *Purāṇas* shows that they belonged to the Northern Deccan. Names of the first two Vākāṭaka rulers are mixed up with the Nāgas of Vidiśā, which, of course, furnishes the pretext for scholars to surmise that they originally might have set up their rule in Central provinces. But the truth is far from it. V.A. Smith, while identifying Vindhyaśakti and Pravira of the *Purāṇas* with Vindhyaśakti I and Pravarasena I, has suggested that the origin of the family can be sought somewhere in Central India. However, he seems to be of the view that the Vākāṭaka had occupied Berar in the fourth century A.D.[2] K.P. Jayaswal holds that the dynastic name of Vākāṭaka has been derived from Vākaṭa, which is identified with Bāgat, a village in the Orcha state in the Jhansi district. It has further been suggested that the founder of the dynasty, Vindhyaśakti, was the first anointed *Brāhmaṇ* king and adopted the name of his own town as his dynastic title.[3] But this evidence can hardly be taken to be conclusive. On the basis of some epigraphic evidence it has also been assumed that the Vākāṭaka prince Vindhyaśakti belonged to the North.[4]

V.V. Mirashi has conclusively proved that the Vākāṭakas belonged to the Southern India. He has also made sincere attempts to prove the historicity of the *Purāṇic* accounts of the Vākāṭakas on the basis of the epigraphic evidence. He has identified Vindhyaśakti I with the Vākāṭaka prince mentioned in the Amrāvati inscription (Guntur district, Andhra Pradesh) dated third century A.D. He takes him as the progenitor of the Vākāṭaka family. Vindhyaśakti I has been described in an inscription in cave XVI at Ajanta as the "banner of the Vākāṭaka family'. He, according to Dr. Mirashi, ruled from 250 to 270 A.D. It is said that he had his base in the Central Deccan from where he occupied some parts of Vidarbha. On the basis of a copper-plate grant of the Vākāṭaka king Vindhyaśakti II, which was discovered from Basin in the Akola district of Vidarbha in 1939, he has proved that after the death of Pravira or Pravarsena I, who ruled from 270 A.D. to 330 A.D. (which is in full accord with the *Purāṇic* length of reign, sixty years), the Vākāṭaka dynasty was divided into four branches. Taking the *Purāṇic* testimony, that he had four sons, as authentic one he has established that his eldest son Gautamiputra could not ascend the throne. But his second son Sarvasena had set up a separate dynasty with his capital at Vatsagulma (modern Basim) in the Akola district of Vidarbha. He ruled from about 330 to 335 A.D. Nothing has been mentioned about the dynasties set up by his other two sons. Pravarasena I was succeeded by his grandson, Rudrasena I (330 to 350 A.D.), the son of Gautamiputra, who was further followed by other rulers like Prithvisena I (350 to 400 A.D.), Rudrasena (400-405 A.D.), Divakarasena (405-420 A.D.), Pravarasena II (420-450 A.D.), Narendrasena (450 to 470 A.D.) and Prithvisena II (470-490 A.D.). In the line of Sarvasena (Pravira's son) there were some other rulers. Sarvasena was succeeded by Vindhyasena, who is called Vindhyaśakti II in the said copper plate. He ruled from about 355 to 400 A.D. He was succeeded by his son Pravarasena II, who ruled from 400 to 415 A.D. His successors ruled up to 500 A.D. After the defeat of Vākāṭakas at the hands of the Kalacuris (descendants of Kārtavirya Arjuna of the Haihaya race mentioned in the epics and the *Purāṇas*) of Māhiṣmati in the second quarter of the sixth century A.D., the dynasty ultimately came to an end or ceased to exist.[5]

### The Guptas

The evidence furnished in the "*Kaliyugarājavṛttānta* (which forms a part of the *Bhaviṣya Purāṇa*) about the origin of the early Guptas, that :

एते प्रणधरसामन्ताः श्रीमद्गुप्तकुलोद्भवाः ।
श्रीपार्वतीयान्ध्रभृत्य नामानश्चक्रवर्तिनः ।।

appears to be vague. Depending exclusively on this evidence, we cannot establish anything positively about the advent of the Guptas. But, on the other hand, we find that some scholars on the basis of the account concerned have attempted to establish that the Andhras were followed by their vassals, the Guptas. It is said that Sri Gupta, the progenitor of the Gupta family came from Sri Parvata or Nepal and joined the service of Vijayasri Sātakarṇi as one of his generals (or as a feudatory chief) and with his help he managed to maintain his tottering kingdom. Sri Gupta was succeeded by his son Ghatotkaca Gupta, whose son Candragupta later ascended the throne. According to the '*Kaliyugarājavṛttanta*', in Sri Gupta dynasty there were seven kings, who are said to have ruled for 245 years from *c.* 328 to 83 B.C.[6] This account cannot be considered as authentic one. We do not have any evidence at our disposal to confirm this account. Hence, it can be disposed of as wholly unworthy of credence.

The origin of the Guptas is, of course, shrouded in obscurity, but it is almost certain that the foundation of the Gupta empire was originally laid on the ruins of the Kuṣāna empire in Uttar Pradesh. The Guptas were the feudatories of the Kuṣānas in Uttar Pradesh and not of the Andhras in the Deccan. The Guptas, of course, subsequently established their sway over some parts of the former dominions of both the Kuṣāns and the Sātavāhanas about the middle of the third century A.D. The kingdom of the Guptas originally comprised only some parts of Uttar Pradesh and Bihar at the end of the third century A.D. The earliest centre of their power was in Uttar Pradesh, which can be confirmed by the discovery of early Gupta coins and inscriptions mainly from this part of India. They gradually expanded from Prayag (U.P.) over the neighbouring regions and the whole of Magadha in South Bihar. The founder of the Gupta dynasty was Sri Gupta, who ruled as a minor chief over a small territory in Magadha from *c.* 275 to 300 A.D. His kingdom possibly comprised some portion of northern or central Bengal. He has been described in the Poona Copper plate inscription of Prabhavati Gupta (daughter of Candragupta II) as the "Ādirājā of the Gupta dynasty". His son and successor, Ghatotkaca (*c.* 300-319 A.D.), also figures in two records of Prabhāvati Gupta. After Ghatotkaca, his son Candragupta I (*c.* 319-335 A.D.) became the sovereign ruler.

We have some reliable accounts in the *Purāṇas* of the Guptas' rule over some parts of U.P. and Bihar. It is said that the Guptas set up their rule over Anugaṅga (the middle Gangetic basin), Prayāga (Allahabad), Sāketa (Ayodhya) and Magadha (south Bihar). This can be confirmed by the following verses :

अनुगङ्गं प्रयागं च साकेतं मगधांस्तथा ।
एतान् जनपदान् सर्वान् भोक्षयन्ते गुप्तवंशजाः ।।[7]

This shows the extent of the Gupta dominions during the time of Candragupta I. This is what almost all the historians have unanimously accepted. While dealing with the date of the compilation of the dynastic account in the *Purāṇas*, Pargiter observed that "The Guptas are mentioned as reigning over the country comprised within Prayāga, Sāketa and Magadha, that is exactly the territory, which was possessed . . . by

Candragupta I, who founded the Gupta dynasty in A.D. 319-20 and reigned till 330 (or 335) perhaps before it was extended by the conquests of his son and successor Samudragupta."[8] The Allabhabad Pillar inscription of Samudragupta (*c.* 335-380 A.D.) also bears reflection of the truth that Candragupta I ruled over eastern Uttar Pradesh, Bihar and Northern Bengal. As the *Purāṇic* account does not touch upon Samudragupta's conquests, we have reason to believe that the narrative was closed during the interval, which elapsed between the time, when Candragupta I extended his authority from Magadha to Tirhut and other parts of Bihar and Oudh as far as Allahabad, and the beginning of Samudragupta's reign. The *Purāṇas* do not furnish any other details except what we have discussed here. Before we close the discussion, it will be in the fitness of things to add that it is historically proven fact that in the imperial Gupta line there were twelve kings (Sri Gupta to Bhanugupta), who ruled for 235 years from 275 to 510 A.D., which is in contradistinction to the *Purāṇic* duration, 245 years of the reigns of seven Guptas, who according to the traditional choronology ruled from *c.* 328 to 83 B.C., as mentioned above. In the Jain works (Yativṛsabha's *Tiloyapaṇṇati*, vv. 95-99; Jinasena's *Harivaṁśa Purāṇa*, Sarga sixty, vv. 487-92, 551-52) the duration of reigns of the Guptas is 231 years. But in *Tiloyapaṇṇati* (vv. 86-94) the Guptas have also been assigned the reign-periods of 255 years.

## References and Notes

1. *Vy.*, 99, 365, 370-72; *Bmd.*, 3, 74, 184-86; *Vṣṇ.*, IV, 24, 56—(only the names of Vindhyaśakti and Pravira are mentioned in the *Viṣṇu*. The other details are conspicuous by their absence); see also H.H. Wilson (tr.) : *Vṣṇ.*, pp. 382-83; Pargiter *PDKA*, p. 44.
2. See his article "the Vākāṭaka Dynasty of Berar in the 4th and 5th Centuries" in *JRAS*, 1914, pp. 317-38.
3. *JBORS*, March-June, 1933, p. 67.
4. Kielhorn's Inscriptions of Northern India, No. 622, *Ep. Ind.*, V, Appendix.
5. V.V. Mirashi, "The Vākāṭaka Chronology" in *IHQ*, Vol. XXIV, pp. 148-55; *CII*, Vol. V (Inscription of Vākāṭakas, ed. by him and pub. by the Archaeological Survey of India, 1963), Intr., also his article in "*Purāṇa*", (pub. by All India Kāshirāja Trust, Rāmnagar, Varanasi), Vol. 1, No. 1, pp. 31-38. For further details see M. Govinda Pai, "Genealogy and Chronology of the Vākāṭakas" in *JIH*, Vol. XIV, 1935, pp. 1-26, 165-204; R.C. Majumdar, "Note on the Genealogy and Chronology of the Vākāṭakas" in *JRASB* (L), Vol. XII, p. 150; S.K. Aiyangar, "the Vākāṭakas and their place in the History of India" in *ABORI*, Vol. V, pp. 31-54.
6. M. Krishnamachariar, *HCSL*, Intr., XLix-XLviii.
7. *Vy.*, 99, 383; *Vṣṇ.*, IV, 24.63; H.H. Wilson, *op. cit.*, p. 385; See also V.A. Smith, *Ind. Ant.*, 1902, p. 258 note; D.R. Patil's paper on "Gupta Inscriptions and *Purāṇic* Tradition" in *BDCRS*, Vol. II, pp. 2-58.
8. *PDKA*, Intr., p. XII and 20.

# 9

# Kingdoms and Dynasties of the post-Harṣa Period

**(c. 650-1200 A.D.)**

THE kingdoms and dynasties of Northern India of post-Harṣa period find mention in the *Prati Sarga Parvan* of the *Bhaviṣya Purāṇa*. According to this *Purāṇa*, the Pratihāras (Parihāras), the Paramāras, the Cāhamānas (Cauhānas) and the Cālukyas or Solankis (Śuklas), representing the four Rajput families, belonged to the *Agnivaṁśa* or *Agnikula*.[1] The theory relating to Agnikula origin of the Rajputs is also propounded in Prithvirāja Raso of Cand Bardai. The historical tradition pertaining to the origin of the Cauhānas (one of the four Agnikulas) is recorded in *Prithvirāja-Vijaya,* attributed to Jayānaka. One of the reasons for their association with Agnikula seems to be that they took vow before *agnikund* or firepit in presence of the *Brāhmaṇas* to defend the territorial integrity of the country by repulsing the foreign invaders. They, actually, dominated the politics of Northern India after the death of Harṣa in 647 A.D. They established their rule in this part of India and founded several petty independent kingdoms, which lasted for nearly five centuries and then one by one succumbed to the Muslim invaders. The *Purāṇa* concerned, virtually, deals with the history of the Rajput period (*c.* 650-1200 A.D.). It does not fall within the scope of this book to present a detailed account of the subject. All that is intended to be done here is to discuss the subject on the basis of only those evidences, which are recorded in the said *Purāṇa* and have some historical value.

The Pratihāras have been described in the *Purāṇa* as the Parihāras. It can be stated without any fear of contradiction that prior to the conquest of Kanauj (Kānyakubja), they established their rule in Avanti (Ujjain). A notable ruler of the Pratihāra dynasty named Vatsarāja (identified by all historians with the father of Nāgabhata II, *c.* 805-33 A.D.), who was a king of Avanti, figures in the *Purāṇa*.[2] The Jain *Harivaṁśa* fairly attests to this fact. He is believed to have ascended the throne in or about 778 A.D. His empire initially comprised Malavā and eastern and central Rajputānā. He gradually established his supremacy over a large part of Northern India. Bhoja I (*c.* 836-85 A.D.) and Bhoja II (*c.* 910-12 A.D.) were also the Pratihāra rulers of Kanauj. We find the description of the

Bhojas in the *Purāṇa*,[3] but neither their periods nor the details of their achievements are given therein. However, the Pratihāras continued to exercise their sway over Kanauj and Madhyadeśa. The last king of this dynasty, Rājyapāla (*c.* 991-1018 A.D.) also figures in the *Purāṇa*.[4] His capital Kanauj was invaded by Mahmud of Ghazni in 1018 A.D., but he could not defend it and fled away out of fear.

The tradition confirms that the Candellas, who established their dominion over the southern parts of the Ganga-Yamuna *doāb* including western Bundelkhand in the tenth century A.D., were feudatories of the great Pratihāra emperors of Kanauj. According to the *Purāṇa*, Kālinjar (which was, earlier, one of the strongholds of the Pratihāras and later occupied by the Candellas) was founded by the king named Parihara, who ruled for ten years. The city of Kālinjar is said to have a circumference of 1½ *yojana*.[5] He was followed by Gaurvarman, Dhirvaraman, Karvarman, Bhogavarman, Kalivarman, Bhojavarman, etc., who ruled over Kālinjar,[6] one of the important cities in the Candella kingdom. The Karvarman of the *Purāṇa* can be identified with Kirtivarman, who ruled some time between 1,100 and 1,129 A.D.

The Paramāras of Malavā, according to the tradition, were the descendants of king Pramara of Avanti. He is said to have ruled over Avantipura (having the extent of four *yojana*) for six years.[7] Munja or Munjavarman (*c.* 974-98 A.D.), who was the seventh king of the Paramāra dynasty, has been clearly mentioned in the *Purāṇa*. He is said to have defeated the Śavaras and Bhilas. The details about Sindhurāja or Sindhuvarman (Sindhula) are also given therein.[8] The most famous king of this dynasty was Bhoja (son of Sindhurāja), who ruled over Malavā with its capital of Dhāra, sixty Km. from Indore. He was popularly known as Rājā Bhoja. He ruled for about forty two years from 1018 to 1060 A.D. The *Purāṇa* explicitly mentions his name as a king of the Paramāra dynasty of Malavā.[9] This can also be confirmed by the testimony afforded by C.F. Wilford on the basis of his researches in the *Purāṇas*.[10] A Jain work, Prabandha-Cintāmani of Merutunga, mentions Bhoja as the immediate successor of Munja, which is not correct. The *Purāṇa* mentions Ranavarman (Naravarman), Citravarman, Dharmavarman, Kṛṣṇavarman, Udaya (Udayāditya), etc. as the later Paramāra kings of Malavā.[11] But the historicity of only two of them, viz. Naravarman and Udayāditya has been established. The copper plate by Naravarman (nephew of Bhojarāja) preserved in archaeological museum of Indore proves that the Paramāra king, Udayāditya (*c.* 1059-1094 A.D.), was brother of Bhoja. According to the *Purāṇa*, Udaya was the founder of Udayapura,[12] which can be amply substantiated by "Udepur" inscription,[13] which describes him as the successor of Bhoja.

The *Purāṇic* accounts of the Tomaras of Delhi and the Cauhānas of Ajmer and Delhi are of considerable historical importance.

According to the *Purāṇa*, the Tomara dynasty, founded by Anangpāl I, ruled in Indraprastha (Delhi region).[14] It is further said that Mahipāla, the founder of Ajmer, ruled for ten years. He was succeeded by his son Tomara, who ruled at Indraprastha. His descendants became known as Tomara Kṣatriyas. Tomara's son, Cauhānasubha, became known as Sāmaladeva, who ruled for seven years. One of his descendants was Ajaya (or Ajayapāla).[15]

It is historically a proven fact that Ajayapāla was one of the Cauhāna rulers of Ajmer. He is credited with having founded the city of Ajmer, which is contradicted by the *Purāṇa*. One of the famous rulers of dynasty, Viśāla Deva (or Vigraharāja IV, 1152-64 A.D.), captured Delhi about 1158 A.D. from the Tomaras. In the *Purāṇic* genealogy of the Cauhāna rulers the name of Viśāla clearly figures. One of his descendants was Jayasimha, who ruled for fifty years. The two other noted rulers, Anandadeva and Someśvara, have been also mentioned.[16] The most illustrious ruler of Cauhāna family, Prithvi Rāja (1179-92 A.D.), who was the king of Ajmer, inherited the kingdom of Delhi from his maternal grandfather, Anangpāl II, the last king of the Tomara dynasty according to the *Purāṇa*. It is clearly stated therein that after the death of Anangpāl he became the full-fledged ruler of Delhi. He made it a fortified city. It was an extensive and magnificent city during his time.[17] He was the last Hindu ruler of Delhi and Ajmer.

According to the *Purāṇa*, Prithviraja's overlordship of Northern India was disputed by Jayacandra (of Gāhaḍavāla dynasty), the king of Kānyakubja or Kanauj (who ruled from 1170 to 1194 A.D.). It is said that Prithvirāja Cauhān of Delhi had turned him into an enemy by forcibly carrying off his beautiful daughter, Saṁyogitā, from her Svayamvara. The rivalry between the two, ultimately, resulted in the battle, which was fought at Sukar. In this battle the soldiers of both sides were killed. The hostility between the two potentates proved to be disastrous for the Agnivaṁśa[18] and blessing for Muhammad Ghori. The *Purāṇa* even records the "death of Prithvirāja at the hands of Sahaddin" (Sihabuddin Ghori),[19] which is an indication towards a well-known fact that the latter after having defeated the former in the second Battle of Tarain (fourteen miles from Thanesar or near Bhatinda) fought in 1192 A.D. captured him near the *Sarsuti* (Sarasvati) and put to death either there itself or at Ghazni. Thereafter, Delhi and Ajmer fell under the occupation of Ghori. Likewise, in 1194 A.D. Muhammad Ghori defeated Jaichandra of Kanauj at Candawar near Agra and conquered his kingdom.

The *Purāṇa* slightly touches upon the Cālukya (called Śukla) dynasty of Ānarta (Gujarat) in western India. The founder of the dynasty, Śukla, is said to have set up his rule at Dvārakā and ruled for ten years. He was followed by Visvakṣena, who ruled for twenty years, Jayasena, who ruled for thirty years and Visena, who ruled for fifty years. There were some other rulers, but details are not provided about them. Their identification and reign-periods cannot be satisfactorily determined.[20]

## References and Notes

1. The *Purāṇic* accounts do not appear to be very much systematic. Several gaps have been noticed in the dynastic and genealogical accounts of the *Purāṇas*. The overlapping of the dynastic accounts is apparent. However, their historical value from the genealogical points of view cannot be dismissed. Moreover, some of the relevant details are in full accord with the facts recorded in history of ancient and early medieval period.
2. *Bhv.* (Supra), Vol. II, p. 165, v. 32.

3. Ibid., Vol. I, pp. 419-20, 425; Vol. II, p. 165.
4. *Ibid.*, Vol. II, pp. 165-66, v. 35.
5. *Ibid.*, Vol. I, p. 336, vv. 1-2; Vol. II, pp. 184-85, vv. 1-4.
6. *Ibid.*, Vol. II, pp. 184-90, vv. 5-37.
7. *Ibid.*, Vol. I, p. 335, v. 49, p. 337, v. 8, Vol. II, pp. 161-62. vv. 13-15.
8. *Ibid.*, Vol. II, pp. 175-77, vv. 25-30.
9. *PK*, p. 385.
10. *As. Res.*, Vol. IX, pp. 176-77.
11. *Bhv.*, Vol. II, pp. 176-77, vv. 31-35.
12. *Ibid.*, p. 176, v. 34.
13. *Ep. Ind.*, Vol. I, pp. 232-38.
14. *Bhv.*, Vol. I, p. 424, v. 5, pp. 429-32, vv. 1-14 (The details about the descendants of Anangpal are given)
15. *Ibid.*, Vol. II, pp. 168-69, vv. 1-6.
16. *Ibid.*, pp. 170-71, vv. 18-22 (the pedigree and progeny of king Viśāladeva are given).
17. *Ibid.*, p. 171, vv. 22-25, Vol. I, pp. 430-34, vv. 1-15, 22-28.
18. *Ibid.*, Vol. I, pp. 432-35, vv. 17-21, 29-38, pp. 435-45, vv. 1-63 (the historical narratives are given in detail); also pp. 424-25, v. 4 (only for Jayacandra, as a king of Kānyakubja).
19. *Ibid.*, Vol. II, p. 171, v. 25 (It is also recorded that after the death of Prithvirāja a large number of women of the Cauhāna family fell into the hands of the Muslims and their descendants were neither pure Āryans nor *mlecchas.* They were rather of mixed parentage. They are represented by the Jātas and Mehans. The other *Kṣatriyas* sprang from the Cauhānas. *Ibid.*, pp., 171-72, vv. 26-28).
20. *Ibid.*, Vol. I, p. 336, v. 4; Vol. II, 172-76, vv. 1-28.

# 10

# Minor Kingdoms and Dynasties

THE peoples of both indigenous and foreign origins and the kingdoms over which they ruled in Northern, Central and Western India and the Deccan, and some minor dynasties including the contemporary ones, which were founded there at different periods of history, are vividly portrayed in the *Purāṇas.* The genealogies and chronology of some dynasties are also given therein.

The later Sātavāhanas (or the successors of the Sātavāhanas) of the Deccan have been referred to in the *Purāṇas* as Andharavṛtyas. They belonged to the lineage of the servants of feudatories of the Andhras. There were seven kings in this line. The Sriparvatiya-Andhras (of Telingana) have been assigned a reign-period of fifty-two years. One of the five minor dynasties that came into being after the dismemberment of the Sātavāhana empire was that of the Abhiras of Western India (Maharashtra). The ten Abhira kings are said to have ruled for sixty-seven years. The kings of the Andhra dynasty (who established themselves in the Deccan and Western India sometime after 236 A.D.) are said to have ruled for over a period of 300 years. The *Purāṇas* also provide description of the foreign invaders of India. The eight Yavana kings (Greek princes of Bactria lying between the Hindu-Kush and the Oxus, who ruled from the third century B.C. to the middle of the first century B.C.) ruled for either eighty or eighty-seven years according to the *Purāṇas.* The eighteen (or 10,16) Śaka kings (Indo-Scythians, second century B.C.-Second century A.D.) are said to have ruled (over different parts of India and Afghanistan) for 183 or 380 years. The fourteen *Tuṣaras* (the tribes on the banks of the river Cakṣu or Oxus, the north-western region) ruled for 500 years. The seven *Gardabhinas* or *Gardabhillas* (tribes of north-west India, who established themselves anterior to the *Śakas*) ruled for seventy-two years. The thirteen *Murundas* (a branch of the Indo-Scythians) of *Mleccha* origin along with other kings of the *Śudra* class ruled for 200 years only and not 450 years, as given in some *Purāṇas.* The eighteen or nineteen Hunas or Maunas ruled for 300 years. The 11 kings of the contemporary mleccha dynasty are said to have reigned for 300 years.[1] The kings of the dynasties mentioned above altogether ruled for 1,090 years, according to the *Viśnu*,[2] and 1,099 years, according to the *Bhāgavata Purāṇa*.[3]

The Murundas were probably the kinsmen of the Kushans. After the Kushan power in north India came to an end around 230 A.D., the Murundas established their rule in some parts of Central India. They continued to rule till the time of Samudragupta (A.D. 335-80), which can be substantiated by the epigraphic evidence and other relevant sources. The Allahabad pillar Inscription confirms that the "Śaka-Maurundas" were one of those foreign powers, who acknowledged Samudragupta as their overlord.[4] They were probably the Śaka lords or chieftains, who were ruling in the regions of Saurashtra and Ujjain at the time of Samudragupta. K.P. Jayaswal has provided the details of "The Murunda Dynasty".[5] B.C. Law has identified the *Purāṇic* Murundas with Moroundai of Ptolemy (150 A.D.). According to him, they occupied an extensive territory comprising some parts of North Bihar on the East of the Ganges. Further, on the authority of Hemacandra's *Abhidhānacintāmani* (IV, 26), he identifies them with the Lampakas, who were located near the sources of the modern Kabul river. It, therefore, follows that they had a settlement in this region as well.[6] According to some Jain sources, the Murundas or "Marudayavaṁsa" ruled for forty years.[7] The Jaina literary tradition corroborates the evidence relating to the flood of Pātaliputra in the time of the Murunda kings (third century A.D.) and the invasion and devastation of Taxila by the Turuṣkas or Tuṣaras (third century A.D.).[8]

The exact identity of the *Gardabhinas* or *Gardabhillas* is not yet firmly established. They are considered to be identical with the Garddabha princes, who once ruled over Malava region of Central India and some parts of Western India.[9] In some of the Jain sources they have been identified with the Gaddabhas, who ruled for 100 years. The Jaina scholars, while providing the accounts of the different dynasties that ruled over Ujjain or Ujjayini, have stated that Balamitra and Bhanumitra jointly ruled for sixty years and Nabavaha ruled for forty years. Then the rule of Gardabhilla dynasty over Ujjain began. This dynasty was in power for 152 years. Gardabhilla Mahendrāditya reigned for thirteen years (74-61 B.C.) and was then expelled by the Śaka kings (in 61 B.C.), whose rule lasted for four years, i.e. up to 57 B.C., when they were in turn expelled by the Malava people under Vikrama.The Śaka kings had displaced the dynasty of Vikramāditya. The Śaka dynasty ruled over different parts of India for 242 years. According to the Jain tradition, Gaddabhilla or Gardabhilla, the father of Vikramaditya, while ruling at Ujjain had abducted Sarasvati, the sister of famous astrologer Kālakācārya. Kālacācārya, being enraged went to the west of the Sindhu and brought ninty five or ninty six chiefs from Pārasakula (Persia) and with their help and the kings of Gujarat declared war against Gaddabhilla, inflicted crushing defeat on him and besieged Ujjayini. Thereafter, the Śaka kings established their supremacy over Malava with its capital at Ujjain. Gardabhilla's son, Vikramāditya, regained his ancestral kingdom of Ujjain by expelling the Śakas after seventeen years of their rule (which began in 75 B.C.), i.e. 58 B.C. Vikramāditya and his dynasty ruled for 135 years.[10]

Wilford's account regarding the parentage of Vikramādiyta is self-contradictory, for in one place he refers to him as the son of Gardabha and in other as the son of Gandh-Rupa.[11]

According to the *Prati-Sarga Parvan* of the *Bhaviṣya Purāṇa*, Vikramāditya, the famous king of Ujjayini or Ujjain (also called Avantipur, the earliest capital of Malava, situated on the bank of Sipra river), belonged to the Panwar or Paramara dynasty. The Panwars constitute one of the four families of Agnivaṁśa. Vikramāditya was the son of Gandharvasena, one of the descendants of "Pramara", (the founder of the dynasty, who ruled for six years only).[12] Vikramāditya ascended the throne twenty four years (= 3,044 *Kali* era) before the composition of "*Jyotirvida-bharana*", an astronomical work, by Kālidāsa in 33 B.C. (= 3,068 *Kali* era), i.e. in 57 B.C. About 600 kings of neighbouring states, both small and big, had acknowledged his sovereignty. He fought against the Śakas and succeeded in driving them out of his kingdom. A new era called *Vikrama Samvat* (also *Malava Samvat*) was introduced to commemorate his victory over the Śakas in 58-57 B.C. According to the *Jyotirvidabharana* (V. 13) and the Jain source-*Prabhāvaka-Carita* (V. 44) of Prabhācandra, he killed ninty-five Śaka kings. His reign-period varies from sixty or sixty-eight to eighty-six or 100 years. Merutunga in his Vicārasreni has stated that Vikramāditya reigned for sixty years and his four successors ruled for forty, eleven, fourteen and ten years respectively. The eighteen kingdoms, which flourished during Vikramāditya's time, included Indra-Prastha, Kuru, Pañcāla, Avanti, etc.

Vikramāditya was succeeded by his son Devabhakta, who ruled for ten years only. He was either overthrown or killed by the Śakas.[13] His son Śālivāhana of the same dynasty flourished 135 years after his grandfather Vikramāditya and ruled for sixty years. After having conquered the Śakas he celebrated his victory by commencing a new era called the *Saka era* in 78 A.D.[14] He not only conquered the Śakas, but also the Cīnas Bāhlikas, Kāmarūpas, Romajas, etc. From *Indra-Prasthiya-Rājavali* (by an anonymous writer) it appears that Śālivāhana was ruling over his kingdom with its capital at Ujjain in thirty two A.D. From the *Bhaviṣya Purāṇa* it is evident that he was followed by Śālihotra (who ruled for fifty years), Śāli-Vardhana, Śakahanta, Suhotra Havihorda, Indrapāla, Mālyavana, Sambhudatta, Bhaumarāja, Vatsarāja and his son Bhojarāja.[15] It is said that there were ten rulers in the Śālivāhana dynasty, who altogether ruled for 500 years. Bhojarāja, the tenth king (who ascended the throne in 542 V.E), was a very powerful king. He conquered Gandharavas, *Mlecchas*, Kasmiras, etc.[16] Bhojarāja was followed by Sambhudatta Vindupāla, Rājapāl, Somaśarma Kāmavarmā, Bhumipāla, Rangapāla, etc.[17] It is said that there were seven rulers in the dynasty of Bhojarāja and their reigns altogether covered a period of 300 years.[18] Eleven kings altogether ruled in Ujjain after king Bhoja and towards the close of the reign of the second of them (733-763 A.D.) the kingdom of Magadha was conquered by the Pāla king in 762 A.D.

The *Purāṇas* refer to the unanointed kings as Kilakila or Kolakila. They are stated to have belonged to either *Yavana* race or *Śudra* class.[19] They, actually, succeeded the Abhiras of Maharashtra after overthrowing them. The *Bhāgavata Purāṇa* (XII, I. 33) mentions Praviraka as a ruler of Kalikila. Sir William Jones takes it to be a city in the

"Mahratta country"[20] An inscription dated A.D. 1058, which refers to Kilakila as the capital of Narasimha Deva, the king of Konkan,[21] confirms his belief. The Kilakila princes were succeeded by the rulers of the dynasty founded by Vindhyaśakti. After the extinction of this dynasty, three Vāhlika kings, Supratika, Nabhira etc., ruled for thirty years.[22] Śākymā was the famous king of Mahiṣa (of Māhiṣmati).[23] The Mekala (situated on the bank of Narmada river) was ruled by seven kings, and Kosala was governed by nine kings. The Naiṣadhas or kings of Niṣadha belonged to the dynasty of Nala,[24] son of Virasena. They were all contemporary provincial rulers.

One of the powerful kings of Magadha, Visvasphani, after having exterminated other kings granted territories to Kaivartas, Pulindas and *Brāhmaṇas* to rule over them under his royal patronage.[25]

There were many other contemporary rulers. The king Devarakṣita and his descendants ruled over Kosala, Andhra, Pundra, Tāmralipti and other cities on the sea-coast, Campā, etc. Kalinga, Mahiṣa (Māhiṣmati) and Mahendranilaya kingdoms were ruled by the rulers of Guha dynasty. The kingdoms of Niṣadha, Yaduka, Saiśita, Naimisa and Kala-Kosaka or Kalatopada were ruled by the dynasty of Manidhānya. Kanka ruled over Muśika. Saurastra and Avanti came under the rule of the Abhiras and *Śudras* and the *Janapadas* on the Narmada fell under the occupation of Vrātyas, Dvija, Abhiras and *Śudras.* Candrabhāga, Kasmira, etc. were occupied by the Vrātyas and other *mleccha* and *Śudra* kings.[26]

According to some *Purāṇas,* the 13 rulers including Puṣyamitra (or Puspamitra) Paṭumitra, Durmitra, Padmamitra and others governed the region of Mekala near the source of the Narmada. They have been distinguished from the other seven rulers of the Mekala. It appears that Puṣyamitras are said to have ruled for thirteen years.[27] Fleet has also placed the Puṣyamitras somewhere along the banks of the Narmada.[28] The Bhitari pillar inscription bears witness to the fact that towards the closing years of Kumāragupta's reign (*c.* 414-55 A.D.) the Puṣyamitras invasion led to the eclipse of the Gupta power. However, it was Skandagupta, who crushed them and restored the fallen fortunes of his family.[29]

K.P. Jayaswal has described the Mitras of the *Purāṇa* texts as the republican communities of Mālavā. On the authority of the *Vāyu Purāṇa* he has concluded that they ruled over their respective states (in Mekala and Māhiṣmati regions) for about thirty years.[30] He has clearly stated that ". . . the Puṣhyamitras rose to such a height of power in the reign of Kumaragupta I that they nearly uprooted the Gupta dynasty. The Puṣyamitras 'developed a great power and wealth' to such an extent that they dealt a blow at the imperial throne from which it could not fully recover. The defeat inflicted by them on the imperial forces under Kumaragupta made the dynasty . . . totter to its fall. Evidently Kumāragupta himself was killed. In the second war Skandagupta remained on the battlefield the whole night . . . The next morning when the battle continued he succeeded in forcing a decision, which entitled him . . . to sovereignty. But it is not claimed that the Puṣyamitras bent their head or became feudatory. It was, therefore, a military defeat at most or rather it was the stemming back of the invading Puṣyamitras . . . The Puṣyamitra retired, but the glory of the Guptas never returned".[31]

## References and Notes

1. For details see *Vy.*, 99, 359-64; *Mats.*, 273, 18-24; *Mats.*, *SBA*, pp. 339-41; *Vṣṇ.*, IV, 24, 51-54 and 58; *Vṣṇ.* (tr.) H.H. Wilson, pp. 380-82; *Bmd.*, 3, 74, 170-79; *Bhāg.*, XII, 1, 27-32; Partiger, *PDKA*, pp. 42-46; Wilford, *As. Res.*, Vol. IX, pp. 116 ff.
   We come across some inaccuracies and discrepancies in the *Purāṇas* with regard to the number of kings of the dynasties concerned and the duration of their rule.
   See also H. Luder's List of Brāhmi Inscription from the earliest times to the second century A.D., *Ep. Ind.*, Vol. X, Appendix nos. 963, 965, 1093, 1123, 1135, 1137, 1140, 1148-49, 1154, 1156, 1162 and J.F. Fleet, *CII*, Vol. III, (Calcutta, 1888), Gupta Inscriptions, p. 14 for Abhiras, Yavanas, Śakas, Murundas, etc.
2. *Visnu Purāṇa*, iv, 24, 53.
3. *Bhagavata Purāṇa*, XII, 1, 30-32.
4. Fleet, CII; Vol. III, no. 1, pp. 1-17; see also J. Allan, *Catalogue of the Coins of the Gupta Dynasties* (London, 1914), Intr., pp. xxix-xxx.
5. See *Mālaviyaji Commemoration Volume*, pp. 185-87.
6. *HGAI*, (Delhi, 1976), p. 112.
7. *Tiloyapaṇṇati of* Yativṛsabha (ed. by A.N. Upadhyaya and H.L. Jain, Solapur, 1951), vv. 95-99; *Harivaṁśa Purāṇa* of Jinasena (Bombay, 1930), Sarga-60, vv. 487-92, 551-52.
8. Cf. *Premi Volume* (Tikamgarh, 1946), pp. 227-49.
9. For details see *As. Res.*, VI, 35; IX, 147; *JASB*, Dec., 1835, p. 688; *JRAS*, Vol. III, p. 385.
10. For details see Yativṛsabha's *Tiloyapaṇṇati*, vv. 86-94, 95-99; Jinasena's *Harivaṁśa, Sarga* 60, vv. 487-92, 551-521 *Pattāvali Samuccaya* (ed. Muni Darsanavijaya, Viramgam, 1933), *Titthogāli-Painna*, p. 197, also the *Tirthoddhāra-Prakarana* and the *Tapāgaccha-Pattāvali*, cf. *Pattāvali Samuccaya*; Merutunga's *Vicāraśreni*; "*Gurjaradeśa-bhupavalī*" (a hand-written document by Rangavijaya V.E., 1886 with 100 Vs.); J.C. Jain *LAIJC*, pp. 457-58; *JIH*, Vol. LVI (April 1978), Pt. I, pp. 51-52; *Mats.*, note p. 1052 (where the view, that Vikramāditya was the son of Gardabhilla, has been supported.
11. *As. Res.*, Vol. IX (Essay IV; Vikramāditya and Śālivāhana : their Respective Eras) pp. 140 and 166.
12. *Bhv.* (Bareilly, 1978), Vol. I, pp. 337-40, vv. 8-26; Vol. II, pp. 161-164, vv. 13-21.
13. *Bhv.* (Supra), Vol. II, pp. 163-64, v. 22.
14. *Ibid.*, pp. 163-64, vv. 23; Vol. I, pp. 416-19, vv. 17-19, 33; See also *Gurjaradeśa-bhupavali*; Wilford, *As. Res.*, Vol. IX, pp. 117-18, 130-40, 161-176; M. Elphinstone, *History of India* (London, 1866); pp. 72, 272; *The Ain-i-Akbari* by Abul-Fazl Allami (tr. and annot. H.S. Jarrett and Sir J.N. Sarkar, Delhi, 1988), Vol. 2, pp. 15, 16, note 22; *AIT*, pp. 154-55.
15. *Bhv.* (Supra) Vol. II, pp. 164-65, vv. 24-32.
16. *Ibid.*, Vol. 1, pp. 419-20, vv. 1-4.
17. *Ibid.*, Vol. II, pp. 165-67, vv. 33-42.
18. *Ibid.*, Vol. I, p. 425, vv. 1-2.
19. *Vy.*, 99, 363-64; *Mats.*, 273, 23-24; *Vṣṇ.*, IV, 24, 55.
20. *As. Res.*, Vol. XI, p. 142.
21. *JRAS*, Vol. IV, p. 282.
22. *Vy.*, 99, 372-73; *Vṣṇ.*, IV, 24, 57 (names are not given).
23. *Vy.*, 99, 374.
24. *Vy.*, 99, 375-77; *Vṣṇ.*, IV, 24, 59-60.
25. *Vy.*, 99, 377-82; *Vṣṇ.*, IV, 24, 61-62; *Bmd.*, 3, 74, 191.

26. *Vy.*, 99, 384-87, also 388-404; *Vṣṇ.*, IV, 24, 64-72; *Bmd.*, 3, 74, 189-90.
27. *Vy.*, 99, 374; *Vṣṇ.*, IV, 24, 58; *Bmd.*, 3, 74, 187-88; Wilson (tr.), *Vṣṇ.*, p. 384; Pargiter, *PDKA*, p. 51, note. 14.
28. *Ind. Ant.*, 1889, p. 228.
29. See Fleet, CII; Vol. III, pp. 53-55; H.R. Divekar's article "Puṣyamitras in the Gupta Period" in *ABORI*, 1919-20, pp. 99-103.
30. *Hindu Polity* (Bangalore, 1981), p. 156; History of India, 150 A.D. to 350 A.D. (Lahore, 1933), p. 85.
31. *Hindu Polity*, p. 157.

# 11

# Conclusion

THE *Purāṇic* accounts of kingdoms and dynasties in ancient India are, incontrovertibly, of great historical value. The period extending from the later *Vedic* age to the twelfth century A.D. saw the rise and fall of many kingdoms, the beginnings and end of many dynasties and the emergence and decay of many towns, cities and various other urban centres, which were founded by different kings in different parts of India, as it appears from the *Purāṇic* records. The historicity of many of them is a well proven fact. The kingdoms of primaeval antiquity still exist, though rulers and their descendants have passed into oblivion.

The rule of the Solar and Lunar dynasties (Suryavaṁśa and Candravaṁśa respectively) over their respective kingdoms in the pre-Bhārata war period are fairly illustrated in the *Purāṇas*. The rulers of the Solar race directly descending from Manu's offspring, Ikṣvāku, established their rule, by and large, in the middle Gangetic plains, whereas, on the other hand, we find that the descendants of Purūravas Aila, the progenitor of the Lunar race, expanded from their original homeland, Pratiṣṭhāna (near Allahabad) over greater parts of Northern, Central, Western and Eastern India, Madhyadeśa or Ganga-Yamana *doāb* and the Sārasvata region. By far the greater part of ancient Indian historical tradition deals with their migration, occupation of different territories, patterns of settlement, mutual political relations, kings' exploits, etc. But the tradition, proportionately, deals more with potentates than populace. The *Purāṇic* description in this regard is too clear to admit of any doubt or debate. It is clearly elucidated in the *Vāyu Purāṇa* (99, 462) that twenty-five dynasties, that reigned in different parts of India, sprang from five sons (Yadu, Turvasu, Druhyu, Anu and Puru) of Yayati in the line of Pururavas.

The *Vedic*, epic, Jain and Buddhist traditions and archaeology corroborate, to a considerable extent, the *Purāṇic* evidence relating to the kingdoms and dynasties of the Solar and Lunar race of the pre-Bhārata war period. For making an accurate historical study of the *Purāṇic* data, as well as for projecting a coherent picture of the subject, we have placed our reliance on those non-*Purāṇic* traditions, which are identical with the *Purāṇic* one.

The first phase of Pauravas' (the descendants of Puru) settlements in Sarasvati and Upper *doab* and Yādavas' settlements in Narmada valley, Malvā, Mathurā, Ganga-Yamuna *doāb*, Kathiāwaḍ (Gujarat), as mentioned in the *Purāṇas*, are archaeologically associated with Ochre-Coloured Pottery (OCP) of late Harappan period (*c.* 2,200-1,700 B.C.) and Black and Red Ware (BRW) ascribed to *c.* 2,000 B.C. respectively. The existence of urban centres like Hastināpur, Indraprastha, Kauśāmbi, Ahicchatra, Kāmpilya, Mathurā, Rājagir, Kāśi (Rājaghat), etc. in the Gangetic valley, as described in the epic and *Purāṇic* literature, have been archaeologically proved, and they have been associated with Painted Grey Ware (PGW) and Northern Black Polished Ware (NBPW) cultures. On the basis of Radio Carbon (14) dating, the archaeologists have placed them in the first millennium B.C., which is not beyond dispute. H.D. Sankalia ("Archaeology and Tradition" in *AIHA*, Delhi, 1977, pp. 277-78), while placing his reliance on the combined testimony of both tradition and archaeology, has reasonably concluded that the antiquity of towns and cities as occurring in the *Mahābhārata* and *Purāṇas* can be proved by archaeological evidence. However, the archaeological description of the patterns of settlement is inconsistent with that of literary tradition. The epic and *Purāṇic* traditions confirm the naming of towns and cities after those kings who founded them. For example, Hastin founded Hastināpur, Kusāmba Kauśāmbi, Vasu Vasumati, Viśāla Vaiśāli, Mithi, Mithilā, Mahiṣmān, Māhiṣmati, Śrāvasta Śrāvasti, Kusāgra Kusāgrapur (one of the earlier names of Rājagṛha or Rājagir), Campā Campāvati, Madhu Madhura of Mathurā, etc., Bhārata's two sons Takṣa and Puṣkara founded Takṣaśilā and Puṣkaravati respectively, and Rāma's son Kuśa Kuśāvati. The existence of most of them have been archaeologically proved.

In the pre-Bhārata war period, from Ikṣvāku to Pāṇḍavas (from Treta yuga to the Dvāpara-yuga) the rulers concerned ruled over their respective kingdoms for about ninty-four or ninty-six generations covering a period, which roughly extends from *c.* 3,000 B.C. to 1,400 B.C.

The credibility of traditional history from the earliest times to the accession of Parikshit II, as recorded in the *Mahābhārata* and *Purāṇas*, has been tested on the touchstone of some relevant historical sources.

The dynasties and kingdoms of the post Bhārata war period extending from the accession of Parkshit II or the beginning of *Kali-yuga* down to the fifth century B.C. include the twenty-eight or twenty-nine Pauravas, who ruled over Hastināpur, Indraprastha and Kauśāmbi, twenty-eight or twenty-nine Ikṣvākus of Kosala including the predecessors and successors of Buddha of Śākya clan, twenty-two Bārhadrathas of Magadha, who ruled for 638 years from *c.* 1151 to 513 B.C., five Pradyotas of Avanti, who ruled for 102 years from 513 to 411 B.C. and other kingdoms like Pañcāla, Śuraśena, Videha, Kāśi, Aṅga, etc. The genealogical accounts of the rulers concerned are also historically important. The details provided in the *Mahābhārata* about the Kuru kingdom of Hastināpur ruled by the successors of Parikshit II are also of considerable historical importance. The Buddhist and Jain sources also throw some light on the subject concerned to a considerable degree.

The *Purāṇic* accounts of the Magadhan dynasties of early historical period are of exceptional value. The ten kings of Bimbisārian and Śaiśunāga dynasties ruled for 200 years from *c.* 543 to 343 B.C. The nine Nandas ruled for twenty two years from *c.* 343 to 321 B.C. The ten Maurya kings ruled for 137 years from *c.* 321 to 184 B.C. The ten kings of the Śuṅga dynasty ruled for 112 years from *c.* 184 to 72 B.C. The four Kāṇvas ruled exactly for forty five years from *c.* 72 to 27 B.C. The twenty-nine or thirty kings of the Andhra or Sātavāhana dynasty ruled over western India (Mahārāshtra) and the Deccan for about 252 years from *c.* 27 B.C. to 225 A.D.

The Buddhist tradition recorded in the Pāli Canon, Chronicles and Commentaries and the Sanskrit-Buddhist texts, and the Jain tradition recorded in both the Canonical and non-Canonical texts, are very helpful for supplementing the *Purāṇic* accounts of the Magadhan dynasties of both Buddhist and post-Buddhist period to the Mauryas and for verifying the correctness of the dynastic chronology of the ruler concerned. There are also some epigraphic and numismatic evidence to confirm the historicity of the Purānic evidence about some rulers up to the Sātavāhanas.

It is worthy of remark that the genealogies of the said dynasties (Bārhadratha, Pradyota, Bimbisārian, Śaiśunāga, Nanda, Maurya, Śuṅga, Kāṇva and Sātavāhana) are chronologically arranged in the *Purāṇas*. Many of the dynasties are historically authenticated. Regnal years and the time span of individual kings are given with slight variations in the *Purāṇas*, which are, no doubt, to a great extent, anachronistical and hence they have been verified with the help of other faithful historical records. The *Purāṇic* length of reigns of the rulers concerned are in most of the cases inflating. However, the *Purāṇic* data concerned are extremely useful for genealogical and chronological reconstruction of ancient Indian history of the periods concerned. The historical authenticity of the *Purāṇic* data from the dynastic, genealogical and chronological points of view have also been acknowledged by many distinguished historians, indologists, archaeologists and other oriental and occidental scholars. The evidences furnished by them on the basis of their researches into the subject concerned are very helpful in substantiating the *Purāṇic* accounts of the historical dynasties.

The *Purāṇas* also deal with the later Sātavāhanas, who established themselves in the Deccan and Western India in the second quarter of the third century A.D. The kingdoms of Northern, Central, Eastern and Western India and the Deccan over which the people of both indigenous and foreign origins ruled for considerable period of time and some minor contemporary dynasties, which were founded there at different periods of history, are also mentioned in the *Purāṇas*. The foreign invaders like the Śakas, Yavanas, Tuṣāras, Gardabhillas, Murundas, Hunas and others of both *mleccha* and *śudra* origin, who ruled in different parts of India between the third century B.C. and the fifth century A.D., are also enumerated in the *Purāṇas*. The rulers of Vikramāditya, Śālivāhana and Bhoja dynasties of Ujjain ruled from the first century B.C. to the sixth or seventh century A.D. The Mitra rulers of Mekala of Kumāragupta's time (*c.* 414-55 A.D.) have also been described in the *Purāṇas.*

The historical reliability of the *Purāṇic* accounts of the Nāga dynasties, that reigned at Vidiśā, Padmāvatī, Mathurā, etc. between the second century B.C. and the fourth century A.D., is beyond doubt. The historicity of many of them has been confirmed by the discovery of the coins also. The *Purāṇas* also make mention of some rulers of Vākāṭaka dynasty of the Deccan, whose historicity is confirmed by the epigraphic records. The extent of the Gupta dominion during the times of Candragupta I (*c.* 319-35 A.D.) also gets reflected in the *Purāṇic* records. The Vākāṭakas ruled contemporaneously with the Gupta from the middle of the third century A.D. to the second quarter of the sixth century A.D. According to the traditional accounts, the seven Guptas ruled for 245 years, which is incompatible with the authentic historical accounts of the subject concerned.

The kingdoms and dynasties of Northern India of post-Harṣa period (*c.* 650-1200 A.D.) find mention specifically in the *Bhaviṣya Purāṇa.* The history of four Rajput families, viz. the Pratihāras of Kanauj, the Paramāras of Mālavā, the Cauhānas of Ajmer and Delhi and the Cālukyas of Gujarat is presented in the above *Purāṇa.* The history of the Tomaras and Cauhānas is prolixly narrated therein.

The dynastic accounts of the *Purāṇas* show that from Yudhiṣṭhira to Prithvirāja Cauhāna there were more than 250 kings belonging to different dynasties, who ruled over different kingdoms altogether for about 4,200 years (the total duration of their reigns).

The details of the ancient Indian kingdoms and dynasties with their genealogies and relative chronology, as provided in the *Purāṇas,* sharply reflect the *Purāṇic* chroniclers' (or Purāṇakāras') sense of history and chronology.

V.A. Smith (*EHI,* 4th revd. edn. by S.M. Edward, London, 1967, pp. 4 f and 10) has fairly attested to the historical value of traditional history, as embodied in literature, but, unfortunately, he like Elphinstone has not acknolwedged the importance of ancient Indian historical tradition anterior to the sixth or fourth century B.C. A.B. Keith (*HSL,* Ist pub., Oxford, 1920, Delhi, 1973, pp. 144-45) and Prof. Maurice Winternitz (*HIL,* 1st pub., Calcutta, 1927, reptd., Delhi, 1977, Vol. I, pp. 29-30) also affirm the historical value of ancient literary traditions of India. A.D. Pusalker in one of his research papers, "Conception of History in Ancient Indian Literature" (pub. in *Our Heritage,* Vol. 12, 1964, pt. 2, pp. 35-52) has strongly advocated the historical validity of the epic and *Purāṇic* data about the various aspects of ancient Indian history and culture. U.N. Ghoshal (*The Beginnings of Indian Historiography and other Essays,* Calcutta, 1944, pp. 21 f and 51) has also attached considerable importance to the historical traditions preserved in the *Vedic,* Epic and *Purāṇic* literature. M. Krishnamachariar (*HCSL,* Delhi, third ed., 1974, pp. 1 ff. 10 ff, 50 f.) strongly supports the historical value of the *Purāṇic* data concerned. Romila Thapar (*AISH,* Hyderabad, 1984, pp. 269-73, 326 f, 352) has also admitted that the *Purāṇas* constitute very faithful record from the dynastic, genealogical and chronological points of view.

The *Purāṇas* constitute an addition to important documents on ancient Indian traditional historiography. On the basis of the richness of historical and chronological data contained in the *Purāṇas*, the views expressed by many Indian and foreign scholars, that ancient Indians—the *Brāhmaṇas*, Jains and Buddhists—lacked the sense of history and chronology, can be disposed of. The statements very often made by some scholars, that ancient Indians did not maintain the records of the past events, can also be dismissed as fanciful. It will be wrong to say that ancient India has not bequeathed to us any historical works. The aspect concerned, strictly speaking, does not fall within the purview of the treatment of the present subject. I have, therefore, discussed this aspect separately at length in *Ancient Indian Historiography*, which is one of my forthcoming books.

I close the discussion with the observation of E.J. Rapson. He has reasonably maintained that the dynastic lists and genealogies preserved in ancient Indian literature attributed to the *Brāhmaṇas*, Jains and Buddhists mark the beginnings of history in ancient India, whose development was carried beyond this rudimentary stage. He also refers to the deficiency of historical material in literature from the standpoint of political events. (*CHI*, Delhi, 1962, Vol. I, *Ancient India*, pp. 51-52.

# APPENDICES

## Chronological Tables of Different

TABLE I : **(Based on the Traditional**

| Sl. No. | Name of the Dynasty | Numer of Kings | Duration as given in the *Purāṇas* | Duration as given by Pargiter |
|---|---|---|---|---|
| 1 | 2 | 3 | 4 | 5 |
| 1. | Bārhadratha | 22 | 1,000 or 1,006 years | 484 years |
| 2. | Pradyōta | 5 | 138 years | 138 years |
| 3. | Bimbisārian and Śaiśunāga | 10 | 360 (or 362) years | 360 years |
| 4. | Nanda | 9 (or 2) | 100 (or 40) years | 100 years |
| 5. | Maurya | 10 (or 12) | 316 years | 137 years |
| 6. | Śuṅga | 10 | 300 (0r 112, 120 years) years | 112 years |
| 7. | Kāṅva | 4 | 85 (or 45) years | 45 years |
| 8. | Āndhra or Sātavāhana | 30 (or 32) | 506 (or 456, 460) years | 460 years |
| 9. | Gupta | 7 | 245 years | — |

**NOTE :** The *Purāṇic* duration of rule of the Bārhadratha dynasty over Magadha, i.e. 1,000 or 1,006 years, as shown above, actually, includes the reign-periods of ten kings of the pre-Bhārata war period and twenty two kings (10+22=32) of the post-war period. The figure is, of course, exaggerated. However, the last ruler of this dynasty, Ripuñjaya, was contemporary of Bimbisāra. The Pradyotas of Avanti ruled contemporaneously with Magadhan rulers of Bimbisārian and Śaiśunāga dynasty for about 102 years and not 138 years. According to *Mahāvaṁśa*, the duration of reigns of kings of Bimbisāra and Śaiśunāga dynasty was 200 years and that of Nanda dynasty was twenty-two years. The *Purāṇic* figures in some cases are too high to be accepted as credible. The duration of reigns of the Mauryas, Śuṅgas and Kāṇvas, as given in all standard *Purāṇa* texts, go well in accord with what we have accepted. It is only the *Kaliyugarājavṛttānta*,

## Dynasties with Supplementary Notes

**and Historical Evidence.)**

| of Reign | | Period of Reign | |
|---|---|---|---|
| as given by V.A. Smith | Accepted | Traditional Dates | Accepted Dates |
| 6 | 7 | 8 | 9 |
| — | 638 years | 3,138-2,132 B.C. | *c.* 1,151-513 B.C. |
| — | 102 years | 2,132-1,914 B.C. | *c.* 513-411 B.C. |
| — | 200 years | 1,994-1,634 B.C. | *c.* 543-343 B.C. |
| 45 years | 22 years | 1,634-1,534 B.C. | *c.* 343-321 B.C. |
| 137 years | 137 years | 1,534-1,218 B.C. | *c.* 321-184 B.C. |
| 112 years | 112 years | 1,218-918 B.C. | *c.* 184- 72 B.C. |
| 45 years | 45 years | 918-833 B.C. | *c* 72 -27 B.C. |
| 289 years | 252 years | 833-327 B.C. | *c.* 27 B.C.-225 AD. |
| 149 years | 235 years | 327-82 B.C. | *c.* 275-510 A.D. |

which provides the exaggerated figures, which have, unfortunately, been accepted by some scholars. The duration of reigns of the Andhras, as given in the *Purāṇas,* has not been accepted on reasonable ground. The Andhrabhṛtyas have sometime been confounded with the Guptas, as it appears from the *Purāṇas.* The exactitude of reign-periods of either of them cannot be ascertained. The *Purānic* variations in respect of the duration of rule may precisely be attributed to interpolation.

V.A. Smith has also not given credence to the long period of reigns, that Purāṇas have assigned to individual kings and the dynasties. After having examined the validity of the *Purāṇic* duration of the dynasties of pre and post-Maurya period (from Nanda to Gupta) with the help of standard historical works and some other epigraphic and numismatic evidence, he adjusted the dates on rational basis,[1] which we have given above. He considers the *Purāṇic* dynasties as historical and not fictitious.

Pargiter has also slightly modified the traditional length of reigns in his monumental work (Dynasties of the Kali Age), which has been partially criticized by Kota Venkatachalam.[2] But the justification, which he has given of his criticism of Pargiter's duration of the dynasties concerned, does not seem to be valid.

The Chronology arranged by Pargiter shows that Senājit Bārhadratha (the seventh Māgadhan king of the post-Bhārata war period) ascended the throne about 850 B.C. and he and other 15 Bārhadratha kings (average 14½ years) ruled for about 231 years. The Pradyotas began their rule about 627 or 619 B.C. The five Pradyotas (average, 10½ years) ruled for 52 years. The Śiśunāgas began their rule about 575 or 567 B.C. The ten Śiśunāgas (average 16½ years) ruled for about 165 years. Mahāpadma Nanda's accession took place in B.C. 402 and he and his eight sons ruled for eighty years. Candragupta's asscession has been ascribed to 322 B.C. He has, however, candidly admitted that there is always a scope for further adjustment or partial modification of the dates concerned.[3]

The traditional chronology as given above is purely based on astronomical proof of the outbreak of the Bhārata war in 3,138 B.C. and the beginning of *Kaliyuga* in 3,102 B.C. It has not been totally discarded, but not accepted either. The dates accepted are relatively more rational and based on the scientific calculation of the data available in all relevant sources, and it is in commensurate with the accepted duration of reign. However, it cannot be denied that the chronology of the pre-Maurya period is, by and large, tentative. Max Muller, while denouncing the Indian Chronology of the period concerned as vague, rightly observed that "all the dates before Chandragupta are to be considered only as hypothetical."[4]

## References

1. *EHI* (Oxford, 1924), pp. 31-33, 46-48.
2. *Chronology of Ancient Hiṇdu History* (Vijayawada, 1957), Pt. 1, pp. 95-96.
3. *AIHT*, (Delhi, 1972), 286-87.
4. *HASL* (Varanasi, 1968), p. 268. According to him, everything in Indian Chronology depends on the date of Chandragupta Maurya's accession, i.e. "315 B.C." V.A. Smith (*EHI*, fourth revd. edn., S.M. Edward, Oxford, 1967, pp. 4, 10-11) is also of the view that no definite date can be determined before *c.* 326 B.C.

TABLE II : **(Based on the Chronological Charts of Sir William Jones[1])**

| Sl. | Name of the Dynasty | Number of Kings | Duration of Reign | Regnal Period |
|---|---|---|---|---|
| 1. | Bārhadratha | 20 | 1,000 years | 3,100-2,100 B.C. |
| 2. | Pradyota | 5 | 138 years | 2,100-1,962 B.C. |
| 3. | Shishunāga | 10 | 360 years | 1,962-1,602 B.C. |
| 4. | Nanda | 1 | 100 years | 1,602-1,502 B.C. |
| 5. | Maurya | 10 | 137 years | 1,502-1,365 B.C. |
| 6. | Shuṅga | 10 | 112 years | 1,365-1,253 B.C. |
| 7. | Kāṇva | 4 | 345 years | 1,253- 908 B.C. |
| 8. | Andhra | 32 | 456 years | 908- 452 B.C. |
| | | | Total : 2,648 Years | |

**NOTE :** In Jan. 1788 William Jones first prepared the dynastic list of kings of the post-Bhārata war period on the evidence of the work "*Purāṇārthaprakāsha*", chiefly based on the *Bhāgavata Purāṇa*, which was composed by Pandit Radhakant Sharma. He learnt from his Sanskrit guide, Pt. Sharma, that according to the *Bhāgvata Purāṇa*, the Hindu concept of Creation goes back to high antiquity; Vaivasvata Manu appeared on the scene tens of thousands of years ago; the *Mahābhārata* war, a landmark in Indian history, was fought more than 3,000 years before the beginning of the Christian era and the Kali-yuga commenced 36 years after the war. All these constitued the foundation of his knowledge about the Hindu Chronology. Out of the four *yugas* of the Hindus he took only the *Kaliyuga* as an historical age and accordingly he began with 3,101 B.C., which marked the beginning of the *Kali* era coinciding with the commencement of the Bārhadrathas rule over Magadha. Ripuñjaya, the last king of the Bārhadratha dynasty, was put to death by his minister 'Sunaca', who placed his own son Pradyota on the throne of his master exactly two years before Buddha's appearance in the same kingdom, which is believed by the Hindus to have taken place 3,888 years ago or 2,001 years before Christ as stated by him. He says that "this revolution constitutes an epoch of the highest importance in our present inquiry".[2]

According to him, after the death of last Sātavāhana king, Chandrabija, which happened according to the Hindus 396 years before Vikramaditya (56 B.C.), i.e. 452 B.C., seven dynasties comprising that of Andhrabhṛtya (Andhras' feudatories in the Deccan), Abhira, Gardabhin, Śaka, *Yavana*, Tuṣāra and Murunda with 76 Princes altogether reigned for 1,399 years. Praviraca, Yasonandi and others reigned in the city of Maharashtra till 1,053 or for 106 years.[3] After Praviraca, the empire was divided among the mlecchas and infidels.

The first table of William Jones, as shown above, was obviously based on the traditional chronology, which he called "the most authentic system of Hindu chronology". But after sometime he began to doubt its authenticity. He later on realised that the *Purāṇic* figures are not fully reliable. He also cast his doubt on the high antiquity of the dynasties concerned, and, thus, he slightly modified some of his earlier dates. Taking B.C. 1,027, the date of Buddha's birth fixed by the Chinese authorities, as the starting point he prepared another chronological chart, according to which Abhimanyu is ascribed to 2,029 B.C., Pradyota 1,029 B.C., Buddha 1,027 B.C., Nanda 699 B.C., Balin (Andhra dynasy) 149 B.C. and Vikramaditya 56 B.C. Taking the date of Buddha from Abul Fazl's *Ain-i-Akbari*, he further placed Abhimanyu 2,368 years before Christ. Fixing the birth of Buddha ten years before the *Kali age*, i.e. Buddha 1,027 B.C. and Parikshit—1,017 B.C., he further suggested that reckoning twenty or thirty generations Pradyota may be ascribed to 317 or 17 B.C. and Nanda 313 or 13 A.D.[4] In his discourses on 28.2.1973 Jones determined Candragupta Maurya's epoch as 300 B.C.

Putting all the blames on the *Brāhmaṇs* for the mistakes, which he committed earlier in his analysis and interpretation of chronological data while fixing the high antiquity of the dynasties, as shown above (Table II), he observed that "Even in the history of the present age (Kali) the generation of men and the reigns of kings are extended beyond the course of nature, and beyond the average resulting from the accounts of the *Brāhmaṇs* themselves, for they assign to a hundred and forty two reigns a period of 3,153 years . . . yet they represent four Kanva princes on throne of Magadha for a period of 345 years; now it is even more improbable that four successive kings should have reigned 86 years . . . then Nanda should have been a king a hundred years . . . Taking Chinese accounts of Buddha's birth (1,027 B.C.) from M. De Guignes . . . I arranged the corrected Hindu Chronology . . . We have given a sketch of the Indian history through the longest period fairly assignable to it, and have traced the foundation of the Indian empire before 3,800 years from the present time; but on a subject in itself so obscure and so much clouded by the fictions of the *Brāhmiṇs*, who, to aggrandise themselves, have designedly raised their antiquity beyond truth, we must be satisfied with probable conjecture and just reasoning from the best attainable data."[5]

It appears that William Jones went on changing his chronological tables without sticking to any particular one. He has not drawn any plausible conclusion regarding the duration of reigns and reign-periods of different dynasties, probably, because of the reasons that he did not take any pain to make a scientific study of the *Purāṇic* chronology and to examine the relevance of other available historical data. The chronology provided by him exposes his ignorance of all the relevant data available in the *Purāṇas*.

Kota Venkatachalam has also doubted Jones' sound knowledge of the *Purāṇas.* He is not in perfect agreement with him so far as the duration of reigns is concerned. But he himself seems to be too much obsessed with the longer period of reigns of the kings of some dynasties, as given in some *Purāṇas.* He has accepted only those higher figures as duration of reign and those traditional dates as period of reign of the *Purāṇic* dynasties,[6] which have been shown in Table I.

## References

1. "On the Chronology of the Hindus" in *As. Res.* (Delhi, 1979), Vol. 2, pp. 107-11; Lord Teignmouth (ed.): The Works of Sir William Jones (London, 1807), Vol. IV, pp. 36-40.
2. *As. Res.*, Vol. 2, pp. 107-8.
3. *Ibid.*, pp. 110-11.
4. *Ibid.*, pp. 112-13; Lord Teignmouth, *op. cit.*, pp. 42-46.
5. Lord Teignmouth, *op. cit.*, pp. 42-46; *As. Res.*, Vol. 2, p. 111-12.
6. The Plot in Indian Chronology (Vijayawada, 1953), pp. 23-27.

B

# Notes on Chronology arranged by F. Wilford and J. Bentley

THE Chronology arranged by F. Wilford and J. Bentley on the basis of the *Purāṇic*, astronomical and other evidences also deserves our notice.

Wilford, while writing on the Chronology of the Hindus sometime between 1790 and 1795 on the basis of the evidences recorded in the *Purāṇas* and the astronomical works, *Vārāhi-Saṁhitā* of Vārāhamihira (*c.* 500-550 A.D.) and *Brahmasphuta-siddhānta* of Brahmagupta (*c.* 598 A.D.), postulated that *Kaliyuga* began about 2,405 years ago or 1,600 years before Christ.[1] Later, he altered the dates. He found that it was B.C. 3,101, which marked the beginning of the *Kaliyuga*. Astronomically, Yudhiṣṭhira lived 3,044 years before Vikramāditya (3,044+56=), i.e. 3,100 B.C. or between 1,500 and 1,370 B.C. or about 1,881 year of the *Kaliyuga*, as stated by him. The various dates, which he has suggested as the beginning of the *Kaliyuga*, are 1,078, 1,219, 1,370 and 1,400 B.C.[2] According to him, the Bārhadrathas ruled for about 1,000 years; the Pradyotas for about 138 or 128 years and the Śiśunāgas for about 360 or 362 years. Mahāpadma Nanda ascended the throne 299 years before Vikramāditya (299+56=), i.e. 355 B.C. and ruled for twenty eight years up to 327 B.C. and his son ruled for twelve years from 327 to 315 B.C. From the birth of Parikshit or the beginning of the *Kaliyuga* to Mahāpadma Nanda's accession to the throne there elapsed exactly 1,015 years. The year 315 B.C. marked the accession of Candragupta Maurya to the throne of Magadha. About 29 rulers of the Andhra dynasty ruled for 456 or 460 years. From Nanda to the last Andhra ruler 'Puloma' there elapsed 836 years.[3] Deriving his authority from *Ain-i-Akbari* he has suggested that Buddha began to reign 1,367 years before Christ.[4] He has further supplied the chronology of some of the successors of Vikramāditya (56 B.C.) and Śālivāhana (78 A.D.) of Ujjain up to time of king Bhoja.[5]

According to John Bentley, Manu Vaivasvata, the seventh Manu, belonged to 1,736 B.C. and *Kaliyuga* or Iron Age began in 1,004 B.C.[6] While writing in 1796, he suggested that the *Kaliyuga* commenced in Feburary in the 906th year of the world. He has placed Yudhiṣṭhira in 2,825th year of the world, which is equivalent to astronomical 1920, and Parikshit in 2,835th year of the world, which is equivalent to astronomical 1,925. He has placed Buddha in 1,002, or 1,043, 1101 year of the astronomical era. While fixing the chronology of different *Purāṇic* dynasties in *Kali* era, he has concluded that the Pradyotas' rule began in 1,095 (it ended in *Kali* era 1,107-8 = B.C. 1,995-94), Śiśunāga in 1,139 (ended in *Kali* era 1,467-68=B.C. 1,635-34) and Nandas' in 1,499 (ended in *Kali* era 1,567-68 = B.C. 1535-34). He has placed Candragupta Maurya in 1,599 (the dynasty ended in *Kali* era 1883-84=B.C. 1219-18). Puṣyamitra Śuṅga has been ascribed to 1736 (the dynasty came to an end in *Kali* era 2183-84=919-18) and Vāsudeva, the founder of the Kāṇva dynasty to 1,848 (the dynasty ended in *Kali* era 2,268-69 = B.C. 834-33). The Andhra dynasty, according to him ended in 2,649 or 2,984 (but, according to other traditional dates, it ended in 2,774-75 of the *Kali* era = B.C. 328-27).[7]

We find some contradictions in his chronological statements. His mode of calculation suffers from the lack of clarity, to some extent. The confusion and darkness, that pervade and overspread the Hindu chronology, have been attributed by him to the fancy of the Brāhmaṇs and poets, who embellished their history with allegory and fiction, and to the modern Hindus' ignorance of several eras and modes of dating, which were made use of by their ancient historians. He observes : "*Brāhmaṇs* and poets in recording past events have blended the whole together into one mass of absurdity and contradiction."[8]

## References

1. "An Essay on the Sacred Isles in the west with other Essays connected with that work". Kings and their Chronology, in *As. Res.* (Delhi, 1979), Vol. ix, p. 84.
2. *Ibid.*, pp. 84-89, 118, 161, 208-10; See also "Chronology of the Hindus" in *As. Res.*, Vol. v, pp. 241 f (for *Purāṇic* Chronology).
3. *As. Res.*, Vol. ix, 87-117.
4. *Ibid.*, p. 88.
5. *Ibid.*, pp. 118-78.
6. "On the Hindu System of Astronomy, and their Connection with History in Ancient and Modern times" in *As. Res.*, Vol. VIII (Delhi, 1979), pp. 225-28.
7. For details see his article, "On the Principal Eras and Dates of the Ancient Hindus" in *As. Res.*, Vol. V (Delhi, 1979), pp. 318-43.
8. *Ibid.*, p. 315.

# C

# Genealogical Tables of the Śiśunāgas as Mentioned in the Purāṇas, with Traditional Dates

| No. | Name | Regnal Years | Regnal Period |
|---|---|---|---|
| 1. | Śiśunāga | 40 | 1,995-1,955 B.C. |
| 2. | Kākavarṇa | 36 | 1,955-1,919 B.C. |
| 3. | Kṣemadharman | 26 | 1,919-1,893 B.C. |
| 4. | Kṣemajit or Kṣatraujas | 40 | 1,893-1,853 B.C. |
| 5. | Bimbisāra | 38 | 1,853-1,815 B.C. |
| 6. | Ajātaśatru | 27 | 1,815-1,788 B.C. |
| 7. | Darśaka | 35 | 1,788-1,753 B.C. |
| 8. | Udāyin | 33 | 1,753-1,720 B.C. |
| 9. | Nandivardhana | 42 | 1,720-1,678 B.C. |
| 10. | Mahānandin | 43 | 1,678-1,635 B.C. |
| | Total | 360 years | |

The traditional dates of the Śiśunāga kings of Magadha are purely based on the astronomical proof and the Saptarsi era. Traditionally, Buddha is ascribed to 1,887-1,807 B.C. and considered to be contemporary of Kṣemajit, Bimbisāra and Ajātaśatru. But, according to the *Mahāvaṁśa* (tr. Geiger, pp. xl-xlvi), Buddha (563-483 B.C.) was contemporaneous with Bimbisāra (558-491 B.C.) and Ajātaśatru (491-459 B.C.).

D

# Dynastic Chronology according to the Jaina Traditions

ACCORDING to the *Tiloyapaṇṇati*[1] or Yativṛṣabha (a Digambara) and the *Harivaṁśa*[2] of Jinasena, Pālaka, the son of king Caṇḍa Pradyota-Mahāsena of Avanti, ruled for sixty years, Puṣyamitra thirty years, Vasumitra and Agnimitra sixty years, the Gaddavas 100 years, the Murundas forty years and the Guptas 231 years.

The dynastic lists given in the *Dhavala* of Virasena, the *Jayadhavala* of Jinasena Svāmi, the *Uttarapurāṇa* (Benaras, 1952) of Gunabhadra, the *Trilokasāra* of Nemicandra and other Digambara works are more or less identical with the corresponding lists of the *Tiloyapaṇṇati* and *Harivaṁśa.*

According to one particular list, as inserted in the *Tiloyapaṇṇati,*[3] the Śaka dynasty ruled for 242 years and the Guptas 255 years.

According to the *Śvetāmbara* tradition, as recorded in the *"Titthogālipainna"*, an old Prākṛt text, Pālaka, the king of Ujjayini, ruled for sixty years, the Nandas 150 years, the Mauryas 160 years, Puṣyamitra thirty five years, Balamitra and Bhanumitra sixty years and the Gaddabhas 100 years.[4]

The lists contained in the *Tirthoddhāra-prakarana* and the *Tapāgaccha-paṭṭāvali* (vv. 1-3) show that Pālaka ruled for sixty years, the Nandas 155 years, the Mauryas 108 years, Puṣyamitra thirty years, Balamitra and Bhanumitra sixty years, Gaddabhilla thirteen years and the Śakas four years.

Merutung (a *Śvetāmbara)* in his *Vicāraśreni* provides an almost identical list with some additions. According to him, Candragupta's accession took place 255 years before Vikrama, i.e. (255+57=) in 312 B.C. *Vikrama* and his dynasty is said to have reigned for 135 years after which came the Śaka king, who displaced the dynasty of Vikramaditya.

Almost the same dynastic lists, as given above, are repeated in Prabhācandra's *Prabhāvakacarita* (ed. Jinavijaya, Bombay, 1940), Jinaprabhā Sūri's *Vividha Tirtha-kalpa* (ed. Jinavijaya, Bombay, 1934) and other *Śvetāmbara* works.

Hemacandra is not in agreement with all others. According to him, M.E. (Mahāvira Era)—sixty marked the beginning of Nanda's rule, i.e. (477-60 ) 417 B.C., and Candragupta Maurya ascended the throne in M.E. 155, i.e. (477-155) 322 B.C.[5]

## References

1. Central Jaina Oriental Library, Arrah, ed. by A.N. Upadhye and H.L. Jain (Solapur, 1951), vv. 95-99.
2. Manikachandra Digambara Jaina Grandhamala Series (Bombay, 1930), Sarga 60, vv. 487-92, 551-52.
3. vv. 93-94.
4. *Titthogāli-painna*, vv. 620-23, cf. *Paṭṭāvali-Samuccaya* (ed. Darsanavijaya, 2 Vols., Viramgram, 1933), p. 197, also p. 17.
5. *Pariśiṣṭaparvan* (*Sthavirāvalicarita*), ed. H. Jacobi, *BIS*, Calcutta, 2nd edn., 1932, VI, 243 and VIII, 339.

# Glossary

| | |
|---|---|
| *Āmā* | The baked bricks were called *Āmā* in the *Ṛgvedic* age. |
| *Amātya* | Minister |
| *Aśvamedha Yajña* | Horse-Sacrifice. |
| *Cakravartin* | A ruler who after having conquered surrounding kingdoms brought them under his imperial authority and established his paramount position over an extensive region. |
| Chakra or Nemichakra | The name stands for Nemicakra, who was popularly known as Nicakṣu, the sixth in descent from Parikṣit II or the son and successor of Adhisimakṛṣna |
| *Dvāpara Yuga,* | One of the four Ages or *Yugas,* according to the traditional Indian concept of time, which began after the *Tretā* and came to an end with the Lord Kṛṣṇa going back to his abode. |
| *Doab* | The land between the Gaṅgā and the Yamunā forming the part of Āryāvarta or Madhya-deśa of the *Upanisadic,* Epic and *Purāṇic* ages. |
| Girivraja | Etymologically it stands for the hill-fortress. But, historically, it signifies the oldest name of the capital of Magadha, which later became famous as Rājagṛha (mod. Rājagir). |

| | |
|---|---|
| *Gotra* | A sect or clan, a branch of the same race or family in the genealogical perspective or the common descendants of the same progenitor. |
| Kali Age or *Kali Yuga* | The accession of Parikṣit II (Arjuna's grandson) to the throne of Hastināpur marked the commencement of the *Kali* Age or *Kali-yuga* thirty-six years before which battle of the *Mahābhārata* was fought. |
| *Kali-Dvāpara Sandhi* | The Saptarṣis maintained their position in the Māgha-Nakṣatra till the end of the *Dvāpara-yuga* or untill the beginning of the *Kali-yuga* (the converging point), which has been referred to as the *Kali-Dvāpara Sandhī* in the *Garga-Saṁhita*. |
| *Kali* Era or *Kali Saṁvat* or *Kaliyuga Saṁvat* | According to traditional date based on an astronomical calculation or speculation it began either in B.C. 3102 or 3101. According to the computations of the *Purāṇic* figures its range can be placed between 1472 and 1370 B.C., and according to the interpretations of the archaeological data it can be ascribed to a period which falls between 1,000 and 800 B.C. |
| *Li* | The Chinese 30 or 40 *Li* is equivalent to one *yojana*, i.e.=4 *Krosas* or *Kosa* (8 miles). |
| *Māgha Nakṣatra* | Asterism. |
| Mahānagara | A great Capital City. |
| *Mahāsena* | Pradyota of Avanti was also known as Mahāsena because of his large army. |
| Mahāvira Era | The date 477 B.C. actually corresponds with Mahāvira Era (M.E.). |
| *Mleccha* | Ethno-culturally, they belonged to a degraded race with lower grade of culture, and linguistically, they represent those whose language is unintelligible or indistinct. |
| *Nirvāna* | Final emancipation or salvation. |

| | |
|---|---|
| *Purānakāras* | The composers of the *Purāṇas*. |
| *Rishis* | The Saptarṣis have been called also the seven *Rishis*. |
| Śaka Era or *Śaka Kāla* | The *Śaka* era is marked by 78 A.D. |
| *Samrāt* | An emperor. |
| *Saṁvat* | It denotes Vikrama *Saṁvat*, i.e., 57 B.C. |
| *Saṇgha* | A confederation of republican community. |
| *Saptarṣi* Era or *Saptarṣi Saṁvat* | The *Saptarṣi* era or *Saptarṣi Saṁvat*, according to some *Purāṇas*, began in 1015 (or 1050, 1115, 1500), which synchronised with the birth of Parikṣit. |
| *Satayuga* | It stands for the *Krita* Age. |
| *Sravana* | One of the *Nakṣatras*. |
| *Śudra* | They represent the lowest social order. |
| *Tretayuga* | It preceded the *Dvāpara-yuga*. |
| *Up-Purāṇas* | Besides the eighteen main *Purāṇas*, some *Purāṇas* were composed in different regions of India at different periods of history, which are called *up-Purāṇas*. |
| *Yajñas* | Sacrifices. |
| *Yavana* | They not only represented the Greeks, but also the despised class or degraded race with lower grade of culture. |
| *Yojana* | One *yojana*=4 *Krosas* or 8 miles. |
| *Yudhiṣṭhira Saṁvat* | This *Saṁvat*, according to astronomical calculations based on the data provided by Varāhamihira and Vṛddha-Garga, began 2526 years before the *Śaka* era, i.e.=B.C. 2448. |

# Index